SAN FRANCISCO
RESTAURANTS

Editor-in-Chief
Alain Gayot

Executive Editor
Sharon Boorstin

Managing Editor
GraceAnn Walden

Associate Editor
Karen Seriguchi

Contributing Editors
Alex Amado, Louis Charles, Lisa Crovo,
Beverly Dubrin, Lisa Hanauer,
Catherine Jordan,
Joel & Amy Levine, Ben Marks,
Marty Olmstead, Joan Simon

Directed By
André Gayot

http://www.gayot.com

GAULT·MILLAU

- Los Angeles ■ New York ■ San Francisco
London ■ Munich ■ Paris ■ Vienna

GAYOT PUBLICATIONS

The Best of Beverly Hills
The Best of Chicago
The Best of Florida
The Best of France
The Best of Germany
The Best of Hawaii
The Best of Hong Kong
The Best of Italy
The Best of London
The Best of Los Angeles
The Best of New England
The Best of New Orleans
The Best of New York
The Best of Paris
Paris, Ile-de-France & The Loire Valley
Paris & Provence
The Best of San Francisco
The Best of Thailand
The Best of Toronto
The Best of Washington, D.C.
The Best Wineries of North America

LA Restaurants,
NYC Restaurants,
San Francisco Restaurants
The Food Paper, Tastes Newsletter

http://www.gayot.com

Copyright © 1996, 1999 by GaultMillau, Inc.

Published by GaultMillau, Inc.
5900 Wilshire Blvd.
Los Angeles, CA 90036

Please address all comments regarding
San Francisco Restaurants to:
GaultMillau, Inc.
P.O. Box 361144
Los Angeles, CA 90036
E-mail: gayots@aol.com

Operations: Harriet Callier
Production: Walter Mladina
Coordination: Ariane Shovers
Illustrations: Bettina Oshiro
Page Layout and Design: Mad Macs Communications

ISSN 1523-4029
Printed in the United States of America

CONTENTS

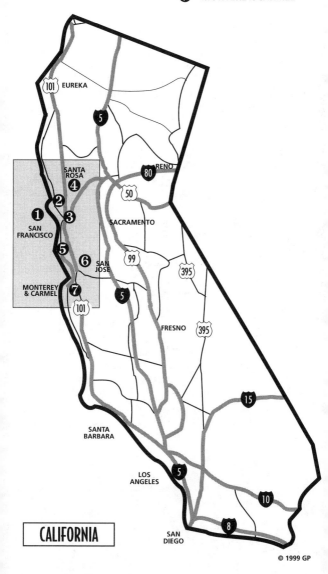

AREAS COVERED

1. SAN FRANCISCO
2. MARIN COUNTY
3. EAST BAY
4. WINE COUNTRY
5. PENINSULA
6. SAN JOSE
7. MONTEREY/CARMEL

CALIFORNIA

© 1999 GP

SAN FRANCISCO
RESTAURANTS

RIGHTS

THANKS

We would like to extend a dear thanks to those who helped to make this book possible: Gregory Balogh of Maison Marques & Domaines; Dr. Su Hua Newton of Newton Vineyards; Tommy McGloin & Paul Volen of Digital City; Philippe Riffi of the Perrier Group; Peter Sears of the Park Hyatt; Elaine Sense of Sense Public Relations; Volker Ulrich of The Pan Pacific Hotel; & Tom Walton of Fortune Public Relations.

DISCLAIMER

The cover of this book was created by and is dedicated to the late Gordon Fiedor, who created distinctive cover illustrations for our publications. Gordon's joy in living was communicated to countless readers through his spirited work. We feel privileged to have published Gordon's work and to have known him as an artist and a friend.

LET A HUNDRED RESTAURANTS BLOOM

More than six million people live in the San Francisco Bay Area. While the City itself is densely populated, housing developments spread out across the suburbs, and in the rural parts of Marin and certainly Mendocino, some people must drive several miles to reach their nearest neighbor. These divergent lifestyles were at one time reflected in the restaurants: San Francisco, long a tourist mecca, featured every manner of eatery, from authentic ethnic venues to haute cuisine restaurants with national reputations. The suburbs made do with casual and affordable chain restaurants, while in the country, there were simple mom-and-pop cafés or small hotel restaurants. For big-deal dining, you had to go to the City.

All that changed over the past ten years. Suburban restaurateurs—whether on the Peninsula, in the East Bay or in Marin—have opened restaurants that rival those in San Francisco. And as suburban populations became more diverse, authentic ethnic eateries opened to serve them. It is no longer necessary to travel to San Francisco's Chinatown for authentic Hong Kong cuisine. You can find it in Millbrae.

The wine country, especially Napa, has seen an explosion of restaurants from transplants like Thomas Keller (**French Laundry, Bouchon**) and the French-born Philippe Jeanty (**Bistro Jeanty**). Sonoma, always more rural than Napa, now hosts a number of excellent chef-opened eateries as well, including **Café La Haye** and the **Girl & the Fig**. Meanwhile, San Jose, which long rivaled San Francisco in size but not sophistication, now hosts multimillion-dollar high-style concept restaurants such as **A.P. Stumps.**

In San Francisco and the East Bay, California cuisine dominated the last 20 years. Today, Berkeley's **Chez Panisse**, led by founder Alice Waters, remains pioneering and minimalistic, but former Chez Panisse chef Jeremiah Tower's **Stars** near the Opera House, has been supplanted by the likes of **Aqua, Farallon, Rubicon** and **Boulevard.** Furthermore, the shift away from the stodgy men's grills and Continental restaurants, coupled with the opening ten years ago of L.A. celebrity-chef Wolfgang Puck's high-energy, high-style **Postrio,** has proven irresistible. Postrio has been followed by at least half a dozen high-concept eateries. But talented chefs still save their pennies and open modest little personalized restaurants: witness the wildly popular (and only 60-seat) **Delfina** or **Globe.**

The result of all this expansion means a wide range of dining possibilities in an ever- increasing geographic area. Several decades ago Chairman Mao endorsed diversity by saying, "Let a hundred flowers bloom." That may have been a difficult principle in politics, but it holds true in the Bay Area dining scene.

OUR RESTAURANT RATING SYSTEM

Clearly, a good many of our restaurants are well worth your time and money, and our team of professional restaurant critics has canvassed restaurants from San Francisco to the Wine Country, from the East Bay to Carmel, to steer you right. In our reviews, we've rated the restaurants (see rating system below) and pointed out details about the decor, look and ambience. We've also recommended some favorite dishes.

What decides the rating of a restaurant? What is on the plate is by far the most important factor. The **quality of basic ingredients** may well be the most telling sign of a restaurant's culinary status. It requires a great deal of commitment and money to stock the finest grades and cuts of meat and the finest quality of fish. There is tuna, for example, and then there's tuna. Ask any sushi chef. One extra-virgin olive oil is not at all the same as the next. Ditto for chocolates, pastas, spices and a thousand other ingredients. High-quality restaurants also attune themselves to seasonal produce, whether it be local berries or truffles from Italy.

Freshness is all-important, too, and another indication of quality. This means not only using fresh rather than frozen fish, for example, but also preparing everything from scratch at the last possible moment, from appetizers through desserts.

What else do we look for? The **details.** If the sauces are all the same, you know that the kitchen is taking shortcuts. The quality of the bread on the table is always a tip-off. Similarly, the house wine can speak volumes about the culinary attitude and level of an establishment. Wine is food, and wine lists and offerings can be a revelation. A list doesn't have to be long or expensive to show a commitment to quality.

In our rating, **creativity and influence** are important, but high quality and consistency of what appears on the plates are also important. A restaurant that serves grilled chicken well is to be admired more than a restaurant that attempts some failed marriage of chicken and exotic produce, or a complicated chicken preparation that requires a larger and more talented kitchen brigade than is on hand. Don't be taken in by attempted fireworks that are really feeble sideshows.

Our Rating System Works as Follows:

Since GaultMillau was founded in Paris more than three decades ago, we have ranked restaurants in the same manner that French students are graded, on a scale of 1 to 20. **The rankings reflect our opinion only of the food; we comment on the decor, service, wine list and atmosphere within each review.** Restaurants ranked 13/20 and above are distinguished with toques (chef's hats) according to the table below. For an index

Exceptional *(4 Toques)* 🎩🎩🎩🎩
(ratings of 19/20)

Excellent *(3 Toques)* 🎩🎩🎩
(ratings of 17/20 and 18/20)

Very good *(2 Toques)* 🎩🎩
(ratings of 15/20 and 16/20)

Good *(1 Toque)* 🎩
(ratings of 13/20 and 14/20)

of every restaurant with a rating of 13/20 or higher, please see the Toque Tally on page 13.

Keep in mind that we are comparing San Francisco's restaurants to the very best in the world. Also, these rankings are relative. A 13/20 (🎩) may not be a superlative ranking for a highly reputed (and very expensive) restaurant, but it is quite complimentary for a small place without much culinary pretension.

We have given a **No Rating** to a few restaurants, primarily because they opened just as we went to press, or underwent some very recent changes. However, we have endeavored to give you an idea of the dishes served at these establishments as well as the ambience, price range and features.

Bargain Bites(¢) are inexpensive eateries where you can stop for a casual meal, and/or eat for $15 per person and under. **Bargain Bites** include lots of terrific places, from burger joints, diners, trendy cafés, noodle shops, happening bars and pizza parlors to ethnic eateries galore. San Francisco and Northern California have literally thousands of good **Bargain Bites**, so we've included only the best. Forgive us if we've left out your favorite—for now, at least, your secret is safe!

Our Pricing System

In our reviews, we code restaurants using one to five dollar signs. **Prices reflect the average cost of a dinner for one person, including appetizer, entrée, dessert, coffee, tax and tip. Not included is wine or any other beverage.**

¢ = under $15
$ = under $20
$$ = under $35
$$$ = under $50
$$$$ = $50-$75
$$$$$ = $75 & up

Symbols

In our reviews, we code restaurants according to the following features:

No credit cards . . . . ⊠

Reservations required or strongly suggested . . . . ☎

Valet parking . . . . 🚗

Great View . . . . 📷

Heart-healthy dishes on menu . . . . ♥

Outdoor dining . . . . ⛱

Jacket/tie suggested . . . . 👔

Romantic ambience . . . . 💃

Serves past midnight . . . . 🦉

Live entertainment . . . . 🎷

Kid friendly . . . . 👫

Full bar . . . . 🍸

Great wine list . . . . 🍷

Private party room available . . . . ⬡

Advice & Comments

CONFUSION CUISINE

Before **Nouvelle Cuisine** was introduced to San Francisco in the '70s, followed by **California** cuisine in the '80s and **New American, Fusion, Pan-Asian, Mediterranean** and **Pacific Rim** cuisine in the '90s, it was easy to classify restaurants by their cuisine—there was **American, French, Italian, Continental, Chinese, Japanese, Greek** etc., period. Today, the lines between the cuisines have blurred. New American and even Fusion have evolved into what is now called **Contemporary.** Futhermore, chefs create their own style of cooking—which might combine elements of some—or all—of the above.

We find it difficult to slap a label on the type of cuisine a restaurant serves, yet we must for the sake of indexing—and so that readers will have a sense of what they'll be served when they dine there. In most cases, we have labeled a restaurant's cuisine according to what its owners and chefs call it. But that does not always make things easier. For we've found that though one restaurant may describe its cuisine as New American, another as Contemporary and another as Eclectic, their dishes are quite similar—innovative takes on new and old themes, concocted of fresh regional ingredients and using a combination of elements from various ethnic cooking styles.

In the long run, who cares what a restaurant's cuisine is called? After all, it's not what type of cuisine you're eating that's important—it's how it tastes. And we hope it tastes great!

JUST HOW DRESSY IS DRESSY?

San Francisco is neither an inordinately formal town (such as New York) nor an altogether laid-back place (such as L.A.). You can be yourself in whatever you genuinely feel comfortable wearing, except in a few of the most elegant venues. In some fancier restaurants, men are still expected to wear jackets and ties; we've pointed these out to you by including a tie symbol (👔) in the listing information. You don't want to underdress for Masa's or the Ritz-Carlton Dining Room. In some upscale restaurants, men may feel more comfortable wearing sports jackets, although ties are rarely required. But in the hipper places, anything goes, from studded leather to tailored worsted, from Adidas sneakers to patent-leather Gucci loafers. You don't want to overdress for Zuni or Hawthorne Lane.

CELEBRITIES IN THE KITCHEN

If you have your heart set on having a famous chef cook your meal, call ahead to make sure he or she will actually be in the restaurant that night. But remember, an executive or owner-chef doesn't cook every dish that comes out of the kitchen. A kitchen consists of a brigade of cooks that the executive chef oversees. If your dining experience isn't as marvelous as our rating would suggest, keep the faith and try again another time (and let us know).

PARKING POSSIBILITIES

Many restaurants in the City offer valet parking. If you use it; it's customary to tip the valet $2 or so—proportionately more if you want your BMW handled with kid gloves. The next best option is to use a parking lot in the area, even if you have to walk a few blocks to dinner. Finding convenient street parking can require lots of time or prodigious good fortune.

NO SMOKING!

Smoking is banned in nearly all enclosed public places in California. Smoking sections in restaurants no longer exist, and a complete ban on smoking in bars, pubs and cocktail lounges is the law. Smokers are pretty much relegated to the sidewalks outside restaurants or bars—some restaurants have placed tables outside to accommodate nicotine fans. But as with any rule, there are exceptions. Some restaurants allow smoking within their outdoor seating (technically illegal), and many neighborhood bars pretend they don't notice their customers smoking. But beware: Violators are subject to a $75 fine and the bars risk a $500 fine. Surprise visits from health inspectors or the police are always a possibility.

11

TIPPING TIPS

Very few Bay Area eateries follow the European custom of adding a set service charge to your bill (Chez Panisse is one). While many restaurants do add a gratuity to the checks of large groups (eight or more) to ensure that servers are properly tipped, in most cases tipping is up to you. Servers are traditionally given 15 to 20 percent of the total bill, before tax. A maître d' who makes special accommodations should also be tipped accordingly ($5 and up), and a helpful sommelier might be acknowledged with $2 or $3 per bottle of wine served, or more for top-notch bottles.

DINING AL FRESCO

You'll find a number of places in (and some out of) the City where you can enjoy a meal al fresco. This could mean a few sidewalk tables or a terrace, patio or courtyard. We've indicated those restaurants with a patio umbrella symbol ( ) in the listing information. For a complete list of restaurants offering al fresco dining, see Outdoor Dining under RESTAURANT INDEXES at the back of this book.

Sample Review

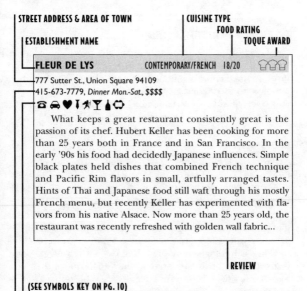

STREET ADDRESS & AREA OF TOWN

CUISINE TYPE

FOOD RATING

ESTABLISHMENT NAME

TOQUE AWARD

FLEUR DE LYS   CONTEMPORARY/FRENCH   18/20

777 Sutter St., Union Square 94109

415-673-7779, Dinner Mon.-Sat., $$$$

What keeps a great restaurant consistently great is the passion of its chef. Hubert Keller has been cooking for more than 25 years both in France and in San Francisco. In the early '90s his food had decidedly Japanese influences. Simple black plates held dishes that combined French technique and Pacific Rim flavors in small, artfully arranged tastes. Hints of Thai and Japanese food still waft through his mostly French menu, but recently Keller has experimented with flavors from his native Alsace. Now more than 25 years old, the restaurant was recently refreshed with golden wall fabric...

REVIEW

(SEE SYMBOLS KEY ON PG. 10)

PHONE NUMBER, DAYS OPEN & PRICE CATEGORY

TOQUE TALLY
TOP RESTAURANTS: FOOD RATING

Restaurants are in San Francisco unless otherwise indicated: **(M) Marin County, (EB) East Bay, (WC) Wine Country, (P) Peninsula, (SJ) San Jose, (M/C) Monterey/Carmel**

18/20 ♟♟♟

Fleur de Lys

The French Laundry (WC)

The Ritz-Carlton Dining Room

17/20 ♟♟♟

Aqua

La Folie

16/20 ♟♟

Boulevard

Charles Nob Hill

Chez Panisse (EB)

Club XIX—Inspired by Hubert Keller (MC)

La Toque (WC)

Masa's

Pacific

Postrio

THE TOQUE, CIRCA 1700

Have you ever wondered about the origin of that towering, billowy (and slightly ridiculous) white hat worn by chefs all over the world? Chefs have played an important role in society since the fifth century B.C., but the hats didn't begin to appear in kitchens until around the eighteenth century A.D. The toque is said to be of Greek origin; many famous Greek cooks, to escape persecution, sought refuge in monasteries and continued to practice their art. The chefs donned the tall hats traditionally worn by Orthodox priests, but to distinguish themselves from their fellows, they wore white hats instead of black. The custom eventually was adopted by chefs from Paris to Peking.

15/20 ♟♟

A. Sabella's
Acquerello
Alfred's Steak House
Antica Trattoria
Anzu Nikko
A.P. Stumps (SJ)
Applewood Inn & Restaurant (WC)
Babette's (WC)
Bay Wolf (EB)
Betelnut
Bistro Jeanty (WC)
Bouchon (WC)
Brazio (EB)
Brix (WC)
Café at Chez Panisse (EB)
Catahoula (WC)
Chapeau!
Cypress Club
Delfina
Domaine Chandon (WC)
Eulapia Restaurant & Bar (SJ)
Farallon
42 Degrees
Fresh Cream (MC)
Fringale
Greens
Hawthorne Lane
Jardinière
Kabuto Sushi
L'Amie Donia (P)
Lark Creek Inn (M)

Left Bank (P)
Mazzini Trattoria (EB)
Mercury
Mixx (WC)
Momo's
101 Main Bistro & Wine Bar (WC)
One Market
Oritalia
Pinot Blanc (WC)
Plumpjack Café
The Restaurant at Meadowood (WC)
Restaurant Sent Sovi (P)
The Ritz-Carlton Terrace & Lobby Lounge
Rose Pistola
Roy's at Pebble Beach (MC)
Sanraku Four Seasons
Shanghai 1930
Sierra Mar (MC)
Silks
Spago Palo Alto (P)
Stokes Adobe (MC)
Tavolino
Terra (WC)
Thep Phanom
Tra Vigne (WC)
Willowside Café (WC)
Yank Sing
Yuet Lee
Zaré
ZigZag (MC)
Zuni Café

Exceptional (19/20)	♟♟♟♟
Excellent (17/20 & 18/20)	♟♟♟
Very Good (15/20 & 16/20)	♟♟
Good (13/20 & 14/20)	♟

14/20 ♟

Ajanta (EB)

Alioto's No. 8

Alta Plaza

Amber Indian Restaurant (P)

Anjou

Aperto

Auberge du Soleil (WC)

Bighorn Grill (EB)

Bistro Aix

Bistro Don Giovanni (WC)

Bistro Ralph (WC)

Black Cat

Brava Terrace (WC)

Bridges (EB)

Bubba's Diner (M)

Buckey Roadhouse (M)

Byblos

Ca' Bianca Restaurant (WC)

Café Beaujolais (WC)

Café Florio

Café La Haye (WC)

Café Lolo (WC)

Casanova (MC)

Cesar (EB)

Christophe

Clementine

The Covey at Quail Lodge (MC)

Crustacean

Cucina Jackson Fillmore (M)

Deuce (WC)

Ebisu

Elba (P)

Elite Café

Emile's (SJ)

Enrico's Sidwalk Café

Eos Restaurant & Wine Bar

Foothill Café (WC)

Germania Restaurant at the Hochburg (SJ)

Girl & the Fig (WC)

Glen Ellen Inn Restaurant (WC)

Grasing's (MC)

Globe

Golden Turtle

Grandeho Kamekyo

Heirloom (WC)

The Helmand

House

India Village (M)

Insalata's (M)

Kasbah Moroccan Restaurant (M)

Kincaid's Bistro (MC)

Kokkari

Lalime's (EB)

Lasalette (WC)

Le Colonial

Le Marquis (EB)

Le Mouton Noir (P)

Left Bank (M)

Lhasa Moon

L'Olivier

Marnee Thai

Maya

MC2

Mecca

The Meetinghouse

Millennium

Miss Millie's

Montrio (MC)

Mustards Grill (WC)

North Beach Restaurant

O Chame (EB)

Oakville Grocery Café (WC)

Obelisque (EB)

Oliveto (EB)

Paolo's (SJ)

Park Grill

Pastis

Piaf's

Plouf

Postino (EB)

Prima Trattoria (EB)

Restaurant Lulu

Restaurant Zibibbo (P)

Ristorante Ecco

Ristorante Ideale

Rivoli Restaurant (EB)

Rose's Café

Royal Thai

Rubicon

Scala's Bistro

Sushi on North Beach

Taste Café & Bistro (MC)

213 Ellsworth (P)

Uncle Yu's (EB)

Universal Café

Valentine's Café

Vineria

Vito's (MC)

The Waterfront Restaurant

Wente Vineyards Restaurant (EB)

Yabbies

Zarzuela

13/20 🎩

Agenda (SJ)

Alamo Square

Albona Ristorante

Alegrías

Amfora Fino (EB)

Angkor Borei Restaurant

Anton & Michel (MC)

Aram's

Arco-Iris (EB)

Asia (SF)

Atlas Peak Grill (WC)

Autumn Moon Café (EB)

Avenue 9

Aya Sushi

Baker Street Bistro

Barcelona

Basil

Battambang (EB)

Bayview Restaurant (WC)

Bella Mia (SJ)

Bella Vista Restaurant (P)

Bergman's (WC)

Bistro Alsacienne (M)

Bizou

Boca Rotis

Boonville Hotel (WC)

Brannan's Grill (WC)

Bravo Fono (P)

Bucci's (EB)

Buffalo Girl (P)

Butterfield's

Café Akimbo

Café Cuvée

Café de Paris L'Entrocôte

Café Fina (MC)

Café for All Seasons

Café Jacqueline

Café Kati

Café La Scala (P)

Caffè Delle Stelle

Caffè Macaroni

Caffè Sport

Carta

Cassis Bistro

Chow

Cibo Ristorante (MC)

City of Paris

Cityscape

Creola—A New Orleans Bistro (P)

Curbside Café

Cypress Grove (MC)

Doug's (EB)

El Paseo (M)

El Zocalo

Elan Vital

Eliza's

Elroys

Empire Grill &
Tap Room (P)

Ever Rain (M)

Fandango (MC)

Fina Estampa

Firefly

First Crush

Flying Saucer

Fog City Diner

Fook Yuen (P)

Fountain Court

Garibaldis

Garibaldi's On College (EB)

Gaylord India Restaurant

Ginger Island (EB)

Gira Polli

Gordon's (WC)

Grand Café

Great Eastern

The Grill at
Meadowood (WC)

The Grille at Sonoma Mission
Inn (WC)

Half Day Café (M)

Hama-Ko

Harbor Village Restaurant

Harris'

Hayes Street Grill

Higashi West (P)

Hong Kong Flower
Lounge (SF, P)

Il Fornaio (SF, P, M)

Indigo

Jackson Fillmore Trattoria

Jakarta

Jeanne D'Arc

John Ash & Co. (WC)

Kathmandu (EB)

Kelly´s Mission Rock

Kenwood Restaurant &
Bar (WC)

Khan Toke Thai House

Kuleto's Trattoria (P)

Kyo-Ya

La Bohème (MC)

La Boucane (WC)

La Felce

La Gondola (MC)

La Note (EB)

La Traviata

Lalita

Lark Creek Café (EB)

Le Charm

Le Cheval (EB)

Le Papillon (SJ)

Liberty Café & Bakery

L'Osteria del Forno

Livefire Grill &
Smokehouse (WC)

Madrona Manor (WC)

Mandalay

The Mandarin

Mangiafuoco

Manora's Thai Cuisine

Matterhorn Swiss Restaurant

Mayflower

Menara Moroccan
Restaurant (SJ)

Mescolanza

Mikayla (M)

Mistral (WC)

Miyake (P)

Mondo's Trattoria (MC)

Napa Valley Grille (WC)

Nepenthe (MC)

Nippon (No Name)

Nob Hill Terrace

North India

North Sea Village (M)

Oberon

Okina Sushi

Oodles

Original Joe's

Osaka Grill

Osho (P)

Osome

Ovation at the Opera

Pacific Café (M)

Pairs Parkside (WC)

Palio D'Asti

Pane e Vino

Park Chow

Parkside Grille (P)

Pearl (WC)

Piatti Ristorante (P)

Ping's (M)

PJ's Oyster Bed

Rasta Dwight's
Barbecue (WC)

Restaurant Peony (EB)

The Rice Table (M)

Ristorante Milano

Robata Grill & Sushi (M)

Rossetti Osteria Romana (M)

Rue de Paris (SJ)

Salute (EB)

Sardine Factory
Restaurant (MC)

Scott's Seafood (SJ)

71 Saint Peter (SJ)

Shen Hua (EB)

Showley's (WC)

The Slanted Door

Soizic (EB)

South Park Café

Speckmann's

Splendido

Stars

Stevenswood Lodge &
Restaurant (WC)

Stillwater's (MC)

Stratta Grill & Café (SJ)

Suppenküche

Sushi Groove

Sushi to Dai For (M)

Swan Oyster Depot

Taiwan

Tapas Sevilla (EB)

Terra Brazilis

Thanh Long

Thep Lela (M)

Thirsty Bear

Ti Couz

Timo's

Tokyo Go Go

Tommaso's

Townhouse Bar & Grill (EB)

Trap Door

Trattoria Contadina

2223 Restaurant

Uzen (EB)

Via Vai

The Village Pub (P)

Vinga

Vivande

Woodward's Garden

Yet Wah (M)

Yo Yo Tsumami Bistro

Zax

Zinzino

The Zodiac Club

The following restaurants
were either too new, or
had major changes at
press time, so we didn't
rate them:

No Rating

The Basin (P)

Bistro Zare

Café Niebaum-Coppola

Campton Place

Filou (M)

Gordon's House of Eats

Lisa Hemenway Bistro (WC)

Manka's Inverness
Lodge (M)

Pacific's Edge (MC)

Rôti/Red Herring

Viognier (P)

Voulez-Vous (EB)

Uva Trattoria Italiana (WC)

The Wine Spectator
Restaurant at
Greystone (WC)

San Francisco

MAP OF SAN FRANCISCO

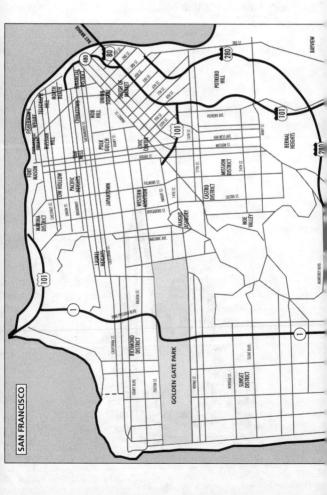

CONTEMPORARY?
ETHNIC? IT'S ALL GOOD!

That San Francisco is a restaurant town nobody can deny. But sheer numbers don't begin to tell the story of the food scene here. With the area's abundant resources and so much collective energy devoted to the pursuit of the best in food and wine, San Francisco has become a playground—even a school of sorts—for chefs, residents and visitors who want to earn an epicurean education.

In recent years, chefs and restaurateurs have responded both to the economy and to demand. Comfort food has made a comeback—roast chicken and mashed potatoes seem to be a staple on many menus. Noodles are big, whether served in chain Italian pasta emporiums, fusion restaurants or trendy pan-Asian restaurants. And grazers can pick and choose from among small plates of European and Asian tapas.

While the interest in Mediterranean food, encompassing dishes from Italy to the Middle East, has waned a little (and we mean just a *little*), the new restaurant comeback kid is the French bistro. And if you're wondering whatever happened to California cuisine—fresh market ingredients, lots of simply grilled items, with pasta and light sauces a prevalent theme—it's still around. But in many cases California cuisine has evolved into what we call Contemporary cuisine. By that, we mean cuisine that uses fresh market ingredients not just from California but from all over the world, often in new ways and in new combinations. Contemporary cuisine may encompass inventive variations on regional American or international dishes: Maryland crabcakes with red-pepper aïoli, Santa Fe-style corn chowder with chile butter, a "tostada" filled with red beans and duck confit, or Chinese dumplings stuffed with foie gras. One note of warning about Contemporary cuisine: the more innovative the concept, the more complicated the combination of ingredients, the more talented the chef needs to be to pull it off!

In addition, those seeking ethnic culinary authenticity will continue to be satisfied in San Francisco. But when you think Italian, think regional: you'll find everything from simple Roman fare to Istrian specialties. And Chinese? Would that be Cantonese, Szechuan or Hakka? When you've worked your way through the wonders of those regional cuisines, Tibetan, Swedish, Argentinean and Burmese will tease your palate. For whether you're seeking innovative contemporary or authentic ethnic cuisine, San Francisco remains a unique and rewarding restaurant town.

FOR GAYOT'S UPDATED SAN FRANCISCO RESTAURANT REVIEWS, GO TO:

Digitalcity.com/sanfrancisco/dining

RESTAURANTS

A. SABELLA'S RESTAURANT   SEAFOOD   15/20

2766 Taylor St. 3rd fl., Fisherman's Wharf 94133
415-771-6775, *Lunch & Dinner daily*, $$$

When the Sabella family emigrated from Sicily in 1871, they made their living by fishing the Bay. They opened this seafood restaurant in 1920, and today the third generation of Sabellas runs the place. The huge banquet-style room has floor-to-ceiling windows overlooking the wharf, and the bar is warmed by a fireplace. Special dishes include live crab; cioppino; a huge crab-shrimp Louie that includes lobster and avocado; bouillabaisse; sautéed fresh Monterey calamari; and abalone fresh from the tanks in the back, served with a lemon-garlic beurre blanc and sautéed spinach. The adjacent lounge features a mystery-dinner theater. Desserts are stylish and delicious.

ABSINTHE   FRENCH   12/20

398 Hayes St., Civic Center 94102
415-551-1590, *Breakfast & Lunch Tues.-Fri., Dinner Tues.-Sun., Brunch Sat.-Sun.*, $$$

The lavish decor is reminiscent of the belle époque at this Opera House-adjacent bar and restaurant. Executive chef Ross Browne's menu is bold, based on cuisine from the south of France with a California accent. On the dinner menu, the ahi tuna with a gribiche sauce is good; try the risotto with langoustine, too, or the roasted half chicken over sage stuffing. Inconsistency unfortunately plagues the kitchen and the service. Desserts are just fair—we recommend the cheese plate for two. The bar serves a solid hamburger, among other late-night-supper dishes, making it a good spot for post-theater dining.

ACQUERELLO   ITALIAN   15/20

1722 Sacramento St., Nob Hill 94109
(415) 567-5432 *Dinner Tues.-Sat.*, $$$$

This is a luxurious restaurant and priced accordingly, but it is luxury as sensuous and inviting as the watercolors that fill the dining room (hence the name). Chef-owner Suzette Gresham's menu is constantly changing. Begin with the veal carpaccio with lemon-egg sauce or the marinated swordfish with Sicilian-style baked onions. Among the splendid pasta dishes is ravioli stuffed with pecorino, Asiago, Mascarpone and ricotta. Of the main courses, we especially like the pork loin encrusted with parsley and pink peppercorns and the oregano-encrusted filet of salmon. The wine list features an award-winning selection of Italian bottlings as well as a number of premium California entries. The well-trained and accommodating staff will help you choose. For dessert, try the warm zabaglione perfumed with orange liqueur.

ALAMO SQUARE SEAFOOD GRILL   FRENCH/SEAFOOD   13/20

803 Fillmore St., Hayes Valley 94117
415-440-2828, *Dinner nightly, Brunch Sun., $$*

This small neighborhood spot is a great place for a reasonably priced meal of good food with a French twist. The menu centers on a mix-'n'-match selection of the fish of the day, sauces and cooking methods. As you would in the venerable Hayes Street Grill, you select one from each column and end up with a plate full of tasty seafood, along with a panoply of wonderful side dishes. The sautéed chicken breast, with a crispy coating, is also nice. The restaurant itself, though tiny, is stylish, sporting saffron walls with brick-colored highlights.

ALBONA RISTORANTE   ITALIAN/ISTRIAN   13/20

545 Francisco St., North Beach 94133
415-441-1040, *Dinner Tues.-Sat., $$*

The menu in this cozy room finished in soft colors, offers a rich blend of Italian and Central European influences—think sauerkraut, goulash and strudel. Chef-owner Bruno Viscovi (from the town of Albona on the Italian-Yugoslavian border) has lovingly re-created the flavors he remembers from his childhood. You'll find chifeleti, pan-fried potato gnocchi in a superb beef sirloin and cumin sauce, and such entrées as braciole di maiale, pork cutlets stuffed with sauerkraut, apples, prunes and prosciutto. The wine list offers mostly Italian varietals, including often overlooked gems from the Friuli and Alto-Adige regions. For dessert try the competent strudel.

ALEGRÍAS   SPANISH   13/20

2018 Lombard St., Marina 94123
415-929-8888, *Dinner nightly, $$*

This cheery restaurant, decorated with hand-painted ceramics and terra-cotta flower boxes, gets better with every visit. We recommend all of the tasty tapas calientes and tapas frias. A plate of escalivada—grilled eggplant, peppers and onions sprinkled with extra-virgin Spanish olive oil—will get your appetite in top gear. Conejo a la cazuela, stewed rabbit with vegetables and wine, is a hot tapa that could make a light entrée. Try the zarzuela de mariscos, shellfish in tomato, garlic, saffron and wine sauce, or the New York steak with blue-cheese sauce. The rice-and-milk pudding is marvelous.

ALEJANDRO'S LA POLLERIA   MEXICAN/PERUVIAN   11/20

2937 Mission St., Mission 94110
415-826-8260, *Lunch & Early Dinner daily, $*

When it was located in the Richmond District, Alejandro's was originally "the" Spanish restaurant in San Francisco. Although Peruvian artifacts line the walls, any attempt at elegance has been lost since it moved to the Mission a few years ago. Instead of paella the menu offers well over a dozen appetizers and several main plates from Peru and Mexico. The ceviche is one of the best, and a rendition of octopus salad is deliciously earthy. The classic Peruvian boiled potatoes, served here with feta and ricotta cheeses, turmeric and lemon-cream sauce, are velvety. Service, however, is almost nonexistent.

ALFRED'S STEAK HOUSE — STEAKHOUSE — 15/20

659 Merchant St., Chinatown 94111
415-781-7058, *Lunch Mon.-Fri., Dinner nightly, $$$$*

For more than 70 years, Alfred's has been offering great steaks and personal service. When the owners moved to a new location, they took everything with them, from the banquettes to the dark wood wainscoting to the ballroom chandeliers to the old-world charm. As they did in their former digs, the deep red wallpaper, the damask tablecloths and the gilded mirrors give the restaurant a stately yet still cozy appeal. The menu is straightforward: a Caesar salad prepared tableside (dressing with or without raw egg), redolent of anchovies and garlic. The entrée section offers more than half a dozen cuts of steak. Arguably the best is the 32-ounce porterhouse called "the King", a juicy tenderloin that practically dissolves on the tongue. The perfect accompaniments are the sinfully rich gratin potatoes and the nutmeg-graced creamed spinach. The wine list is deep with big, beefy reds. Dessert is superfluous.

ALIOTO'S NO. 8 — ITALIAN/SEAFOOD — 14/20

8 Fisherman's Wharf (at Taylor St.), Fisherman's Wharf 94133
415-362-7733, *Lunch & Dinner daily, $$$$*

Just because it's been on touristy Fisherman's Wharf forever, doesn't mean Alioto's is strictly for the tourists. Locals love the place, especially those of Italian extraction, for in addition to seafood, the kitchen turns out one of the best cioppinos in town and such robust Sicilian specialties as calamari topped with a mélange of bread crumbs, garlic and anchovies. The wine list is extensive and well chosen; wine expert Nunzio Alioto is one of three dozen Master Sommeliers in the United States. You'll no doubt pay dearly for both food and drink.

ALTA PLAZA — CALIFORNIA — 14/20

2301 Fillmore St., Pacific Heights 94115
415-922-1444, *Dinner nightly, Brunch Sun., $$*

The clientele is primarily gay, but all are welcome in this inviting spot on Fillmore Street's busy shopping strip. The dining room is a square, airy room overlooking the bar. The menu changes daily, but expect chef Amey Shaw to prepare rib-sticking dishes such as calf's liver with applewood-smoked bacon, Jack Daniels onions and mashed potatoes, or a pan-roasted duck breast with a winter vegetable purée and grilled radicchio napped by a sour-cherry-Chianti sauce. Shaw also favors vegetable juices as the base of her sauces, so many entrées are low in calories. Alta Plaza is a pleasant spot for a nightcap after a foreign flick at the nearby Clay Theater.

ANGKOR BOREI RESTAURANT CAMBODIAN 13/20

3471 Mission St., Outer Mission 94110
415-550-8417, *Lunch Mon.-Sat., Dinner nightly, $*

The first-rate cuisine in this bare-bones white stucco room is Cambodian, one of the least explored Asian cuisines in the Bay Area. Less elegant than Vietnamese and spicier than Thai, the offerings here include a grilled beef balls stuffed with fresh water chestnuts and served with pickled vegetables, and a crêpe of tofu, bean sprouts, ground pork and coconut with a lemon-garlic sauce and a shredded vegetable salad. Whole fried fish topped with a sweet-hot sauce is typically Cambodian, as are rich clay-pot entrées containing shrimp and vegetables.

ANJOU FRENCH 14/20

44 Campton Pl., Union Square 94108
(415) 392-5373 *Lunch & Dinner Tues.-Sat., $$*

Just steps from Union Square, this wonderful bistro is a favorite hideaway for shoppers and suits. Chef Pierre Morin looks to his Loire Valley home of Anjou for inspiration and turns out such favorites as warm duck confit with endive and watercress, and grilled steak with perfect frites. Cassoulet takes on a new meaning here: Morin uses lobster, monkfish and lingo beans in a crayfish sauce to lighten the traditionally heavy dish. Desserts include Morin's specialty, Anjou pears in a warm sabayon. The exposed-brick walls, brass trim and pale yellow fabric may look très 1980s, but the quiet dining room is a relief from the hustle and bustle outside.

ANTICA TRATTORIA ITALIAN 15/20

2400 Polk St., Russian Hill 94109
415-928-5797, *Dinner Tues.-Sun., $$*

Chef-owner Ruggero Gadaldi has developed a real neighborhood treasure, a casually sophisticated space with huge windows looking out on busy Polk Street. One brilliant starter is the sliced fennel with blood oranges and red onions. Main courses change frequently, but if they're available, try the braised veal short ribs or the bigoli, a spelt wheat spaghetti with a wild-boar sauce bolognese. The wine list is more than adequate, with fair prices and a good selection.

ANZU NIKKO STEAK/SUSHI 15/20

Nikko Hotel, 222 Mason St., Union Square 94102
415-394-1100, *Breakfast Mon.-Fri., Lunch & Dinner daily, Brunch Sun., $$$$*

Anzu Nikko manages to reinvigorate the cliché of "surf and turf." Anzu offers expertly prepared sushi appetizers and entrées of prime aged steak. The stars of the entrées are the prime cuts of steak, ranging from 6 to 16 ounces, all basted with a house marinade and cooked to order. Each is served with a choice of sauces, including a caramelized onion and a slightly sweet hoisin-barbecue sauce. Fire-roasted ratatouille and a wild-mushroom bread pudding are wonderful accompaniments. Overlooking the lobby of the elegant Hotel Nikko, Anzu Nikko has neutral checkerboard walls spiced up with blond and ebony wood highlights and detailing in malachite greens.

APERTO — CALIFORNIA/ITALIAN — 14/20

1434 18th St., Potrero Hill 94107
415-252-1625, *Lunch & Dinner daily, Brunch Sat.-Sun.,* $

The open kitchen in this small space gives customers a chance to get very close to their dinner even before it's served. The surroundings are pleasant, and the changing menu offers top-notch pastas and good roast chicken, served with baskets of warm homemade focaccia. Desserts, particularly the fruit tarts, are worth a look. The wine list is more than adequate. As they don't take reservations, prepare to wait for a table.

AQUA — CONTEMPORARY/SEAFOOD — 17/20

252 California St., Financial District 94111
415-956-0662, *Lunch Mon.-Fri., Dinner Mon.-Sat.,* $$$$

Aqua feels like a New York restaurant. That is, you can expect to see seriously dressed-up patrons here—and to spend serious money. It's a beautiful space with salmon-colored walls, a long curved bar and stunning floral arrangements. The restaurant specializes in creatures from the sea. And whether it's skate, black cod, swordfish, lobster or ahi tuna, it is some of the freshest seafood in San Francisco. The dishes are always very well prepared, and the meals taste ethereal under the direction of executive chef Michael Mina. Seasonal ingredients are incorporated into the menu, so, for example, heirloom tomatoes will appear in a soup during the summer months. Signature appetizers include black mussel soufflé and tartare of ahi tuna. Main courses that almost never come off the menu are the various fish enrobed in crispy potato "scales"; a tuna, foie gras and potato-cake napoleon; and the totally indulgent whole roasted foie gras. The wine list is impressive, the service professional. Desserts are a must, mostly classic French—sorbets, an espresso mousse, a sabayon or a charlotte—with the random humorous treat such as a root beer float.

ARABI AT RINCON ANNEX — MIDDLE EASTERN — ¢

100 Spear Street #22, Embarcadero 94105
415-243-8575, *Lunch Mon.-Fri.*

The Caféteria-style format belies the complexly seasoned and incredibly delicious Palestinian food served here. Crispy cumin-scented falafel and tender shwarma in pillowy soft pita are the best of the genre, especially when anointed with shatta, a fiery hot sauce. Wonderful salads, daily soups, grilled shish kebabs with vegetables, and saffron rice are not to be missed. A honey-dripping diamond of baklava is just one more jewel.

ARAM'S MEDITERRANEAN 13/20

3665 Sacramento St., Presidio Heights 94118
415-474-8061, *Dinner Tues.-Sat., Brunch Sun.*, $$$

This intimate restaurant is a well-kept secret in Presidio Heights. Tucked away behind a scenic landscaped courtyard, Aram's serves wonderful Mediterranean food. If you go in a large party, your best appetizer bets are the savory Taster Plates—sharing-size dishes of garlicky hummus, spanakopita, dolmadakis, and other Middle Eastern delicacies. The entrées are flavorful and occasionally innovative. Try the wine-braised lamb shank, which falls off the bone and dissolves in your mouth. It's served with white beans and a tangy mushroom relish. A tasty surprise is the lemony artichoke risotto.

ARINELL PIZZA PIZZA ¢

509 Valencia St., Mission 94110
415-255-1303, *Lunch & Dinner daily*

In this comfortable, noisy Mission storefront, Arinell specializes in thin-crust New York-style pizzas layered with traditional toppings and sprinkled with oregano, by the slice or whole. Keep the combinations to a minimum to enjoy the sharp flavors, subtle spices and properly crisped crust.

ASIASF FUSION 13/20

201 Ninth St., SoMa 94103
415-255-2742, *Dinner nightly*, $$

It takes seriously good food to keep your attention with everything else going on at AsiaSF. For one thing, the decor is outrageous, a sort of Asia-meets-the-Jetsons motif. Luminous shoji screens slowly change colors against two walls, while a sparse bamboo forest is set in front of another wall. Did we mention the waitresses? Every last one of them is an Asian male in drag. They're called "gender illusionists," and they're a big part of AsiaSF's appeal, especially when they mount the back bar and lip sync. The grilled shrimp and herb salad is good, as is the quesadilla filled with smoked duck and Jack cheese served with---believe it or not---a sun-dried-cherry crème fraîche dipping sauce that really works. The best way to do AsiaSF is to bring a gang and share the small dishes, then wait for the entertainment to begin.

ATLAS CAFÉ AMERICAN ¢

3049 20th St., Mission 94110
415-648-1047, *Lunch & Dinner daily*

Smack in the middle of the "Mission industrial zone," once a blue-collar Spanish-speaking neighborhood with a smattering of artists and photographers that has begun to show signs of yuppie/loft erosion, lies this bohemian enclave. Coffee drinks, homemade soups, generous salads, steamed eggs and a variety of sandwiches are the fare. Vegetarian choices are well represented on the sandwich board: you'll find roasted yams with feta, cilantro, onion and garlic olive oil on a baguette. Join the literati scene on the sunny back patio.

AVENUE 9   CALIFORNIA   13/20

1243 Ninth Ave., Sunset 94122
415- 664-6999, *Lunch Mon., Dinner nightly, Brunch Sun., $$*

Avenue 9 is part of the bumper crop of new restaurants in the Inner Sunset. This busy spot has managed to satisfy its clientele with solid, straightforward food like seared ahi tuna, Sonoma duck confit, Niman-Schell burgers and grilled salmon. We also recommend the house "pizzettas" of caramelized onion and roasted garlic, or barbecued duck. The servers are knowledgeable and friendly, and the wine list features a mix of California, Aussie and French labels.

AYA SUSHI   JAPANESE/SUSHI   13/20

2084 Chestnut St., Marina 94123
415-929-1670, *Lunch & Dinner Tues.-Sun., $$*

With a cheerful greeting, Aya's chef-owner Hiro Tanabe welcomes all to his small, unintimidating Japanese restaurant. Tanabe runs a tight ship: he mans the sushi bar; the solo waitress (literally) runs the beers and dishes to the handful of tables in the dining room; the behind-the-scenes cook turns out crisp seafood and vegetable tempura and moist and flavorful teriyaki. For singles and couples, the sushi bar is where you want to be. The rich sesame dressing on the green- and purple-cabbage house salad is positively addictive; order it separately or have it as part of the sushi combination plate. The dining room looks onto a bamboo garden, a nice respite from busy Chestnut Street. Expect harried service during peak hours.

BACKFLIP   CALIFORNIA   11/20

601 Eddy St., Tenderloin 94109
415-771-3547, *Dinner Tues.-Sat., $$*

The apotheosis of '90s hip makes its home at Backflip, the bar and restaurant hidden in the transitional Tenderloin. (The space, part of the Phoenix Hotel, once housed Miss Pearl's Jam House.) More L.A. than S.F., Backflip's decor is vibrant with shades of aquamarine and overlooks the motel's outdoor swimming pool. This place is hot with singles, so it's no surprise that the drink menu is nouveau martini bar. Backflip serves a tapas-style "cocktail cuisine" that roams the culinary map—hummus, sushi, prawn tamales—and is delivered via dim-sum trolley. The grilled vegetables, house-smoked salmon and minted Moroccan lamb show imagination but not consistency.

BAHIA CABANA | BRAZILIAN | 12/20

1600 Market St., Civic Center 94102
415-626-3306, *Dinner nightly, $$*

You can get the real flavor of Brazil here, not only through the food but also in the live music Thursday through Saturday, and from the huge, vibrant paintings on the wall. Hot peppers, cilantro, coconut and tropical fruits are staple ingredients of this cuisine. For an authentic taste of Brazil, try the feijoada completa, a rich stew of various meats, black beans and herbs, simmered all day and served with rice, farofa (toasted manioc flour and spices sautéed in garlic and olive oil) and couve (collards sautéed the same way). If you only want a quick bite, drop in for some tapas and a Xingu (Brazilian black beer) or two.

BAKER STREET BISTRO | FRENCH | 13/20

2953 Baker St., Marina 94123
415-931-1475, *Lunch & Dinner Tues.-Sun., $$*

Hearty French fare is the strength of this tiny restaurant just off Lombard Street's motel strip. We love the snails sautéed in garlic with cream for a starter, followed by a flavorful lamb stew or the superb rabbit in mustard sauce. At lunch, baguette sandwiches and a lovely quiche are satisfying. The traditional crème brûlée for dessert is worth a trip across town.

BALBOA CAFÉ | AMERICAN | 12/20

3199 Fillmore St., Cow Hollow 94123
415-921-3944, *Lunch & Dinner daily, $$$*

Billy Getty and Gavin Newsom of PlumpJack Café bought this venerable bar and eatery and gave it a beautiful face-lift. The society crowd and their kids are coming again to rub shoulders, grab a bite, and down a few. The menu mostly centers on unfussy American food: roasts, chops, seafood and poultry. The burger is still terrific, but make sure you get it on a hamburger bun; trying to eat one on a baguette will run up your cleaning bill.

BANGKOK 16 | THAI | 11/20

3214 16th St., Mission 94103
415-431-5838, *Dinner nightly, $*

The Mission is particularly rich in Thai restaurants, and the diminutive Bangkok 16 is a neighborhood favorite: spend a few moments inside and you'll know why. The hook is the charming, home-style dining room—it feels more like a living room—and the friendly, exceptionally gracious service. One appetizer, meang-kom, is startling and delicious. A plethora of ingredients—ginger, lemon, coconut, peanuts, onions and dried shrimps—come with spinach leaves for you to roll your own. The Bangkok 16 crêpe is similarly delicious; all the dishes on the extensive menu are artfully presented and served.

BARCELONA   SPANISH   13/20

7 Spring St., Financial District 94104
415-989-1976, *Lunch Mon.-Fri., Dinner Mon.-Sat., $$*

If you can find your way to tiny Spring Street, you'll find Barcelona, a stylishly fanciful restaurant hidden among the towers of the Financial District. Inside is a riot of iconic Spanish images: Picasso and Miró prints battle for your attention above impossibly plush booths. The menu features dishes with a level of style that sets Barcelona apart from other would-be tapas palaces. Try the succulent Moorish-style lamb in almond-garlic sauce, or the scallops grilled in the shell over saffron-laced onions. Entrées such as zarzuela a la Catalonia, a rich seafood stew, and the churrasco à la parilla, a grilled Angus steak topped with wood-roasted piquillo peppers, receive tasteful treatment. Entertainment, from disco to live salsa bands, is often featured in the back room.

BARAONDA   ITALIAN   11/20

2162 Larkin St., Russian Hill 94109
415-447-0441, *Dinner nightly, $$$*

The epitome of a cozy trattoria, Baraonda is comfortable and calming. In fact, the taupe walls, white tablecloths and copious candlelight make it a romantic place to dine. The extensive menu offers a number of traditional dishes and more than a dozen nightly specials. Starters include tuna tartare and a Belgian endive shrimp salad. Entrées range from a braised veal shank on a bed of fettuccine to more original plates like grilled salmon piled high with mango, avocado and pineapple. While some of the dishes are good, the kitchen is inconsistent. Sadly, Baraonda's food falls far short of its superior sister restaurant, Bella, in the Richmond District.

BASIL   THAI   13/20

1175 Folsom St., SoMa 94103
415-552-8999, *Lunch Mon.-Fri., Dinner nightly, $$*

The deep purple banner flapping outside this South of Market eatery gives you the first clue that this is something more than a run-of-the-mill Thai restaurant. Basil has put together a stylish and contemporary interior of midnight blue walls, bright yellow columns, chrome wall sconces and enormous flower arrangements. Happily, the interior is also home to exceptionally good food. Start with an appetizer of tender fried calamari served with a spicy dipping sauce. From the grill, you might opt for the flavorful slab of marinated skirt steak topped with a Thai peanut sauce. Complete the meal with a side of refreshing cucumber salad and jasmine rice.

FOR GAYOT'S UPDATED SAN FRANCISCO RESTAURANT REVIEWS, GO TO:

Digitalcity.com/sanfrancisco/dining

BASTA PASTA   ITALIAN   11/20

1268 Grant Ave., North Beach 94133
415-434-2248, *Dinner nightly*, $$

At his nearby North Beach Restaurant, Lorenzo Petroni is as much a draw as is his partner Bruno Orsi's food. Petroni nightly welcomes regular longtime patrons and a host of movers and shakers. Because of Petroni's long track record and high profile, the reopening of his 20-year-old Basta Pasta after a beautiful remodeling was much anticipated. Changing about every six weeks, the menu features pastas and pizzas, seafood and meats, and of course hot and cold antipasti. Unfortunately, the food does not match the beautiful interior. The wine list has 500 choices, including 70 from Italy, and—mama mia!—72 grappas. Recently, they stopped serving lunch but added live jazz on Thursday nights.

BEACH CHALET   AMERICAN/BREWPUB   12/20

1000 Great Hwy., Richmond 94121
415-386-8439, *Lunch Mon.-Sat., Dinner nightly, Brunch Sun.*, $$

The draw here is not the food or house-made microbrews, although the brews are tasty; it is the spectacular 180-degree view of the waves crashing on Ocean Beach. The Beach Chalet opened in 1997 after massive renovations to the vintage beach-side building that now doubles as a restaurant and historic site. The dining room stretches across the second floor, while the main floor houses the history of Golden Gate Park and a collection of restored Depression-era murals. Arrive during daylight hours to appreciate the view. The food pairs nicely with the microbrews, but the execution can be hit or miss—stick to basics like the roast chicken and the Niman-Schell burger.

BETELNUT   PAN-ASIAN   15/20

2030 Union St., Cow Hollow 94123
415-929-8855, *Lunch & Dinner daily*, $$$

There's an air of drama and excitement at Betelnut, as if you were dining in an exotic bar with a Raffles look, replete with paintings of beautiful Asian women and overhead fans lazily swirling. The food is pan-Asian with a bow to European techniques. It's always good, sometimes great. Start with sun-dried anchovies, wok-tossed with peanuts, chiles and garlic, or the chile-encrusted calamari. Move on to the orange-glazed beef with Szechuan peppercorns or the hot-and-chile'd Singaporean whole crab. There's a whole range of delightfully sinful drinks, and the wine list matches the firecracker flavors of the food, offering a good example of what can be done with serious wines and Asian food.

BIG NATE'S   BARBECUE   ¢

1665 Folsom St., SoMa 94103
415-861-4242, *Lunch & Dinner daily*

This bright yellow building, owned by basketball Hall of Famer Nate Thurmond, is one of a handful of barbecue outlets in San Francisco. Big Nate was a very good basketball player, and you want his barbecue to be good, too, but it's only fair. The sauce is very tomatoey and barely spicy. The meat is over-smoked and hard under the sauce, with no tender juiciness.

BILL'S PLACE   AMERICAN   ¢

2315 Clement St., Richmond District 94121
415-221-5262, *Lunch & Dinner daily*

This longtime favorite doesn't serve the best burger in town, but the place is comfortable and friendly. Bill's also does well by other lunch-counter staples: French fries, malts and shakes, tuna or egg salad sandwiches and a variety of green salads. The flower-filled patio is wonderful on a sunny day.

BISTRO AIX   FRENCH   14/20

3340 Steiner St., Marina 94123
415-202-0100, *Dinner nightly, $$*

Chef-owner Jonathan Beard has created a welcoming French bistro with a high-tech look. All those hard surfaces mean that the noise level can be high, but the food is so delicious that you may not notice. Starters are faves like mussels in a white-wine-shallot broth, Entrées include "cracker crust" pizzas, and tarragon-perfumed roast chicken with mashed potatoes and ratatouille. The $11.95 prix-fixe dinner Sundays to Thursdays from 6 p.m. to 8 p.m. is a good draw. Desserts are delightful—try the tarte tatin or the caramel mousse cake with chocolate ganache. The heated patio is alluring.

BISTRO CLOVIS   FRENCH   11/20

1596 Market St., Civic Center 94102
415-864-0231, *Lunch Mon.-Fri., Dinner daily, $$*

The look here is that of a sedate and cozy French bistro. House-made pâté with onion marmalade, a sturdy onion soup and a lamb salad are well made. Main dishes can be hit-or-miss: the rabbit braised in Chardonnay is paired with a creamy shallot-enriched sauce, but an uninspired goat-cheese-stuffed chicken breast can leave you cold. Desserts include old standbys like tarte tatin and crème brûlée.

BISTRO ZARE   MEDITERRANEAN   NO RATING

1507 Polk St., Polk Gulch 94109
415-775-4304, *Dinner nightly, $*

Bistro Zare is Hoss Zare's new second restaurant, which follows Zare on Sacramento Street. Starters include carpaccio

de Ladoucette Pouilly-Fumé: "Subtle green plum, mineral and herb with notes that carry through from start to the long, mouthwatering finish. Appealing for its subtlety and grace." - *Wine Spectator*

SETTING THE STANDARD FOR THE WORLD'S WHITE WINES.

de Ladoucette

Pouilly-Fumé
France

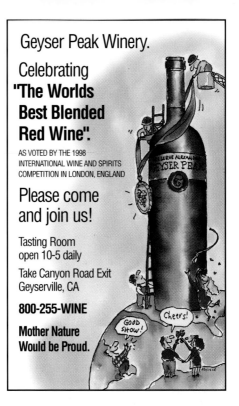

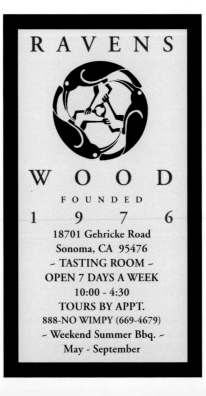

dishes, and the fish entrées are somewhat do-it-yourself. Choose a fish and match it with a sauce of your choice, like a spicy puttanesca. Sandwiches, pastas and the roast chicken are also well-done. Unlike the cavernous Zare, this restaurant (the former Aromi) has a enclosed brick patio looking out onto Polk Street—perfect for people watching.

BITTERROOT   AMERICAN   12/20
3122 16th St., Mission 94110
415-626-5523, *Breakfast & Lunch daily, Dinner Tues.-Sat., $-$$*

Inside this airy Bohemian storefront overlooking the heart of the Mission, the flavors are big, reminding you of a roadside diner somewhere in the Midwest—only lots better. Try barbecued pork spare ribs, served with crisp roasted potatoes, spicy coleslaw and yam chips. Bitterroot also serves a great American-style breakfast.

BIX   AMERICAN   12/20
56 Gold St., Financial District 94133
415-433-6300, *Lunch Mon.-Fri., Dinner nightly, $$$*

Squint and you can well believe that F. Scott Fitzgerald and his party are waiting for a table at the end of the bar. This 1920s-style supper club, with its burnished dark wood and polished brass, its white-jacketed wait staff and jazz pianist, serves what might be described as classic American cuisine. Try the chicken hash or an inventive Waldorf salad—here with apples, walnuts and blue cheese. When is the last time you saw a wedge of iceberg lettuce doused with a creamy blue-cheese dressing? Other classics include roasted chicken, braised lamb shank and rib-eye steak.

BIZOU   MEDITERRANEAN   13/20
598 Fourth St., SoMa 94107
415-543-2222, *Lunch Mon.-Fri., Dinner Mon.-Sat., $$*

In a city suddenly overflowing with bistros, Bizou is a delicious blend of French tradition and freewheeling California accents. It is a small but airy space, and the food is terrific and reasonably priced. There's a wood-burning oven at the heart of Bizou's menu, so try the pizzas with special toppings. An appetizer of batter-fried green beans with fig dipping sauce is a surprising but tasty combination. We recommend such country-style dishes as the braised beef cheek. Desserts such as the clafoutis or the bittersweet-chocolate vacherin continue the French bistro theme. The wine list is brief but well-selected.

BLACK CAT   CONTEMPORARY/SEAFOOD   14/20
501 Broadway, North Beach 94133
415-981-2230, *Lunch & Dinner daily, $$$*

Reed Hearon's latest restaurant is a swinging, bi-level American brasserie that recaptures North Beach's '50s Beatnik look, from the spindly graphics to the Lawrence Ferlinghetti poem that's graffitied on the brick wall outside (the poet is a regular lunch patron). The menu is an appealing mix "from the four corners of Broadway," which means Italian, seafood, Asian and old-fashioned American. You'll find everything from oysters and Dungeness crab to steak frites, Hong Kong-style chow mein, Italian pastas and such sophisticated specials as tuna au poivre with red wine sauce and foie gras. The downstairs lounge is dark and sexy, the perfect setting for a martini while grooving to cool live jazz. The wine—dare we call it a list? It's more like a book, a comprehensive and varied selection of nearly 200 wines.

BLOWFISH SUSHI TO DIE FOR   JAPANESE   12/20

2170 Bryant St., Potrero Hill 94110
415-285-3848, *Lunch Mon.-Fri., Dinner nightly, $$*
☎

This stylish sushi bar brings to mind '80s L.A. Sleek lacquered wood and traditional saké pots are set against giant video screens playing Japanese animation. Add a pulsing techno soundtrack and you're blown away before you've taken your seat. The restaurant's name alludes to its dish of northern puffer, a harmless cousin to the poisonous fugu. Offerings from the kitchen are hit-or-miss—stick with the sushi plates.

BLUE POINT RESTAURANT   SEAFOOD   12/20

2415 Clement St., Richmond District 94122
415-379-9726, *Dinner Tues.-Sun., $$*
💆

As the name of this neighborhood restaurant suggests, the emphasis here is on fish and shellfish. The steamed sea bass with chopped rosemary and garlic is one of the better dishes, as are the pan-seared shrimp with goat cheese and sun-dried tomatoes. Despite the attention to fish, one of the house specials is a rib-eye steak, grilled to perfection.

BOCCA ROTIS   MEDITERRANEAN   13/20

1 W. Portal Ave., West Portal 94127
415-665-9900, *Lunch & Dinner daily, $$*
☎ 💆 🍶

Jesse James, the owner of Aperto on Potrero Hill, opened his second restaurant in a former bank—the high ceilings, lack of carpeting and soft surfaces bring the noise levels way up when it's busy. But the lavender-honey chicken from the rotisserie and quite possibly the best lemon meringue pie in the city are worth it. Early in the evening the tables are packed with families.

BOMBAY ICE CREAM & CHAAT   INDIAN   ¢

522 Valencia St., Mission 94110
415-431-1103, *Open Tues.-Sun.*
💆

Chaat is an Indian word meaning snack. We love the samosas, fried stuffed pastry turnovers, the aloo poori, mini

wheat bread pockets filled with potato, onion, cilantro and
yogurt. This little café (only two tables—this is walking food)
also has a collection of the most unusual ice cream flavors
you're likely to ever stumble on, like kesar pista (saffron and
pistachio), cardamom, fig, chai (spiced tea), rose and cashew
raisin. The curry lunch specials are a mega-bargain.

BOTANA   MEXICAN   ¢

422 Haight St., Lower Haight 94117
415-863-9113, *Lunch & Dinner Tues.-Sun.*

Botana (a little bite) is an apt name for this modest gem.
Every little bite is filled with big flavor, each sauce and salsa is
more complex and distinctive than the last. Highlights include
a vegetarian's dream tamale, with black beans, roasted chiles
and mixed vegetables, and fish tacos of cornmeal-coated, fried
mahi mahi paired with a crispy shredded-cabbage salad. One
drink, agua fresca de sandia, is the essence of ripe watermelon.
Buñuelos, crispy, cinnamon-sugared tortilla strips, provide a
sweet ending.

BOULEVARD   CONTEMPORARY   16/20

1 Mission St., Embarcadero 94105
415-543-6084, *Lunch Mon.-Fri., Dinner nightly, $$$$*

Owner-designer Pat Kuleto designed an elegant brasserie
for his partner, chef Nancy Oakes. The long bar is usually
packed. Curved brick ceilings give way to bistro seats at the
dining bar; to the rear, sparkling tiles and a view of the Bay
enhance the experience. The food on the daily-changing
menu is big and usually presented in some sort of tower shape.
You'll find great wood-oven-roasted items like a duck breast
served with a duck leg confit, spit-roasted pork loin and grilled
Hawaiian swordfish. Desserts, such as a marvelous espresso-fla-
vored angel food cake, have the same high standards as the
regular menu. The brilliant wine list is emphasizes California
selections, especially Chardonnay. Our only complaint on a
recent visit: slow service with attitude to boot.

BRASSERIE SAVOY   FRENCH   NO RATING

Hotel Savoy, 580 Geary St., Union Square 94102
415-441-8080, *Breakfast & Dinner daily, $$*

Large, brightly colored paintings bring this dining room to
life and contribute to an overall feeling of bonhomie. The
most recent chef and the best, Fabrice Canelle, left for the Big
Apple, and the future of the restaurant, which suffers from its
location—it's a little too far from the heart of the theater dis-
trict—is up in the air. Meanwhile, you'll find dishes on the
order of crispy sweetbreads with risotto, and desserts that run
from rich to refreshing, with lemon-crunch éclairs on the one
hand and passion-fruit sorbet on the other.

THE BRAZEN HEAD RESTAURANT   FRENCH   12/20

3166 Buchanan St., Marina 94123
415-921-7600, *Dinner nightly, $$*

Got an itch for escargot at midnight? This modest and romantic restaurant serves until 1 a.m. nightly. Tables have fresh flowers and are lit by candlelight. You can also order a garlicky Caesar or a solid onion soup with bubbling Gruyère. Chicken is done in a brandy sauce, and the filet mignon comes with dreamy scalloped potatoes. Because it serves late, restaurant workers flock here.

BRISAS DE ACAPULCO   MEXICAN/SALVADORAN   ¢

3137 Mission St., Mission 94110
415-826-1496, *Breakfast, Lunch & Dinner daily*

This friendly little place is open until midnight weeknights and until 3 a.m. on weekends, making it the perfect Mission drop-in for seafood with a Latin American accent. Served beneath a bold mural and a lively open kitchen, most dishes are well under $10. Try the fresh ceviche, tasty seafood soups, pupusas and seafood tostadas.

BROTHER-IN-LAW'S BAR-B-QUE   BARBECUE   ¢

705 Divisadero St., Western Addition 94115
415-931-7427, *Lunch & Dinner Tues.-Sun.*

Pilgrims from all over town line up at this brick smokehouse for the 'cue. Eugene Ponds and Demo Adams' slow-cooked pork ribs (the fat-free short ends are worth the extra charge), fork-tender beef brisket, chicken and lean beef links all carry a deep but never overpowering smoky taste. Ask for the mixed hot-and-mild sauce, plus sweet baked beans and corn muffins.

BRUNO'S   CALIFORNIA   12/20

2389 Mission St., Mission District 94110
415-550-7455, *Dinner Tues.-Sat., $$*

Bruno's is a pre-World War II Mission District hangout, brought to life by a couple of hip locals. The wonderful red leather booths from a restaurant that closed long ago, the retro light fixtures and the hostess decked out in 1950s garb give it a comfortable, clubby feel. The setting may be in a time warp, but the Cal-Med-style food is up-to-date. Go for the grilled chicken or the pork chops. The kitchen has not seemed to recover the spark it once had since the founding chef left. The bar area features music most nights.

FOR GAYOT'S UPDATED SAN FRANCISCO RESTAURANT REVIEWS, GO TO:

Digitalcity.com/sanfrancisco/dining

BUBBLE LOUNGE   GOURMET BAR FOOD   ¢

714 Montgomery St., Financial District 94111
415-434-4204, *Open Mon.-Sat., $-$$$$*

A branch of a Manhattan-based bubbly-and-snack venue, this hip spot concentrates on Champagne and sparkling wines: 20 bubblies by the glass are available plus a stock of more than 300 Champagnes and sparkling wines. The food is just nibbles, albeit good ones: oysters, caviar, pâté, spring rolls and cheese plates.

BURMA SUPER STAR   BURMESE   12/20

309 Clement St., Richmond District 94118
415-387-2147, *Lunch & Dinner Tues.-Sun., $*

The audaciously titled Burma Super Star has a lot to live up to: it's one of only a handful of restaurants that claim to serve authentic Burmese cuisine. Try lat pat doke, a salad of pickled green-tea leaves, tomatoes, cabbage, and roasted nuts, or moo hing nga, considered Burma's national dish: a rich stew of catfish and soft noodles in a spicy broth. Service, though occasionally forgetful, is unfailingly friendly.

BUTTERFIELD'S   SEAFOOD   13/20

Above Third St. Station Bar
202 Townsend St., SoMa 94107
415-281-9001, *Lunch Mon.-Fri., Dinner Tues.-Sat., $$*

At first glance, Butterfield's seems to be trapped in an out-of-the-way location, hidden over a bar in an old brick building. But when the Pac Bell baseball park is completed—the new home of the San Francisco Giants— Butterfield's will be a stone's throw away. The restaurant specializes in fresh seafood, prepared in a no-fuss, almost retro fashion: chowder, crab-cakes, oysters on the half shell, steamed Maine lobster and several blackened-fish offerings. If you're not a fan of fish or seafood, you'd best avoid Butterfield's—the lone non-fish entrée is a BLT sandwich.

BYBLOS RESTAURANT   LEBANESE   14/20

1910 Lombard St., Marina District 94123
415-292-5672, *Dinner nightly, $$*

Once you've been to Byblos you become part of the family. Local artists often display their paintings, and the whole feeling is so friendly that we just keep going back. You can choose from more than 20 little starters, ranging from a selection of pickled vegetables to lambs' tongues to the best dolmadakia in the city. They make their yogurt fresh daily. If you can put together a party of 12, you can special-order a whole roast lamb, which comes with all the mezes you want. The wine list is small but thoughtfully chosen; it includes Château Musar, the famed and hard-to-find wine from Lebanon.

CAFÉ AKIMBO   FUSION   13/20

116 Maiden Ln. Third Fl., Union Square 94108
415-433-2288, *Lunch & Dinner Mon.-Sat., $$*

☎

    This third-floor aerie is where East meets West with panache. The soft yellow walls are nicely set off by rainbow-painted support beams. We like the salad of mixed greens, balsamic vinaigrette, Gorgonzola, dried mission figs and spiced pecans. Another good choice is the grilled prawns with a kiwi-mint sauce. The ever changing menu has lots of good choices: braised beef short ribs; seared scallops and fusilli with a mushroom-macadamia-nut cream sauce.

CAFÉ BASTILLE   FRENCH   12/20

22 Belden Pl., Financial District 94104
415-986-5673, *Lunch & Dinner Mon.-Sat., $$*

☎ 🖥

    Located on a pedestrian side street, this French-kissed casual café has the best seats on the street itself. On pleasant days it's almost a slice of Paris, with patrons enjoying bistro favorites such as salade niçoise, onion soup, mussels and pâté. The wine list is just adequate.

CAFÉ CLAUDE   FRENCH   12/20

7 Claude Ln., Financial District 94111
415-392-3505, *Lunch & Dinner Mon.-Sat., $$*

☎

    If this feels like an authentic Parisian bistro, right down to its zinc-topped bar, that's because it is. Café Claude used to be Le Barbizon in Paris, until owner Steve Decker bought the place lock, stock and pastis pitchers—and shipped it to San Francisco. The sandwiches, soups and salads are good enough at lunch, but we prefer the value-priced food at dinner. The cassoulet is robust and savory, the chocolate mousse rich and silky. The crôque monsieur is the perfect snack.

CAFÉ CUVÉE   CALIFORNIA   13/20

2073 Market St., Castro 94114
415-621-7488, *Breakfast & Lunch Tues.-Fri., Dinner Tues.-Sat., Brunch Sat.-Sun., $$*

☎ 📷 👥 🍷 🍸

    Café Cuvée's chef is Anne O'Driscoll, a native San Franciscan. Seating 30 in two rooms with an open kitchen, O'Driscoll changes her menu monthly but always features local and organic ingredients. We recommend the simple soups, salads and rustic stews. The small wine list is surprisingly international. The weekend brunch spans everything from fluffy omelets to walnut crêpes.

CAFÉ DE LA PRESSE   FRENCH   12/20
352 Grant Ave., Downtown 94108
415-249-0900, *Breakfast, Lunch & Dinner daily, $$*

Café de la Presse has expanded into the space formerly occupied by Aïoli, the adjacent Mediterranean restaurant, and Sebastian Urbain, who ran both kitchens before, has greatly enlarged the menu. There's still a very French tilt to the food, which can be quite good. Look for the braised rabbit with apples, prunes and Calvados sauce, or the classic lamb shank. The wine list is just decent.

CAFÉ DE PARIS L'ENTRECÔTE FRENCH   13/20
2032 Union St., Marina 94123
415-931-5006, *Lunch & Dinner daily, $$$*
☎🚗🖥🏃

The specialty at this traditional French brasserie is the L'Entrecôte de Paris, a charbroiled New York steak served with a garlicky, buttery green sauce that you just can't get enough of. This entrée also comes with a butter lettuce salad and a continuous supply of wonderfully thin, extra crispy French fries. Start with the French onion soup, done right with crispy croutons and bubbling over with Gruyère. The glassed-in dining patio looks out onto bustling Union Street.

CAFÉ ETHIOPIA   ETHIOPIAN   ¢
878 Valencia St., Mission 94110
415-285-2728, *Lunch & Dinner daily*
☎👥

Café Ethiopia doesn't promise much with its modest coffee-shop decor, but it's a welcome addition to the Mission. Eighteen dishes run the gamut from the hearty kitfo, a buttery Ethiopian steak tartare, to the delicate alecha ater, a rich purée of yellow split peas.. Diners use chunks of injera, a spongy fermented crêpe, to scoop up the flavorful food.

CAFÉ FLORE   AMERICAN   ¢
2298 Market St., Castro 94114
415-621-8579, *Open daily*
✕🖥

This casual café looks like a large greenhouse surrounded by a fenced patio and perched on a sunny corner in the Castro. The habitués are as eclectic as San Francisco itself: gays, straights and the pierced and tattooed. The sandwiches, egg dishes and salads are good, but it is the espresso drinks and the scene that draw the crowds.

CAFÉ FLORIO   FRENCH   14/20
1915 Fillmore St., Fillmore 94115
415-775-4300, *Dinner nightly, Brunch Sat.-Sun., $$$*
☎👥🍸🍾

French food is making a comeback big time. Florio, one of the latest bistros to open, is one of the nicest. Owner Doug

Biederbeck, who also owns Bix, has taken a space that housed Oritalia and transformed it. Art deco lamps, gold-toned walls and lots of burgundy set the scene for the brasserie-inspired food. We loved the steak frites, the roast chicken and the mussels. Chef David Shawn does retro apps like radishes with buttered bread and salt. Other treats include a bracing lobster bisqueand—fusilli with braised oxtails. The wine list has many hard-to-find European choices and good values on California selections.

CAFÉ FOR ALL SEASONS   AMERICAN   13/20
150 W. Portal, West Portal 94127
415-665-0900, *Lunch & Dinner Mon.-Fri., Brunch & Dinner Sat.-Sun.*, $$

This all-American café is a no-fuss, untrendy place where diners can eat (rather than dine on) good solid burgers and pastas. You'll find entrées such as a simple grilled trout topped with herb butter and served with crispy french fries. Owner Donna Katzl studied with the late James Beard, and the menu and style of this restaurant reflects her training. We highly recommend the apple cake with warm caramel sauce.

CAFÉ JACQUELINE   FRENCH   13/20
1454 Grant Ave., North Beach 94133
415-981-5565, *Dinner Wed.-Sun.*, $$

Jacqueline Margulis works miracles with soufflés—and only soufflés (with soup and salad on the side). In short, this small, warm, romantic space in the heart of North Beach is the holy grail if you are a soufflé fancier. The heavy hitter is the pricey black truffle version, but no less memorable are the cauliflower, wild mushroom, prosciutto, corn, broccoli…and so on. The salad of mixed greens with pine nuts and bacon is a perfect way to begin. Desserts are spectacular; among them are a chocolate soufflé.

CAFÉ KATI   CONTEMPORARY   13/20
1963 Sutter St., Western Addition 94115
415-775-7313, *Dinner Tues.-Sun.*, $$

Chef-owner Kirk Webber indulges in cross-cultural stylings and dramatic presentations. Occasionally a dish doesn't work, but it's often rewarding to choose between unique creations such as a miso-marinated Chilean sea bass with tempura Japanese squash, and roasted salmon with a portobello mushroom, tomato confit, Kalamata olives and salsa verde. Desserts run to the classic with twists, like a butterscotch pudding with a Tina Turner wig of spun sugar. The wine list matches the wide range of tastes offered here, with helpful tips from the chef.

CAFÉ MARIMBA   MEXICAN/CALIFORNIA   11/20
2317 Chestnut St., Marina 94123
415-776-1506, *Lunch Tues.-Sun., Dinner nightly*, $$

Unlike the city's plethora of taco and burrito places, Café Marimba attempts, sometimes successfully, to present authentic Mexican regional cuisine. The moles and special sauces are brought in from Mexico. The snapper ceviche can be good, and when they take care, the dishes with the imported moles shine. The owner has put together a good tequila list and a thoughtful wine list. The trendy crowd can seem very *Melrose Place*.

CAFÉ NIEBAUM-COPPOLA   ITALIAN   NO RATING

916 Kearny St., North Beach 94133
415-291-1700, *Open daily, $$*

Near press time, Café Niebaum-Coppola opened in the Sentinel Building, which also houses Francis Ford Coppola's film company. The café serves casual, rustic Italian fare. The modest menu includes pizza, sandwiches and a couple of pasta dishes. A heated terrazzo sidewalk and a bright red heated canopy make the outdoor seating fun for people watchers. The extensive wine list offers wines by the glass, flights of wine and bottles. It's not a late-night bistro, though, closing at 8 p.m.

CAFÉ PESCATORE   ITALIAN   11/20

The Tuscan Inn, 2455 Mason St., Fisherman's Wharf 94133
415-561-1111, *Breakfast & Lunch Mon.-Fri., Dinner nightly, Brunch Sat.-Sun., $$*

Savor the garlic wafting into the dining room from the large open kitchen. Chicken cacciatore is a specialty at this hotel trattoria: here the boneless breast of the bird is infused with a zesty porcini mushroom sauce and ladled over a slab of polenta. Try the wood-fired pizza, followed by a dessert "calzone" filled with brandied apples and raisins.

CAFÉ TIRAMISU   ITALIAN   12/20

28 Belden Pl., Financial District 94104
415-421-7044, *Lunch Mon.-Fri., Dinner Mon.-Sat., $$*

When the sun is out, the breeze is gentle, and you've got an hour or two to spare, having lunch at one of the tables set out in front of Café Tiramisu is a joyful reminder of why you love San Francisco. The simple fare is perfect for light dining—rustic bruschetta, spaghetti pomodoro, penne doused with a deliciously garlicky tomato sauce. For dessert, have the tiramisu.

CAFFÈ TRIESTE   CAFÉ/DESSERTS   ¢

601 Vallejo St., North Beach 94133
415-392-6739, *Open daily*

An eclectic clientele of bohemians, locals and tourists flock here for the cappuccino and pastries. A limited number of sandwiches, like turkey or ham and cheese on focaccia, are nice at lunch. The company imports, roasts and distributes its own beans in a retail shop next door. Every Saturday afternoon at 1 p.m. the restaurant holds a sing-along, with patrons and staff performing arias together.

CAFFÈ DELLE STELLE   ITALIAN   13/20

395 Hayes St., Hayes Valley 94102
415-252-1110, *Lunch Mon.-Sat., Dinner nightly*, $$

Its walls lined with wine bottles and stacks of canned toma-
toes, Caffè Delle Stelle serves basic Italian fare in the heart of
Hayes Valley. Location alone could keep this place busy—it's
close to the Performing Arts Center. Lunch might mean roast-
ed pumpkin-and-ricotta ravioli or any of a number of reason-
ably priced pasta dishes. At dinner, homemade gnocchi with
smoked chicken-apple sausage, seafood risotto, osso buco and
braised lamb on polenta, are good bets. Wines comprise a mix
of Tuscan reds and big-name California favorites.

CAFFÈ MACARONI   ITALIAN   13/20

59 Columbus Ave., North Beach 94133
415-956-9737, Lunch Mon.-Fri., Dinner Mon.-Sat., $$

This tiny, cramped space—with a mezzanine dining area—
offers rustic Italian fare much like you'd find on a busy side
street in Naples, where the owner hails from. You'll find every
imaginable size and shape of macaroni plastered on the ceiling; and the charming Italian waiters ensure that any visit is
bound to be pleasant. We recommend the reasonably priced
pasta, pizza and hearty daily specials like the mélange of
seafood over pasta "dyed" with squid ink The wine list is surprisingly deep, with an Italian accent.

CAFFÈ SPORT   ITALIAN   13/20

574 Green St., North Beach 94133
415-981-1251, *Lunch & Dinner Tues.-Sat.,* $$$

Caffè Sport continues to be a favorite for delicious south-
ern Italian food, like the garlic-laden seafood platters, pastas
and probably one of the best cioppinos in the city. The festive
Sicilian-inspired artifacts and artwork, and the twinkling
Christmas lights, will get you in a festive mood. Because the
prices are not cheap and the portions so big, it's best to come
here in groups of four or more.

CALIFORNIA CULINARY ACADEMY   MEDITERRANEAN   11/20

625 Polk St., Tenderloin 94102
415-771-3536, Lunch & Dinner Mon.-Fri., Buffet Fri. & Sun., $$

If you have a sense of adventure, this is the place for you.
All of the meals served in both of the restaurants here (plus
the goodies available in the café/deli) are prepared by students in the school's 16-month professional-chef training program— with mixed results. The Academy Grill features simple
salads, soups, burgers and other grilled dishes prepared by the
freshman class. In the Carême Room, upperclassmen produce
an ambitious, ever-changing menu that recently assumed a
more Mediterranean bent. Your servers are also students, who
are required to learn all aspects of restaurant operations.

CAMPO SANTO   MEXICAN   ¢

240 Columbus Ave., North Beach 94133
415-433-9623, *Open daily*

Food influenced by the Mayan region of the Yucatan peninsula is Santo's specialty. Try the quesadilla Cancun, made with nopale cactus, rock shrimps and corn, the grilled chicken marinated in achiote and sweet chiles, or the daily fish specials. You'll dine within bright blue and yellow adobe walls decorated with candles and statues with a Día de Los Muertos theme.

CAMPTON PLACE   FRENCH   NO RATING

Campton Place Hotel, 340 Stockton St., Union Square 94108
415-955-5555, *Breakfast, Lunch & Dinner daily, Brunch Sun.,* $$$$

This hotel dining room has had a fine tradition of great chefs, including Bradley Ogden. Recently, new chef Laurent Manrique began adding his signature dishes to the menu. Specialties include monkfish roasted Basque-style with red and yellow peppers and Serrano ham, and striped bass enlivened with caramelized fennel and tomato confit. This destination restaurant is richly comfortable, offering the kind of fine-dining experience that is rare in these rushed times. The staff is always helpful. Campton Place has always been renowned for its breakfast and brunch, which features a delectable smoked-salmon omelet. The small bar off the entrance is a pleasant place. The extensive wine list is pricey, but shows great depth in California offerings.

CANTO DO BRASIL   BRAZILIAN   12/20

41 Franklin St., Civic Center 94102
415-626-8727, *Lunch Mon.-Fri., Dinner nightly,* $$

Life is a Carnaval! You can celebrate the vibrant, zesty flavors of Brazil at this colorful and cheery little spot. Duck under the blazing yellow awning and into the cozy cobalt and terracotta environs enlivened with Gauguin-esque murals. A traditional Brazilian specialty, feijoada completa, a thick black bean stew, is available on weekends. Another favorite is sautéed prawns or red snapper in a tasty coconut sauce. Entrées are served with rice, beans and farofa (toasted manioc flour). If you're still yearning for a taste of Brazil, head around the corner to Bahia Cabana, one of the city's best dance clubs, also owned by the Neto family.

CAPP'S CORNER   ITALIAN   11/20

1600 Powell St., North Beach 94133
415-989-2589, *Lunch Mon.-Fri., Dinner nightly,* $

From the photographs of the DiMaggio brothers to the long bar, you can tell Capp's is about local color, not food. A tossed salad, tartly dressed and full of canned kidney beans, follows the soup. If it's on the daily special board, osso buco is one of the best dishes. Entrées are served with mixed vegetables and a plate of pasta. Wash it all down with an inexpensive

Chianti. Not great food, but Capp's is fun and the price is right.

CARNELIAN ROOM · FRENCH/CALIFORNIA 12/20

Top of the Bank of America Bldg.
555 California St., Financial District 94104
415-433-7500, *Dinner nightly, Brunch Sun., $$$$*

Fifty-two floors above the city is surely one of the most spectacular settings imaginable for a restaurant. The menu varies but holds no surprises. Appetizers include ahi carpaccio and oysters on the half shell; salmon comes peppered, grilled and drizzled with lemon butter; duck is twice-roasted in a sour-cherry-citrus glaze. The wine list is heavily French and has some older treasures, if you are willing to pay. The bar has the same magnificent view and is frequented by a younger, after-work crowd.

CARTA · ECLECTIC · 13/20

1772 Market St., Civic Center 94102
415-863-35162, *Lunch Mon.-Fri., Dinner Tues.-Sun., Brunch Sun., $$*

Every two months this small restaurant cooks a different world cuisine. Usually the chefs offer a series of small plates or appetizers and four larger entrées planned around the theme. They've recently expanded their space and added a bar. As for the food, one of the best attempts has been with the flavors of Spain and Morocco: appetizers such as vegetable rice empanadas and merguez Moroccan lamb sausages, entrées of paella; zarzuela or Spanish-style mussels.

CASSIS BISTRO · FRENCH · 13/20

2120 Greenwich St., Cow Hollow 94123
415-292-0770, *Dinner Tues.-Sat., $$*

Unpretentious Cassis looks to southern France for inspiration. More often than not, the small dining room echoes with both English and French. Expect smallish portions of simple classics like homemade pâté, endive salad with goat cheese, and garlicky escargots in puff pastry. Entrées include a savory lamb stew, rosemary-scented braised rabbit and simple sautéed swordfish. The friendly staff moves efficiently.

CHA CHA CHA · LATIN AMERICAN · 12/20

1801 Haight St., Haight-Ashbury 94117
415-386-5758, *Lunch Mon.-Fri., Dinner nightly, $$*

A mainstay of the wild and crazy Haight, Cha Cha Cha brims with primary colors and lots of noise and loud music—it's definitely a place for the young. The eclectic selection of tapas-inspired dishes ranges from mouth-tingling calamari to deep-fried new potatoes. Other tapas are Cuban inspired, such as the fried plantains with black beans. The daily specials board almost always features fish and some form of barbecue.

CHAPEAU! FRENCH 15/20

1408 Clement St., Richmond District 94118
415-750-9787, *Dinner Tues.-Sun.*, $$

Minimally decorated with white tablecloths, this bistro serves lusty French country food. The menu usually offers two or three prix-fixe menus and a bargain-priced early-bird special. Splendid appetizers like sautéed sweetbreads or a silken lobster bisque pave the way for such main courses as crispy salmon on lentils or pork loin steak in a persillade crust. Desserts at Chapeau! are similarly fabulous, especially the berry napoleon. The wine list is amazing for such a small place, with over 300 wines offered.

CHARANGA LATIN/TAPAS ¢

2351 Mission, Mission 94110
415-282-1813, *Dinner Tues.-Sat.*

This noisy, colorful little hole-in-the-wall is located near the popular Bruno's in the newly hip part of the Mission. Many small plates make up the menu: ahi tuna with three flavorful sauces; sautéed mushrooms perfumed with garlic and shallots; a calamari and shrimp sauté redolent of garlic and ginger, surrounded by green pea shoots, with a mound of coconut rice in the center of the plate. Larger plates might feature a seafood stew or a risotto flavored with Spanish Manchego cheese instead of Parmesan. Desserts tend toward the homey but are very good. An ample list of inexpensive wines allows grazers to explore various wine and food pairings.

CHARLES NOB HILL FRENCH/CALIFORNIA 16/20

1250 Jones St. at Clay, Nob Hill 94109
415-771-5400, *Dinner Tues.-Sun.*, $$$$

Chef Ron Siegel's sophisticated cuisine pairs well with the elegant, romantic setting of this upscale offshoot of Restaurant Aqua. We favor the cozier side room facing the street. Foie gras makes several appearances on the menu, but none is better than the sautéed foie gras paired with a huckleberry compote, black pepper jus and brioche crouton. The rich alliances continue in the main courses: local prawns with lobster ravioli, filet mignon with a crispy polenta cake and hen-of-the-woods mushrooms. Other choices might include potato-crusted halibut, pan-seared squab breast and sautéed black bass. Desserts are often upscale versions of homey tastes, like the warm brioche bread pudding. Try one of the tasting menus, complemented with wines from the well-selected but expensive list.

CHEF JIA'S   CHINESE   ¢

925 Kearny St., Chinatown 94133
415-398-1626, *Lunch & Dinner daily*

Though it adheres to the Formica-and-linoleum school of decorating, Chef Jia's serves first-rate, inexpensive Chinese food. Perennial favorites include spicy string beans with yams, mu shu (pancake-wrapped) dishes and a braised whole fish, the most expensive entrée at $10.95.

CHOW   AMERICAN   13/20

215 Church St., Castro 94114
415-552-2469, *Lunch & Dinner daily, $*

This addition to the Castro's collection of mediocre restaurants has soul-satisfying food at bargain prices. Not everything works, but if short ribs are on the menu, make a bee-line. The hot meatball sandwich is very filling. Pizza by the slice, a good burger and fresh salads are winners. The no-oil Thai salad is one of the healthy dishes on the menu. For anyone who's ever been annoyed by $16 pasta dishes, the pastas here, all priced under $8, will be a welcome sight. **Also Park Chow at 1240 Ninth St.**

CHRISTOPHE   FRENCH   14/20

415 Mason St., Union Square 94104
415-771-6393, *Dinner nightly, $$$*

A favorite pre- and post-theater choice, Christophe is romantic, elegant and relaxing. Soft mauve walls, candlelight and fresh flowers combine to create intimacy above the hum of Union Square's bustling theater district. The well-priced prix-fixe menu allows a choice of entrées, including the delicate salmon Wellington, the roasted duck with a tangy orange and raspberry glaze, or the tender, succulent herb-crusted rack of lamb. For dessert try the profiteroles, a house specialty.

CITRUS CLUB   FUSION   11/20

1790 Haight St., Haight 94117
415-387-6366, *Lunch & Dinner Tues.-Sun., $*

Tropical surrealist art and Vietnamese bordello chic set the decorative tone for this cozy storefront restaurant. The menu tours Southeast Asia by way of enormous bowls of noodles at bargain prices. Start with the addictive wasabi-roasted peas and a minty, rice-noodle-wrapped spring roll. The Thai-inspired hot-sour shrimp noodle soup is enough to feed a small family. This is hippie chow come of age.

FOR GAYOT'S UPDATED SAN FRANCISCO RESTAURANT REVIEWS, GO TO:

Digitalcity.com/sanfrancisco/dining

CITY OF PARIS FRENCH 13/20
101 Shannon Alley, Union Square 94102
415-441-4442, *Breakfast, Lunch & Dinner daily, $$*

Reasonably priced, rustic, bistro-style cuisine served in a lovely dining room is the draw here. A large open kitchen—backed by a huge rotisserie—faces the dining room. Start with the Roquefort-spiked red cabbage salad or the onion-fennel soup gratinée. Recommended entrées include a crispy but virtually greaseless duck confit and a tender grilled salmon. The rotisserie chicken was disappointing on a recent dinner, but they do a good hamburger. Save room for desserts.

CITYSCAPE AMERICAN 13/20
San Francisco Hilton & Towers, 333 O'Farrell St., Union Square 94102
415-923-5002, *Dinner nightly, Brunch Sun., $$$*

Perched on the 46th floor of the San Francisco Hilton, Cityscape offers great views plus traditional American fare nightly, but we're most excited about their lavish $42 per person Sunday buffet brunch. The Champagne flows while guests make their way from food station to food station, sampling an array of dishes inspired by cuisines from all over the world. Crave caviar? You'll find five kinds to choose from. Interested in Italian? Try the prosciutto di Parma with grilled eggplant. There's also Japanese sushi, Chinese smoked duck and Australian lamb chops, plus chicken from nearby Petaluma served with a Thai-coconut-chile sauce.

CLEMENTINE FRENCH 14/20
126 Clement St., Richmond District 94118
415-387-0408, *Dinner Tues.-Sun., Brunch Sun., $$$*

Newish Clementine brings an elegant measure of French charm to this area, and serves delicious bourgeois dishes at reasonable prices. Decorated with vintage posters, Clementine has neighborhood appeal: diners range from business people to romantic couples to families with young children, all out for a bite of wonderful French country cooking. One signature starter is the richly delicious walnut-crusted sweetbreads topped with duxelles. Try the beef bourguignon or the roast salmon with a mussel sauce. A distinctive dessert is the Far Breton, a dense French custard filled with prunes and raisins.

COLUMBUS RISTORANTE ITALIAN 11/20
3347 Fillmore St., Marina 94123
415-781-2939, *Dinner Tues.-Sun., $$*

May Ditano moved her North Beach eatery to the Marina several years ago. Whereas her snappy counter chat went over well at her counter-based restaurant on Broadway, the upscale neighborhood and fancier digs don't seem to be as good a match. In an open room with a long hallway of tables (it's the former space of Café Adriano), Ditano offers an appetizer of bread topped with mozzarella grilled until it's melted, finished with a butter-anchovy dressing, plus creamy risotti and tender osso buco. Ditano herself often patrols the dining room.

CRUSTACEAN   SEAFOOD/VIETNAMESE   14/20

1475 Polk St., Polk Gulch 94109
415-776-2722, Dinner nightly, $$

A 270-foot neon wave spans the exterior of this stylish Vietnamese restaurant, named for the house specialty—Dungeness crab. Inside, a massive, vividly colored mural effectively turns the entire restaurant into an undersea wonderland. Crab is prepared three ways: roasted, drunken (poached in three wines and scallions) or sweet and sour. Each style is rewarding, but the garlicky roast crab, the house's signature dish, is especially tempting. Another signature is the irresistible garlic noodles dish—so secret the recipe is prepared in a separate "secret" kitchen. Other good entrées on the Euro-Asian menu are the chicken stuffed with pork, almonds, mushrooms and onions, and the curried prawns.

CURBSIDE CAFÉ   CALIFORNIA/FRENCH   13/20

2417 California, Fillmore District 94115
415-929-9030, Open daily, $

Competition for the good food at this charming eatery can be fierce—it has only ten tables. Start the day with a hearty serving of Curbside's stellar bourbon-baked French toast, or one of the variations on eggs Benedict. For an inexpensive lunch or dinner, try one of the best hamburgers in the city. In the evening, some French specials compete with California-ish dishes. They also have wonderful house-made brownies.

CURBSIDE TOO   FRENCH/CALIFORNIA   14/20

2769 Lombard St., Marina 94123
415-921-4442, Dinner nightly, Brunch Sat.-Sun., $$

Curbside Too is intimate, cozy and simple in design but with a warm, slightly rustic interior. Outdoor tables overlook the Presidio. Area locals have discovered this little neighborhood treasure, delighting in the rack of lamb and the filet mignon. While the dinner menu leans toward authentic French cuisine, including a ratatouille-filled crêpes and escargots de bourguignon, brunch offers decidedly more California fare—egg-white omelets, crab Benedict, even huevos rancheros.

CYPRESS CLUB   CONTEMPORARY   15/20

500 Jackson St., North Beach 94133
415-296-8555, Dinner nightly, $$$

The setting is 1940s American supper club seen through a George Lucas *Star Wars* lens. Large ginger-jar shaped columns support the copper-accented room, which is encircled by a robust '40s-style mural. More style comes from the custom-made chairs and red velvet banquettes, and light fixtures that look like Madonna's breastplates. You may go once to gawk at this restaurant-as-theater, but you'll return for the food and the wine. Chef Stephen Janke does a lively tuna tartare, and a deep-flavored sweetbread tartlet with caramelized cauliflower. The $60 tasting menu is a culinary trip, offering such choices as arctic char, Peking duck breast and lamb pot-au-feu. The cheese plates feature artisanal selections, and pastry chef Erik Souza does trendy desserts like an oozing chocolate cake. The wine list is rich in U.S. and imported wonders, and a jazz combo plays near the bar nightly.

DALLA TORRE — ITALIAN — 11/20

1349 Montgomery St., Telegraph Hill 94133
415-296-1111, *Dinner Wed.-Sun.*, $$$
☎ 🚗 📷 🎿 🍷 ⬭

Perched atop Telegraph Hill, this space affords a view of the entire Bay. Unfortunately, patrons can't dine on the view. Since its opening, it has had a revolving door of chefs, and the food seems to be on a definite downward slide. The menu includes crabcakes, carpaccio and steamed clams. Fettuccine is paired with scallops in a cream sauce, but the smoked-chicken ravioli seemed to be missing the main ingredient. Main courses range from a crispy salmon to rubbery baked lobster tails. The cavernous main dining room is adorned with murals, a vaulted ceiling and large windows looking onto the Bay below.

DAME, A RESTAURANT — CALIFORNIA — 12/20

1815 Market St., Castro 94114
415-255-8818, *Dinner Tues.-Sun., Brunch Sun.*, $$
☎ 🙌

Opened in 1995 by caterers James and Kelly Dame, this restaurant serves uncomplicated, Cal-Ital-inspired cuisine to an eager clientele. Although the dishes sometimes miss the mark, the good prices, excellent service and inviting décor—squash orange walls and paper-covered tables—tip the balance in the restaurant's favor. The menu features a winning potato-encrusted salmon filet on spinach with spicy tomato sauce and a hickory-smoked pork loin on Gorgonzola-laced polenta. Desserts have improved since our last visit—we love anything here made with chocolate. The wine list features value-priced bottlings. Don't miss dame's excellent brunch offerings on Sunday.

DELANCEY STREET RESTAURANT — AMERICAN — 11/20

600 Embarcadero, South Beach 94107
415-512-5179, *Lunch & Dinner Tues.-Sun.*, $$
☎ 🚗 🖥 🙌 ⬭

The Delancey Street Restaurant is an offshoot of one of the most successful halfway-house rehabilitation programs ever. Located in the condo-packed South Beach area, the restaurant offers a stunning waterfront view of the Bay. The Delancy Street residents, many of whom are former convicts and drug users, staff the front of the house and kitchen. The moderately priced food is traditional American fare highlighted by specialties drawn from the ethnic and regional backgrounds of the residents. You might be offered anything from salmon mousse to potato latkes to barbecued baby back ribs. Desserts range from sweet-potato pie to apple pie. Because the help eventually goes on to lives outside Delancey Street, the restaurant has a lot of turnover, which means inconsistency is a problem.

DELFINA MEDITERRANEAN 15/20

3621 18th. St., Mission District 94110
415-552-4055, *Dinner nightly, $$*

Chef Craig Stoll, who manned stoves at several popular Bay Area restaurants, finally has his own little spot which he runs with partner Anne Spencer. The menu is short, seasonal and farmer's market-driven. It leans to Italian-Mediterranean flavors, like those in a starter of fried squash blossoms stuffed with sheep's-milk ricotta and in a main course of braised rabbit with pine nuts and olives. Fresh sorbets and chocolate concoctions make delightful finales.

DES ALPES RESTAURANT BASQUE 11/20

732 Broadway, Chinatown 94133
415-391-4249, *Dinner Tues.-Sun., $*

Lifted straight out of a late-19th-century Nevada sheepherder's hotel, Des Alpes is the last family-style Basque restaurant—Spanish in this case—in San Francisco. The set-price meal always includes a large bowl of soup and hearty fare like roast chicken, braised beef tongue and oxtail stew. After dinner enjoy a sol y sombra (made of brandy and anise) in the funky front bar, where you can sometimes hear four languages spoken at the same time-Basque, English, French and Spanish.

DOIDGE'S AMERICAN/BREAKFAST 12/20

2217 Union St., Cow Hollow 94123
415-921-2149, *Breakfast & Brunch daily, $*

Arguably one the city's most elegant breakfast nooks, Doidge's serves eggs, pancakes and omelets to those wise enough to make reservations beforehand. From the outside, Doidge's looks charming, with a welcoming bench and café curtains dressing the windows. Once inside, guests pass by the long, diner-style counter to enter the bright, New England-style dining room, with tasteful artwork, white tablecloths and fresh flowers. Servers rush about with coffeepots and pewter creamers, while diners enjoy buttermilk pancakes with fresh strawberries, rich eggs Benedict with hollandaise, and home-fried potatoes. Omelets with avocado, artichoke hearts and chicken-apple sausage will also entice you, as will the french toast.

DOTTIE'S TRUE BLUE CAFÉ — AMERICAN — 12/20
522 Jones St., Downtown 94108
415-885-2767, Breakfast Wed.-Mon., Lunch Mon.,Wed.-Fri., $
☎ 👥

Great breakfasts are the lure at this homey spot. Chintz curtains and decorative plates help to create the atmosphere. The typical breakfast fare has inventive twists, and carnivores and vegetarians will be happy with the lunch offerings.

DRAGON WELL — CHINESE — ¢
2142 Chestnut St., Marina 94123
415-474-6888, Lunch & Dinner daily
☎ 👥

Interesting photos of San Francisco's Chinatown greet diners at this pleasant newcomer. Sunny yellow walls and comfortable seating set the stage for pretty ordinary Chinese fare, unfortunately. But if you're in the neighborhood . . .

E & O TRADING COMPANY — PAN ASIAN — 12/20
314 Sutter St., Union Square 94108
415-693-0303, Lunch Mon.-Sat., Dinner nightly, $$
☎ ♿ 👥 🍷 ⟳

This pan-Asian venue has a lot going for it. It's a microbrewery, a good snack place for shoppers, and a restaurant that offers delicious dinners and live entertainment every night. E & O's spacious dining room evokes the colonial spirit that drives its food. Taking inspiration from India, Indonesia, Thailand and Japan, the dishes are split, tapas-like, into small and large plates. The salty, Indian-style naan breads are quite good, and fried items like the crisp squid with a subtle tomato-sambal dipping sauce are expertly prepared. Main dishes fuse delicious elements: seared sushi-grade ahi is paired, for example, with a dome of green-onion-spiked rice, baby bok choy and shiitake mushrooms. The house-made beers and sodas are quite good. Live music entertains patrons every night.

EASTSIDE WEST — ECLECTIC — 11/20
3154 Fillmore St., Cow Hollow 94123
415-885-4000, Lunch & Dinner daily, $$$
☎ 🍴 ♿ 🍷 ⟳

This ambitious restaurant located in the "Bermuda Triangle"—so named because of the lively singles restaurant-bars on three corners of the intersection—attempts to bring an East Coast sensibility to the dining scene. What does that mean? Lotsa clams on the menu, for one—baked Cherrystones casino and also an entrée of fusilli pasta with clams, mussels and ham hocks. Other big plates run from a striped bass with clam fritters to very good fusilli pasta with braised rabbit. Desserts are forgettable. With a long list of specialty drinks, a raw bar and live music, this new venue has been packed from day one, but we fear the novelty will soon wear off.

EBISU   JAPANESE/SUSHI   14/20

1283 Ninth Ave., Inner Sunset 94122
415-566-1770, *Lunch & Dinner daily*, $$

Ebisu is a longtime favorite with sushi connoisseurs. Four master sushi chefs make suggestions and occasionally dispense amusées bouches of seafood treats. If it's available, get the toro—fatty tuna belly—at all costs; the succulent meat seems to melt in your mouth. The yellowtail, sea urchin, and sweet shrimps are reliably excellent (the last served with their tempura-fried heads), and the oysters, served with lemon and ginger, are unbelievably good. Kitchen dishes are well prepared, but don't distract yourself from the sushi. Ebisu is no secret, and the no-reservations policy means long...long...waits.

EDDIE RICKENBACKER'S   AMERICAN   12/20

133 Second St., SoMa 94105
415-543-3498, *Lunch Mon.-Fri., Dinner Mon.-Sat.*, $$

This is a cross between a sports bar and a classic San Francisco grill. Its look is very manly, with Harleys suspended from the ceiling plus lots of brass and wood. Some office workers come for the 5-7 p.m. happy hour, when the house puts out a spread that includes chicken wings, egg rolls, calamari and ribs. This is one of the few places in town where you can order celery Victor, a classic San Francisco appetizer. Grilled chops and braised meat round out the menu.

EL BALAZO   MEXICAN/CENTRAL AMERICAN

1654 Haight St., Haight-Ashbury 94117
415-864-8608, *Lunch & Dinner daily*

Painted in vibrant murals and featuring "Jerry's" and "Bob's" (of the Grateful Dead) specialty burritos, El Balazo is just right for the neighborhood. Fillings such as Mexican goat cheese, nopales cactus, and sautéed rock shrimps bring the offerings up a notch from the cheap-meat burrito circuit. Add an excellent salsa bar, plus an extensive soda, agua fresca, and Central American beer selection, and set it all in two attractive dining rooms, and you've got one great burrito joint.

EL FAROLITO   MEXICAN

2777 Mission St., Mission 94110
415-824-7877, *Open daily*

The prospect of a first-rate taco or burrito after a night of bar-hopping or sight-seeing makes the trip to El Farolito an entirely worthwhile adventure. On weekends burritos can be ordered until 3:45 a.m. The grilled steak is fantastic. If watching your quesadilla cook on the griddle doesn't spark your appetite, nothing will. You'll be well fed and content for under $5. **Also 4817 Mission St., 415-337-5500.**

EL NUEVO FRUITLANDIA CUBAN/PUERTO RICAN ¢

3977 24th St., Mission 94110
415-648-2958, Lunch Tues.-Sat., Dinner Tues.-Sun., Brunch Sun.

Fruitlandia was on the scene long before the Caribbean food trend surfaced. It's a hopping place, particularly on weekends, when there is often live music with no cover. The delicious food is mildly spiced, with hefty portions of Cuban- and Puerto Rican-inspired fare. Main courses emphasize beef, pork or seafood; most come with black beans and rice. The house specialty is ropa vieja, shredded flank steak cooked in a mild Creole sauce. There are decent Spanish wines and many beers.

EL ZOCALO SALVADORAN 13/20

3230 Mission St., Mission District 94110
415-282-2572, Lunch & Dinner daily, $

This unpretentious restaurant-with its fake leather booths crammed into a narrow, deep room-is undoubtedly one of the few places in the Bay Area where you can get a decent, whole steamed or fried red snapper at 2 a.m. If you aren't in a fish mood, go for the Bonanza, a top sirloin served with Salvadoran sausage, beans, rice and salad. A must-try is the Salvadoran pupusas, grilled patties of fresh cornmeal batter filled with your choice of stuffing—chicken, beef, cheese, pork, beans. They are utterly delicious eaten with a spicy cabbage salad called cortido. **Also at 1633 El Camino, South San Francisco.**

ÉLAN VITAL CALIFORNIA 13/20

1556 Hyde St., Russian Hill 94109
415-929-7309, Dinner nightly, $$

Élan vital means "spirit of life," an appropriate name for this intimate, softly lit restaurant perched atop Russian Hill. Chef-owners Will Dodson and Ruth Schimmelpfennig also run the acclaimed Frascati across the street, but Élan Vital is the cozier of the two. Depending on the season, selections might include Sonoma foie gras with a vibrant kumquat gastrique, marvelously rich pan-seared spinach gnocchi, or an excellent-quality salmon tartare with tobiko.

ELEPHANT BLEU VIETNAMESE ¢

3232 16th St., Mission 94110
415-553-6062, Lunch & Dinner Tues.-Sun.

One of the Mission's rare Vietnamese restaurants, Elephant Bleu serves food with a hearty, home-cooked slant. There's a wide selection of filling vermicelli dishes and first-rate barbecued pork. The eatery is open until midnight on Friday and Saturday, which makes it a good late-night stop.

ELITE CAFÉ   CREOLE/CAJUN   14/20

2049 Fillmore St., Pacific Heights 94115
415-346-8668, *Dinner nightly, Brunch Sun.,* *$$$*

Chef Donald Link is working some Cajun-Creole magic at this venerable Fillmore Street eatery. Baton Rouge born and bred, he flys in tasso, andouille sausage, shrimp, blue crab and crawfish from the Big Easy. His gumbo is a deep chocolate brown; his crawfish etouffée tingles on the palate. For your main course, go with the daily special or one of the Cajun classics: blackened redfish, shrimp etouffée or crabcakes with caper tartar sauce. Overall, the service by the youthful, white-jacketed waiters is efficient. For dessert, ask one of them to bring you the sturdy bread pudding with bourbon sauce.

ELIZA'S   CHINESE   13/20

1457 18th St., Potrero Hill 94107
415-648-9999, *Lunch & Dinner daily,* *$*

A neighborhood favorite on 18th Street's restaurant row, Eliza's updates Hunan and Mandarin cooking without sacrificing an iota of the cuisine's hot, sweet, salty and pungent appeal. In fact, the low prices seem out of place in this airy, arty eating space. Potted plants, colorful paintings and whimsical sculpture vie for your attention, while the food arrives on attractive, hand-painted dishes. The menu includes many warhorses: kung pao chicken, mu shu pork, Buddah's delight. But they receive fresh treatment in the form of light sauces and crisp vegetables. In all, Eliza's delivers the goods and without benefit of MSG. **Also 205 Oak St., 415-621-4819.**

ELLA'S   AMERICAN   12/20

500 Presidio Ave., Presidio Heights 94115
415-441-5669, *Breakfast & Lunch daily, Dinner Mon.-Fri., Brunch Sat.-Sun.,* *$*

Ella's is a classy little place decked out in spiffy navy blue awnings and weathered shingles. It promises neoclassical American cooking and delivers the goods: grilled pork loin, meatloaf with gravy and chicken pot pie. Ella's serves breakfast, lunch and dinner to regulars from the neighborhood, but the big deal here is weekend brunch. On Sunday mornings, diners sit cheek-by-jowl, vying for Ella's open-face omelets. Fresh fruit, buttermilk pancakes, homemade sticky buns and coffee cake get washed down with bottomless cups of coffee. Service is calm and organized despite the weekend pandemonium.

ELROYS   CALIFORNIA   13/20

300 Beale St., SoMa 94105
415-882-7989, *Lunch Mon.-Fri., Dinner nightly,* *$$*

Elroys space-age decor appeals to the young movers and shakers from the nearby Financial District, who commandeer this warehouse-size restaurant and bar as a fun after-work watering hole. A new chef, Marc Valiani, may breathe new life into the menu. The small plates include a steaming bowl of mussels, Dungeness crabcakes and spicy coconut-curry noodles. Main courses have definitely been upscaled: black-pepper pasta with duck confit, herb-encrusted salmon and a cured pork porterhouse. The drink list includes 13 martinis, 9 margaritas and 11 draft beers, as well as some pretty decent wines. Throw in a huge heated patio, a view of the Bay and a second level for pool tables, and you've got a SoMa hot spot.

EMPRESS OF CHINA   CHINESE   12/20

838 Grant Ave., Chinatown 94108
415-434-1345, *Lunch & Dinner daily*, $$

Locals typically prefer neighborhood Chinese restaurants to this aging dowager, but that doesn't mean that the Empress is not very busy, especially with banquets. Other places might be a dollar or two cheaper, but you can't beat this fourth-floor eatery, high above bustling Chinatown's Grant Avenue, for a spectacular view. The menu concentrates on fresh Cantonese food—meaning an emphasis on seafood. The view and the efficient service by jacketed waiters make the Empress appealing. In the elevator lobby, photos of past celebrities and dignitaries who have dined here grace the walls.

ENRICO'S SIDEWALK CAFÉ   ECLECTIC   14/20

504 Broadway, North Beach 94133
415-982-6223, *Lunch & Dinner daily*, $$

Broadway is still lined with girlie shows, but Enrico's and the nearby Hi-Ball Club—and two new restaurants, Moonshine and Black Cat—draw swingers for the jazz and the food. At Enrico's, select a couple of the tapas for starters, like the smoked-salmon bruschetta or the fiery potatoes bravas. A generous bowl of steamed mussels or the wonderful salt-cod gratin with crostini, would also be a good starter, or a meal in itself. The pizzas, and hamburgers served on focaccia, are always a treat. Main courses, from pastas to a hearty lamb shank, cover the world. The wine list has a good selection of California wines along with lesser-known European bottlings.

ENTROS   FUSION   11/20

270 Brannan St., SoMa 94107
415-495-5150, *Dinner nightly*, $$

This Seattle import is an experiment in fusion, but not the kind of fusion you might think. Entros defines itself as "a venue where exceptional food and drink are combined with smart, social entertainment for groups of four to four hundred." And what exactly does that mean? Basically, the two-level building, decorated in a mix of modern industrial and American nostalgia, attempts to fuse food and fun by applying high-tech gaming to your culinary experience. You can play InterFace 3.0, a multimedia version of the old standby blind-man's bluff, or Big Toy Arcade, a game that calls for physical agility and perfectly timed teamwork. Not surprisingly, the much overlooked cuisine is also considered fusion—a strange but tasty mix of Asian and southwestern food that includes the likes of duck mole spring rolls and Cantonese tequila-marinated grilled chicken.

EOS RESTAURANT & WINE BAR   FUSION   14/20

901 Cole St., Haight-Ashbury 94117
415-566-3063, *Dinner nightly, $$$*
☎ 🍸

Chef-owner Arnold Wong grew up in his family's Ashbury Market, a neighborhood store that has offered residents fine produce and wines for many years. The artfully presented food reflects Wong's Chinese heritage and classical French training. Green-papaya spring rolls get a peanut-plum-kumquat sauce, the grilled marinated steak comes with a mound of yellow Finn mashed potatoes, and tiramisu is enlivened with bananas. The adjacent wine bar is a good place to wait for your table, since the restaurant is always busy, and there are pages of wines to choose from.

ESPERPENTO   SPANISH   12/20

3295 22nd St., Mission District 94110
415-282-8867, *Lunch & Dinner daily, $$*
✕

The name of this usually jammed place is a Spanish word referring to a ridiculous person or situation, but we find nothing funny about the tapas here. Our favorites are the thick and filling torta de patata—a classic Spanish tapa of potatoes, eggs and olive oil prepared like a hard omelet—the plump mussels in a tangy red-pepper vinaigrette, and the chicken livers in red-wine sauce. Main-course specials and paellas are also available, but stick with the tapas. House-made flan is the dessert of choice; try either sangría or one of the good Spanish wines.

EVITA CAFÉ   ARGENTINEAN   12/20

199 Gough St., Hayes Valley 94102
415-552-7132, *Lunch Tues.-Fri., Dinner Tues.-Sat., Brunch Sat.-Sun., $$*
☎ 🚶 👫

The brick-red and taupe walls of this casual Argentinean restaurant are covered in framed memorabilia evoking Eva Perón Duarte. Portraits, photographs, and posters from various productions of the Rice/Webber musical are just a start. The food is also a testament to Evita's memory. Authentically prepared dishes like the garlic soup with puffs of potato are mouth-puckering good. For an entrée, consider pastel de choclo Lucia, a traditional Chilean dish consisting of a creamy corn pie with chunks of tender chicken and beef, custard, hard-boiled egg, raisins and green olives.

FARALLON   CONTEMPORARY   15/20

450 Post St., Union Square 94108
415-956-6969, *Lunch Mon.-Sat., Dinner nightly, $$$$*

Famed Bay Area restaurant designer Pat Kuleto teamed up with chef Mark Franz to open this spectacular restaurant in 1997. The decor has an underwater theme, with light fixtures that resemble jellyfish suspended from the ceiling, just one part of Kuleto's over-the-top fantasia. Farallon's daily-changing menu features all manner of shellfish. A cornmeal blini is topped with smoked salmon, sturgeon, salmon gravlax and house-made caviars plus a dab of chive cream. For the main course, the roasted Northern walleye, seared Louisiana Gulf prawns, roasted Sterling salmon and lovely Atlantic skate are all wonderful. The single non-seafood item recently was stuffed Sonoma quail. The scrumptious desserts, such as an apple pithivier or a hot-fudge chocolate cake, are by Emily Luchetti, who is, like Franz, a Stars restaurant alum.

FATTOUSH   MIDDLE EASTERN   12/20

1361 Church St., Noe Valley 94114
415-641-0678, *Lunch & Dinner Tues.-Sun., Brunch Sun., $$*

Abed Amas opened Fattoush in 1998, and the name is the same as the meal: grilled eggplant mixed with tomatoes, mint, cucumber, Italian parsley and green onion, sprinkled with sumac and tossed in a special lemon vinaigrette. It's traditionally the first meal eaten after the yearly Ramadan fast. The chef is Manal Al-Shafi, formerly of YaYa's; and here she does feast foods from Palestine, Syria, Iraq and Morocco. One intriguing dish is the Palestinian mansaf, a nomadic creation of lamb cooked in aged yogurt with rice, roasted almonds and pine nuts. Add $12 to any entrée price and the "royal" feast, with many more side dishes plus dessert and mint tea, is yours.

FAZ RESTAURANT   MEDITERRANEAN   12/20

161 Sutter St., Financial District 94104
415-362-0404, *Lunch Mon.-Fri., Dinner Mon.-Sat., $$*

Chef-owner Faz Poursohi has built a tempting menu around pizza, pasta, basmati rice and grilled specialties ranging from jumbo prawns to juicy lamb shank braised with garlic, onion and tomatoes. Try the marinated and grilled boneless chicken, which comes with jeweled rice and vegetables. The perfectly crisp-edged grilled eggplant pizza is also a fine dish. The plombière (semifrozen cream blended with pineapple, maraschino cherries and sponge cake), provides a sweet finale.

FINA ESTAMPA   PERUVIAN   13/20

2374 Mission St., Mission 94110
415-824-4437, *Lunch & Dinner Tues.-Sun., $*

One of the great things about eating out in San Francisco is the range of ethnic food. At any given time you can probably find a half dozen Peruvian restaurants—they come and go—in the city, but Fina Estampa remains one of the best. The menu comprises the entire food palette of Peru, with wonderful seafood soups from the Pacific and a whole fried fish with hot green salsa. From the mountains come a number of potato varieties, beef heart and beef and chicken dishes, all perfectly cooked. **Also at 1100 Van Ness Ave., 415-440-6343.**

FIOR D'ITALIA   ITALIAN   11/20

601 Union St., North Beach 94133
415-986-1886, *Lunch & Dinner daily, $$$*

Opened in 1886, this restaurant welcomes casual eaters to its bar area and many dining rooms, including one dubbed the Tony Bennett. You'll find risottos, pastas and other solid old-fashioned Italian fare, including a host of veal dishes. Stick with the sweetbreads or chicken livers and you won't go wrong.

FIRECRACKER   CHINESE   12/20

1007 1/2 Valencia St., Mission 94110
415-642-3470, Dinner Tues.-Sun., Brunch Sat.-Sun., $

This newcomer to the rapidly gentrifying Valencia strip has already won a devoted following, which unfortunately makes it hard to get a table. A soothing, pastel vision of late Imperial China, Firecracker's artful iron chairs and fanciful underlit stools beckon to the clusters of hungry diners outside. The menu includes old standbys but veers toward the unexpected. Yin Yang prawns bring to the table half an order of walnut-tossed prawns and half an order of spicy-hot tossed shrimp. Service is warm and professional.

FIREFLY   ECLECTIC   13/20

4288 24th St., Noe Valley 94114
415-821-7652, *Dinner nightly, $$*

Chef-owner Brad Levy creates home cooking without borders, bringing life to hearty, balanced foods. Though plenty of protein can be found here, some of the kitchen's best work is found in its vegetarian selections: a smoky kale and beluga-lentil stew is paired with griddled pesto-laced grits, and porto-bello mushrooms replace beef in an eminently satisfying Wellington. Shrimp and scallop pot stickers are a textural delight, as are carefully composed salads employing top-notch produce. The wine list leans toward excellent value-priced bottles, and we highly recommend the artful desserts.

FIREWOOD CAFÉ   ITALIAN   12/20

4248 18th St., Castro 94114
415-252-0999, *Lunch & Dinner daily, $$*

Firewood encompasses two elements that usually don't go together: a well-appointed interior and reasonable prices. The limited menu features well-prepared salads, pizza, pasta and chicken. The price you pay for the bargain is that you order at the counter; a runner brings the food to the table. We recommend the fire-roasted potatoes, redolent of garlic and herbs; the citrus-stuffed baked chicken; and any of the pasta dishes.

FIRST CRUSH   CONTEMPORARY   13/20

101 Cyril Magnin St., Downtown 94102
415-982-7874, *Dinner nightly*, $$$

A culinary and oenological shrine to the California wine-making industry, this is a serious wine restaurant that doesn't take itself too seriously. The walls of the cozy upstairs bar—which serves 30 wines by the glass, wine flights and spirits—are hung with photographs of early California vintners. Candlelight reflects from the mirrored walls of the subterranean, serpentine dining room onto the wine-colored columns and carpet. A first course of warm, poached oysters served on the half shell with pancetta, baby red chard and cream is like a delicate oyster stew from a slipper. Moist horse-radish-crusted Atlantic cod is perfectly paired with a Viognier. Save room for the sun-dried blueberry crème brûlée.

FLEUR DE LYS   CONTEMPORARY/FRENCH   18/20

777 Sutter St., Union Square 94109
415-673-7779, *Dinner Mon.-Sat.*, $$$$

What keeps a great restaurant consistently great is the passion of its chef. Hubert Keller has been cooking for more than 25 years both in France and in San Francisco. In the early '90s his food had decidedly Japanese influences. Simple black plates held dishes that combined French technique and Pacific Rim flavors in small, artfully arranged tastes. Hints of Thai and Japanese food still waft through his mostly French menu, but recently Keller has experimented with flavors from his native Alsace. Now more than 25 years old, the restaurant was recently refreshed with golden wall fabric punctuated by cleverly placed mirrors, custom-made wall scones and a gigantic central floral arrangement—all adding up to a palatial feeling. The amuse-bouche might be a tiny crabcake on salsify. Alsatian choucroute enrobes a small piece of salmon perched on warm potato salad dressed with whole-grain mustard. Surprises at every turn on the tasting menu include a tender venison filet set off by a black-barley cake and disks of roasted apples, napped with a Cabernet sauce. Keller's wife, Chantal, and co-owner Maurice Rouas supervise the front of the house. You can have a completely different experience each time you dine at Fleur de Lys: Give serious consideration to a prix-fixe tasting menu and the vegetarian menu. The quality of the desserts matches the other remarkable courses, the service is top-notch, and the splendid wine list can make a dent in your wallet.

FLYING SAUCER ECLECTIC 13/20

1000 Guerrero St., Mission District 94110
415-641-9955, *Dinner Tues.-Sat., $$$*

☎ ▮ ✿

As the name hints, the food at this neighborhood store-front is somewhat otherwordly. The tiny kitchen in the center of the restaurant is like a laboratory, and chef Albert Tordjman a mad chemist. Dishes such as the prawn-shiitake pot stickers and the roast rack of lamb with ratatouille-basil confit reflect Tordjman's travels and his flamboyant style. The portions are huge, so bring an appetite, especially for the enormous, exquisitely constructed desserts, which taste as good as they look. The wine list is brief but well thought out. Service can be slightly spaced out (to fit the theme?), but all in all, Flying Saucer is an amusing and ambitious place—a worthy original.

THE FLY TRAP AMERICAN 12/20

606 Folsom St., SoMa 94107
415-243-0580, *Lunch Mon.-Fri., Dinner nightly, $$*

☎ ⚲ ▾

The nether regions of Folsom Street might not be the first place you think for dinner, but if you're craving solid, old-time food in a clean, well-lit environment, Fly Trap is the place for you. The walls are decorated with antique maps and botanical prints, and the menu concentrates on simple, old-style favorites: sweetbreads with pancetta, sautéed calf's liver with bacon and onions, a hangtown fry. Lighter offerings include a San Francisco favorite, celery Victor. The desserts are winners.

FOG CITY DINER AMERICAN 13/20

1300 Battery St., Financial District 94111
415-982-2000, *Lunch & Dinner daily, $$$*

☎ 🚗 👥

This gleaming magnet for the young and the restless of all ages is a romantic cross between a 1930s roadside diner and a 1940s big-city bar and grill. Created by Cindy Pawlcyn of the Real Restaurants group and Pat Kuleto, the well-known restaurant owner and designer, Fog City was packed when it opened ten years ago, and it is still popular. Order from small plates, including a delicious pork satay, mu shu pork burritos and a vegetarian quesadilla. Large plates always include a lovely cioppino, a roast half chicken, barbecued quail and a grilled steak with very crispy french fries. Kids will dig the Diner chili dog.

42 DEGREES MEDITERRANEAN 15/20 ♟♟

235 16th St., Potrero Hill 94107
415-777-5559, *Lunch Mon.-Fri., Dinner Wed.-Sat., $$*

☎ 🖥 ⚲ 👥 ▾ ▮ ✿

Located in a free-standing building and hidden away in the parking lot of the Esprit outlet, this exciting industrial-style space offers delightful Mediterranean dishes. One starter is truly unique: roasted veal bones with their marrow intact are served with toast points for a real European taste. For entrées, the grilled pork chop with grilled portobello mushrooms and steak fries is super, as is the lamb shank with eggplant. The wine list is excellent, with a number of little-known bottlings.

FOUNTAIN COURT   CHINESE/SHANGHAI 13/20

354 Clement St., Richmond District 94118
415-668-1100, Lunch & Dinner daily, $

The regional Chinese fare here is wonderful. A good way to start is with the Shanghai steamed buns filled with ginger-laced pork and herbs. Braised beef is redolent of five-spice powder, and the lion's head is a well-executed classic: five browned balls of ground pork arranged over crunchy bok choy. Another standout is the plump prawns combined with rice wine, garlic, ginger, and minced pork.

FOURNOU'S OVENS   CALIFORNIA   11/20

Renaissance Stanford Court Hotel
905 California St., Nob Hill 94108
415-989-1910, Breakfast, Lunch & Dinner daily, Brunch Sat.-Sun., $$$$

For several years, food has been up and down at this once highly rated hotel restaurant. Service, too, seems robotic at times. The best advice we can give is to order anything that comes out of the huge rustic ovens situated in one of the dining rooms. The menu changes seasonally, although the rack of lamb has become a signature dish and remains one of the best in the city. There's a good selection of wines by the glass, chosen from an extensive wine list.

FRANCISCAN   SEAFOOD   12/20

Pier 43 1/2 at the Embarcadero, Fisherman's Wharf 94133
415-362-7733, Lunch & Dinner daily, $$$

This venerable wharfside restaurant has recently been remodeled, creating an interior with beautiful theater-style raised seating that affords a view of the Bay. The appetizers include sparkling fresh oysters on the half shell and a delicious ahi tuna carpaccio dressed with a drizzle of wasabi crème fraîche. We like the pastas, especially an Alfredo with crabmeat. On the entrée side are reasonably priced fish and chips, a fisherman's stew and sautéed scallops with a sweet-pepper risotto. Desserts are not always made in-house at Wharf restaurants, but they are here. Don't miss the chocolate mousse cake.

FRASCATI   CALIFORNIA   12/20

1901 Hyde St., Russian Hill 94109
928-1406, Dinner Tues.-Sun., $$$

A popular neighborhood gathering place, this charming restaurant was purchased by Will Dodson and Ruth Schimmelpfennig, who decided to not change the name. But the menu has moved away from the former Italian concept, which may be confusing to the uninitiated. The food, however, is not confusing at all. A meltingly tender honey-mustard pork chop entrée comes with pineapple sauerkraut. The fusilli with a grilled salmon filet will satisfy any Italian-food urges.

FRINGALE FRENCH 15/20

570 Fourth St., SoMa 94107
415-543-0573, *Lunch Mon.-Fri., Dinner Mon.-Sat., $$*

Serving homey, deceptively simple bistro-style fare from all the regions of France, including his native Basque countryside, chef and co-owner Gerald Hirigoyen has maintained the highest quality as well as moderate prices since he opened Fringale seven years ago. Soups such as the potato-garlic are balanced and flavorful. A starter of Dungeness crab salad is brightened with mangoes and fresh herbs; another starter of house-cured salmon is redolent of fresh dill. When you come to the main course, try the shredded duck confit topped with bits of toasted walnuts and sandwiched in a mound of mashed potatoes, or the Roquefort ravioli with basil and pine nuts. At lunch, the ahi tuna burger with a dab of aïoli is as good as it's been since day one here. A handsome curved bar stands near the entrance of the cozy 50-seat dining room, and reservations are a good idea. The wine list is short but focused, and it includes rare bottlings from French Basque wineries.

FUZIO UNIVERSAL NOODLES ¢

469 Castro St., Castro 94114
415-863-1400, *Open daily*

Everyone loves noodles—that's the theory behind the Fuzio concept. This chain is sleek, efficient and pleasant, though clearly formulaic. The pasta section is truly international: you'll find everything from linguini with meatballs and marinara sauce to pad thai to a bowl of udon with tofu and vegetables. The desserts include the Black & White Affogato—something like an ice cream and espresso float. What Fuzio lacks in soul and personality, it makes up for in good value and wholesome food. **Also in the Marina (2175 Chestnut St., 415-673-8804), North Beach (1548 Stockton St., 415-392-7601) & Embarcadero (1 Embarcadero Center, 415-392-7995).**

GARDEN COURT CALIFORNIA 11/20

Sheraton Palace Hotel, 2 New Montgomery St., Downtown 94108
415-546-5010, *Breakfast daily, Lunch Mon.-Sat., Dinner & Tea Wed.-Sat., Brunch Sun., $$$*

There's no prettier room in San Francisco than this one in the lobby of the Sheraton Palace hotel. Beneath a spectacular glass roof, a sea of elegant tables, chairs, and willowy palms is arranged over a richly patterned carpet. The optimum time to visit is for afternoon tea, when the aristocratic aura and attentive service bring a Victorian fantasy to life. Sunday brunch is also a very good experience, but lunch and dinner are by rote.

GARIBALDIS CALIFORNIA 13/20

347 Presidio Ave., Presidio Heights 94115
415-563-8841, *Lunch Mon.-Fri., Dinner daily, Brunch Sun., $$*

This charming neighborhood restaurant has an understated decor and windows that open onto Presidio Avenue. Great appetizers include luscious crabcakes and a perfect Caesar salad. The burgers, filet mignon and lamb tenderloin are appealing. Many pastas tempt the locals that flock here. Portions are homey and huge. **Also in Oakland.**

GAYLORD INDIA RESTAURANT INDIAN 13/20

900 North Point St., Ghirardelli Square 94109
415-397-7775, *Lunch & Dinner daily, $$$*

Chef Santok Kaler has been turning out reliable North Indian specialties in this Ghirardelli showplace, part of a worldwide chain, since 1981. The dining room is elegantly and comfortably appointed, with windows overlooking the Bay. The food is as steady and respectable as the restaurant's reputation promises, and some consider it the best Indian restaurant in San Francisco. Chicken makhanwala, with tomatoes and fenugreek, is one of the more savory curry dishes. Freshly baked Indian breads (naan) as well as lamb chops and chicken arrive hot from the tandoor.

GIRA POLLI ITALIAN 13/20

659 Union St., North Beach 94133
415-434-4472, *Dinner nightly, $$*

This North Beach gem takes the humble chicken, stuffs it with oranges, lemons and herbs, and roasts it rotisserie-style. The result is one of the best birds in town. The meat is juicy and tender; it's too bad the side vegetables are bland. Meals also can be made of appetizers: prosciutto-wrapped melon; a tomato-and-mozzarella salad; an antipasto of fresh artichokes, roasted red peppers, basil, Gorgonzola and olives. The counter help is friendly, and the service is both smooth and casual. **Also in Mill Valley & Walnut Creek.**

GLOBE CONTEMPORARY 14/20

290 Pacific Ave., Financial District 94111
415-391-4132, *Lunch Mon.-Fri., Dinner Mon.-Sat., $$$*

Mary Klingbeil and former Spago chef Joseph Manzare have taken a former brick livery stable and turned it into a comfortable, warm restaurant that serves until 1 a.m.—the kind of place where chefs (and waiters) from some of the city's top spots go after their own kitchens close. Besides daily pizza specials, the changing lunch menu includes items like grilled salmon on a parsnip purée with salsa verde and house-made spaghetti with roasted new potatoes and basil pesto. For dinner you might start with baked mussels, bay scallops and rock shrimp with basil and garlic butter, then continue with a tasty braised veal shank on lemon risotto or a pork chop.

GOLDEN TURTLE   VIETNAMESE   14/20

2211 Van Ness Ave., Van Ness 94109
415-441-4419, *Dinner Tues.-Sun., $$*

This attractive space contains easily one of the top Vietnamese restaurants in San Francisco. Chef-owner Kim-Quy Tran's distinguished Vietnamese cuisine employs simple, fresh flavors in a marvelous complexity further enhanced by sweet and savory sauces. Try the charbroiled prawns, the Look Luck beef, or the catfish in a clay pot. Don't miss such house specialties as the five-spice chicken, the Saigon pork chops and the shrimp-and-pork salad roll with its pronounced cilantro tang. In fact, there is almost nothing that isn't a treat. Check the vegetarian menu for such exotica as lotus blossom salad.

GORDON BIERSCH   AMERICAN/BREW PUB   11/20

2 Harrison St., Embarcadero 94105
415-243-8246, *Lunch & Dinner daily, $$*

See review in PENINSULA chapter.

GORDON'S HOUSE OF EATS   ECLECTIC   NO RATING

500 Florida St., Potrero Hill 94107
415-861-8900, *Dinner daily, $$$*

"Eclectic" is truly the word for the offerings of Gordon's House of Fine Eats, which opened at press time. Chef-owner Gordon Drysdale, who cooked for years at Bix, has created a menu that ranges from comfort food (good fried chicken) to luxury (foie gras). The sleek design at this high-style concept in a neighborhood formerly bereft of large fun restaurants is drawing crowds.

GRAND CAFÉ   FRENCH/CALIFORNIA   13/20

Hotel Monaco, 501 Geary St., Union Square 94109
415-292-0101, *Breakfast, Lunch & Dinner daily, $$*

Grand Café captures the turn-of-the-century feel of a Parisian brasserie. The dining room, once a hotel ballroom, has the whimsical yet impressive look of the belle époque, and Denis Soriano's cuisine fits right in. Standout starters from the lunch menu include ahi tuna tartare and a polenta soufflé with a wild mushroom ragoût and Cambozola fondue. For main course selections, choose the pheasant ravioli with sautéed wild mushrooms and duck consommé. At dinner, the braised beef cheeks is a sure winner, as is the sweetbread fricassée.

ENHANCE

THE

Experience.

Vittel®

YOUR SOURCE *of* VITALITY.

GRANDEHO KAMEKYO   JAPANESE/SUSHI   14/20

943 Cole St., Haight Ashbury 94117
415-759-8428, *Lunch & Dinner daily*, $$

This hidden treasure draws patrons from all over the city for its sparkling fresh fish. The look of GRANDEHO and the food set it apart. The walls have a gold tone, a lavender ceiling and light-wood sushi bar and canopy. Chef Yoshihiko Fujita, who worked at the acclaimed Kyoya in the Sheraton Palace Hotel, creates a good selection of vegetarian sushi, including asparagus with flying-fish roe (tobiko), plus interesting combinations of pickled and fresh vegetables. Many of the rolls feature cooked rather than raw fish—good choices are the smoked salmon or fried soft-shell crab. Main courses often have creative twists, like the panko-encrusted chicken.

GREAT EASTERN   CHINESE   13/20

649 Jackson St., Chinatown 94133
415-986-2500, *Lunch & Dinner daily*, $$

As in most Hong Kong restaurants, seafood is the draw here, and it couldn't be fresher—it comes straight from the restaurant's briny aquariums. The tanks are filled with crabs, abalone, prawns, oysters, scallops, frogs, and various fin fish, which are priced by the pound. Order a whole steamed fish, and the waiter will bring the flopping creature to the table for your inspection. The prawns are incredible prepared with a generous dose of minced garlic. Among the non-seafood dishes, both quail and squab are popular.

GREENS   VEGETARIAN   15/20

Fort Mason, Bldg. A, Marina 94123
415-771-6222, *Lunch Tues.-Sat., Dinner Mon.-Sat., Brunch Sun.*, $$$

If you are looking for a "view" restaurant with outstanding food, cast your eyes toward Greens. The staff puts together the freshest ingredients available—seasonal produce and herbs and flowers from local organic growers—to create bright, innovative dishes. The menu changes daily, but offerings might include such starters as a white-corn salad served with guacamole, tortilla chips and mango salsa, or a grilled tomato-jalapeño-chile soup with cucumbers, scallions, cilantro, mint and crème fraîche. For main courses, we recently enjoyed enchiladas verdes with mushrooms, peppers, corn, red onions, and cheeses; and a linguine with cherry tomatoes, artichokes, red onions and garlic bread crumbs. Greens serves a prix-fixe menu on Saturday evening and a Sunday brunch featuring such goodies as black-bean chile and a mesquite-grilled corn on the cob with basil butter. Culinary artistry, impeccable service and a spectacular bay view make this one of San Francisco's most celebrated dining adventures.

HAMA-KO JAPANESE/SUSHI 13/20

108-B Carl St., Haight-Ashbury 94117
415-753-6808, Dinner Tues.-Sun., $$

This tiny restaurant turns out some of the best sushi in the city. Chef-owner Ted Kashiyama does his shopping daily and has excellent sources for fish and shellfish such as giant clams. You can either order from the menu or call ahead and ask that Kashiyama prepare a special menu, often a series of hot and cold courses. The service is gracious and welcoming. One is never made to feel rushed even when the space is filled.

HARBOR VILLAGE RESTAURANT CHINESE 13/20

4 Embarcadero Center, 2nd level, Financial District 94111
415-781-8833, Lunch & Dinner daily, $$

Come to this vast, well-appointed Embarcadero Center restaurant, the first American outpost of the Hong Kong-based Harbor View Group, for the most elegant dim sum lunch in the city. Perfectly composed in bamboo steamers, the pristine dumplings, pork-stuffed tofu and nor mi gai (chicken-studded rice in lotus leaves) lead a superior lineup of always fresh dim sum. At night, the teak and rosewood interior, and the linen, crystal and china table settings, promise attentive service and consistently good food. Everything we've tried has been delicious, but we especially recommend anything with bones or shells: squab, duck, catfish, rock cod, and crab netted from aquariums on the premises.

HARD ROCK CAFÉ AMERICAN ¢

1699 Van Ness Ave., Van Ness 94109
415-885-1699, Lunch & Dinner daily

There's a Hard Rock in every major city in the world these days, yet tourists and non-locals flock to each one seeking an experience all their own. Centrally located and always packed, this place is famous for rock memorabilia, the sales of which outstrip the food sales. Simple things like the hamburgers and milkshakes are fine.

HARRIS' STEAKHOUSE 13/20

2100 Van Ness Ave., Van Ness 94109
415-673-1888, Dinner nightly, $$$

Along with supper clubs and jazz, red meat seems to have come back in style. If you want to catch the trend, check out this clubby and comfortable restaurant. Steak's the thing here. Harris' buys whole sides of corn-fed, midwestern beef, ages it in its own temperature-controlled cases, then grills up all manner of cuts to juicy, savory, primordial perfection. Non-carnivores can get basic but well-prepared seafood and poultry dishes, and the list of red wines is substantial and nicely chosen.

HARRY DENTON'S AMERICAN 11/20

161 Steuart St., Embarcadero 94105
415-882-1333, *Breakfast & Lunch Mon.-Fri., Dinner nightly, Brunch Sat.-Sun.*, $$

Monday through Saturday nights this SoMa spot hops with live music and dancing in the bar area. Thursday through Saturday nights there's also a live DJ to the rear of the dining room. Fancy cocktails, all that entertainment and a straightforward American menu make this place appealing to young professionals. At lunch, too, the place is packed. It's too bad that this handsome eatery has seen such a revolving door of chefs. However, the dinner menu still offers Harry's yummy "world famous" pot roast with buttermilk mashed potatoes.

HARRY DENTON'S STARLIGHT ROOM GOURMET BAR FOOD 12/20

Sir Francis Drake Hotel, 450 Powell St., Union Square 94105
415-395-8595, *Open nightly*, $

Close to the Theater District and many hotels, this is a fun place to go dancing, have a snack and sip a few cocktails. In addition to the live music provided by a rock band, there's a spectacular, almost 360-degree view from this hotel aerie. The snacks include smoked salmon, caviar, prawns and oysters.

HAWTHORNE LANE CONTEMPORARY 15/20

22 Hawthorne St., SoMa 94105
415-777-9779, *Lunch Mon.-Fri., Dinner nightly*, $$$$

This dramatic space was opened in 1995 by former Wolfgang Puck chefs David and Anne Gingrass, who left Postrio to launch their own restaurant. The space is huge: the entry, which houses an oval bar, could be a restaurant in itself. The other half is dominated by enormous steel ceiling beams and an alluring open kitchen. The cooking is American with an Asian touch, like Chinese-style roasted duck with green-onion buns and fresh Mandarin orange marmalade. Certain dishes come and go according to the season, but if you can, do have the excellent duck schnitzel with crème fraîche risotto, the wood oven-roasted chicken breast, or the fried whole black bass. Of the daily desserts, favorites include the warm spice cake or the weird-sounding but utterly delicious chocolate malted crème brûlée. The wine list is a superb and lengthy collection dominated by California Chardonnays and Cabernets.

HAYES & VINE WINE BAR ¢

320 Hayes St., Hayes Valley 94102
415-626-5301, *Open nightly*

This sleek wine bar is a lively place to explore the wines of the world. You'll find 140 rotating wines by the glass; flights of companionable wines, and rare vintages to enjoy with the small plates of cheeses or pâté. They stay open until 1 a.m. on Friday and Saturday but close early on Sunday.

HAYES STREET GRILL   AMERICAN/SEAFOOD   13/20
320 Hayes St., Hayes Valley 94102
415-863-5545, *Lunch Mon.-Fri., Dinner nightly, $$$*
☎ 🍷 🍶

Visitors to the Bay Area think they have to go to the Wharf for seafood, but this restaurant, as well as Yabbies and Aqua, does an excellent job. The comfortable setting, the black-and-white photos of local celebrities, and the easy pace also contribute to this being one of the city's favorite dining rooms. The formula here is to leave conducting the dinner up to the patron. A daily changing menu offers about a dozen fresh fish and a handful of sauces. Or you can choose from one of the daily meat specials, including a great burger. Our pick of the traditional desserts—when it's in season—is the homey peach shortcake with strawberry sauce. The wine and beer lists are extensive.

THE HELMAND   AFGHAN   14/20
430 Broadway, North Beach 94133
415-362-0641, *Dinner nightly, $$*
☎ 🚗 🚶 🍶

Here, in the heart of North Beach, you'll find this pretty, romantic place with flowers on each table and low-key service. A specialty is lamb served three ways: sautéed with yellow split peas, onions, and vinegar; speared into kebabs, marinated with onion and sun-dried baby grapes, and charbroiled; or marinated, sliced, and served on Afghan bread with sautéed eggplant. One popular dish, aushak, is a kind of Afghan ravioli. The combinations seem exotic, but the flavors work, and a good wine list matches the refined food. Turkish coffee prepared tableside is an elegant end to any meal here, especially with a couple of cardamom pods popped into the brew.

HERBIVORE   VEGAN   12/20
983 Valencia, Mission 94110
415-826-5657, *Lunch & Dinner daily, $*
☎ ❤ 💻 🧑

Come up to the counter at Herbivore, where the menu reads like an ethnic food festival: lasagne, shish kebab, kung pao, falafel, tacos, curry, pad Thai. The hook? It's all vegan, relying on extremely fresh ingredients, many organic vegetables, and absolutely no animal products, including butter or cheese. Top starters from the global vegetarian menu include toast with pesto and sun-dried tomatoes, and charbroiled corn on the cob seasoned with a lemon-cayenne mixture. Entrées include filling dishes like mushroom lasagna with tofu ricotta, a good pad Thai, plus charred portobello mushrooms served with tomatoes, zucchini and garlic aïoli on French bread.

HONG KONG FLOWER LOUNGE   CHINESE   13/20

5322 Geary Blvd., Richmond 94121
415-668-8998, *Lunch & Dinner daily, $$*

☎ 🍸 ⇄

See review in PENINSULA chapter.

HOUSE   FUSION   14/20

1269 Ninth Ave., Inner Sunset 94122
415-682-3898, *Lunch Tues.-Fri., Dinner Tues.-Sun., $$*

☎ 👬

One look at the exterior of House, with its angled window mimicking the restaurant's logo, and you know that something about this place is a little different. As it turns out, that "something" is just about everything—from the top-notch food, to the austere industrial decor, to the excellent service. If you like chicken wings, don't miss the garlic-crusted chicken wings. Another favorite is the hot five-spice calamari, served with a cooling buttermilk dipping sauce. A good fish dish is the grilled Chilean sea bass with braised green beans and jasmine rice. An exciting alternative is the Australian rack of lamb flecked with Korean red pepper. The creamy tapioca is soft and rich, topped with a generous layer of cold cream and mango purée. **Also in North Beach (1230 Grant Ave. 415-986-8612).**

HOUSE OF NANKING   CHINESE   ¢

919 Kearny St., Chinatown 94133
415-421-1429, *Lunch Mon.-Sat., Dinner nightly*

⊠

While its cooking is tailored to the Caucasian palate, there's no denying that Nanking is popular with students and tourists, who line up for the inexpensive, spicy food. Try the good spring-onion cakes or the spicy, dry-cooked string beans. Dishes include shrimp cooked in Tsing Tao beer, with thick, chewy noodles. If it's ambience you crave, you're out of luck: the bare-bones restaurant is always busy, the service notoriously curt. We don't understand the cult status, but go if you must.

HOUSE OF PRIME RIB   STEAKHOUSE   12/20

1906 Van Ness Ave., Van Ness 94109
415-885-4605, *Dinner nightly, $$*

☎ 🍴 👬 🍸 ⇄

If you're looking for a serene atmosphere, this is not the place; but if you want prime rib, it is. You get the works here, from the icy salad dressed at the table to the slabs of rare to well-done prime rib, carved tableside, plus baked potato and Yorkshire pudding. Order a side of the creamed spinach. For the price—none of the prime rib dinners is over $25—this place can't be beat. In the windowless room, you could be back in the 1950s, but you know exactly what you're getting. The wine list is up to the challenge of roast beef and there's a full bar.

HUNAN RESTAURANT   CHINESE   12/20

924 Sansome St., North Beach 94133
415-956-7727, *Lunch & Dinner daily, $*

Chef-owner Henry Chung introduced Hunan cuisine to San Francisco in 1974, and his fans' lips have been tingling ever since. We suggest you start with the signature deep-fried flour cake filled with pork, cheese, vegetables and minced onions. You can hardly go wrong with any of the entrées, but make sure to try the house-smoked duck, which is always lean, moist and flavorful. The fiery bean curd stewed with meat sauce or the house-smoked ham is guaranteed to bring your body temperature up a few degrees. **Also at 674 Sacramento St. (415-788-2234), and 1016 Bryant St. (415-861-5808).**

HUNGARIAN SAUSAGE FACTORY   HUNGARIAN   ¢

419 Cortland Ave., Bernal Heights 94110
415-648-2847, *Lunch Sat.-Sun., Dinner Tues.-Sun., Brunch Sat.-Sun.*

When this place opened seven years ago, the owners had two tables inside and a couple outside on nice days. Eventually they expanded and now have 28 seats and the same homey, delicious menu of schnitzel, goulash, house-made sausages, rib-sticking potato side dishes and unique salads. Since they don't take reservations, be prepared to wait on weekends.

HYDE ST. BISTRO   FRENCH   12/20

1621 Hyde St., Russian Hill 94109
415-292-4415, *Dinner Tues.-Sun., $$*

A young couple—he's French and she's American—bought this spot not too long ago and have turned it into a little southern French retreat on Russian Hill. The nightly prix-fixe dinner (three courses for $22) is a good deal. Among the appetizers, we recommend the luscious sautéed snails with gnocchi and pistou sauce or the simple frisée salad with smoked bacon and poached egg. Of the main dishes, the hanger steak is enticing. Desserts are refined and tied to seasonal ingredients.

IL FORNAIO   ITALIAN   13/20

1265 Battery St., Financial District 94111
415-986-0100 *Breakfast, Lunch & Dinner daily, Brunch Sun., $$*

See review in PENINSULA chapter.

INDIAN OVEN   INDIAN/CALIFORNIA   12/20

233 Fillmore St., Haight-Ashbury 94117
415-626-1628, *Dinner nightly, $$*

A lot of imagination is at work on the menu of this small restaurant, which gives a California twist to the average Indian menu. The vegetable curries—including an unusual mushroom

curry—can be a treat. Also worth ordering is the pakora, bat-
tered and fried leaves of spinach and onion rings in a dish of
spicy yogurt. Some of the tandoori dishes tend to be dried out.
The open kitchen of this popular spot provides a great show.

INDIGO	CALIFORNIA	13/20	

687 McAllister St., Civic Center 94102
415-673-9353, *Dinner Tues.-Sun.*, $$

Indigo joined the pre-theater dinner crowd in 1997 and
hits the right notes with an unpretentious, airy, blue-toned din-
ing room and a pre-theater fixed-price menu of $23.95. Expect
California cuisine with lots of seasonal local produce, grilled
and roasted fish and seafood. For starters, try the lobster-fen-
nel soup or oak-smoked salmon. Entrées include barbecued
Gulf prawns, fresh asparagus in a tart lemon vinaigrette and
roasted trout with a wild rice and dried cranberry stuffing.
Desserts are rich and fruity, from bananas Foster to poached
pears with sorbet. Wine selections reveal a love of California.

IRRAWADDY BURMESE CUISINE	BURMESE	12/20

1769 Lombard, Marina 94123
415-931-2830, *Dinner nightly*, $$

This place is busy in fits and starts, but the food is always
delightful. Perhaps the location on busy Lombard is not right
for the concept, but Irrawaddy has lasted several years in spite
of it. Look for dishes such as daikon soup, smoky eggplant, ginger or tea salad, and sea bass steamed in banana leaves. Opt for
beer with this cuisine.

ISOBUNE	JAPANESE/SUSHI	12/20

Kintetsu Mall, 1737 Post St., Japantown 94115
415-563-1030, *Lunch & Dinner daily*, $$

The idea—and boy, is it fun for kids—is that diners pluck
their selections from little boats floating around the counter
while two sushi chefs continuously replenish the stock. At the
end of the meal the waitress counts the empty trays in front of
each diner and tabulates the bill. Unfortunately, the sushi
leaves a little to be desired. Keep an eye on what the chef
places on the boat and nab it quickly to avoid any raw fish
that's circled the counter too many times.

IZZY'S STEAK & CHOPHOUSE	STEAKHOUSE	12/20

3349 Steiner St., Marina 94123
415-563-0487, *Dinner daily*, $$$

Izzy's looks from the outside like a saloon, but once you are
seated in the comfy banquettes, you'll spy a shelf holding what
looks like every steak sauce ever manufactured. That's your
clue: order steak, although the chops and other entrées aren't

bad. The assortment of accompaniments—potatoes, roasted carrots and onions, and especially the creamed spinach—are winners. Service can be impersonal.

JACK'S   AMERICAN   11/20

615 Sacramento St., Financial District 94111
415-421-7355, *Lunch Mon.-Fri., Dinner Mon.-Sat.,* $$$
☎ 🚗 🍸 ♻

Abraham Lincoln was president ehen Jack's opened in 1864, and virtually ever since it's been the darling of San Francisco's political and business elite. Since the beautiful remodeling by the Konstin family, the food and service here have had their ups and downs. Stick with the simple grilled fish or meat. For small parties, reserve one of the upstairs dining rooms and pretend it's 1925.

JACKSON FILLMORE TRATTORIA   ITALIAN   13/20

2506 Fillmore St., Pacific Heights 94115
415-346-5288, *Dinner nightly,* $$
☎ 🎎 🍶

Chef-owner Jack Kreitzman's love of Italy is apparent. He travels there often to research new regional recipes. Because of the trattoria's diminutive size and Kreitzman's local following, it's best to go early and be prepared to wait. Try the starter of carpaccio di zucchini, sliced zucchini topped with curls of pecorino cheese, a swirl of olive oil and toasted pecans. Our favorite entrée is the chicken O.O.A., a zesty preparation involving olive oil, caramelized onions and anchovies. The wine list offers reasonably priced Californian and Italian wines.
Also in MARIN: see Cucina Jackson Fillmore.

JAKARTA   INDONESIAN   13/20

615 Balboa St., Richmond District 94118
415-387-5225, *Lunch Tues.-Fri., Dinner Tues.-Sun.,* $$
☎ 🗡

This charming restaurant, comprising a series of small rooms, offers an extensive menu of Indonesian dishes made with fresh ingredients and high-quality meats. The shrimp cakes, dotted with corn and hot peppers, or the grilled brochettes, marinated and grilled beef, or chicken served with peanut sauce (reminiscent of a Thai satay), are fine choices to start. We recommend the deep-fried squid, grilled rockfish, braised beef served with various vegetables and a very spicy-hot fried chicken in chile sauce.

JARDINIÈRE   FRENCH/CALIFORNIA   15/20

300 Grove St., Civic Center 94102
415-861-5555, *Dinner nightly,* $$$$
☎ 🚗 🗡 🎵 🍸 🍶

Restaurant designer Pat Kuleto's stellar creation is a joy. Jardinière's theme is celebration: an inverted Champagne glass soars above the bar and the oval dome sparkles like rising bubbles. A balcony-level dining area offers the best view of the party scene below. The menu, created by Traci Des Jardins, includes such innovative dishes as ahi tuna carpaccio à la niçoise and a terrine of foie gras with pear salad and toasted brioche. For main courses, try the pork chop with sweet potatoes, apples and braising greens with a whole-grain mustard sauce—a perfect marriage. In addition to serving fanciful desserts, Jardinière is one of the few restaurants in the country with a cheese cellar to keep its superb collection of cheeses at the right temperature. One night the choices ranged from an aged goat's milk from Northern California to a sheep's-milk cheese wrapped in chestnut leaves from Washington state.

JASMINE HOUSE   VIETNAMESE   12/20

2301 Clement St., Richmond District 94121
415-668-3382, *Lunch & Dinner nightly, $$*

Warm and tasteful, Jasmine House is on a busy stretch of Clement Street. The delicious Vietnamese food draws neighborhood families and couples. Fried imperial rolls are served with wrappers of lettuce, cucumber and mint and a sweet-and-sour dipping sauce. During the crab season (November through April), dig in to a fresh local Dungeness—roasted and bathed in a butter-black-pepper sauce. Service is friendly.

JEANNE D'ARC   FRENCH   13/20

715 Bush St., Union Square 94108
415-421-3154, *Dinner Mon.-Sat., $$*

This romantic dining room in the Cornell Hotel transports you to a charming 15th-century hideaway in the French province of Lorraine, decorated with artifacts relating to Joan of Arc. The prix-fixe dinner menu features old-style, simple, country French cuisine. Begin with a hearty soup du jour, followed by your choice of well-prepared salads. The sautéed prawns and scallops were uninspired on a recent visit, but the filet mignon was tender. Enjoyable desserts include a black currant and passion fruit mousse cake. A well-priced, appropriate California-French wine list is available.

JOHN'S GRILL   AMERICAN   11/20

63 Ellis St., Downtown 94102
415-986-0069, *Lunch Mon.-Sat., Dinner nightly, $$*

Owner John Konstin has (smartly) gotten a lot of mileage from the fact that this venerable grill was a favorite hangout of author Dashiell Hammett, as well as Hammett's fictional character, Sam Spade. Like all grills of the period, its food has an Italian flavor. Specialties include grilled steaks, pork chops and fish. The chicken Jerusalem is a good classic, and the seafood dishes are satisfying, especially the shrimp Louie. Pasta dishes round out the menu. Take time to peruse the memorabilia.

JUBAN   JAPANESE/GRILL   12/20

Japan Center, 1581 Webster St., Japantown 94115
415-776-5822, *Lunch & Dinner daily, $$$*
☎

   This is a do-it-yourself yakiniku restaurant, where diners
cook their meals on built-in table grills. It's a popular barbe-
cue-style operation that traveled to Japan from Korea some 30
years ago. The elegant modern environment, almost austere, is
highlighted by dramatic flower arrangements. A typical meal
consists of meats, seafood or vegetables that diners grill them-
selves. Accompaniments are Juban's secret dipping sauce,
small plates of mild kim chee, soup and rice. Particularly
appealing was the thinly sliced raw beef tongue, grilled and
eaten with a squeeze of lemon juice. The sliced rib-eye cooks in
about 20 seconds. **Also in the PENINSULA chapter.**

JULIE'S SUPPER CLUB   CALIFORNIA   12/20

1123 Folsom St., SoMa 94103
415-861-0707, *Lunch Mon.-Fri., Dinner nightly, $$*
☎ ⚷ 🍸 🍾

   The two dining rooms at this SoMa hot spot are usually
packed with a diverse and fashionable clientele. The menu
includes a wide range of small plates such as the appealing avocado and grapefruit with grilled marinated shrimp, or the
seductive smoked salmon in ravioli with a broth of grilled shiitake mushrooms. Among our favorite main courses are the
roasted breast of free-range chicken with risotto and a fresh
tarragon and tomato sauce, and the grilled breast of duckling
with wild rice and almonds in a sauce of chiles and fresh
orange. Dave's burger, served on a sourdough baguette, is perfect with a glass of Zinfandel from the short but excellent wine
list. Live jazz plays here on the weekends.

JULIUS' CASTLE   ITALIAN/CONTINENTAL   11/20

1541 Montgomery St., Telegraph Hill 94133
415-392-2222, *Dinner nightly, $$$$*
☎ 🚗 📷 🍴 🏃 🍸 🍾 ↻

   Perched on the city's most charming hill and commanding
a majestic view of the Bay Bridge, Alcatraz and Treasure Island,
Julius' Castle is the place to go when you want to pop the question or impress out-of-town guests. In 1995, the castle underwent $1 million worth of renovations, adding new marble and
an exhibition kitchen. Two Victorian-style dining rooms display
glittering chandeliers, ornate moldings and comfy chairs, plus
there's a turret room that seats ten. The menu features fancy
Italian/Continental dishes with imperial prices. Starters
include beluga caviar, Dungeness crab gnocchi and seared
Atlantic scallops. Main courses are rack of lamb, poached
Maine lobster and roast Muscovy duck breast. The wine list
earns accolades and the service is old-world and solicitous.

JUST FOR YOU CAFÉ   AMERICAN

1453 18th St., Potrero Hill 94107
415-647-3033, *Breakfast & Lunch daily, Brunch Sat.-Sun.*

In a simple, straightforward manner, Just For You serves up hearty breakfasts and lunches to those lucky enough to get in. No reservations are accepted; the minuscule restaurant boasts only a couple of tables and a very skinny counter for eat-in service. Lucky customers enjoy the grits, huevos rancheros and hot cakes. Decor is kept to a minimum, but the café exudes a cheery, laid-back charm.

KABUTO SUSHI   JAPANESE/SUSHI   15/20

5116 Geary Blvd., Richmond District 94121
415-752-5652, *Dinner Wed.-Sun.,* $$

☎

Kabuto is probably the best sushi bar in San Francisco, its reputation built on the talents and personality of master sushi chef Sachio Kojima. In our experience, the sushi here has been uniformly excellent—immaculately fresh and meticulously prepared with the kind of grace and showmanship few other sushi chefs can match. The selection of fresh seafood and crustaceans is unmatched anywhere else in the city. One friendly note: the chef always offers diners a complimentary tidbit to whet the appetite. Among the exceptional offerings is the white tuna topped with flying-fish roe and a raw quail egg nestled in the middle. A full Japanese menu is also available.

KAM PO HONG KONG KITCHEN   CHINESE/BARBECUE

801 Broadway, Chinatown 94133
415-982-3516, *Breakfast, Lunch & Dinner*

⋈

Kam Po is a Chinese deli with tables. Its main feature is the hanging sides of crispy roast pork, roast soy-sauce- and salt-baked chickens, and luscious roast ducks. The take-out is very good, especially the roast pork and poultry and the stir-frys. If you eat here, expect almost no English and your dining companions to be mostly local Chinese working men. This place is as bare bones as they get, but cheap and good. Having a party? Order a whole pig and a few stir-frys and feed 50 for $3 a head. Be aware that this store-café closes at 8 p.m.

KATE'S KITCHEN   AMERICAN   12/20

471 Haight St., Haight-Ashbury 94117
415-626-3984, *Breakfast & Lunch daily,* $

This unpretentious little restaurant, with hand-painted walls and geographical artifacts, attracts the breakfast club for Kate's famous ginger-peach pancakes. The hush puppies are surprisingly good, and soul food such as greens, beans and rice are made with a practiced hand. Don't mind the downscale digs: no reservations, no credit cards, a long wait and a walk through the kitchen to the bathroom are part of the bargain.

KATIA'S, A RUSSIAN TEA ROOM   RUSSIAN   12/20
600 Fifth Ave., Richmond District 94118
415-668-9292, *Lunch & Dinner Tues.-Sun.,* $$
☎ ♟

This place really isn't a Russian tearoom—it's actually a full-service restaurant, serving Russian home-style favorites lightened with a Californian touch. Look for very good smoked salmon, tender blini with salmon caviar, flaky piroshki and cabbage stuffed with beef and rice. Katia's is located on a sunny corner with windows that look out on the neighborhood. Flowers on every table and mirrors make it a pleasant spot.

KELLY'S MISSION ROCK   CALIFORNIA   13/20
817 China Basin, China Basin 94107
415-626-5355, *Lunch & Dinner daily, Brunch Sun.,* $-$$
☎ 📷 🖥 🍴

Those who remember the old Mission Rock are in for a surprise. The funky, dilapidated building has been transformed, and all that remains of the original is one wooden deck jutting out into the Bay. The new building, shiny and aluminum, is split into two. Downstairs, in the Dockside Café, the spirit of the old rowdy jeans-and-flannel-shirt Mission Rock lives. You can get a pitcher of beer, a basket of fish 'n' chips, burgers or garlic fries while you play pool or hang out on the deck and listen to live music. Topside is a completely different concept. This upstairs restaurant has flavorful and creative food, and it's quite a bit more expensive than downstairs. Sunday brunch is reasonable, with choices like the wonderful fresh-crab BLT.

KHAN TOKE THAI HOUSE   THAI   13/20
5937 Geary Blvd., Richmond District 94121
415-668-6654, *Dinner nightly,* $$
☎ ⚁ ♿

You enter the candlelit labyrinth of dining rooms in your stocking feet—you've been asked to check your shoes at the door. The opulent, romantically lit dining room is lushly appointed with thick carpeting and elegant wood carvings. You can sit on the floor or at traditional tables. Choice appetizers include a green-papaya salad laced with fresh chiles and a spicy squid salad shot with mint. Khan Toke's curries (red, green or yellow) infuse vegetables or meats (chicken, prawns and beef) with fragrant, layered flavors. And the wine list is up to the spicy food.

KITARO   JAPANESE/SUSHI   12/20
5850 Geary Blvd., Richmond District 94121
415-386-2777, *Lunch & dinner daily,* $
☎

With an inviting decor, Kitaro offers sushi and traditionally prepared dishes that are worth considering if you're in search for an inexpensive Japanese meal. Diners can sit at any of the half dozen tables or at the sushi bar, where you can get a close-up view of the sushi chef at work. Try the maguro nigiri or the spider rolls. Also consider the house special rolls, which change daily. The entrées include tasty dishes like chicken teriyaki and grilled salmon served in bento boxes.

KOKKARI   GREEK   14/20

200 Jackson St., Financial District 94111
415-981-0983, *Lunch Mon.-Fri., Dinner nightly, $$$*

Named for a small fishing village on the Aegean Sea, Kokkari is owned by the partnership that runs the successful Evvia Estiatorio restaurant in Palo Alto. The impressive multi-million-dollar design presents a large welcoming fireplace, lots of wood and pottery, and floor lamps that lend a sophisticated, intimate look. One homey feature is a 20-foot-long family table near the semi-open kitchen. Chef Jean Alberti, who hails from Alsace but has traveled extensively in Greece, creates tradition-al favorites like phyllo-encased spinach-cheese spanakopita, grilled octopus and moussaka. Start with an appetizer of crisply fried smelts.

KOREA HOUSE   KOREAN/BARBECUE   12/20

1640 Post St., Japantown 94115
415-563-1388, *Lunch & Dinner daily, $*

This is Asian soul food with enough heat to blow both Thailand and the Hunan province right off the map. Each of the many tables has its own gas barbecue for grilling marinated meats and fish. Everything is served with pickled vegetables and a peppery broth. The method here is simple: you grill the meat, place it in a leaf of lettuce and add some of the relishes supplied—for the Korean version of a taco.

KOWLOON VEGETARIAN RESTAURANT   CHINESE/VEGETARIAN   ¢

909 Grant Ave., Chinatown 94108
415-362-9888, *Lunch & Dinner daily*

Dining here is informal at best, though an attractive and incense-laden Buddha watches over the utilitarian dining room. Vegetarian "M & M" refers to mushrooms cooked with sea moss, a tiny seaweedlike vegetable that raises the dish from the ordinary. Vegetarian eel contains crispy pieces of eel (actu-ally mushrooms) tossed with bean sprouts. Be sure to try the dim sum.

KULETO'S   ITALIAN   12/20

Villa Florence Hotel, 221 Powell St., Union Square 94102
415-397-7720, *Breakfast, Lunch & Dinner daily, $$$*

Pat Kuleto is a restaurateur phenomenon-about-town. He began as a designer (Fog City Diner and Postrio) and also did the design for this beautiful trattoria and lent his name to it,

but he is no longer involved. It is quintessential Kuleto: marble, turtleback chandeliers and burnished wood. Focal points are a high, Florentine-style painted ceiling and a mahogany bar with a forest of hanging salamis, pastas, herbs and garlic garlands. The kitchen's best starter is grilled radiccio wrapped in pancetta, but our favorite is the house-made focaccia, a bulb of roasted garlic and an order of fried calamari. We also like the thick-crust pizza with cheese, pancetta and pine nuts.

KYO-YA JAPANESE/SUSHI 13/20
The Sheraton Palace Hotel, 2 New Montgomery St.
 Financial District 94105
415-546-5090, *Lunch Tues.-Fri., Dinner Tues.-Sat., $$$$*

Regarded by some as one the best Japanese restaurants in San Francisco, Kyo-ya is part of a chain. You can go either for a full lunch or dinner or simply stick to sushi. The sushi option is more expensive but worth the splurge. The sea urchin roe is an exquisite treat if you have the taste for it; you'll also find fresh yellowtail and tuna belly. The grilled butterfish with soybean sauce is a favorite for lunch or dinner. Service is professional, but the restaurant's atmosphere is cold and businesslike, unlike the friendlier, family-owned neighborhood sushi venues that dot the city.

LA CUMBRE MEXICAN ¢
515 Valencia St., Mission 94110
415-863-8205, *Open daily*

In its heyday 20 years ago, this was the best taqueria in town. The owners opened more outlets over the years, and the style has become Americanized. But the food is still pretty good: The made-to-order burritos weigh in at well over a pound each, the carne asada (beef) is a winner, and the burritos made with tongue or fried pork have legions of fans.

LA FELCE ITALIAN 13/20
1570 Stockton St., North Beach 94133
415-392-8321, *Lunch Mon., Tues.-Fri., Dinner nightly, $-$$*

Once North Beach was overcrowded with family-style restaurants like La Felce, but sadly, they closed as trendier places opened. For the price of an entrée, diners can order soup or salad, plus dessert and a beverage. Antipasti are à la carte. We highly recommend the osso buco, the veal saltimbocca and the crispy fried calamari. The wonderful fettuccine Alfredo and spinach gnocchi are made in-house.

LA FOLIE FRENCH 17/20
2316 Polk St., Russian Hill 94109
415-776-5577, *Dinner Mon.-Sat., $$$$*

Chef-owner Roland Passot creates what is perhaps the most inspired French food in San Francisco. Witness a lovely parsley-garlic soup encircling an escargots-stuffed tomato, or cauli-flower soup garnished with curried pears, lobster and osetra caviar. Lyon-born chef Roland Passot, like Hubert Keller of Fleur de Lys, began his apprenticeship at the age of 14 in France. Later he cooked in Paris, Chicago and Dallas before opening this handsome restaurant almost ten years ago with the help of his wife, Jamie, and brother and sommelier, George. The intimate, whimsically decorated dining room has a painted blue sky overhead; a recent remodeling added blond wood accents and antique hand puppets. But the decor is no match for the drama of Passot's plates. Signature dishes include lobster with spicy mango-citrus vinaigrette, tender roasted quail stuffed with foie gras, blanquette of sweetbreads and lobster and roasted venison. Desserts are inventive, and George handles the wine list masterfully; it encompasses many little-known French treasures and limited-production California bottles.

LA RONDALLA   MEXICAN   ¢

901 Valencia St., Mission 94110
415-647-7474, *Lunch & Dinner Tues.-Sun.*

It's always Christmas at this crazy-quilt restaurant, amply decorated with Christmas tree lights, balloons, stuffed birds, fake Tiffany lamps and other kitsch. From its long counter, La Rondalla's open kitchen serves fine Mexican food, including a rare-grilled steak—smothered with fresh onions, potatoes and tomatoes—and an equally tasty birria, slow-cooked goat in a rich thick sauce. Roving mariachis and unflappable waitresses in red ruffled blouses add to the fun.

LA TAQUERIA   MEXICAN   ¢

2889 Mission St., Mission 94110
415-285-7117, *Open daily*

With its distinctive whitewashed facade, street-side seating and gleaming tiles, La Taqueria is perhaps the most visually appealing bargain in the Mission. Yet no one comes for the decor: rather, they line up for perfectly composed burritos and tacos and perhaps the most authentic fruit drinks in the Bay Area. The carnitas cooked in lard are meltingly tender; the chorizo sausage is spicy and lean; and the carne asada may be the best in the neighborhood. If we could give a Bargain Bite three toques, La Taqueria would be the first to get them.

LA TRAVIATA   ITALIAN   13/20

2854 Mission St., Mission 94110
415-282-0500, *Dinner Tues.-Sun.,* $$

Who woulda thought? Here's a romantic, refined Italian restaurant in the heart of the Mission District, with excellent tortellini and an opera theme. It's fun perusing the opera memorabilia and photos of top tenors and sopranos, some of whom have graced the tables here. Besides the luscious pasta dishes, look for veal, poultry and seafood entrées with a northern Italian accent. The house tiramisu is sinfully good.

LALITA   THAI   13/20

96 McAllister St., Civic Center 94102
415-552-5744, *Lunch Mon.-Fri., Dinner nightly, $$*

The high ceilings, hardwood floors and painted jungle murals of Lalita make you feel as if you've stepped into another world. The grimy street outside fades as you come under Lalita's charm. Start with the stuffed angel wings filled with ground pork and rice noodles. Be sure to try Lalita's specialty: Thai beef jerky with a chile sauce. The dish has a smoky, spicy flavor. The house drinks are also worth a look, especially the Thai ice tea with rum and a dollop of coconut ice cream.

LE CENTRAL   FRENCH   12/20

453 Bush St., Financial District 94108
415-391-2233, *Lunch & Dinner Mon.-Sat., $$*

With its functional, no-frills decor and menu scrawled on the mirror, Le Central is an homage to the French bistro. The traditional country dishes warm the soul and fill the stomach. The individual onion tart is tasty, if a little soggy, but the roast chicken with watercress, grilled tomatoes and french fries is a treat. Unfortunately, the once famous cassoulet has gone downhill and the desserts are uninspired.

LE CHARM   FRENCH   13/20

315 Fifth St., SoMa 94107
415-546-6128, *Lunch Mon.-Fri., Dinner Mon.-Sat., $-$$*

The bright, airy room fills regularly for lunch and dinner, creating a din as diners and an open kitchen compete for air space. Still, if you're craving classics such as frisée aux lardons, steamed mussels or salade niçoise at a good price, you've come to the right place. Lunch can be enjoyed either in the dining room, or on the back patio, when it's warm. At night, Le Charm features a three-course ($20-$24) fixed-price menu with lots of choices: perhaps fish soup provençale followed by steak frites, or gravlax followed by duck confit and an orange crème brûlée. Fresh flowers, capable service and an interesting crowd make Le Charm a worthwhile trip.

LE COLONIAL   VIETNAMESE   14/20

20 Cosmo Place, Downtown 94109
415-931-3600, *Lunch Mon.-Fri., Dinner Mon.-Sat., $$$*

Sitting on the historic site long occupied by Trader Vic's, Le Colonial had a lot of tradition to overcome when it opened. The lush decor is designed to bring diners a taste of tropical elegance reminiscent of the French colonial era in

Southeast Asia. Patchwork tile floors, rattan furniture, a stamped-iron ceiling, shuttered windows and palm trees all contribute to the illusion of being a world away from the city outside. The food, prepared by chef Dieu Ho is top-notch. One pleasant starter is goi cuon, a soft rice crêpe filled with pork and shrimp, served with a sweet-hot hoisin peanut sauce. Entrées include a delicious roast chicken with a lemon-grass glaze, and a rich red-curry dish of simmered prawns with slices of mango and eggplant. The desserts include a banana spring roll served with a coconut-milk tapioca sauce.

LEFT AT ALBUQUERQUE   SOUTHWESTERN   11/20

2140 Union St., Cow Hollow 94123
415-749-6700, *Lunch & Dinner daily*, $

See review in PENINSULA chapter.

LHASA MOON   TIBETAN   14/20

2420 Lombard St., Marina 94123
415-674-9898, *Lunch Thurs.-Fri., Dinner Tues.-Sun.*, $$

This charming little restaurant is an exciting find on outer Lombard. Try the steamed momo buns, a kind of dumpling stuffed with meats or vegetables and flavored with basil, mint and chives. You'll find a large selection of vegetarian dishes, including bean-thread strings, potatoes and celery, sautéed with ginger and emma, a kind of Tibetan peppercorn. Try several breads, including bhaley, a dry fried flatbread, and loko momo, a steamed bread. Meat dishes include kongpo shaptak, a hot, spicy, cheese-flavored beef and chile-pepper dish, and gutse rithuk, a hearty pasta dish cooked in a lamb stew. A glass of Tibetan-style rice wine makes a perfect apéritif.

LIBERTY CAFÉ & BAKERY   AMERICAN   13/20

410 Cortland Ave., Bernal Heights 94110
415-695-8777, *Lunch Tues.-Fri., Dinner Tues.-Sun., Brunch Sat.-Sun.*, $$

Before the Liberty, Bernal Heights residents used to have to leave the neighborhood for a comfortable sit-down dinner. At lunch you'll find homey chicken pot pie and a sandwich of deep-fried clams on crusty French bread. We loved the warm goat-cheese salad on baby greens drizzled with a walnut-oil and sherry vinaigrette. Another good appetizer is the fried sand dabs with onion rings and spicy catsup. For a main course try the braised beef served with Gorgonzola mashers. Everyone lines up for the warm apple turnovers and sticky buns on the brunch menu. Check out the bakery in a cottage to the rear of the restaurant—it becomes the wine cottage at night.

LITTLE CITY ANTIPASTI BAR   ITALIAN   12/20

673 Union St., North Beach 94133
415-434-2900, *Lunch & Dinner daily*, $$

This was one of the first places in San Francisco to pioneer the concept of antipasti for dinner, and by and large the quality has been maintained. You can sip a glass of sparkling wine at the bar and share an appetizer like the perennial favorite, baked Brie cheese, a whole roasted garlic bulb and bread. Small plates reign here: try the grilled asparagus with pistachio tahini sauce, the Szechuan lamb sausages and the grilled prawns borrachos marinated in tequila and lime. The Caesar salad is one of the best in the city.

LONGLIFE NOODLE COMPANY & JOOK JOINT   PAN ASIAN   ¢

139 Steuart St., Embarcadero 94105
415-281-3818, *Lunch Mon.-Fri., Dinner Mon.-Sat.*

The contrast of red and black accents, mediated by grays, gives this new place a slick look. As you might guess, the restaurant specializes in noodle dishes, taken from all over Asia. For starters try a plate of "overstuffed" pot stickers with a singularly tasty ground-pork filling. Alternatively, you might choose the minced chicken in lettuce cups with veggies. For a main course, try the enchanted heat, a large bowl of hot and sour soup with barbecued pork, various vegetables and ginseng—all brought together as a hangover cure. Also try the house-made specialty drinks, like ginseng ginger ale.

L'OLIVIER   FRENCH   14/20

465 Davis Ct., Financial District 94111
415-981-7824, *Lunch Mon.-Fri., Dinner Mon.-Sat.,* $$$

This popular place for business lunches becomes a romantic dining spot by night. The main dining room sets the mood: dark-wood antiques, dramatic chandeliers, oil paintings of the French countryside, and white linen draping the tables. Most important, the tables are generously spaced and the noise level allows conversation. The special bouillabaisse dinner on Friday and Saturday nights is a big draw. For starters we recommend the crabcakes or classic lobster bisque. Entrées include grilled salmon in Pinot Noir sauce and tournedos of filet mignon with truffle sauce. For dessert, we recommend the L'Olivier soufflé. Service is professional, and the wine list is extensive.

L'OSTERIA DEL FORNO   ITALIAN   13/20

519 Columbus Ave., North Beach 94133
415-982-1124, *Lunch & Dinner Wed.-Mon.,* $$

Here you'll find some of the best food in North Beach in a space the size of a large walk-in closet. You will almost always experience a wait for a table, but it's worth it. L'Osteria hardly has a real kitchen—the cooking is all done in one oven—but that hasn't stopped the owners from presenting an imaginative, ever changing menu. L'Osteria is famous for its focaccia bread and milk-braised pork roast, a Tuscan favorite. The pizzas come with crisp thin crusts. A short but good selection of Italian wines is available by the glass.

LOTUS GARDEN   CHINESE/VEGETARIAN   11/20

532 Grant Ave., Chinatown 94108
415-397-0707, *Lunch & Dinner Tues.-Sun., $*

Carnivores and vegetarians alike flock here for the inexpensive rice plates such as braised bean curd with chiles and mushrooms in sesame oil, or bean curd sautéed in curry sauce. The house vegetarian chow mein is always good, as is the sizzling rice soup. Somewhat unusual but nevertheless appetizing is a dish of whole black mushrooms stuffed with cabbage, Chinese cilantro and gluten.

LUCKY CREATION   CHINESE/VEGETARIAN   12/20

854 Washington St., Chinatown 94108
415-989-0818, *Lunch & Dinner Thurs.-Tues., $*

There's little left to chance at this hole-in-the-wall space with a handful of seats, though carnivores may disagree: the restaurant serves only vegetarian cuisine. Deep-fried taro rolls are winners. Lucky Creation's forte, however, is its clay pot dishes. Essentially Chinese versions of hearty stews, all are excellent, though the braised eggplant with bean sauce is a standout. This is probably the best vegetarian Chinese restaurant in the city.

MACARTHUR PARK   AMERICAN   12/20

607 Front St., Financial District 94111
415-398-5700, *Lunch Mon.-Fri., Dinner nightly, $$*

MacArthur Park was once a hot spot, but in recent years the food has gone south. The ribs are OK, steamed tender but lacking any discernible smoky flavor. Whatever you order, a good side of crispy fried Bermuda onion strings are addictive. Desserts (apple pie, shortcake) are fine. The bar is still popular after office hours, but later in the evening the dining room suffers from a dearth of patrons. The restaurant, located in a former brick warehouse, has a classic look and its large windows afford a view of the park across the street.

MAGNOLIA PUB & BREWERY   AMERICAN/BREWPUB   12/20

1398 Haight St., Haight-Ashbury 94117
415-864-7468, *Lunch & Dinner daily, $$*

This newish brewpub has down-to-earth food like well-filled sandwiches and great burgers. More adventurous dishes such as the grilled sesame-soy eggplant with Fontina-stuffed risotto cakes and a spicy tomato jam are exciting if a little short on presentation. The house-made (Mayor) Willie Brown ale and several other brews are very good. Perhaps the best comes last--desserts are homey, generous and excellent. Be sure to try the warm blood-orange upside-down cake if it's offered.

MAMA'S ON WASHINGTON SQUARE · AMERICAN/BREAKFAST 12/20

1701 Stockton St., North Beach 94133
415-362-6421, *Breakfast & Lunch Tues.-Fri., Brunch Sat.-Sun.,* $

This is one of the most popular breakfast stops in San Francisco, and the lines start early on the weekends. Don't miss the banana-bread french toast or the generous omelets with the works, including a slice of melon. Although the food may be stuck in the 1980s, it's wholesome and comes in large portions. In one modern concession they also feature low-cholesterol egg-white omelets. Well-stuffed sandwiches are popular at lunch as are the huge salads.

MANDALAY · BURMESE 13/20

4348 California St., Richmond District 94118
415-386-3895, *Lunch & Dinner daily,* $

Mandalay was the first Burmese restaurant in the city, and its decor needs freshening, but the food is packed with pungent flavors. Our favorite dishes include the Mandalay prawns and the chicken in garlic sauce. Salads are particularly tasty. Try the tea-leaf salad: artfully arranged portions of peanuts, split beans, fried garlic, fried coconut, roasted sesame seeds, dried shrimp and special tea leaves, which patrons toss together. Rice and noodle dish plus curries round out the menu.

THE MANDARIN · CHINESE 13/20

900 North Point St., Ghirardelli Square 94109
415-673-8812, *Lunch & Dinner daily,* $$$

This is simply one of the most beautiful restaurants in San Francisco—a palatial space with exquisite Chinese antiques and artifacts, and an exquisite view of the Bay. A new owner added California touches to the menu, but we still like the classics like Peking duck, flaky green-onion pancakes and shrimp-filled rice paper rolls. We love the tea-smoked duck and prawns stir-fried with honeyed walnuts, an upscale banquet dish.

MANGIAFUOCO · ITALIAN 13/20

1001 Guerrero St., Mission 94110
415-206-9881, *Dinner nightly,* $$$

Mangiafuoco means fire eater, and this small, corner restaurant serves credible Italian specialties at good prices. A wood-fired oven spans half a wall and yields some of the best dishes on the menu: try the Sonoma lamb chops with a mustard and huckleberry sauce, or the fettuccine with seafood baked in parchment paper. An incredible risotto, featherweight gnocchi, and good pasta dishes round out the offerings. The decor is charmingly hip, with bright miniature lamps circling the room. A mostly Italian wine list covers the bases.

MANORA'S THAI CUISINE   THAI   13/20

1600 Folsom St., SoMa 94103
415-861-6224, *Lunch Mon.-Fri., Dinner nightly,* **$**

Manora's serves innovative and affordable Thai food. Classic—including the ubiquitous pad Thai, galanga and tom yan gung soups—receive simple and artful treatment. Other dishes include pong pang, a seemingly bottomless clay pot of seafood cloaked in a hot chile sauce. Reservations are only accepted for parties of four or more, so you may have to cool your heels a few minutes. Few other restaurants offer that perfect balance of heat, sweetness, spice and vibrant herbal flavors that make a great Thai meal. **Also in SoMa (3226 Mission St., 415-826-4639).**

MARIO'S BOHEMIAN CIGAR STORE   ITALIAN   ¢

556 Columbus Ave., North Beach 94133
415-362-0536, *Lunch & Dinner daily*

Don't believe it when cynics proclaim the death of North Beach: as long as Mario's is around, the neighborhood's spirit is alive. Wonderful cappuccinos, delicious focaccia sandwiches and a lemony ricotta cheesecake are served at the bar or one of the small tables. One of the most European of North Beach's cafes, it's a favorite with locals and European tourists in particular. Sit at the bar and enjoy the Sinatra CDs and have a punt e mes or the best cappuccino on the Beach. **Also Mario's on Polk St. (2209 Polk St., 415-776-8226).**

MARNEE THAI   THAI   14/20

2225 Irving St., Sunset District 94122
415-665-9500, *Lunch & Dinner Wed.-Mon.,* **$**

In traditional dress, May Siriyan, wife of chef-owner Chaiwatt Siriyan, choreographs the flow of cooks, waiters and customers with the skill of a dancer. The taste buds join the frolic, too, as Siriyan turns out some of the city's most vivid Asian food. The deep-frying at this perpetually crowded Sunset restaurant is superlative, as the greaseless corn cakes and spicy angel wings attest. Try the green papaya, its fiery jolt offset by lettuce leaves, and the chan pad poo, a silken rice- noodle dish brimming with crab meat, green onion and egg. In season, end your meal with mangoes paired with warm sticky rice.

MASA'S   FRENCH/CONTEMPORARY   16/20

Hotel Vintage Court, 648 Bush St., Union Square 94108
415-989-7154, *Dinner Tues.-Sat.,* **$$$$$**

In August 1998, chef Julian Serrano gambled on opening Picasso restaurant in the Bellagio Resort in Las Vegas, and sous chef Chad Callahan was promoted to chef. You can still dine well here, but Masa's is not as good as it once was. Some dishes have annoyingly prominent salt crystals; the wine service seems at times to be less focused, although the pricey and deep list is still great; and waiters seem at times to have lost their passion. Many of Serrano's dishes remain with Callahan's twists: for example, a warm lobster salad is napped with a truffle vinaigrette instead of Serrano's citrus accompaniment. Serrrano's foie gras sautéed with a Madeira-truffle sauce still appears on the menu but lacks the balance and execution it once had. Another Serrano-era dish is the venison with caramelized apples in a pungent Zinfandel sauce. There's a tasting menu at $85 as well as an $80 prix-fixe. The decor, in a difficult space off a hotel lobby, was spruced up a couple of years ago. The walls are a rich red, and modernistic paintings and heavy drapes create a romantic atmosphere. We hope that Masa's regains its equilibrium and that we can once again award it one of our highest ratings.

MATTERHORN SWISS RESTAURANT   SWISS   13/20

2323 Van Ness Ave., Van Ness 94109
415-885-6116, Dinner Tues.-Sun., $$$

Matterhorn is fondue central: nine kinds are available, served in traditional style with a bubbling pot of oil and broth and accompanied by side dishes and condiments. But there is more to life here than fondue. We love the fish, poultry and veal dishes, particularly the julienned veal with mushrooms. For dessert, go for a chocolate fondue. The interior appointments are all Swiss-manufactured; Alpine scenes are painted on glass panes that divide the dining rooms.

MAX'S DINER   AMERICAN   ¢

311 Third St., SoMa 94107
415-546-6297, Lunch & Dinner daily

This ersatz deli-diner has huge sandwiches, traditional blue-plate diner specials, low-fat dishes and lots of salads. Cakes, pies and crisps in huge portions are gooey and good. Jewish-style deli mavens, however, will be disappointed. **Also 18 other locations around the Bay Area.**

MAYA   MEXICAN   14/20

303 Second St., SoMa   94107
415-543-6709, Lunch & Dinner Mon.-Sat., $$$

The Sandoval brothers run the successful Maya in Manhattan, and decided to open one here. They decorated the odd-shaped space in a SoMa high-rise with lovely silver accessories and a wall of flowers in mounted vases, then wrapped the entire package in a peach-tinted interior. You'll find Mexican flavors but also the elegance of French presentation. The guacamole is served in a silver accented volcanic-rock molcajete. One great starter is the shrimp-stuffed chile relleno brightened with crème fraîche. We recommend such entrées as the mariscada---succulent sea scallops, mussels, prawns and clams with black rice---and the luscious mole poblano. Crepas de cajeta drenched in a sauce of caramelized goat's milk are a wonderful dessert.

MAYE'S ORIGINAL OYSTER HOUSE   ITALIAN/SEAFOOD 11/20

1233 Polk St., Polk Gulch 94109
415-474-7674, Lunch Mon.-Fri., Dinner Mon.-Sat., $$

Opened in 1867, Maye's is San Francisco's second-oldest restaurant. These days, it serves predictable old-style dishes: veal Parmigiana, lobster thermidor and shrimp Newburg are prominently featured. But this old war-horse has undeniable charm. Genial, barrel-chested waiters seat you in a dark, cozy room filled with photos of old San Francisco, where you can get comfortable with oysters Rockefeller or the signature pan-fried sand dabs. The regal bar is a good place to find yourself at happy hour.

MAYFLOWER   CHINESE/SEAFOOD   13/20

6225 Geary Blvd., Richmond District 94121
415-387-8338, Lunch & Dinner daily, $$

A good buy here is the seafood dinner for four people, which includes steamed crab, sautéed conch and scallops. Other recommended dishes are minced squab, shrimp accompanied by fried milk (cubes of milk curd that are crisp outside and barely set inside) and roast chicken. Uncooked sushi-style fish is served over a plastic-wrapped bed of ice and with an interesting spicy soy sauce dip. Crystal chandeliers and jacketed waiters make this an upscale Hong Kong–style venue.

MCCORMICK & KULETO'S   SEAFOOD/AMERICAN   11/20

900 North Point St., Ghirardelli Square 94109
415-929-1730, Lunch & Dinner daily, $$

This restaurant in Ghirardelli Square offers panoramic views of the city's waterfront and Bay, of which designer Pat Kuleto's theater-style seating takes artful advantage. The menu is as expansive as the restaurant—maybe too expansive, as the best dishes tend to be the simplest. Have oysters for starters, then anything in season that's grilled and minimally sauced fish. Coho salmon, for example, comes blackened and drizzled with a citrus-shallot vinaigrette. The wine list is both expansive and expensive, with an emphasis on California Chardonnays as well as a fine "reserve" list and a selection of half bottles.

MC^2 CALIFORNIA/ASIAN   14/20

470 Pacific Ave., North Beach 94133
415-956-0666, Lunch & Dinner daily, $$$$

Detractors call the slick design "too L.A." The style may lend energy to the scene, but it also means a noisy dining room. Another small but important complaint is the unupholstered seating, uncomfortable for multicourse dining. Experienced chef Yoshi Kojima has a light hand with sauces and stays away from overly fussy presentations. The fennel salad with ripe, bursting-with-flavor tomatoes and shaved Parmesan is simple and tasty. Seared tuna is married with a green-pepper vinaigrette. Tender beef cheeks are overworked here, braised with whole black tea leaves and paired with celeriac purée, a port sauce and caramelized apples. Kojima grills salmon and naps it with a Pinot Noir sauce to create a classic. Desserts are really special: we loved the warm soufflé.

MECCA — CONTEMPORARY — 14/20

2029 Market St., Castro 94114
415-621-7000, *Dinner nightly, $$$*

The heavy velvet curtains and the long horseshoe bar in the middle of the restaurant make diners feel as if their tables are part of a stage at this upscale Castro supper club. Mecca is the first high-style restaurant to open in the predominately gay Castro, but it's not exclusive; both mixed and same-sex couples enjoy the food here. Mike Fennelly, the new chef, brings his New Orleans roots and love of Asian flavors to the menu. He does a spicy bouillabaisse and adds a little heat to an ahi tuna filet paired with green-chile mashed potatoes. The small plates are popular, especially at the large 28-seat bar: barbecued oysters, spicy pecan salad, pizzas and shrimp dumplings are all delightful. The bar is a flirt-scene late at night.

THE MEETINGHOUSE — AMERICAN — 14/20

1701 Octavia St., Western Addition 94109
415-922-6733, *Dinner Tues.-Sat., $$$*

As austere and solid as any Shaker design, the Meetinghouse reminds us of what restaurants were like before glitz took over. The wood gleams, lights glow softly and fresh flowers add a note of indulgence to the otherwise unadorned room. The brief menu changes often but could include a lovely asparagus bisque, roasted duck breast with a red-onion marmalade, and various chicken, fish and chops. Surprisingly there are more desserts than entrées, including a rhubarb crisp, double-chocolate bourbon bread pudding and a warm banana tart. The wine list takes the best of Northern California vineyards, and prices are reasonable.

MEL'S DRIVE-IN — AMERICAN — ¢

2165 Lombard St., Marina 94123
415-921-2867, *Open daily*

Looking like something straight out of the movie *American Graffiti*, this local chain of diners serves up milkshakes, terrible burgers and good breakfast egg dishes (late) and snacks. A favorite for prom kids and bar hoppers. **And also 3355 Geary Blvd., Richmond District 415-387-2255 and 1050 Van Ness Ave., Van Ness 415-292-6357**

MERCURY   CONTEMPORARY   15/20

540 Howard St., SoMa 94105
415-777-1419, *Dinner Mon.-Sat.* $$$$

The sleek, metallic, dramatic 1940s supper-club look is appropriate—velvet, glass, brushed metal and leather in shades of black, gray and silver make Mercury visually stunning. The food, while not as far-out as the decor, is satisfying. For a starter, consider the earthy mushroom medley over toast, or the flaky lobster spring rolls. One unusual starter, reflecting the chef's time in Hawaii, is the tuna po'ke, "cooked" in a marinade of lime, soy and garlic. Not to be missed is the enormous and savory filet mignon crowned with foie gras, or the monkfish with black bean vinaigrette. For dessert, chocoholics will revel in the "chocolate galaxy," a sampler of fondant, pot de crème, chocolate macadamia tartlette, cookies, truffles and ice cream. After dinner, descend into the **Mercury Lounge** nightclub (bypassing the usual $20 cover charge), and marvel at the decor; if anything, it's even further out than the restaurant's.

MESCOLANZA   ITALIAN   13/20

2221 Clement St., Richmond District 94121
415-668-2221, *Dinner nightly*, $$

Clean and contemporary, this restaurant is decorated with saffron-tinted walls and a timeless architectural mural. The food is both traditional and hearty. As an appetizer to share, you can't beat any one of the seven thin-crust pizzas: mozzarella, goat cheese, pear, walnuts and prosciutto for the adventurous, or a simple mozzarella with tangy tomato sauce and fresh basil. Any number of the pastas are worth trying, especially the house specialty linguine with a lemon-cream sauce. For a more substantial entrée, try the veal Marsala, browned slices of veal in a rich wine reduction with shallots and mushrooms. The desserts are good and uncomplicated, like the crème caramel.

MIFUNE   JAPANESE/NOODLES   ¢

Kintetsu Mall, 1737 Post St., Japantown 94115
415-922-0337 *Lunch & Dinner daily*

People line up for quick bites at this inexpensive noodle emporium featuring 20 hot dishes, a dozen cold, and about as many donburi rice bowls. Each noodle dish comes with either white udon noodles or buckwheat soba noodles, both made in-house. Service is quick and efficient, helping this place remain a solid favorite for 20 years.

MILLENNIUM   VEGAN/CALIFORNIA   14/20

246 McAllister St., Civic Center 94102
415-487-9800, *Dinner nightly*, $$

Millennium draws a diverse clientele: animal rightists in canvas shoes, heart patients mending their ways, and the curious. The softly lit room and comfortable seating mean that someone has finally created the right setting for healthy and inventive food. Appetizers might include grilled vegetables with focaccia and aïoli or an empanada stuffed with tempeh chile, olives and raisins. Entrées are equally intriguing: the winter-harvest purse is a light pastry stuffed with roast veggies, and the Asian-style napoleon has layers of crisp sesame phyllo, oyster mushrooms, Japanese eggplant, asparagus and smoked tofu. Millennium hosts vegan holiday dinners.

MISS MILLIE'S AMERICAN 14/20

4123 24th St., Noe Valley 94110
415-285-5598, Breakfast, Lunch & Dinner Tues.-Sat., Brunch Sun., $

Breakfast is a big deal here, featuring wonderful baked goods: sticky cinnamon rolls, flavored scones, and French toast topped with bananas, whipped butter and real maple syrup. And don't miss the lemon ricotta pancakes with blueberry syrup! Healthier alternatives are also available, such as a side dish of roasted root vegetables instead of meat with the egg dishes. Dinner choices include seafood and chicken. Expect long waits on the weekend.

MOBY'S FISH & CHIPS IRISH/SEAFOOD ¢

494 Haight St., Haight-Ashbury 94117
415-522-6629, Open daily

Nautical objets d'art, seat cushions covered in mod velvets and leopard prints, and hefty handmade tables furnish the interior of this bright, Irish 'chipper' (fish and chip shop) owned and operated by three ex-pats. The menu features a full range of Irish pub specialties such as pasties, sausage rolls and beans, but the main draw is the crispy beer-batter-encased fish (sparkling fresh cod purchased directly from local fishermen) and the crispy chips. A selection of beers and ciders is on hand. Moby's stays open until 3 a.m. on weekends.

MOMO'S AMERICAN 15/20

760 Second St., China Basin 94107
415-227-8660, Lunch Mon.-Fri., Dinner nightly, Brunch Sat.-Sun., $$$

The lofty ceiling with exposed rafters, warm earth tones on the walls, leather banquettes and historic city photos make this large eatery near the new ballpark a seductive destination. Happily, the feeling of comfort also extends to the food. The exhibition kitchen turns out exceptional modern American fare. Start with crispy onion strings and baby back ribs with a tangy bourbon-barbecue sauce. Entrées include a tender grilled pork chop; the crisp thin-crust pizzas are also good. End your meal with a tangy blackberry crisp or an espresso-chocolate ice cream sandwich covered in caramel sauce. Twenty wines by the glass and a well-selected list hit a homer.

MOONSHINE — BARBECUE — 10/20

498 Broadway, North Beach 94133
415-982-6666, *Lunch Mon.-Fri., Dinner nightly, $$*

It's no secret that San Francisco is short on great barbecue restaurants, though there are some good ones are in Oakland. So hopes were high when this southern theme restaurant opened on Broadway. The look of the place, in the the long-closed Vanessi's, is almost perfect: a pressed-tin ceiling, wooden wainscoting, antique light fixtures and comfy booths replicate a southern jazz-era roadhouse. The expensive smoker could be a great asset, but all the meats that emerge from it are way oversmoked. Except for a few items like the shucked oysters, steamed peel-and-eat shrimp, the coleslaw or the Tabasco onion rings, the rest of the menu is best ignored. Have some shucked oysters and enjoy the live music and dancing.

MORTON'S OF CHICAGO — STEAKHOUSE — 12/20

400 Post St., Union Square 94108
415-986-5830, *Dinner nightly, $$$$*

Although this upscale steak chain offers a great piece of beef, diners pay a high price. And even at that price, the meat comes ungarnished; every side dish carries a separate price tag. Waiters are trained to put on a dog-and-pony show of the menu while displaying the raw ingredients. For dessert, avoid the soufflés and stick with the Key lime pie. The basement setting, with dark woods and low lighting, has a men's club mood.

MO'S GOURMET BURGERS — AMERICAN — ¢

1322 Grant Ave., North Beach 94133
415-788-3779, *Open daily*

Prepared over a revolving coal-fired grill, the top hamburger in the area has a slightly smoky flavor with a crusty exterior and juicy interior. The old-fashioned shakes served in metal containers are winners, too. Don't miss the frothy root-beer float. Breakfast is also served, but we stick with the burgers.

NEW AUX DELICES — VIETNAMESE/FRENCH — ¢

1002 Potrero Ave., Potrero Hill 94110
415-285-3196, *Lunch & Dinner Mon.-Sat.*

Blink and you might miss this little gem near General Hospital. Pink linens cover the tables, and lacy curtains cover the windows facing the street. A huge menu offers an array of delicious soups, appetizers, meat and vegetarian dishes, and seafood (including abalone sautéed with vegetables). Among a few French specialties are duck à l'orange (at $8.95!) and a charbroiled eight-ounce steak, served with French onion soup. The imperial rolls will keep you coming back. Soups are flavorful and soothing. Best of all, you can feast like royalty here and barely making a dent in your wallet.

NIPPON (NO NAME)   JAPANESE/SUSHI   13/20

314 Church St., Mission District 94114
No phone, *Lunch & Dinner daily*

This homey little box just off Market Street is almost always crowded with voracious diners. The plain tuna, salmon and in particular unagi (roasted veel with a sweet-salty ponzu sauce) are quite good. Vegetarian selections are available, from simple sliced cucumbers to sour umeboshi plum- and natto-fermented soybeans. Arrive early or stand in line outside. If you prefer alcohol to the excellent toasted-rice and green tea, brown-bag it from nearby stores before you're seated.

NOB HILL TERRACE   CALIFORNIA   13/20

Mark Hopkins Inter-Continental Hotel,
999 California St., Nob Hill 94108
415-616-6944, *Breakfast, Lunch & Dinner daily*, $-$$$$

For lovers of San Francisco tradition, a stop at The Mark on Nob Hill is a must. The hotel's dining room remains happily tradition bound, with dark-wood-paneled walls, smartly dressed tables and fine silver and china. At lunch the menu tries to hit all the right notes with good sandwiches and a selection of well-priced entrées. The appetizers we've enjoyed are tea-smoked foie gras, the seared-scallop napoleon and the risottos. Recent entrées ranged from a pan-steamed salmon with a Pinot Noir sauce to a roasted rack of lamb. After dinner, enjoy the view at the famous **Top of the Mark** cocktail lounge.

NORTH BEACH RESTAURANT   ITALIAN   14/20

1512 Stockton St. North Beach 94133
415-392-1587, *Lunch & Dinner daily*, $$$

The million-dollar remodeling of this North Beach eatery brings its look and style into the nineties. Longtime chef-owner Bruno Orsi and owner Lorenzo Petrone present some of the most delicious northern Italian food in the city. Enjoy any veal dish, the chicken cooked under a brick, the pastas and house-cured prosciutto. Dine upstairs surrounded by handsome wood wainscoting or downstairs in the private dining areas. The basement has a small prosciutto curing room with a couple of hundred hams hanging overhead. The owner is a wine fancier, so the list has a range of Italian and California winners.

NORTH END CAFFÈ   CAFÉ/SNACKS   ¢

1402 Grant Ave., North Beach 94133
415-956-3350, *Open daily*

Joe Parrilli is a young restaurateur with a sense of history—hipster history. The menu for his cute little café features pizzas: the Frank Sinatra has garlic, tomatoes and provolone; the Dean Martin is slapped with pesto; and the Sammy Davis Jr. has smoked salmon and dill. The rest room is an homage to the King—Elvis, of course. The menu also includes egg dishes and sandwiches. A new wave of bohemians hang out day and night.

NORTH INDIA — INDIAN — 13/20

3131 Webster St., Marina 94123
415-931-1556, *Lunch Mon.-Fri., Dinner nightly, $$*

The twin dining rooms in this warm, family-run operation are almost always full. North India's reputation is based on its curries and its jumbo prawns prepared in a variety of hot sauces. The curries in particular have an intriguing delicacy and complexity. We also find the boti kebab, skewered, spiced lamb from the tandoor oven, surprising in its subtlety. Classic accompaniments include good matar paneer (cheese and peas in a mild sauce) and exceptional breads, especially the onion kulcha. A wide range of appetizing vegetarian dishes are also available.

NORTH STAR RESTAURANT — AMERICAN — 12/20

288 Connecticut St., Potrero Hill 94107
415-551-9840, *Lunch Tues.-Sun., Dinner Tues.-Sun., Brunch Sat.-Sun., $$*

The sunny yellow, wood-paneled walls of this cozy bistro are portents of the comfort food to come; the sleek, miniature zinc bar alludes to the modern sensibility of the menu. Whole-leaf romaine with a creamy lemon vinaigrette and roasted onions is a fine alternative to the ubiquitous Caesar. A juicy hamburger with Gruyère at lunch, and the braised short ribs, mashed potatoes and greens at dinner make this a neighborhood destination. From the adjoining Little Dipper Bakery come banana-chocolate cream pie and ricotta poppyseed cake. The wine list is heavily California with a drizzle of Oregon.

OBERON — CALIFORNIA/MEDITERRANEAN — 13/20

1450 Lombard St., Cow Hollow 94123
415-885-6555, *Dinner nightly, $$*

If lamb is a favorite of yours, this is a good stop: you'll find rack of lamb, lamb shank and an appetizer of skewered ground lamb with mint and garlic. Other dishes include a roast half chicken with couscous and steamed clams. The dining room is a charming three-room space hidden behind the facade of a dreary-looking motel, but there's plenty of free parking. From time to time, the owners invite in groups to entertain.

OKINA SUSHI — JAPANESE/SUSHI — 13/20

776 Arguello Blvd., Richmond District 94118
415-387-8882, *Dinner Wed.-Sat., $*

A meal at Okina offers a primer in Zen. Don't look for any fancy rolls here. You won't find tempura or even miso soup. It's simply sushi and it's perfect. Chef-owner Akio Matsuoka's dedication to simplicity is apparent in the sparse yet tasteful decor: traditional Japanese light wood and paper, clean and organic. A master of his craft, Matsuoka has been serving generous slabs of the freshest sashimi at this location since 1981. Ask him what's good today and treat yourself

OLD KRAKOW   POLISH   12/20

385 W. Portal Ave., West Portal 94127
415-564-4848, Lunch Sat.-Sun., Dinner nightly, $$

   As far as we know, this is San Francisco's only Polish restaurant. The original artwork by Polish artists and the rustic furniture help create an appropriate atmosphere. The food is rib-sticking: huge cabbage rolls stuffed with seasoned ground beef and rice, a sausage dinner, and tender pirogi. Cheesecake and poppyseed cake are both good choices for dessert.

ONE MARKET   CONTEMPORARY   15/20

1 Market St., Embarcadero 94105
415-777-5577, Lunch Mon.-Fri., Dinner nightly, Brunch Sun., $$$

   Owner-chef Bradley Ogden created this beautiful restaurant. Now Rabah Abusbaitan is executing the dynamic menu. Recommended starters include Bradley's Caesar, the salmon tartare with fresh horseradish and quail egg, and the Maine lobster tortellini. The entrées span from a flavorful chanterelle mushroom risotto to a double-cut pork chop with caramelized-apple chutney. A five-course tasting menu is worth the tab of $55, $85 with wines and brandy. One great dessert is the made-to-order Tahitian vanilla bean ice cream dressed up with hot fudge, caramel and strawberry toppings. One Market has a daily wine list that offers a number of nice selections by the glass, as well as the "expanded list and cellar selections" which comprise an astoundingly broad range of American wines.

OODLES   FUSION   13/20

900 Bush St., Union Square 94108
415-928-1888, Dinner Mon.-Sat., $$$

   As you might guess from the name, this restaurant is a study in whimsy, from the relentlessly colorful stemware to the Day-Glo uniforms of the wait staff, down to the small plastic animals clinging to the edges of the glasses. The menu is an ambitious pan-Asian mishmash of dishes, some brilliant, some falling short. It works if you're having the delicious chawan mushi, a loose custard of chicken confit, scallops and gingko nuts. Another success is the sautéed foie gras served with star anise, sugared grapes and a Thai-influenced caramel sauce. Entrées worth considering include a punchy pancetta-wrapped pork loin with spicy clams and Chinese sausage.

ORGANICA — VEGAN — 12/20

1224 Ninth Ave., Inner Sunset 94122
Dinner, Tues.-Sun., $

☎ 👬

This is an unusual restaurant in a town full of unusual restaurants. Not only is it 100 percent vegan—meaning no dairy products are used—but it also serves only uncooked food, save that which is baked by the sun. Sound terrible? Guess again: Raw's new-agey treats are surprisingly satisfying, even those like the cold "fat mushroom" soup featuring yellow tomatoes and portobello mushrooms. Pizzas are built on a sun-dried buckwheat crust; toppings include sea palm, house-made kraut and marinated eggplant. Complement your meal with hot shots of puréed pepper juice. The restaurant itself is a perfect slice of California, overgrown with lush plants, framed photos of reclining goddesses and a techno soundtrack.

ORIGINAL JOE'S — ITALIAN — 13/20

144 Taylor St., Tenderloin 94102
415-775-4877, *Lunch & Dinner daily, $$*

☎ 🚗 🦉 🍸

Take a walk on the wild side, the Tenderloin, that is, to experience this old-timey Italian-American spot. The Tenderloin is a slowly improving neighborhood that still carries a rather rough reputation, but adjacent valet parking is helpful. The red vinyl booths and moody lighting likewise speak of another era. In vintage tuxedos, the waiters are grumpy but good. The excellent, huge hamburger is served on a hollowed-out French roll. Italian-American classics—lasagne, veal dishes and pasta—make up the balance of the menu.

ORITALIA — FUSION — 15/20

586 Bush St., Union Square 94108
415-782-8122, *Dinner nightly, $$*

☎ 🚗 🎷 🍸 ▲ ○

While many have attempted to fuse, few have pulled it off as successfully as chef Brenda Buenviaje, a Filipina Creole transplant from New Orleans. Though distinctly more "or" than "italia," the menu is full of subtle, delicate and creative combinations. For starters, the nori-wrapped Maine blue-crab cakes in a lemon-grass cream are good, and the poached rock-shrimp wontons in roasted garlic sesame broth are addictive. Even better is the Thai curry beef. You don't get very much, but the plump gnocchi with Maine lobster dressed in a lime buerre blanc is delicious. Another winner is the saké-steamed sea bass in a black bean sauce. Desserts are edible works of art. The wine list of more than 80 selections also offers many wines by the glass. Dramatic ochre-colored walls are accented with contemporary art in the warren of dining areas.

OSAKA GRILL   JAPANESE/GRILL   13/20

1217 Sutter St., Van Ness 94109
415-440-8838, *Lunch Mon.-Fri., Dinner nightly, $$*
☎

Inside this attractive, minimal space, meals are prepared on hibachis while the customer watches. Chef-owner Noel Mok has created a light cuisine that keeps people coming back for more. Highlights include the shrimp appetizer, sea bass with ginger sauce, and a terrific steak in garlic sauce. Grilled scallops are always perfectly cooked and deliciously fresh.

OSOME   JAPANESE/SUSHI   13/20

1923 Fillmore St., Pacific Heights 94115
415-346-2311, *Dinner nightly, $$*
☎ 🏃

Osome vies with Kabuto in the Richmond District as the best sushi venue in the city. Though small, it boasts an extensive menu, and the food is consistently delectable. The maguro (tuna) is some of the freshest, richest-tasting sashimi we've had, and the "rock and roll" made of grilled eel and avocado is a rare delight. The beef roll of thinly sliced sirloin wrapped around Asian chives and served with teriyaki sauce and shredded cabbage is similarly not to be missed. Forty-something varieties of fun sushi are prepared here, as well as tempura, shabu-shabu and kaiseki dinners.

OVATION AT THE OPERA   FRENCH   13/20

Opera Hotel, 333 Fulton St., Civic Center
415-863-8400, *Breakfast, Lunch & Dinner Mon.-Sat., Brunch & Dinner Sun. $$$*
☎ 🚗 🏃

One of the most beautiful rooms in the city is located at the Inn at the Opera hotel. It's filled with wonderful oil paintings and flower arrangements, an ornate bar, dark wood, an oversize fireplace and comfy banquettes. Despite its location near the Performing Arts Center, this restaurant has had its ups and downs. New owners offer a classic French menu: foie gras terrine, coquilles St. Jacques and escargots. Soups are wonderful: shellfish bisque, traditional onion and a daily special. The entrées are classics with a twist: Dungeness crab and lobster ravioli come with an interesting lemon-grass butter, and sautéed sweetbreads sparkle under a port wine sauce.

At the heart of the most

Beautiful city in the world,

More than a hotel, ours is a

Departure from the ordinary.

Here, architecture rewards the eye, calms the spirit. Service is gracious, smiles genuine. There is the luxury of a personal valet and a chauffeured limousine. Like the City itself, it is soothing, sophisticated, unique in every respect.

THE PAN PACIFIC HOTEL
San Francisco

A block from Union Square at 500 Post Street
For reservations call your travel planner
or 800-533-6465

PACIFIC   CONTEMPORARY   16/20

Pan Pacific Hotel, 500 Post St., Union Square 94102
415-929-2087, *Breakfast Mon.-Sat., Lunch & Dinner daily, Brunch Sun.,*
$$$

This hidden gem on the third floor of the Pan Pacific Hotel has a serene dining room. The kitchen is headed by Michael Otsuka, who worked with L.A. superchef Joachim Splichal. Otsuka brings a perfect sensibility to the Asian-kissed menu. Consider this starter: a salad of smoked eastern black cod with Yukon potatoes and caviar. Or how about an asparagus-potato soup with portobello mushrooms and corn? For main courses, we recommend the Chilean turbot with mushroom gnocchi, the lobster napped with a garlic-lemon emulsion, and the lamb done as a rack and as a strudel with Moroccan spices. Desserts continue the theme with Asian flavors and French technique. All this, in combination with a fine, reasonably priced wine list, makes this a top choice for comfortable dining.

PALIO D'ASTI   ITALIAN   13/20

640 Sacramento St., Financial District 94111
415-395-9800, *Lunch Mon.-Fri., Dinner Mon.-Sat., $$$*

Colorful flags reminiscent of Siena's Palio delle Contrade, the famous horse race dating back to medieval times, fly in this sleek restaurant. A glassed-in kitchen dominates one side of the dining room, while a charming curved bar sits near the entrance across from the wood-fired pizza oven. Start with a selection of house-made antipasti. Main courses include -a pan-fried salmon with toasted orzo, English cucumbers and tomato coulis, and a brick-cooked chicken with spinach and creamy tomato. For dessert, try the berries macerated in Pinot Noir with zabaglione. The first-rate wine list includes a nice selection of dessert wines.

PALOMINO EURO BISTRO   CALIFORNIA   11/20

345 Spear St., Embarcadero 94105
415-512-7400, *Lunch Mon.-Fri., Dinner nightly, Brunch Sun., $$*

The offshoot of a Seattle chain, this eatery in Hills Brothers Plaza affords diners a good view of the Bay Bridge. The menu revolves around the wood-burning oven: pizzas have cracker-thin crusts, and two of the best main courses are spit-roasted chicken and cedar-planked salmon with a smoky perfume. Even the apple tart gets a turn in the wood oven and comes out with a bronze glaze; it's topped with a drizzle of caramel sauce. This is very much an after-work destination.

FOR GAYOT'S UPDATED SAN FRANCISCO RESTAURANT
REVIEWS, GO TO:

Digitalcity.com/sanfrancisco/dining

PANCHO VILLA TAQUERIA   MEXICAN   ¢

3071 16th St., Mission District 94110
415-864-8840, *Open daily*

   Don't be deterred by the line out the front door: It moves fast. Mission locals and out-of-the-neighborhood fans flock to this taqueria for some of the best Mexican food in town. Burritos and soft tacos are the main draws; the house special is a huge flour tortilla filled with rice, red or black beans, grilled chopped steak, guacamole and fresh salsa. You'll also find chicken, pork with prawns, red snapper and vegetarian dishes.

PANE E VINO   ITALIAN   13/20

3011 Steiner St., Cow Hollow 94123
415-346-2111, *Lunch Mon.-Sat., Dinner nightly, $$*

   Appealing food brings the rustic, inviting dining rooms of Pane e Vino to life. An appetizer of grilled prawns is bathed in a sauce of feta cheese, lime and mint so zesty that we drizzle it on the crusty sourdough. For entrées, we particularly like the tender lamb chops served with roast potatoes, the spicy house-made Italian sausages surrounded by sweet stewed peppers and polenta, and a whole grilled striped bass dotted with rosemary, peppercorns and other aromatic spices, deboned tableside. The wine list offers a good selection of Italian vintages.

PARK CHOW   AMERICAN   13/20

1240 Ninth Ave., Inner Sunset 94122
415-665-9912, *Lunch & Dinner daily, $*

   See the review of Chow above.

PARK GRILL   CALIFORNIA   14/20

Park Hyatt Hotel, 333 Battery St., Financial District 94111
415-392-1234, Breakfast, Lunch & Dinner daily, Brunch Sun., $$$

   In a town with several Hyatt Hotels, the Park Hyatt's restaurant has distinguished itself for its fine wine program. In addition to a formidable wine and sake list, the Park Grill hosts frequent winemakers dinners. The restaurant is a comfortable and elegant spot for a business lunch. In balmy weather, you can enjoy dine al fresco on the garden terrace. Dinner is also restful, with tables spaced comfortably apart around the handsome dining room. First courses range from a tuna and rock shrimp napoleon given an Asian accent paired with crisp wontons and a soy vinaigrette. We like the Caesar salad, but we love the tea-smoked scallops in a spinach salad enhanced by a lemon-grass vinaigrette. Entrées include a three-pepper flavored tuna, grilled Angus steak and delightful porcini-encrusted sea bass. The staff is sharp and wine savvy. Dive into the award-winning wine list—you won't be disappointed.

PARMA RISTORANTE	ITALIAN	12/20

3314 Steiner St., Marina 94123
415-567-0500, *Lunch & Dinner daily, $$*

Parma's robust pastas and hearty Italian red wines keep this Marina favorite hopping late into the night. The wait staff is a lively bunch whom you half expect to break into a chorus of *That's Amore* as they dash from table to table. Crusty, thick-cut Italian bread arrives with a dish of herbs and olive oil for dipping; linguine alla vongole is heaped with clams and mussels in a garlicky white-wine sauce; the risotto, however, can be lackluster. Once the place fills up, no one seems to notice the noise.

PASTA POMODORO	ITALIAN	¢

655 Union St., North Beach 94133
415-399-0300, *Open daily*

This pasta house offers incredible deals and generous portions. The gnocchi, coated in Gorgonzola sauce and spiked with diced tomato, is better than preparations that cost twice as much. The dozen or so pastas include penne puttanesca (with black and green olives and a slightly spicy tomato sauce); rigatoni with roast chicken, cream, mushrooms and sun-dried tomatoes; and spaghetti with calamari, mussels and scallops. The Caesar salad is light on garlic and anchovies, but big shavings of Parmesan compensate. We like the pasta so much, we forget that they also serve sandwiches. **Also in the Marina (2027 Chestnut St., 415-474-3400), Castro (2304 Market St., 415-558-8123), Richmond District (3611 California St., 415-831-0900), Haight-Ashbury (598 Haight St., 415-436-9800), Inner Sunset (816 Irving St., 415-566-0900), Polk Gulch (1865 Post St., 415-674-1826), Cow Hollow (1875 Union St., 415-771-7900), Noe Valley (4000 24th St., 415-920-9904), and Oakland & San Rafael.**

PASTIS	FRENCH/CALIFORNIA	14/20	

1015 Battery St., Financial District 94111
415-391-2555, *Lunch Mon.-Fri., Dinner Mon.-Sat., $$*

Pastis is the second restaurant from Gerald Hirigoyen of Fringale. The chef is Isabelle Alexandre, originally from Toulouse, who worked for Michel Richard in Los Angeles. The menu offers gutsy fare like boneless oxtail rouelle, an onion-and-cheese tart and escargot ravioli. Alexandre has a good hand with fish: the moist striped bass with lemon and coriander is a treat, as is the seared salmon paired with a potato risotto. A veal chop is lovingly wrapped in bacon with a shallot sauce. The wine list is a good mix of French and California. The industrial space is warmed by the use of color.

PATIO ESPAÑOL   SPANISH   12/20

2850 Alemany Blvd., Outer Mission 94112
415-587-5117, *Lunch & Dinner daily, $$*

Even native San Franciscans rarely venture into this outlying reach of the city, but it is worth a visit. Located between the Excelsior and Daly City, Patio Español is in the Spanish Cultural Center, a rambling white building that could be a roadside hotel in central Spain. It has a large bar with small tables for tapas, and a big dining room for full lunches and dinners. The paella is quite good, but we like the tapas: grilled prawns in garlic sauce, squid in its own ink, grilled sausages, slices of ham. The selection of reasonably priced Spanish wines is probably the best in the Bay Area.

PAULINE'S PIZZA   PIZZA   ¢

260 Valencia St., Mission District 94103
415-552-2050, *Dinner Tues.-Sat.*

Thin-crust pizzas here are topped with everything from homemade sausage to garden-fresh salad toppings. Daily specials include vegetarian pizzas such as a roasted eggplant with Fontina. Salads, delicious breads and a decent wine selection add to the draw, but the yummy pesto pizza is what made Pauline's famous.

PAZZIA   ITALIAN   12/20

337 Third St., SoMa 94107
415-512-1693, *Lunch Mon.-Fri., Dinner Mon.-Sat., $$*

This sunny little trattoria isn't big on furnishings: the tiled dining room might be described as "stylishly barren." What Pazzia does excel in are thin, crisp-crusted pizzas—some say they're the city's best—and rustic pastas and panini. Around lunchtime, the café is filled with office workers; on sunny days, a lucky few get to enjoy the sidewalk tables. Dinner is a little less harried. Peruse the excellent Italianate wine list; entrées as good as the rosemary-grilled lamb chops deserve an apt bottle.

PERRY'S   AMERICAN   12/20

1944 Union St., Cow Hollow 94123
415-922-9022, *Breakfast & Lunch Mon.-Fri., Dinner nightly, Brunch Sat.-Sun., $$*

One of the first singles bars in the city, Perry's now caters to an older crowd, more likely to be discussing Barry Bonds' batting average than chatting up the person on the next stool. If the noisy barroom isn't your scene, ask to be seated in back. Perry's has perhaps the best hamburgers in town, served on a poppyseed roll with all the messy trimmings. The menu, however, runs the gamut from quesadillas to chile and grilled ahi tuna to linguine with clams. **Also near Union Square (185 Sutter St., 415-989-6895).**

PIAF'S   FRENCH   14/20

1686 Market St., Civic Center 94102
415-864-3700, *Dinner Tues.-Sat., Brunch Sun.*, $$

Sounds from Piaf records or a live pianist playing her beautiful songs set the atmosphere at this restaurant/cabaret. The decor is accentuated by plum-colored walls, splashes of gold, a cherry-wood bar, white fringed lamps and Piaf memorabilia. The cooking is authentic Paris bistro style. Everyone gets an outstanding, complimentary lobster bisque to start. The grilled quail with quince and a lavender-honey vinaigrette makes an enjoyable starter. Other choices include seared foie gras, salade lyonnaise and a fine coq au vin garnished with oh-so-good truffled potatoes. Make sure to Sample the scrumptious chocolate tureen with crème anglaise. A reasonably priced, bistro-appropriate French-California wine list is available.

PJ'S OYSTER BED   CREOLE/CAJUN   13/20

737 Irving St., Inner Sunset 94122
415-566-7775, *Lunch & Dinner daily*, $$

It's always Mardi Gras at PJ's and the style and taste of the food are close to the New Orleans original. We liked the iron-skilleted Avery Island shellfish roast, blackened catfish, spicy jambalaya and oyster-bar selections. Unfortunately, space is at a premium and those without reservations will have to wait upwards of an hour (many wait across the street at Yancy's Saloon) for one of the cramped tables. If you can finagle a seat at the counter, you can watch the chefs at work.

PLANET HOLLYWOOD   AMERICAN   11/20

2 Stockton St., Downtown 94103
415-421-7827, *Lunch & Dinner daily*, $$

Number 25 in this worldwide chain of eateries owned by Sylvester Stallone, Arnold Schwarzenegger and Bruce Willis, this spot is strictly for the fanatical movie buff. Cluttered with movie photos, costumes, and artifacts from *Raiders of the Lost Ark*, one of the half-human robots from the *Terminator* series, and lots of costumes and props, it's more of a theme park than a restaurant. But kids (and kids at heart) will probably have a good time, especially with an ice cream soda and a burger.

PLOUF   SEAFOOD   14/20

40 Belden Pl., Union Square 94109
415-986-6491, *Lunch Mon.-Fri., Dinner Mon.-Sat.*, $$$

Plouf bills itself as a seafood bistro, and the buckets of tender mussels and clams prove it: the preparations range from marinière (garlic, white wine and parsley) to poulette (cream, shallots, white wine and parsley). The menu changes daily, reflecting what's available in the market. The fish offerings start with fish and chips with aïoli and include a traditional bourride, a stew from southern France. The restaurant also features delightful outdoor dining.

PLUMPJACK CAFÉ   CALIFORNIA   15/20

3127 Fillmore St., Cow Hollow 94123
415-563-4755, *Lunch & Dinner Mon.-Sat., $$*

   The food is solid California fare, but one extremely attractive draw for oenophiles is the incredibly priced wine list—absolutely the best in the Bay Area. In some cases you pay equal to what you would at retail. Maria Helm, the talented chef, incorporates fresh seasonal produce into the menu; it shines in dishes such as a risotto with English peas, sweet corn, spring onions, fines herbes and grana; a warm artichoke-and-chèvre tart; a thyme-roasted rabbit with shallots, morels and braised greens. You'll also find a very good Caesar salad and a grown-up hamburger served on focaccia. The creamy crème brûlée and the fruit crisp are exemplary desserts.

PLUTO'S   HOFBRAU   ¢

627 Irving St., Inner Sunset 94117
415-753-8867, *Open daily*

   This budding chain is a modern hofbrau done with a light hand. Service is cafeteria-style, so you can check out the large salad area, fresh roasted turkey and hearty sides. The very good Caesar is made on the spot. The desserts are forgettable. **Also in the Marina (3258 Scott St., 415-775-8867).**

POMELO   INTERNATIONAL/NOODLES   12/20

92 Judah St., Upper Haight 94122
415-731-6175, *Lunch & Dinner daily, $*

   Not much bigger than a bento box, Pomelo is where noodles and grains meet to form a menu for the new food pyramid. Start in Phnom Penh for a refreshing rice noodle, mint and carrot salad with grilled tiger prawns. On to Lanzhou for gingery, thick egg noodles and seared ahi tuna. A foray into Bangkok garners fried rice with egg, sweet onions and strips of pork. From Shanghai we recommend noodles with a spicy pork and shiitake ragoût. In many of the vegetarian dishes, virtue and deliciousness are happy traveling companions. Wines are available by the glass, but the iced ginger-lemon-grass tea is refreshing.

POSTRIO   CONTEMPORARY   16/20

The Prescott Hotel, 545 Post St., Union Square 94108
415-776-7825, *Breakfast, Lunch & Dinner daily, Brunch Sat.-Sun., $$$$*

   Now celebrating its tenth year, L.A. celebrity-chef Wolfgang Puck's wildly popular San Francisco outpost is better than ever under co-executive chefs Steven and Mitchell Rosenthal. The design by Pat Kuleto screams "Celebration!" and the massive modern painting, the landscaped greens spied through the windows, and the central staircase, designed to create grand entrances, add to the buzz. The menu always reflects Puck's vision: Asian flavors, twists on traditional dishes like Chinese roast duck and creative designer pizzas. You might find an appetizer of sautéed sea scallops with a surprising coffee-mushroom jus, roasted salmon with a Maui onion marmalade and squab with baby artichokes. Pastry chef Susan Brinkley is a master of satisfying desserts, such as a warm banana-chocolate pie with cashew brittle ice cream. Postrio is a great spot for an after-theater snack in the bar, and you can always find several excellent wines by the glass from the creative list.

POWELL'S PLACE   SOUTHERN/SOUL   11/20

511 Hayes St., Hayes Valley 94102
415-863-1404, *Breakfast, Lunch & Dinner daily*, $

For more than 20 years, Powell's has served soulful Southern food to locals who want a break from the city's trend-setting restaurant scene. Occasionally, gospel singer Emmit Powell is on hand to welcome you to his comfortable, frill-free Hayes Street restaurant. If your spirit cries out for crisp and tender fried chicken, black-eyed peas with sausage, corn muffins, red beans or mashed potatoes and greens, Powell's offers redemption. Sweet-potato pie makes a rousing finish; blues and R&B play on the jukebox.

PUCCINI & PINETTI   CALIFORNIA/ITALIAN   ¢

29 Ellis St., Downtown 94102
415-392-5500, *Open daily*

Operated by the Kimpton hotel group, which manages more than a dozen restaurants around town, this casual dining spot presents a menu that emphasizes straightforward pasta dishes, a few salads and well-prepared panini, all at reasonable prices. Particularly good menu choices are angel hair pasta with roasted vegetables and basil oil, spicy spaghetti puttanesca and grilled chicken breast with rosemary potatoes.

R & G LOUNGE   CHINESE   12/20

631 Kearny St., Chinatown 94108
415-982-7877, *Lunch & Dinner daily*, $

Downstairs is a family-style Chinese restaurant with astonishingly cheap prices and daily Cantonese lunch specials, like five-spice oxtail soup, that are unbelievably tasty. Upstairs is a serene and rather elegant dining room where you can order fish plucked right from the tank. Start with the crisp and delicious salt-and-pepper shrimp. The vegetables are always perfectly cooked. Private rooms are popular for business confabs.

RED DEVIL LOUNGE   AMERICAN   ¢

1695 Polk St., Russian Hill 94109
415-921-1695, *Dinner Mon.-Sat.*

A slice of New Orleans with black walls, lipstick-red accents and dancing neon demons at the entrance, this is a fun and visually stunning spot for dining or dancing to the eclectic mix of live bands. Good dishes on the short menu include red-hot chile poppers covered in beer batter and served with a super-spicy sauce with sweet undertones. The macho nachos are also a good deal: they're smothered in tomato, green onions, jalapeños, black beans, guacamole, sour cream and cheese.

RESTAURANT LULU   MEDITERRANEAN   14/20

816 Folsom St., SoMa 94105
415-495-5775, *Lunch & Dinner daily, $$$*

This "Riviera-style" eatery, founded by Reed Hearon, has been a grand success since it opened in 1993. Aside from the lofty, open space, moderate prices, good service, wood-burning oven and semi-open kitchen, what has seemed to thrill diners most is the family-style food service. Jody Denton's changing menu includes a number of wood-oven-roasted specials and great pizzas. A selection of antipasti, skillet-roasted mussels, or marinated grilled sardines is a good way to begin. An order of the butternut-squash gnocchi with sage brown butter and Parmesan will leave you satisfied. The intriguing wine list has some good bargains, and offers a wide range of wines by the glass. A new wine bar with 70 wines under a cruvinet system is a great addition. The noise level can be incredible.

RINCÓN PERUANO   PERUVIAN   ¢

3364 26th St., Mission District 94110
415-824-2673, *Lunch Mon.-Fri., Brunch Sat.*

This tiny family-owned joint on the outskirts of the Mission is one of the few places in the city to get authentic Peruvian food. Homespun crafts adorn cheerful orange walls, and since there's only four tables, the food is generally taken out. Peruvian specialties include sudado de mariscos (a tasty, spicy seafood soup), bistek apanado (a breaded steak served with rice and salad) and pescado frito (fish fried with onions and spices). Lunch specials vary, and Saturday's menu includes empanades, Peruvian tamales and a pork-and-onion sandwich.

RISTORANTE ECCO   ITALIAN   14/20

101 South Park, SoMa 94103
415-495-3291, *Lunch Mon.-Fri., Dinner Mon.-Sat., $$*

This is a warm, relaxing space tucked away on the east side of South Park. Across the greenery from South Park Café, Ecco has some of the same hip feeling: the staff is young and friend-ly, the ambience easy, and the food equally satisfying. The antipasti are large enough for two; or you might try a starter of salmon carpaccio drizzled with olive oil, topped with red caviar and served with crostini and fluffy, horseradish-scented Mascarpone. We especially like the linguine dell'Ecco, a flavorful combination of pears, pecans, Gorgonzola, mint and Reggiano. Desserts are terrific: try the warm chocolate pudding with Mascarpone cream.

RISTORANTE IDEALE   ITALIAN   14/20

1309 Grant Ave., North Beach 94133
415-391-4129, *Dinner Tues.-Sun.,* $$

This has rapidly become one of the most popular Italian restaurants in San Francisco, and for good reason. This artsy restaurant fits in well on funky Grant Avenue, lined with eclectic boutiques, coffee houses and blues bars. The daily-changing menu includes simple Roman specialties: fettuccine in a creamy tomato sauce with big chunks of lobster, or pappardelle with lamb. The rabbit is always good; the sliced pork loin with roasted potatoes and vegetables is another crowd-pleaser.

RISTORANTE MILANO   ITALIAN   13/20

1448 Pacific Ave., Russian Hill 94109
415-673-2961, *Dinner Tues.-Sun.,* $$

This small, romantic space is always jammed, but because of the charming staff and the good food, you don't notice that you may be gazing deep into the eyes of your significant other while the guy at the next table has his elbow in your bread plate. The pastas are a treat, as are the skewered chicken livers. The selection of Italian wines is good.

THE RITZ-CARLTON DINING ROOM   FRENCH   18/20

The Ritz-Carlton Hotel, 600 Stockton St., Nob Hill 94108
415-296-7465, *Dinner Mon.-Sat.,* $$$$$

The Dining Room has been among the best restaurants in San Francisco since it opened in 1990. Its exquisite decor, top-of-the-line wine list, ultra-professional service and live dinner music combine to create a showcase for the food, which has passed from the hands of chef Gary Danko to those of former Le Cirque chef Sylvain Portay. Portay's food is more classically French than any other French chef's in San Francisco. We recommend the chilled lobster-almond gazpacho, the crispy vegetable tart with goat cheese or the rabbit ballotine. A salt-baked cod with gribiche sauce is inspired, as is a rabbit shoulder stuffed with fresh herbs. It's difficult to choose from the many wonders on the menu, which offers game, fish and the best in meat from all over the country. Desserts come in two categories—fruits and chocolate—but the extraordinary cheese cart should not be overlooked. Master Sommelier Emmanuel Kimiji will walk wine connoisseurs and novices through the extensive menu to find the right wine pairing. The six-course tasting menu is $78 and well worth it.

THE RITZ-CARLTON TERRACE   MEDITERRANEAN   15/20

The Ritz-Carlton Hotel, 600 Stockton St., Nob Hill 94108
415-296-7465, *Breakfast, Lunch & Dinner daily, Brunch Sun.,* $$$

Guests are pampered here at breakfast, lunch and dinner, but the meals most worth coming for are the Friday night seafood buffet and the Sunday brunch. The Terrace boasts one of the largest and most attractive outdoor dining areas in the Bay Area, often utilized for the superlative Sunday brunch, at which you'll find egg dishes, roast beef, caviar, smoked fish and even sushi. With unlimited Champagne, it is well worth the $40 tab. On Friday nights the seafood celebration is spectacular: all-you-can-eat shellfish, a seafood pasta station, smoked fish and terrines, seafood salads, chowder and a Caesar salad station—all for $49. In the **Lobby Lounge**, sushi and sashimi are served from 5:30 to 8 p.m every night but Sunday to the accompaniment of live cafe-society piano music. Live jazz at brunch as well as most evenings, plus excellent service, makes the Terrace a special place.

ROSE PISTOLA   ITALIAN   15/20

532 Columbus Ave., North Beach 94133
415-399-0499, *Lunch & Dinner daily,* $$$

Chef-owner Reed Hearon created this handsome space with wood beams, an open kitchen, a wood-burning oven, a huge bar, and simple but sophisticated cuisine featuring such Ligurian dishes as farinatas, chickpea-flour pizzas with toppings like caramelized onions and sage. House-cured salmon and anchovies are a good snack or side dish. Grilled items such as the wood-oven-roasted rabbit with white runner beans, and the chicken cooked under a brick, are excellent. The changing fish special comes with garlic-perfumed spaghetti. The Italian varietal list is well chosen. Live jazz is performed most nights.

ROSE'S CAFÉ   ITALIAN   14/20

2298 Union St., Cow Hollow 94123
415-775-2200, *Breakfast, Lunch & Dinner daily,* $$

Rose's offers a casual Italian take on breakfast, lunch and dinner in a casual Cow Hollow setting. Homemade Italian breads are a success, especially the strawberry-black-currant focaccia. For breakfast, don't miss the "breakfast pizza," a thin blistered-crust torte topped with ham, Cheddar and eggs. At lunch, several sandwiches will entice you including the grilled chicken with roasted tomatoes and aïoli, and the steak with blue cheese, radicchio and roasted onion. The fresh salads are also good; try the goat cheese with arugula and tapenade bruschetta. Rose's now offers comfortable seating on the heated and covered sidewalk patio.

ROOSEVELT TAMALE PARLOR   MEXICAN   ¢

2817 24th St., Mission 94110
415-550-9213, *Lunch & Dinner Tues.-Sun.*

This 24th Street institution has been in business since 1922. Order the huge servings of pork or chicken tamales à la carte or on a dinner plate, along with a wide range of other Mexican specialties. Several tasty moles are house-made daily.

RÔTI/RED HERRING   SEAFOOD   NO RATING

155 Steuart St., Embarcadero 94105
415-495-6500, *Lunch Mon.-Fri., Dinner daily, $$*

This attractive new restaurant has a terrific Bay view, an open fireplace and traditional bistro decor. Chef James Ormsby left the popular Bruno's in the Mission to head it up. At press time, it wasn't clear whether it would be called Rôti or Red Herring, with the focus shifting to seafood.

ROYAL THAI   THAI   14/20

951 Clement St., Richmond District 94118
415-386-1795, *Lunch Mon.-Fri., Dinner nightly, $$*

In 1988, Pat and Jamie Disyamonthon opened this San Francisco clone of their successful and well-regarded Royal Thai in San Rafael. The split-level dining room cleverly manages to give each table a feeling of intimacy, a mood enhanced by soft lighting from candles. Check out the stained-glass lobster that dominates the room and nibble on crispy krupuk (rice wafers) with a tangy tamarind sauce while waiting for your order—perhaps marinated, barbecued squid or a crunchy, refreshing, incendiary green-papaya salad.

RUBICON   FRENCH/CALIFORNIA   14/20

558 Sacramento St., Union Square 94111
415-434-4100, *Lunch Mon.-Fri., Dinner Mon.-Sat., $$$$*

With two of the major backers in this restaurant being Francis Ford Coppola and Robin Williams, it makes you wonder why the space isn't more attractive. It's very SoHo, all hard surfaces and hard wooden chairs. The food, under the direction of former chef Traci Des Jardins (who went on to Jardinière), garnered rave reviews, but lately it seems the energy is gone. Two lovely appetizers, though, are the lobster salad with upland cress, and the bacon- and corn-stuffed quail. The lamb shank comes with cream mashed potatoes one time, a more Provençale taste another. The dessert cart is fun, if a bit heavy on the chocolate. A lot of people come to Rubicon just for the wine, which is brilliantly selected by Master Sommelier Larry Stone. You'll discover many older vintages available from California and around the world.

SACRIFICE ECLECTIC 12/20

800 S. Van Ness, Mission District 94103
415-641-0990, *Dinner nightly, $*

This funky Mission bar got its name when the new owners responded to an ad selling a ridiculous amount of restaurant equipment at a "sacrifice." Dark and red, it has a tribal, pagan feel. Huge trippy murals and masks decorate the walls, table-tops are painted works of art, and in one corner is little bamboo lounge referred to as the "tiki room." The eclectic menu includes voodoo pasta (linguine, shrimp and Parmesan in a spicy creole sauce), Hawaiian grilled shrimp, Jamaican jerk chicken served with pineapple salsa, and barbecued rum ribs.

SAM'S GRILL SEAFOOD/GRILL 12/20

374 Bush St., Financial District 94104
415-421-0594, *Lunch & Dinner Mon.-Fri., $$$*

Established in 1867, Sam's Grill is a living piece of San Francisco restaurant lore. From the wood-paneled dining room to the worn linoleum floor, Sam's is a monument to the old days of leisurely two- or three-martini lunches. The trick to dining here is to stick with the basics—whatever is fresh, broiled or pan-fried with minimal saucing. Start with Sam's signature asparagus with mustard sauce. The broiled swordfish and salmon are first-rate, as are the sand dabs and rich cheesecake.

SAN FRANCISCO BAR-B-Q BARBECUE 12/20

1328 18th St., Potrero Hill 94107
415-431-8956, *Lunch & Dinner Tues.-Sun., $ NK*

From chicken to frogs' legs and from scallops to squid, everything comes off the grill moist, succulent and full of flavor from a garlicky Thai marinade. A finely shredded carrot salad and sweet rice accompany the full dinners. For lunch we always gravitate toward the Bar-B-Q duck noodles, a glass bowl full of perfect egg noodles, lettuce and chunks of fat-free duck dressed in a light sauce and sprinkled with chopped peanuts.

SANRAKU FOUR SEASONS JAPANESE/SUSHI 15/20

704 Sutter St., Downtown 94109
415-771-0803, *Lunch Mon.-Fri., Dinner nightly, $$$*

Sanraku almost never gets any publicity, but it is full every night with mostly Japanese diners. Besides the sparkling fresh sushi and sashimi, you'll find more than a dozen appetizers, from a crispy soft-shell crab to the refreshing cold ohitashi, cooked spinach with shaved bonito flakes. The menu offers teriyaki, tempura and donburi, along with several combination plates. Sanraku also offers artful kaiseki meals, an eight-course series of small dishes, tied to the season.

SCALA'S BISTRO ITALIAN 14/20

Sir Francis Drake Hotel, 432 Powell St., Union Square 94102
415-395-8555, *Breakfast, Lunch & Dinner daily, $$*

Opened in 1995, Scala's is a glitzy Italian show-stopper in the heart of the city, and yet you'll feel comfortable for all the drama. The restaurant has drawn rave reviews but along with a few quibbles about service and some of the dishes. However, things do seem to be coming together, and it is fun, after all. To begin at the end, don't leave Scala's without trying the Boston cream pie. (You didn't know that was an Italian dessert, right?) The calamari with fennel is a stunning dish, the sweetbreads are rich and succulent, and the pastas come off very well.

SCOMA'S SEAFOOD 12/20

Pier 47, Fisherman's Wharf 94133
415-771-4383, *Lunch & Dinner daily, $$$*

Believe it or not, this venerable but somewhat rundown-looking seafood house is the highest-grossing restaurant in San Francisco, packing people in just about every day of the year. It's the kind of joint where rushed waiters sling your food at you on the run. As for the food, the fish is very fresh, and portions are generous. Your best bets are the grilled fish steaks. Most of the fish is the catch from the restaurant's two boats.

SCOTT'S SEAFOOD GRILL & BAR SEAFOOD/GRILL 12/20

3 Embarcadero Center (Promenade level), Financial District 94111
415-563-8988, *Lunch & Dinner daily, $$*

This restaurant's successful formula is simple: fresh seafood, friendly service, sensible prices. Grilled salmon corncakes are irresistible, as are the shrimp and crab Louies. The fried seafood dishes, a disaster at most places, are wonderful here; live Maine lobsters are available daily; and a fresh fish menu changes twice daily. But Scott's best dishes are the seafood sautés, especially the scallops or prawns. Some nice but overpriced California wines and a few uninteresting desserts round out the menu.

SEARS FINE FOODS AMERICAN 12/20

439 Powell St., Union Square 94108
415-986-1160, *Breakfast & Lunch daily, $*

With its classic breakfasts, bare-bones environment and motherly waitresses, the place is an institution, and hordes line up to get in daily. A popular dish is the Swedish pancakes.

SHANGHAI 1930 CHINESE 15/20

133 Steuart St., Embarcadero 94105
415-896-5600, *Lunch Mon.-Fri., Dinner Mon.-Sat., $$$*

Walking through the dramatic entranceway and descending the steps to this restaurant is like stepping back in time and across the Pacific. From the lacquered mahogany accents and the dark-wood booths with inlaid metal fittings to the Chinese area rugs, everything is evocative of decadent Shanghai in the years before 1949. Start with such traditional side dishes as spinach with bean cake pieces or "eight delicacies" which include pork, shrimp, bean curd and black mushrooms. Consider entrées like the fish pillows, puffs of cod in a rice-wine sauce, and the whole steamed fish with ginger and scallions. The Shanghai banana foster has an unusual jasmine-caramel sauce.

SILKS   FUSION   15/20

The Mandarin Oriental Hotel, 222 Sansome St., Financial District 94111
415-986-2020, *Breakfast & Lunch Mon.-Fri., Dinner nightly, $$$*

Silks has long been an undiscovered treasure, turning out tasty Pacific Rim food in a lovely, secluded room on the second floor of the Mandarin Oriental Hotel. New executive chef Dante Boccuzzi, though young, has experience in top Manhattan restaurants, and has brought a new look to the cuisine. We went ga-ga over his seared tuna: it's like the old breakfast dish where an egg cooks in the center of a piece of bread—only the surprise is a center of silky foie gras terrine on a pool of port reduction. Another winner is the crab ravioli in a saffron-infused broth. The potato-wrapped sturgeon is set off by a garlic-cream sauce. Desserts feature fresh fruit and chocolate (don't miss the cocoa-crusted banana tiramisu). The wine list is spectacular, with many domestic and imported choices.

THE SLANTED DOOR   VIETNAMESE   13/20

584 Valencia St., Mission District 94110
415-861-8032, *Lunch & Dinner Tues.-Sun., $*

This is not your typical Vietnamese restaurant: the wine list is thoughtfully paired with the food, the decor is sleek, the art is large, and the pastry chef makes an amazing chocolate cake. The food, however, is creative with authentic flavors. Crispy imperial rolls served with mint, lettuce, vermicelli and a light vinaigrette are the perfect way to begin. The chicken simmered in a clay pot with caramel sauce, ginger and shallots, or the "shaking" beef, tender cubes of filet mignon stir-fried with garlic and served over lettuce, are both excellent. In addition to the wine list, beers and specialty teas are offered.

THE SLOW CLUB   ECLECTIC   12/20

2501 Mariposa St., Potrero Hill 94103
415-241-9390, *Lunch Mon.-Sat., Dinner Thurs.-Sat., $$*

Named after the bar in the cult classic film *Blue Velvet*, this hangout of the young and restless is a study in industrial chic: the walls are gun-metal gray and the concrete floors shiny black. The menu reads like haiku: two salads, an antipasto plate, four entrées and a couple of specials make up the "nite" offering. Our favorite dish is the ever changing antipasto plate, which might contain wax beans with red-chile flakes and fennel seed, toasted brioche, a hunk of feta, grilled red and yellow peppers and a half-head of roasted garlic. Unexpectedly good choices are the burger and, for dessert, brownies. The bar whips up heady cocktails, but the wine list is meager.

SOUTH PARK CAFÉ   FRENCH   13/20
108 South Park, SoMa 94107
415-495-7275, *Breakfast & Lunch Mon.-Fri., Dinner Mon.-Sat.,* $$

This place can be fairly busy, especially at lunch time, but if you can get a table, it's worth the wait. The food has had its ups and downs, but it is solidly Left Bank bistro and quite wonderful now. There's a marvelous roast chicken with perfectly done french fries, although we have a hard time ordering anything but the boudin noir sautéed with apples and watercress. You'll find crispy, perfectly cooked sweetbreads, lamb shanks and an excellent crème brûlée for the finale.

SPECKMANN'S   GERMAN   13/20
1550 Church St., Noe Valley 94131
415-282-6850, *Lunch & Dinner daily,* $$

This is one of about three German restaurant in San Francisco, and it's by far the best. The interior dark paneling and tables draped in red-and-white checkered tablecloths set the scene. All dinners come with a hearty bowl of soup. The Sauerbraten is properly sweet and sour, and the crunchy potato pancakes are perfect. Wiener Schnitzel is fried to a crisp and topped with egg. Wash it all down with German beer.

SPLENDIDO   ITALIAN   13/20
4 Embarcadero Center, Financial District 94111
415-986-3222, *Lunch Mon.-Fri., Dinner nightly,* $$$

One of the city's best Italian restaurants is hidden in the massive Embarcadero complex. It's a shame too, since the restaurant, designed by Pat Kuleto, is in stark contrast to its surroundings. Chef Giovanni Perticone imports hard-to-find fish from abroad. Among the dishes we've enjoyed are the seafood soup, the ahi tuna tartare and a perfect carpaccio. From the oak-fired oven comes an array of pizzas, such as the folded rosemary version with prosciutto and wild arugula. Braised veal shank comes perched on saffron risotto, while the pan-seared rabbit is paired with savory oven-roasted vegetables. Share the whole roasted fish with a mixed grill of seafood. The house-made breads are some of the city's best, and the desserts are exceptional. The wine list is deep with good selections.

STARS   CONTEMPORARY   13/20
555 Redwood Alley, Civic Center 94102
415-861-7827, *Lunch Mon.-Fri., Dinner nightly,* $$$$

Jeremiah Tower sold his interest in Stars to a corporate group that is aiding him in opening Stars around the world.

The recent re-do is a disappointment: Gone is Tower's vanity wall covered with awards and celebrity photos. The mirror overlooking the bar has been axed. The new look includes origami-like star-shaped chandeliers and blond furniture. Still, Stars is where some of San Francisco's political, business and social elite meet to schmooze. The straightforward American menu, with some Asian touches, offers everything from swell burgers and perfect oysters to a lovely steak tartare. Another starter, a leek fritter with a black-olive vinaigrette left us cold, however. Look for fresh fish, crispy roast chicken and large, tender steaks.

STRAIT'S CAFÉ   SINGAPOREAN   12/20

3300 Geary Blvd., Richmond District 94118
415-668-1783, Lunch & Dinner daily, $$
☎

See the review in the PENINSULA chapter.

SUPPENKÜCHE   GERMAN   13/20

601 Hayes St., Hayes Valley 94102
415-252-9289, *Dinner nightly, Brunch Sat.-Sun., $$*
☎ 👥

This place inspires an interest and a taste for German food. Minimally decorated and recently expanded, the restaurant has pine picnic benches that you share with fellow diners, most of whom are young and appreciate beer. The entrées are robust, of course, with smoked pork chops at the top of the list. But don't start there. The fresh salads, dense breads, hearty sauerkraut and sausages, Spätzle with oxtail stew, chunky mashed potatoes—even the fish specials—are delicious and satisfying, best savored with a hearty German beer.

SUSHI GROOVE   JAPANESE/SUSHI   13/20

1916 Hyde St., Russian Hill 94109
415-440-1905, *Dinner daily, $$*
☎

When sushi gets really hip, it lives here. The ten counter seats are backed by an illuminated golden Plexiglas wall, lending a sunset glow to the room. Amber crushed-velvet café drapes and rust pillows add style. High-quality fish is handled with a level of artistry not often found at mid-price sushi restaurants. Dig into any of the nightly specials, which might include a refreshing octopus, bonito and cucumber salad or tofu-skin-wrapped salmon and scallions. Ask for the prized toro (tuna belly) if it's available. A thoughtful selection of sakés and Japanese beers whets your wasabi-scorched palate.

SUSHI ON NORTH BEACH   JAPANESE/SUSHI   14/20

745 Columbus Ave., North Beach 94133
415-788-8050, *Lunch Mon. and Wed.-Fri., Dinner nightly, $$*
☎ 👥 🍷

Chef-owner Katsu Matsuda not only knows his fish, but he is also a connoisseur of fine saké—he stocks more than 30. Uni

(sea urchin roe) is like scotch, an acquired taste for some and
for others an addiction. Matsuda doesn't offer it unless it is
sweet and fresh. Hamachi (yellowtail), sea eel and fresh scallops are all winners. Many maki or sushi rolls are available.
You'll also find teriyaki, tempura and curry, but sushi is the star
here. The dining room is traditional, but the background
music ranges from Andrea Bocelli to soothing Celtic singers.

SWAN OYSTER DEPOT — SEAFOOD — 13/20

1517 Polk St., Polk Gulch 94109
415-673-1101, *Lunch & early Dinner Mon.-Sat.*, $$

The Swan Oyster Depot is a true San Francisco landmark;
it's been selling and serving fresh, frill-free seafood since 1912.
Behind the marble counter, convivial employees shuck impec-
cably fresh oysters. Steamed crab, shrimps, and lobster are also
offered, but don't expect any fancy preparations. A couple of
draft beers, including San Francisco's own Anchor Steam, com-
plete the dining experience. You may have to wait for one of
the few wooden stools, but the place is so nondescript from the
outside most tourists miss it . Closing time is 5 p.m.

SWEET HEAT — MEXICAN — ¢

3324 Steiner St., Marina 94123
415-474-9191, *Open daily*

At Sweet heat, spicy chicken wings are paired with a
cilantro-yogurt dipping sauce, and roasted corn is slathered
with either cilantro pesto or hot chipotle salsa. Tacos are
stuffed with calamari or scallops, and burritos are plumped
with fish or one of several other combinations, all at very rea-
sonable prices. Even the Caesar salad gets a zippy twist with
chile-flecked croutons, salsa and Mexican cheese. **Also in
Haight-Ashbury (1725 Haight St., 415-387-8845), & Polk Gulch
(2141 Polk St., 415-775-1055).**

TADICH GRILL — SEAFOOD/GRILL — 12/20

240 California St., Financial District 94111
415-391-1849, *Lunch & Dinner Mon.-Sat.*, $$$

Revered by locals and tourists alike---and thus usually
packed—Tadich has been around since 1849. The look is San
Francisco grill: private wooden booths, lots of counter seating,
and professional no-nonsense waiters, many of whom have
worked here for decades. The menu features honestly prepared seafood, including a robust cioppino, a flavorful calamari steak and a juicy grilled swordfish steak. Thick clam chowder is available daily. Occasionally when the crunch is on, some
of the food can come out sloppily prepared. Desserts are as
simple as everything else: baked apples and cheesecake.

TAIWAN — CHINESE — 13/20

445 Clement St., Richmond District 94118
415-387-1789, *Lunch & Dinner daily*, $

This restaurant and its North Beach sibling are always
crowded, for they're among the few Taiwanese restaurants in

the Bay Area. Irresistible dumplings filled with juicy pork are one of the big attractions. The pot stickers and noodles are also super, soups are delicious, and the stir-fries are worth coming for every day. For a full meal, try the crispy chicken in a rich brown sauce with a side dish of dry-fried long beans. **Also in North Beach (289 Columbus Ave., 415-989-6789).**

TAQUERIA SAN JOSE   MEXICAN   ¢

2830 Mission St., Mission District 94110
415-282-0203, *Open daily*

Fill up on some of the most delicious burritos and tacos around, fashioned from grilled beef, chicken, carnitas and the more exotic lengua (tongue) and sesos (brains). The high-ceilinged space has no ambience, except for the colorful patrons and a kickin' jukebox stocked with Selena. Open until 3 a.m. on weekends. **Also at 2839 Mission St., 415-282-0283, which closes at 11 p.m.; and in North Beach (2257 Mason St., 415-749-0826), which closes at 9 p.m.**

TAVOLINO   ITALIAN   15/20

401 Columbus Ave., North Beach 94133
415-392-1472, *Lunch & Dinner daily, $$*

In a city crowded with Italian restaurants, they've successfully snuck in a new concept in Italian cuisine—cicchetti, the Venetian version of Spanish tapas. The unique wedge shape of the property, combined with the large windows facing onto bustling Columbus Street, makes for some of the best people-watching in the city. The mahogany paneled walls, Italian floor tiles and large chandeliers give the space an elegant feel. Consider starting with the savory fried olives stuffed with anchovy. From there, your options are as limitless as you can get with about 25 hot and cold cicchetti. Try the marinated sea bass, fried but served cold with pine nuts and pickled onions, the beef tenderloin in a potent arugula and green-olive pesto, and the succulent pork loin. The wine list has some affordable Italian wines as well as good California bottlings.

TERRA BRAZILIS   BRAZILIAN   13/20

602 Hayes St., Hayes Valley 94102
415-241-1900, *Dinner Tues.-Sun., $$*

With whimsical hand-blown glass light fixtures, distressed furniture and brick walls dotted with native Brazilian art, Terra Brazilis is a lot of fun. The cuisine pays homage to its Brazilian origins but is modified for the California palate, and includes "small plates," like the beet (not beef) carpaccio served with candied walnuts, watercress, and goat cheese in a tangy blood-orange vinaigrette. Large plates include deliciously braised oxtail with a pomegranate-infused jus. Unfortunately the Brazilian national dish, feijoada, is only served on weekends. Try the crème brûlée topped with a Brazilian sugarcane glaze.

THANH LONG — VIETNAMESE — 13/20

4101 Judah St., Outer Sunset 94122
415-665-1146, *Dinner Tues.-Sun.*, $$

The predecessor of the sleek Crustacean, and still going strong after 27 years, Thanh Long is known for its secret-recipe garlic noodles and wonderful whole-roasted Dungeness crab. The crab is served either with sweet and sour sauce or "drunken" (in a wine broth with green onions). Diners can also opt for Saigon beef, the meat rolled around cooked onions, or a flavorful lemon-grass chicken.

THEP PHANOM — THAI — 15/20

400 Waller St., Lower Haight 94117
415-431-2526, *Dinner nightly*, $

Thep Phanom is perennially voted the top Thai restaurant in the city; one taste and you'll know why. Don't miss the fried quail or the chicken wings stuffed with glass noodles. The meat salads, particularly the chicken and beef, are dressed with fish sauce, lime and herbs. Try the tom kha gai, chicken stewed in coconut milk with galangal root, lime and chiles, or the larb phed, a fiery salad of ground duck cooled by mint leaves.

THIRSTY BEAR — SPANISH — 13/20

661 Howard St., SoMa 94103
415-974-0905, *Lunch Mon.-Sat., Dinner nightly*, $$

This zesty brewpub with a Spanish accent has proved a huge success, popular with young office workers and singles. The look is industrial chic, with lots of hard surfaces and metal sculpture gracing the brick interior. Like the two floors that make up its dining room, Thirsty Bear's food has its ups and downs, with the paella mostly down, but such specials as house-cured salt cod and shrimps sautéed with garlic and white wine quite tasty.

TI COUZ — FRENCH/CRÊPES — 13/20

3108 16th St., Mission District 94110
415-252-7373, *Lunch & Dinner daily*, $

This place (the name means "old house" in Gaelic as spoken in Brittany) basically serves one thing, crêpes: the traditional earthy buckwheat crêpes of Brittany and the more traditional white-flour crêpes served all over France, filled with the likes of tomato and basil or cheese and slivered almonds. The best crêpes are the simplest, like one spread with savory cheese. The onion soup makes a good starter. The dessert crêpes are exceptional; one is filled with apple slices sautéed in Calvados, as well as vanilla ice cream. Wines include reasonably priced French classics as well as a low-alcohol French cider.

TIMO'S   SPANISH   13/20

842 Valencia St., Mission District 94110
415-647-0558, Dinner nightly, $$

Tapas, tapas and more tapas—100 in all—is what Timo's is all about. Owner-chef Carlos Corredor has a solid background in Spanish and Latin American cooking and it shows in his duck-leg confit and his bacalao of salt cod and potatoes, which he serves with a cilantro-mint salsa. You'll find marvelous sweetbreads, grilled quail and sautéed kidneys. The decor benefits mostly from a colorful paint job.

TOKYO GO GO   JAPANESE/SUSHI   13/20

3174 16th St., Mission District 94103
415-864-2288, Dinner Tues.-Sun., $$

Whether you're looking for traditional sushi or offbeat Japanese entrées, Tokyo Go Go is a quirky and fun spot for indulging your wasabi cravings. With decor that jumps from '60s futuristic to '90s contemporary, this newcomer manages to attract a diverse crowd. Try the marinated sake (salmon) or hotategai (scallop) to get your taste buds going. A plate of prawn-stuffed soft-shell crab with mango chutney is excellent. Sushi traditionalists may chafe at some of the far-out combos.

TOMMASO'S   ITALIAN   13/20

1042 Kearny St., North Beach 94133
415-398-9696, Dinner Tues.-Sun., $$

This family-owned place most likely had the first wood-fired pizza oven in the Bay Area two generations ago. To start, ask for the marinated roasted peppers, glistening string beans or whatever vegetables are in season—never have vegetables tasted brighter. And order a bowl of vinegar-accented steamed "coo coo" clams for the table. Then get serious with pizzas and calzones from the wood-fired oven. A light house red wine is served in ceramic pitchers.

TOMMY TOY'S CUISINE CHINOISE   CHINESE/FRENCH   11/20

655 Montgomery St., Financial District 94111
415-397-4888, Lunch Mon.-Fri., Dinner nightly, $$$$

This restaurant was the first high-style Chinese restaurant to open in the city. The look is Asian antiques with a heavy overlay of French style, which extends to the food, sometimes favorably and sometimes not. They offer the special dinner for $49.50, which brings all the favorites this restaurant is known for. Two dishes from it are the seafood bisque presented in a whole coconut under a puff pastry "lid," and a Maine lobster shelled and sautéed with pine nuts and mushrooms on a bed of angel-hair pasta. The wines will give your wallet a workout.

TOMMY'S   MEXICAN   ¢

5929 Geary Blvd., Richmond District 94121
415-387-4747, *Lunch & Dinner daily*

Tommy's family is from the Yucatán, a part of Mexico known for delightful, distinctive foods. While there's nothing wrong with this restaurant's basic menu—the usual selections of beans and rice, tacos and burritos—ask for the Yucatán specials. And order a margarita: for the price, theirs is the best in town.

TON KIANG   CHINESE/HAKKA   11/20

5821 Geary Blvd., Richmond District 94118
415-386-8530, *Lunch & Dinner daily*, $

Ton Kiang specializes in daily dim sum, even at night. We like the delicious steamed Shanghai-style dumplings. This successor to the original, which closed, is a little more upscale, with white tablecloths and sparkling chandeliers, but the food has slipped. The steamed salt-baked chicken arrives pale and soft. Prawns in a delicate wine sauce are also a delight. Special Hakka-style casseroles come in clay pots; among our favorites are rock cod with tofu and duck with bean thread. Don't miss the wonderful vegetables, especially the sugar pea tips.

TRAP DOOR   ECLECTIC   13/20

3251 Scott St., Marina 94123
415-776-1928, *Dinner nightly*, $

Many of the after-work establishments in the Marina are either blatant pick-up joints, venues offering an overpriced cuisine du jour, or one of a number of chain eateries (can you say "wrap"?). The Trap Door miraculously manages to avoid these pitfalls by concentrating on drinks, eclectic food and fun. It is a great place for friends to sit by the gas-jet fireplace, order lots of inexpensive, family-style dishes, and unwind over California wines, draft beer, tequila, or carafes of the house sangría.

TRATTORIA CONTADINA   ITALIAN   13/20

1800 Mason St., North Beach 94133
415-982-5728, *Dinner nightly*, $$

Chef Salvatore Parra infuses both his tried-and-true and more adventurous offerings with a practiced, elegant touch. The restaurant itself is a comfortable wood-paneled refuge from the madness of Columbus Avenue below; genuinely gracious service and large portions will further soothe the ruffled traveler. On the "must try" list is fettuccine alla Salvatore: imported noodles, smoked chicken, Mascarpone, peas and sun-dried tomatoes. Desserts can stray from typical Italian bittersweet models to outright richness.

TRULY MEDITERRANEAN   MIDDLE EASTERN   ¢

3109 16th St., Mission District 94103
415-252-7482, *Open daily*

    You can eat at a small counter or take food out, but it's hard to go wrong in this bargain-priced falafel joint. Falafel sandwiches—with or without pungent feta, fried eggplant or potatoes—are cheap, quick and hot, while the rotating cone of roasting shwarma sells fast. The carrot juice is renowned, though the salty garlic/mint/yogurt drink makes an unusual and refreshing substitute. **Also in Haight-Ashbury (1724 Haight St., 415-751-7482).**

2223 RESTAURANT   CALIFORNIA   13/20

2223 Market St., Castro District 94114
415-431-0692, *Lunch Mon.-Fri., Dinner nightly, Brunch Sun.,* **$$**

    Melinda Randolph left after making her mark as a chef at 2223 and is now back as an owner. She has created an appealing menu with an "American" base; one dish combines herb-roasted chicken with garlic-mashed potatoes and fried onion rings. But how about the nori roll of salmon enrobed in a shiitake mushroom vinaigrette? Or the pecan-maple-glazed pork chop. Some dishes have one too many ingredients, but that hasn't stopped the neighborhood from coming in droves.

UNION ALE HOUSE   AMERICAN   ¢

1980 Union St., Cow Hollow 94123
415-921-0300, *Open daily*

    This popular pub has a great bargain bite every Monday night. For only $5 penny-pinchers can order a pint of choice and a half-pound Niman Ranch cheeseburger with a side of fries. On Tuesdays appetizers are half-price all night; and Wednesday through Friday, appetizers are half-price during happy hour. The appetizers range from chicken skewers to shrimp cakes. The younger set that hangs here keeps the pool table, video games, dart boards and pinball machines busy.

UNIVERSAL CAFÉ   CONTEMPORARY   14/20

2814 19th St., Mission District 94110
415-821-4608, *Breakfast, Lunch & Dinner Tues.-Sun., Brunch Sat.-Sun.,* **$$**

    This is a fun and joyful place to eat, but regulars would go for the food even if it were served in a garage. At lunch you'll find a daily-changing list of chalkboard specials in addition to pizzas and focaccia sandwiches. Chef Julia McClaskey stretches a bit more at dinner, offering an eclectic selection including, on one visit, sautéed Gulf prawns with grilled baby artichokes. Her roast chicken with lemon risotto is outstanding.

VALENTINE'S CAFÉ   VEGETARIAN   14/20

1793 Church St., Noe Valley 94131
415-285-2257, *Dinner Wed.-Sun., Brunch Sat.-Sun.*, $$
♥ ▲

Good vegetarian restaurants aren't all that easy to find even in San Francisco. Valentine's does a fairly good job of it, and what it lacks in subtlety it makes up for in warmth and earnestness. The little restaurant doesn't accept reservations; once inside, you'll be charmed by the softly lit and homey dining room. Try the portobello scaloppine with a lemon "butter" (actually a canola-oil roux) or the mushroom korma. A list of inexpensive wines—including some gems from South Africa, where the owners are from—pairs nicely with the menu.

VIA VAI   ITALIAN   13/20

1715 Union St., Cow Hollow 94123
415-441-2111, *Lunch Mon.-Sat, Dinner nightly*, $$$
☎ ▦

Via Vai is a spin-off of the popular Pane e Vino a few blocks away. The big difference here is that the owners have invested in a wood-burning oven for pizzas, roast fish and chicken. The bright yellow walls and glass light fixtures give the place a warm glow. And after a few bites of the crisp fried calamari, you'll understand why it's so crowded. The pizzas are made with a thin and crispy crust and covered in exquisite toppings. The entrées are hearty and well prepared—try the grilled Italian sausage with polenta and spinach.

VICOLO PIZZERIA   PIZZA   ¢

201 Ivy St., Civic Center 94102
415-863-2382, *Open daily* K

The fresh ingredients and crisp cornmeal crusts served at this high, square, industrial-style alleyway eatery add up to one of San Francisco's most interesting pizzas. Available whole or in slices, a typical pie comes topped with zucchini, red onion, sun-dried tomatoes and basil. A Greek model might include olives, feta, peppers and rosemary. More traditional standards are available, as are great salads.

VINERIA   ITALIAN   14/20

13228 16th St., Mission District 94110
415-415-552-3889, Dinner Wed.-Sun., $$
☎ ♟ ▲

This sleek trattoria has made quite a splash since its opening in 1997; its success is due in large part to dishes taken from its parent restaurant, L'Osteria del Forno in North Beach. Both serve simple, refined pan-Italian fare, but Vineria updates (and enlarges) the tiny North Beach eatery's home-style digs. Almost everything is excellent, from antipasti and salads to elegant pastas and crisp pizzas. The heady salad of tuna, white beans, celery and oregano, begs to be mopped off the plate with crusty slices of focaccia. Grilled whole sea bass is moist and deliciously simple. The Italianate wine list is brief but purposeful, with many selections available by the glass.

VINGA   SPANISH/CATALAN   13/20

320 3rd St., SoMa 94107
415-546-3131, *Lunch Mon.-Fri., Dinner Mon.-Sat.,* $$

☎ 🍸 ♦

Chef Antonio Buendia comes from a small town near Barcelona, where he learned the basic skills of Catalan cooking. Vinga means "come here" in Catalan, and you'll want to come here and taste the tapas: sizzling chorizos, spinach with pine nuts and raisins, shrimp in a garlic and chive olive oil, steamed mussels. Unfortunately, the entrées such as paella or braised duck miss the mark some nights. The "pica pica" tapas are served between lunch and dinner. Vinga's wine list is most impressive for a small, family-owned venue.

VIVANDE   ITALIAN   13/20

670 Golden Gate Ave., Opera Plaza, Civic Center 94122
415-673-9245, *Lunch & Dinner daily,* $$

☎ 🚗 🍸 ♦ ♻

Carlo Middione's Vivande Porta Via on Fillmore Street is still humming along (see the entry under "San Francisco Food Shops"), but the new Opera Plaza restaurant is a magnificent space, and the food, after stumbling a bit when it opened in 1995, is hitting its stride. It's a great place for a pre-theater or pre-opera dinner, and you can get a late supper until midnight. Start with the assorted antipasti, or, in springtime, the risotto with artichokes. Rack of lamb and chicken gallantine are good entrées. The wine list features rare Italian wines, many available by the glass.

WASHINGTON SQUARE BAR & GRILL   AMERICAN   12/20

1701 Powell St., North Beach 94133
415-982-8123, *Lunch & Dinner daily, Brunch Sat.-Sun.,* $$

☎ 🚗 🍸

People sometimes forget that this legendary hangout (a big, curtained room with stodgy, early-20th-century decor) also has pretty good food, especially if you stick with simpler selections like a barbecue-glazed meatloaf sandwich with fries. The pastas are reliable, and the osso buco is first-rate. Chef Timothy Au also does a spectacular job with a banana bread ice cream sundae.

THE WATERFRONT RESTAURANT   FUSION   14/20

Pier 7 on the Embarcadero, Embarcadero 94111
415-391-2696, *Lunch Mon.-Fri., Dinner nightly,* $$$$

☎ 🚗 📷 🍸

Yes, it really exists: a view restaurant with great food. The Waterfront affords views of San Francisco Bay and the Bay Bridge, and its decor is contemporary, with accents of Asian antiques and culinary-themed artwork. The menu is fusion "lite" with some vivid flavors. Highlights include the ahi tuna seared with pumpkin seeds, lotus-braised monkfish, grilled filet of beef with taro gnocchi, smoked sturgeon with osetra caviar and a roast-beet terrine in tomato gelée. Try the honey-soy cured steelhead trout salad frisée. The dessert menu sparkles with standouts like the tangerine-cheesecake tart. Founding chef Bruce Hill has left but still consults on the menu.

WOODWARD'S GARDEN   CALIFORNIA   13/20

1700 Mission St., Mission District 94110
415-621-7122, *Dinner Wed.-Sun.*, *$$*

This little jewel is the creation of four young partners. The small space is artfully designed, but what holds your interest is the food. The menu changes weekly but could include items like a vegetable saffron risotto, ravioli with potato and black truffles, or duck breast on lentils. The inexpensive wine list is full of surprises.

WORLD WRAPPS   ECLECTIC   ¢

2257 Chestnut St., Marina 94123
415-563-9727, *Open daily*

The Marina location has a terrible layout made worse by the habitually long but fast-moving line out the door. The wraps phenomenon seems to have had its day, but some fans like the burritos filled with grilled salmon, Thai chicken or teriyaki tofu. **Also in Polk Gulch (2227 Polk St., 415-931-9727).**

YABBIES   SEAFOOD/CALIFORNIA   14/20

2237 Polk St., Russian Hill 94109
415-474-4088, *Dinner nightly*, *$$$*

Yabbies are crayfish in Australian argot, and you'll find lots of them at this sleek Polk Street restaurant. Chef Mark Lusardi often adds subtle Asian flavors such as ginger, chile, Thai basil and curry. The best appetizers come from the ice bar, including six kinds of shucked oysters, peel-and-eat shrimps and cracked Dungeness crab. Less work (but less fun) are the Rhode Island chowder and crabcakes. The entrées might feature shrimps and scallops with ginger, chiles and Thai basil, or grilled ahi tuna with spicy sesame-shiitake soba noodles.

YANK SING   CHINESE/DIM SUM   15/20

427 Battery St., Embarcadero 94111
Lunch Mon.-Fri., Dinner Mon.-Sat., *$$*

Sure, there are dim sum palaces in the Richmond District and Chinatown that pack them in all weekend, but from Monday to Friday, Yank Sing rules–and it's not even in Chinatown. The dim sum trolley rolls by with more than 80 items. Choices range from pristine shrimp dumplings to savory barbecued pork buns to smooth braised chicken feet. Moist slices of Peking duck are served from one trolley: sandwich the meat between steamed buns and use the scallion brushes to dab on some hoisin sauce. Office workers from the surrounding Financial District keep this place busy.

YO YO TSUMAMI BISTRO   FUSION   13/20

Miyako Hotel, 1611 Post St., Japantown 94115
415-922-7788, *Breakfast, Lunch & Dinner daily*, $$

Yo Yo has had more rebirths than a yogi. The concept is an East/West tapas (yes, that's how they describe it) menu with a few main courses. Favorites include the roast duck confit with sherry-onion jam and the lettuce-wrapped squab. Entrées range from a seafood and vegetable tempura to a lemon-grass chicken. Noodles also play a part: we liked the tea-smoked chicken gyoza with tomatoes and eggplant. A J-town pizza has Asian toppings that work.

YUET LEE   CHINESE   15/20

1300 Stockton St., Chinatown 94133
415-982-6020, Lunch Mon. & Wed.-Sat., Dinner Mon. & Wed.-Sun., $

In the fluorescent glare of the original Chinatown branch, the crowds keep coming until 3 a.m. for some of the cleanest-tasting Hong Kong-style seafood to be found. At the newer Noe Valley branch—which boasts, marvel of marvels, a parking lot—closing time is 11 p.m. Maine lobster and Dungeness crab, two of Yuet Lee's best dishes, are netted from a tank and quickly stir-fried with black beans and chiles or with ginger. Vegetable dishes are good bets, as is the crispy-style Hong Kong chow mein. **Also in Noe Valley (3601 26th St., 415-550-8998).**

ZARÉ   MEDITERRANEAN   15/20

568 Sacramento St., Financial District 94111
415-291-9145, *Lunch Mon.-Fri., Dinner nightly*, $$

Chef-owner Hoss Zaré's Mediterranean cuisine has won raves since he opened in '97. At lunch, the warm, cavelike room fills with suits who love Zaré's braised rabbit with mushrooms and artichokes in tarragon cream sauce or grilled lamb sirloin. Zaré uses bold flavors in unusual combinations: a foie gras appetizer is wrapped in salmon and matched with a port wine reduction; a napoleon of artichokes and Dungeness crab meat is melded with a spicy chive-infused oil. Half the fun is watching Zaré and his crew work at the open kitchen. Desserts include Champagne zabaglione and a chocolate soufflé with Mascarpone. **Also see Bistro Zare in this chapter.**

ZARZUELA   SPANISH   14/20

2000 Hyde St., Russian Hill 94109
415-346-0800, *Dinner, Mon.-Sat.*, $$

Chef-owner Lucas Casco has created what could be taken for a bustling tapas bar in the heart of Madrid's Old Quarter, and it's one of the very best tapas places in the City. Almost anything is good, but croquettes—either chicken or ham—pan con tamate, escalivada (cold grilled marinated vegetables), duck leg, poached octopus and the classic tortilla Español are favorites. The restaurant takes its name from a seafood stew, which is always available. The wine list has a number of good Spanish bottlings, including a decent sherry selection.

ZAX   CALIFORNIA   13/20

2330 Taylor St., North Beach 94133
415-563-6266, *Dinner Tues.-Sat.,* $$

This is a family-run restaurant in an out-of-the-way corner of North Beach. The room, with the feeling of a charming French country restaurant, is calming, and the food can frequently be stunning. The menu changes monthly depending on what's in season. Starters might be a Caesar-esque salad of romaine, anchovies, lemon, garlic and Parmesan; or a twice-baked goat-cheese soufflé with a salad of apples, celery and fennel. Specials might include roast rabbit, a Niman-Schell flat-iron steak with spicy onion rings, or the fresh fish of the day. The inexpensive wine list is appropriate for the food.

ZEIN NOODLE CLUB   NOODLES   ¢

2031 Chestnut St., Marina 94123
415-771-5888, *Open daily*

Whether they're being dished up at a chain Italian pasta house or one of the new-wave Asian noodle houses, noodles are a genuine Bay Area fad. The tiny interior is a nice shade of lime green with colorful prints relieving some of the hard-edged high-tech look. The calamari here is paired with a spicy peanut sauce; another good starter is the green-onion pancakes. An array of noodle dishes make up the heart of the menu: noodles in soup, stir-fried or boiled and served cool. One of the best dishes is the noodle pillows pressed into a small cake and fried and topped with a curry-coconut sauce.

ZINZINO   ITALIAN   13/20

2355 Chestnut St., Marina District 94123
415-346-6623, *Dinner Tues.-Sat., Brunch Sat.-Sun.,* $$

Owned by former Visa executive Kenneth Zankel, Zinzino is a long, narrow, bustling restaurant literally a block deep. An enormous bar greets you, along with Italian posters and the smell of a wood-fired oven churning out tasty pizzas. Best bets are those topped with fennel sausage and caramelized onions, or mozzarella, Fontina, radicchio, arugula and thinly sliced prosciutto. Other good options are the crispy calamari, the unusual salad of shaved fennel and mint, and the pastas .

THE ZODIAC CLUB ECLECTIC 13/20

718 14th St., Castro 94114
415-626-7827, *Dinner nightly, $$*

Manhattan is the theme-restaurant capital, and Zodiac could have been transplanted straight from Tribeca, with its astrological-sign motif and totally cosmic connections. Dim lighting, sensual drapery, ambient music and muted acoustics lend the air of an illicit romance. The menu, which changes often, is small, but the portions most definitely are not. One visit yielded a salad with an abundance of grilled baby octopus in a tasty vinaigrette. Most striking about the food here is the skilled and deliberate contrast of texture. Each dish, like a constellation, is made up of several stars.

ZUNI CAFÉ CONTEMPORARY 15/20

1658 Market St., Civic Center 94102
415-552-2522, *Breakfast, Lunch & Dinner Tues.-Sun., $$*

After 20 years, Zuni is still one of the most popular restaurants in San Francisco. Its loyal clientele hangs out at the long copper bar, downing freshly shucked oysters with their Champagne. Then they stroll past the wood-burning oven in this complex of eccentrically added rooms and take a seat to dig into a sumptuous Sunday brunch, warming winter supper, or, late at night, the hamburger on focaccia. Owner-chef Judy Rodgers has been refining her cooking since 1987; her fondness for the rustic style of southern France and Italy is apparent in the grilled duck breast, and the oxtails and beef cheeks braised in white wine with garlic, green olives and orange served over fettuccine. The Caesar salad, made with anchovies cured in-house, is justly famed. In fact, we don't know of any other menu where we find so many hearty, satisfying dishes.

GOURMET SHOPS & MORE

BAKERIES: BREAD & PASTRIES

THE BAGELRY

2134 Polk St., Polk Gulch 94109
415-441-3003, *Open daily*

For 20 years, owner Mareva Newhouse has taken an artisan's approach to making her dozen or so flavors of bagels. She hand-retrieves the shaped dough from its bath of boiling water, then lines up the bagels-to-be on redwood boards before putting them on stone racks in the bakery's oven. When cooled, the finished bagels are ready to enjoy with Pacific salmon lox cured by a local chef. The Bagelry also carries dynamite chocolate chip and oatmeal cookies.

BOB'S DONUT & PASTRY SHOP

1621 Polk St., Polk Gulch 94109
415-776-3141, *Open daily*

When we were children it was easy to find well-made doughnuts, plain or filled. Now there is only Bob's, where golden, raised donuts and cake-like, old-fashioned ones topped with icings and sprinkles in all the classic flavors pour forth all day and night long—they're open around the clock.

BOUDIN SOURDOUGH BAKERY & CAFÉ

156 Jefferson St., Fisherman's Wharf 94133
415-928-1849, *Open daily*

Maybe because this family owned-bakery was founded in 1849, Boudin is one store that kept the flame alive when the rest of the country had forgotten the goodness of real sourdough bread. Boudin's loaves get their chewy texture and slightly sour flavor from a naturally occurring sourdough starter, and they contain no yeast or preservatives. Visitors can observe the work in the baking room through a large window, where long baguettes, breadsticks and the small rounds (which also double as clam chowder bowls) are molded and baked. **Numerous other locations.**

DIANDA'S ITALIAN AMERICAN PASTRY

2883 Mission St., Mission District 94110
415-647-5469, *Open daily*

A family business since Elio Dianda brought his recipes from Lucca, Italy, Dianda delights everyone with its traditional Italian pastry. You'll find nut-and-fruit-studded panforte, an Italian-style fruitcake, and a profusion of cookies such as meltingly tender biscotti with anise, almonds or fruit. The traditional Italian Christmas bread, panettone, is baked year-round.

DANILO BAKERY

516 Green St., North Beach 94133
415-989-1806, *Open daily*

Exchanges between employees at this venerable North Beach bakery are likely to be in Italian, and the beautiful baked goods still maintain an authentic old-world flavor. Big country-style breads buttress the smaller, hollow rosette behind the well-worn counter. A variety of cookies such as crisp, chewy biscotti and meringue-based ossi di morti are also on hand. Don't neglect the fresh-baked handmade breadsticks.

GOLDEN GATE BAKERY

1029 Grant Ave., Chinatown 94133
415-781-2627, *Open daily*

Yellow custard tarts are displayed in just about every Chinatown bakery and on every dim sum cart in the city, but the best are at this tiny, crowded shop. Tarts, cookies, steamed buns and fat, round moon cakes filled with black bean paste round out the selections.

IL FORNAIO

Levi's Plaza, 101 Greenwich St., Financial District 94111
415-391-4622, *Open daily*

Il Fornaio, "the baker" in Italian, makes award-winning handmade breads daily. Whether it's for the fat, crusty filone (the pride of generations of Italian bakers), an olive or rosemary loaf, multigrain cereals, or even a buttery French croissant labeled cornetto, Il Fornaio is worth seeking out. If you can't make the trip to this location, the breads are also sold at other gourmet food shops and even at some of the larger grocery stores.

JUST DESSERTS

3 Embarcadero Center, Lobby Level, Financial District 94111
415-421-1609, *Open daily*

Just Desserts is San Francisco's hometown bakery. The community-minded owner is active in many charities, and his wares are refined classics: the black-bottom cupcakes, brownies, blondies, triple lemon cake and frosted poppyseed cake are just about perfect. The dense, rich cheesecake with an almond-butter crust that launched the shop in 1974 comes in a rainbow of flavors. Numerous other locations.

LA NOUVELLE PÂTISSERIE

2184 Union St., Cow Hollow 94123
415-931-7655, *Open daily*

Classic French pastry from the hand of maître pâtissier Jean Yves Duperret overflows in this welcoming tea salon, where tiny tables offer a place to rest and enjoy your favorites. Glistening fruit tarts with raspberries, kiwi slices, strawberries, apricots and mixed fruits on a light layer of pastry cream line the shelves next to the flakiest palmiers in the city. **Also Downtown (895 Market St., 415-979-0553.)**

LA VICTORIA

2937 24th St., Mission District 94110
415-550-9292, *Open daily*
⊠

Sweet breads, fruit and custard-filled empanadas and cookies line the windows here. Grab a pair of tongs and a tray and make your choices. Inside you'll find a few groceries, including imported Cuzcatlan and Jarritos fruit-flavored sodas.

LIGURIA BAKERY

1700 Stockton St., North Beach 94133
415-421-3786, *Open daily*

Focaccia, and nothing but focaccia, has made this bakery a North Beach institution. A rich, fluffy square of dough is given a brush of oil and baked plain, or topped with green onions, raisins or, pizza style, with tomato sauce and scallions. Hours vary, because when the focaccia runs out, they close.

MOSCOW & TBILISI BAKERY

5540 Geary Blvd., Richmond District 94121
415-668-6959, *Open daily*

You need not pawn your jeweled Fabergé eggs to shop here. Prices are excellent, and so is the selection of traditional Russian baked goods. Pastries with fanciful names such as Lady's Caprice, Bird's Milk, Madonna and Bonaparte (a Russian napoleon) are joined by fresh loaves of white and light-rye bread, cheese blintzes, fried chebureks (flaky sweet pastry) as big as elephant's ears, and rolled coffee cakes with traditional fillings of poppyseed, apples or cherries.

NOAH'S NEW YORK BAGELS

100 Bush St., Financial District 94104
415-433-9682, *Open Mon.-Sat.*

Spot a Starbucks and a Noah's is likely to be in an adjacent storefront. Noah's makes 14 types of bagels, and they're best eaten fresh and hot from the oven. We're not crazy about the wimpy crust—the result of spraying the raw bagels with hot water rather than boiling them, the old-fashioned way, before baking them. Cream cheese shmears are made with lox, chives, garlic and herbs, strawberries, sun-dried tomatoes and basil, and walnut and raisins. **Numerous other locations.**

NOE VALLEY BAKERY & BREAD CO.

4073 24th St., Noe Valley 94114
415-550-1405, *Open daily*

Double-sized muffins adorned with dried fruits or nuts, and flaky cinnamon twists, join a long roster of well-crafted breads. For staples, there's a crusty white loaf and a whole-wheat sour-dough, but do venture beyond for flavors like onion-sesame and walnut-multigrain.

NOW AND ZEN BISTRO & BAKERY

1826 Buchanan St., Japantown 94115
415-922-9696, *Open daily*

Owner Miyoko Nishimoto Schinner creates gourmet delights using no eggs, sugar or dairy products. It's hard to call a quiche by its name when the eggs, cream and cheese have been removed, but the Zen look-alike is a satisfying dish made with tofu and soy milk, packed with mushrooms and spinach. The vegan Black Forest cake will delight those who eschew animal products while craving good flavors. For a healthy breakfast, try the nonfat muffins made with whole-grain flour, fresh fruits and vegetables.

VICTORIA PASTRY CO.

1362 Stockton St., North Beach 94133
415-781-2015, *Open daily*

Cakes like chocolate roulade and the ubiquitous princess cake (featured at nearly every baptism, first communion or birthday in North Beach) are made here as well as tasty cannoli, deep-fried pastry shells stuffed with ricotta cheese laced with candied fruit. Traditional favorites such as tiramisu and zabaglione sit alongside zuccotto, a sponge cake bearing an overload of cherry liqueur, chocolate cream with hazelnuts, and whipped cream topped with crushed almond macaroons. The St. Honoré cake is the signature treat.

CAVIAR

TSAR NICOULAI/CALIFORNIA SUNSHINE FINE FOODS

144 King St., SoMa 94107
800-95-CAVIAR, 415-543-3007, *Open Mon.-Fri.*

This caviar wholesaler, whose products are served at crème de la crème restaurants in the city, will happily sell its jars and tins of fresh maslossol Tsar Nicoulai caviar to retail customers from its South of Market offices. Most clients call in their order, then pick it up. Smoked sturgeon, smoked Norwegian salmon, dried wild mushrooms and mother-of-pearl caviar spoons and servers can be bought as well as beluga, sevruga, osetra, "gold pearl" salmon roe and American sturgeon caviar.

CHEESE

CREIGHTON'S CHEESE & FINE FOODS

673 Portola Dr., Twin Peaks 94127
415-753-0750, *Open daily*

What do you do when you've just about perfected the cheese shop? Set out to perfect the picnic box. Creighton's combines its cheeses with deli meats, prepared salads, breads and desserts in enticing combinations for dining al fresco.

LEONARD'S 2001

2001 Polk St., Polk Gulch 94109
415-921-2001, *Open daily*

The refrigerator cases beckon with half-pound to three-quarter-pound slices of cheese, pre-cut for convenience. Choices include raw milk Raclette and Cotswold, an English double Gloucester speckled with chives and onions. Imported French and Italian butter is joined by the professional baker's choice, Plugra. The spacious, bright store stocks dozens of bins with bulk grains, beans, nuts and candies as well as dried pasta, cookies, jams and other gourmet treats.

SAY CHEESE

856 Cole St., Haight-Ashbury 94117
415-665-5020, *Open daily*

If you think you've seen it all when it comes to cheese, a visit to Say Cheese will restore your sense of wonder. Besides the most complete roster of blues, French triple creams, chèvres, and sheep's-milk cheeses, you'll find at least 10 pâtés, and clutches of olives.

TWENTY-FOURTH STREET CHEESE

3893 24th St., Noe Valley 94114
415-821-6658, *Open daily*

Sampling can be great fun here, for this is probably the best cheese store in the city. Patrons can choose from more than 280 kinds of cheese and 30 kinds of crackers and bread sticks. The store also carries wine and olives.

CHOCOLATE & CANDY

THE CANDY JAR

210 Grant Ave., Union Square 94108
415-391-5508, *Open Mon.-Fri.*

Truffles come in two styles here: "traditional" soft truffles whose flavored ganache fillings have a creamy texture akin to fudge, and "deluxe" truffles whose thick chocolate shells cover meltingly soft flavored centers. Or you can choose from the great selection of European wrapped candies.

GHIRARDELLI CHOCOLATE & SODA FOUNTAIN

900 North Point St., Ghirardelli Square 94133
415-771-4903, *Open daily*

Visitors should not miss this chocolate manufacturer's retail outlet with origins that reach back to 1852. Wind your way through the shelves full of truffles and chocolate bars in 14 flavors. At the soda fountain, you can enjoy ice cream, special sundaes or hot chocolate made with Ghirardelli's chocolate.

GODIVA CHOCOLATIER

San Francisco Shopping Center
865 Market St., SoMa 94103
415-543-8910, *Open daily*

Despite the plethora of artisan chocolates in the Bay Area, Godiva, from the renowned Belgian firm, has found enduring success. Aside from the famously silky confections packaged in the trademark gold boxes, Godiva also offers a collection of beautifully boxed chocolates for holidays. They will deliver within San Francisco and do mail-order. **Also in the Stonestown Galleria (3251 20th Ave., 415-566-5058).**

JOSEPH SCHMIDT CONFECTIONS

3489 16th St., Castro District 94114
415-861-8682, *Open Mon.-Sat.*

This shop is surprisingly unassuming considering the exquisite confections turned out by Swiss-trained master chocolatier Joseph Schmidt. The egg-shaped truffles are not dainty—allow four bites at least—and their chocolate coating is thick and substantial with a definite snap. Seasonal treats are charmingly inventive, from the life-size chocolate tulips in chocolate vases that grace the shelves in spring to the chocolate-coated fortune cookies at Chinese New Year's.

SEE'S CANDIES

3 Embarcadero Center, ground floor 94111
415-391-1622, *Open Mon.-Sat.*

Homegrown See's has been a California favorite since its founding in Pasadena decades ago. We go out of our way for See's traditional creams and nougats, the mainstay of Christmas-morning chocolate treats. Some other good treats are the dark chocolate or milk chocolate nuts and ginger. Numerous other locations, some open only Mon.-Fri.

ST. FRANCIS FOUNTAIN & CANDY

2801 24th St., Mission District 94110
415-826-4200, *Open Mon.-Sat.*

See review under "Ice Cream."

TEUSCHER CHOCOLATES OF SWITZERLAND

255 Grant Ave., Union Square 94108
415-398-2700, *Open Mon.-Sat.*

The ultimate indulgence for Valentine's Day or New Year's Eve, Champagne truffles have been perfected by this international chocolate retailer. They are flown weekly to San Francisco from Switzerland, along with about a dozen other types of lightly flavored truffles, each one a gem.

XOX TRUFFLES INC.

754 Columbus Ave., North Beach 94133
415-421-4814, *Open daily*

Jean-Marc Gorce was the chef de cuisine at Fringale until he suffered a severe heart attack. His wife, Casimira, already a food salesperson, asked, Why don't you make something I can sell? In a closet-size shop in North Beach, Gorce produces truffles the way they would be made in France, in small bites of delicious chocolate ganache, here in a multitude of flavors.

YAMADA SEIKA CONFECTIONERY

1955 Sutter St., Japantown 94115
415-922-3848, *Open Tues.-Sun.*

Sometimes intensely sweet, sometimes faint and elusive, the flavors of traditional Japanese confections go well with hot green tea. Baked pastries filled with chestnut purée, blocks of plum-wine gelatin (umeshu-kan) made with agar-agar, and twice-cooked egg cake (shigure) are tastes worth trying. Packaged cookies, candies and crackers are also available.

COFFEE & TEA

CAFFÈ ROMA

526 Columbus Ave., North Beach 94133
415-296-7662, *Open daily*

When the roasting and blending equipment is in use—which is often—inhale deeply and take in the aroma of the fresh beans that make up Caffè Roma's unique blends. With names like Frascati, Via Veneto and dark roast Sicilian Gold, the coffees conjure up images of Italy. **Also in SoMa (885 Bryant St., 415-431-8555, Open Mon.-Fri.)**

COFFEE ROASTERY

2331 Chestnut St., Marina District 94123
415-931-5282, *Open daily*

The smell of roasting coffee will draw you into this spacious shop, in the back of which customers can see the gleaming roasting and blending equipment. You'll find ten varietals, from the legendary Colombian Supremo to the delightful Jamaican Blue Mountain. **Also in Cow Hollow (2191 Union St., 415-922-9559).**

FREED, TELLER & FREED

1326 Polk St., Polk Gulch 94109
415-673-0922, *Open Mon.-Sat.*

Reputedly the oldest coffee roaster west of New York (it was established in 1899), Freed, Teller & Freed has the look of an old-time apothecary. Teas fill display cases of dark polished wood and glass bearing gold lettering that describes the exotic contents: smoky Lapsang souchong, fruity teaberry and about 45 other teas. **Also in the Financial District (Embarcadero Center, West Towers, 415-986-8851, Open Mon.-Fri.)**

GRAFFEO COFFEE ROASTING CO.

735 Columbus Ave., North Beach 94133
415-986-2420, *Open Mon.-Sat.*

Coffee loses much of its flavor and aroma just a few days after the beans have been roasted. That's why Graffeo, a North Beach fixture since 1935, roasts its coffees daily. They offer just one blend, a mixture of Arabica beans from Colombia, Costa

Rica and New Guinea—light dark roast. The Swiss water-process decaffeinated is made from Colombian beans.

IMPERIAL TEA COURT

1411 Powell St., Chinatown 94133
415-788-6080, *Open daily*

This is an authentic Chinese teahouse where the service of rare and legendary teas is treated with great care. Experiment with teas like scented Jasmine Pearls or the elegant Monkey-Picked oolong. You can buy all manner of teas or enjoy a pot with Chinese tea cookies. The owners have tea grown and processed to their specifications in China.

PASQUA COFFEE

4094 18th St., Castro District 94114
415-626-6263, *Open daily*

The trays of ready-made sandwiches at Pasqua, including fresh mozzarella with pesto sauce or slim white tuna, remind us of the panini sold in busy Italian coffee bars at lunch time. Chase one down with the Italian after-lunch beverage of choice, a single espresso or macchiato. Pasqua keeps its selection of coffee beans small but well-chosen. **Numerous other locations.**

PEET'S COFFEE & TEA

22 Battery St., Financial District 94111
415-981-4550, *Open Mon.-Fri.*

In 1966, when the Berkeley social scene was fueled by black coffee and heady conversation, Alfred Peet kept the talk well lubricated with his first Peet's Coffee store. Expansion has been kept slow and well managed, so the quality of beans purchased is still first-rate and freshness never slips. Peet's is also an excellent source of fine teas and a good place to buy grinders, filters, infusers and pots. **Numerous other locations.**

ROYAL GROUND COFFEES

2216 Polk St., Polk Gulch 94109
415-474-5957, *Open daily*

Neighborhood types love this newspaper-strewn café where serious coffee rules. First on the menu is the Depth Charge, a cup of coffee boosted by a shot of espresso. Caffè latte made with soy milk is an option. **Numerous other locations.**

STARBUCKS

442 Geary St., Union Square 94108
415-922-9086, *Open daily*

Can't start your day without your nonfat, half-caf, grande latte? Rainy Seattle started the gourmet coffee craze that has swept the nation, all because of the folks at Starbucks. At the modern yet comfy outlets of the now ubiquitous roaster/retailer, the service is friendly and efficient, and you can choose from among dozens of varieties of consistently good coffee, from Indonesian Sulawesi to Arabian Mocha Java to decaffeinated Viennese, along with coffee-making paraphernalia and mugs, teas, assorted baked good and sometimes sandwiches. We're partial to their iced frappéed coffee drinks, as well as their rich coffee ice creams, Chai tea—and now Starbucks chocolate. "Starbucks" doesn't just mean a cup of coffee—it's become a way of life. **Numerous other locations.**

ETHNIC MARKETS & DELIS

BEROZKA   RUSSIAN

5612 Geary Blvd., Richmond District 94121
415-668-3442, *Open daily*

This Russian delicatessen carries a raft of smoked turbot, shad, sable fish and salmon, ideal for sprinkling into a fluffy omelet. The owners make savory piroshki, those flaky Russian turnovers filled with beef and mushrooms that go so well with vegetable soup or borscht. And Berozka is the source for many staples of the Russian kitchen, such as hot horseradish, strong mustard, kasha (grains) and kefir.

BOMBAY BAZAAR   INDIAN

548 Valencia St., Mission District 94110
415-621-1717, *Open Tues.-Sun.*

The air is perfumed with the scent of curry spices, which are abundant in this large, orderly market. Stock up on special flours for making pooris (deep-fried bread) and chapatis (crackers), plus dhal, basmati rice, pappadums (prepared crackers) and tea. Row upon row of shelves proffer chutneys, pickles, sauces and other exotic condiments, including the edible gold-and-silver leaf called vark.

CASA LUCAS MARKET   LATIN AMERICAN/CARIBBEAN

2934 24th St., Mission District 94110
415-826-4334, *Open daily*

Whether you're cooking Caribbean, Spanish, Central American or Latin American dishes, Casa Lucas has everything you'll need. The goods range from guava juice to sausages, including longaniza Mexicana, mild chorizo español and hot salvadoreño. Cones of raw brown sugar, dried salt cod (bacalao) and other ingredients fill the shelves and freezers, plus more than 100 herbs, spices, chiles and seeds.

HAIG'S DELICACIES   MIDDLE EASTERN/GREEK/INDIAN/ARMENIAN

642 Clement St., Richmond District 94118
415-752-6283, *Open Mon.-Sat.*

All manner of Middle Eastern, Armenian, Greek and Indian groceries fill the shelves in stunning and sometimes confusing array. Curry pastes from warm to fiery, heavy Greek olive oil, salty feta cheese, jasmine rice, falafel mix and packaged Turkish coffee are shelved in no particular order, so shopping can be an adventure.

HANS SPECKMANN'S RESTAURANT & DELICATESSEN GERMAN

1550 Church St., Mission District 94131
415-282-6850, *Open daily*

Wursts are the best at this German specialty shop: Bratwurst, Bockwurst and Weisswurst. The Swiss specialty Bündnerfleisch, an air-dried lean filet of beef sliced paper thin, can be found, as well as smoky Black Forest ham. Buy cheeses from Switzerland, Denmark, Holland and Finland and prepared sauerkraut seasoned with caraway. German wines and beers make this a destination for all foods Teutonic.

HAPPY SUPERMARKET   CHINESE/THAI/FILIPINO

1230 Stockton St., Chinatown 94133
415-677-9950, *Open daily*

Both locations are packed with all kinds of Chinese, Thai and Filipino ingredients. The produce includes mustard greens with their yellow flowers intact, big water chestnuts, and delicate pea shoots. Fresh meat and fish are featured, and frozen foods include sausages, dim sum and grated coconut. Also available are durian, green soy beans, canned and powdered curries and hundreds of sauces. **Also in the Richmond District (400 Clement St., 415-221-3195).**

K. UOKI SAKAI   JAPANESE

1656 Post St., Japantown 94115
415-921-0514, *Open Mon.-Sat.*

You'll find what you need for a Japanese dinner at this family-owned emporium: fresh fish, dried wasabi and nori for sushi, sachets of bonito for making soup stock, seasoned vinegar, white rice and noodles, plus green-tea ice cream for dessert. The freezer case holds a variety of convenience foods.

LA PALMA MEXICATESSAN   MEXICAN

2884 24th St., Mission District 94110
415-647-1500, *Open daily*

Watch the woman in the open kitchen pat out the corn or wheat-flour dough before plopping it deftly onto the griddle for fine fresh tortillas. La Palma also sells staples like masa, dried chiles (both ground and whole) and corn husks for tamales. Cooked rice, beans, fresh salsa and guacamole are available to take home, too. Few of the staff speak English.

MOLINARI DELICATESSEN   ITALIAN

373 Columbus Ave., North Beach 94133
415-421-2337, *Open Mon.-Sat.*

Here's the North Beach that time forgot. This dazzlingly overstocked Italian deli and wine shop is run by a gregarious staff. Fresh pastas, hand-formed tortellini, wines from all regions of Italy, numberless olive oils, fresh sausages and a flank of massive salamis and coppas hanging over the deli counter all promise an authentic Italian experience. Order your sandwich on a crusty roll with roasted sweet peppers.

PRUDENTE & COMPANY   ITALIAN

1462 Grant Ave., North Beach 94133
415-421-0757, *Open daily*

Formerly Iacopi's, this Italian delicatessen has an updated selection of Italian tortas (concoctions of Mascarpone cheese layered with sun-dried tomatoes and basil). The staff still makes three kinds of fresh and dried sausages: mild Sicilian, hot Calabrese and garlic Toscano, as well as pancetta (Italian-style bacon) in both hot and mild. In addition to entrées to go, the Prudente folks make the best meatball sandwich in the city.

VIVANDE PORTA VIA   ITALIAN

2125 Fillmore St., Pacific Heights 94115
415-346-4430, *Open daily*

The name means "food to go," and when you peruse the glass deli cases packed with vegetable and pasta salads, tortas, pâtés, cheeses, sausages and pastries, you'll want to take all of it home. Carlo Middione, owner, author and teacher, knows good food. His torta Milanese offers savory layers of ham, spinach frittata and cheese. Or try a celery mushroom salad or a Sicilian eggplant relish with raisins and pine nuts. Every dessert is a winner.

YUEN'S GARDEN   CHINESE

1131 Grant Ave., Chinatown 94133
415-391-1131, *Open daily*

Beautiful roasted birds decorate the windows of this Chinese deli. The tea-roasted quail, the walnut-hued squab cooked with the head on, soy-sauce chicken, poached chicken, roasted Rock Cornish game hens, tea-smoked duck, and pressed duck are all terrific. A steam table holds several stir-fried dishes to go.

FARMERS' MARKETS

FERRY PLAZA FARMERS' MARKET

Front St. parking lot (near Green St.), Financial District 94111
510-528-6987, *Open Tues. & Sat. year-round*

We imagine that heaven looks exactly like this market, but with more parking. Vendors bring all manner of pampered produce, artisanal breads, unusual meats and sausages and exotic fruits. You'll find handmade sheep's-milk cheese by Bellwether Farms and fresh goat's-milk cheese from Redwood Hill. The market is known for its special programs such as Shop with the Chef and Market Cooking for Kids. A number of restaurants have booths selling snacks.

HEART OF THE CITY CERTIFIED FARMERS' MARKET

United Nations Plaza, Market St. at 7th, Civic Center 94102
415-558-9455, *Open Wed. & Sun. year-round*

For 15 years this modest market has stood as a beacon in a dicey neighborhood. Small truck farmers come to offer honey, nuts, eggs, Asian produce, cherries, asparagus, pumpkins and squash in their seasons. The values are good, especially if you get there early in the morning.

SAN FRANCISCO FARMERS' MARKET

100 Alemany Blvd., Outer Mission 94110
415-647-9423, *Open Sat. year-round*

The 70 or so vendors who come here in winter swell in number to about 140 in summer. In addition to local oranges, strawberries, lettuces and such, the market features three bakeries. Try the Vital Vittles Real Bread. Jim Salter in Half Moon Bay provides crabs in the winter and spring and salmon in the summer and fall.

ICE CREAM

BEN & JERRY'S

543 Columbus Ave., North Beach 94133
415-249-4684, *Open daily*

Fans can go straight to the source at these ice-cream counters. San Francisco–inspired flavors like Cherry Garcia and Wavy Gravy join national favorites such as Chunky Monkey in pints and quarts as well as cups and cones. New sorbet flavors provide a low-fat alternative. **Numerous other locations.**

CIAO BELLA GELATO

685 Harrison St., SoMa 94107
415-541-4940, *Open Mon.-Fri.*

Genuine, rich, Italian-style gelato is served at this small café along with fresh, icy sorbets. The New York company recently came West to supply some of the city's top restaurants. The café menu of about two dozen flavors changes seasonally. New gelato flavors include honey, rose petal, and fig and port. New sorbets like raspberry with Zinfandel are appealing.

DOUBLE RAINBOW

1653 Polk St., Polk Gulch 94109
415-775-3220, *Open daily*

The richest and best classic ice cream flavors are joined by seasonal treats like white pistachio and lychee nut. Michael Sachar and Steven Fink created this home-grown ice cream empire (well, duchy) in the late seventies, and it continues to change with the times. Current delights include the memorable sorbets, like marionberry, or the completely harmless (read: no fat, no cholesterol, no lactose, no caffeine, no refined sugar) crème glacé. **Numerous other locations.**

JOE'S ICE CREAM

5351 Geary Blvd., Richmond District 94121
415-751-1950, *Open daily*

With ice cream made on the premises, this soda fountain is a delightful place for thick, old-fashioned milkshakes that barely make it up the straw. This is also the place to find Joe's It, a version of the locally famous It's It, an ice cream sandwich constructed with oatmeal cookies and doused in chocolate.

LATIN FREEZE

3338 24th St., Mission District 94110
415-282-5033, *Open daily*

Mario and Norma Rodriguez know the secret of all good food: keep it simple and fresh. With just fruit, sugar and water, they concoct paletas, refreshing frozen-fruit treats. Flavors include passion fruit, watermelon and papaya.

POLLY ANN ICE CREAM

3142 Noriega St., Sunset District 94122
415-664-2472, *Open daily*

Judging by the loopy signs in the window and the promise of free ice cream cones for dogs, the owner's unusual sense of humor and generosity make people love it. Polly Ann plays with exotic flavors—taro, red bean and avocado—and sometimes they get it just right, as with Sabra, a magnificent chocolate-orange ice cream.

ST. FRANCIS FOUNTAIN & CANDY

2801 24th St., Mission District 94110
415-826-4200, *Open Mon.-Sat.*

Remember lemon custard, black raspberry marble and butter brickle ice cream? This soda fountain does. Nestled in one of its wooden booths, you can savor ice cream made just as it used to be. Buy a quart of your favorite to enjoy at home. The candy counter tempts you with house-made chocolate-covered cherries, peanut brittle and other old-time favorites.

GOURMET MARKETS

EPICURE

Neiman-Marcus, 150 Stockton St., Union Square 94108
415-362-3900 ext. 2175, *Open daily*

With gourmet food available in lots more places, including upscale supermarkets, Neiman-Marcus has scaled back this section of the store. But N-M is still a convenient place to buy various types of caviar, smoked fish, tinned foie gras and luscious chocolates. A small bakery has artisanal cakes and scones, but the main deli is ordinary. Wines are available for steep prices.

MOLLY STONE'S

2435 California St., Pacific Heights 94115
415-567-4902, *Open daily*

The Grand Central Market has become a Molly Stone's, and the quality of the meat department, cheeses, wine selection and produce has definitely gone up several notches. A large parking lot makes this store a Pacific Heights destination.

TRADER JOE'S

555 Ninth St., SoMa 94103
415-863-1292, *Open daily*

Trader Joe's doesn't really like being referred to as a gourmet market. They aim to bring more and finer food to the general public at the best possible prices by jumping on bargains and selling great quantities of private-label foods. Consequently, availability can be spotty, but shopping is always an adventure. You may, or may not, find Turkish apricots or Chilean wine, crumpets or frozen gyoza (pot stickers).

HEALTH FOOD/ORGANIC MARKETS & JUICE BARS

JAMBA JUICE

22 Battery, Financial District 94111
415-438-3321, *Open Mon.-Fri.*

Jamba's lovely fresh-squeezed juices include organic orange and carrot, grapefruit, lemonade and Jambrosia, a blend of nine vegetable juices. Some 22 blended-to-order smoothies round out the menu, as do hot vegetable broth, soups and hot juices. The neighborhood juice bars are usually open everyday. **Numerous other locations.**

RAINBOW GROCERY COOPERATIVE

1745 Folsom St., Mission District 94103
415-863-0620, *Open daily*

This collectively owned grocery store has flourished since the 1970s and has expanded over the years to this present location. You will never find meat or seafood here, although the cheese selection has gotten better. Huge selections of culinary and medicinal herbs are sold from glass jars. Produce, much of it organically grown, is labeled in Spanish and English. Prices are rock-bottom. Bulk bins abound, with 16 types of rice, 7 seaweeds, flours and grains, dried fruits, and organic coffees.

THOM'S NATURAL FOODS

5843 Geary Blvd. Richmond District 94121
415-387-6367, *Open daily*

In business for more than 30 years (at this location for about a dozen), Thom's carries a fine selection of produce, including such hard-to-find items as Spanish black radishes and burdock root, as well as cheese and hormone-free fresh chickens. Bulk foods are nicely stored.

WHOLE FOODS MARKET

1765 California St., Pacific Heights 94109
415-674-0500, *Open daily*

The enormous space housing the latest Bay Area branch of this natural-foods market is stocked with fine products. The prepared foods are better than at some restaurants. There's a farmers' market's worth of organic produce, hormone-free meats and poultry, and a great selection of bulk goods. An in-house bakery makes terrific breads and pastries. **Numerous other locations.**

KITCHENWARE

BIORDI ART IMPORTS

412 Columbus Ave., North Beach 94133
415-392-8096, *Open Mon.-Sat.*

The hand-painted Deruta pottery is ornate and the prices are high, but one magnificent platter or serving bowl from Biordi will prove its worth over the years. Brightly colored Desimone pottery from Sicily looks like something Picasso could have done. Not surprising: Desimone knew Picasso, and the question is who influenced whom.

COOKIN'

339 Divisadero, Western Addition 94117
415-861-1854, *Open Tues.-Sun.*

Cookin' is a dimly lit, cram-packed treasure trove of used apparatus for the kitchen. Amateurs scout the shop for all kinds of cooking equipment—juicers, ricers, bakeware, cake molds, copper mixing bowls, soup tureens: anything and everything is possible. There's a small library of cookbooks, too.

CRATE & BARREL

125 Grant Ave., Union Square 94108
415-986-4000, *Open daily*

It's hard to beat Crate & Barrel for stocking the kitchen or beautifying your tabletop. It carries everything from aperitif glasses to fine crystal. This place is packed with bargain hunters during sales.

FILLAMENTO

2185 Fillmore St., Pacific Heights 94115
415-931-2224, *Open daily*

Lovers of contemporary urban style will find their heart's desire among Fillamento's table settings. Much attention is paid to the imaginative use of bright color, and the store goes out of its way to offer witty and elegant merchandise. We love it that Fillamento is a little more daring than the national chains.

GINN WALL COMPANY

1016 Grant Ave., Chinatown 94108
415-982-6307, *Open Wed.-Mon.*

This all-purpose hardware and kitchen store has the right tools for preparing Chinese food: huge cleavers, small paring knives, rectangular blades for vegetables, plastic mandolins for thin slicing, cast-iron grill pans for sizzling dishes, rice cookers and prickly ginger graters. A wide variety of rolled steel woks in sizes for preparing dinner for one or a dozen are well priced.

GREEN WORLD MERCANTILE

2340 Polk St., Polk Gulch 94109
415-771-5717, *Open daily*

This store features earth-friendly items for your bed, bath, garden and kitchen. You'll find bubbly recycled glass for the table and natural-cotton kitchen towels. It's a lovely place to find a gift for an environmentally conscious friend.

HOMECHEF COOKING SCHOOL & KITCHEN STORE

3525 California St., Laurel Heights 94118
415-668-3191, *Open daily*

Catering to the home cook who can afford the best, HomeChef carries a full line of Kaiser bakeware from Germany, Le Creuset and other top-quality French cookware, and tools of the trade. The school offers a full schedule of cooking classes taught by guest chefs both here and in **Corte Madera, Palo Alto, Walnut Creek and San Jose.**

NAOMI'S

1817 Polk St., Polk Gulch 94109
415-775-1207, *Open Tues.-Sat.*

Owner Naomi Murdach has been here for 28 years, trading in American art pottery. This is a special place to find heaps of the bright Bauer dishware popular in the thirties, as well as other native California pottery. Look for pastel LuRay pieces and the modernistic Raymor pattern by Roseville to set an authentic 1950s table. Look for Hall Company's Coconuts, the cups that places like Trader Vic's used for their fruity cocktails.

SOKO HARDWARE CO.

1698 Post St., Japantown 94115
415-931-5510, *Open Mon.-Sat.*

The lower level of this extremely organized hardware store is devoted to kitchenware, much of it unavailable elsewhere. Thirty-eight sizes of Japanese knives—from the 330-millimeter yanigi-ba to the 90-millimeter ajikiri hocho—stand beside the best European cutlery. There are bamboo mats and wooden molds for shaping sushi, and sturdy metal Mongolian hot pots, sporting handles and wooden lids, with capacities ranging from single servings to about eight quarts. Upstairs you can find ikebana flower-arranging supplies, beautiful platters and trays for hors d'oeuvres or sushi, and delicate tea sets.

TERRA MIA

2122 Union St., Cow Hollow 94123
415-351-2529, *Open daily*

Terra Mia is a do-it-yourself pottery studio offering amateur artists the opportunity to decorate their own baby mugs and latte bowls, casseroles and salad bowls, pet dishes and dinnerware. Patrons choose from a good selection of ready-to-glaze pottery, pick out brushes, sponges and glazes, and then sit down at a clean table and paint as boldly as they like. The pottery is fired by Terra Mia and ready within one week. Visitors can arrange to have items shipped home. **Also in Noe Valley (4037 24th St., 415-642-9911).**

WILLIAMS-SONOMA

150 Post St., Union Square 94108
415-362-6904, *Open daily*

Chuck Williams opened the first Williams-Sonoma store more than 30 years ago, and the chain has since spread across the nation. The shops have always been a dependable source for good-quality basic cookware as well as colorful pottery tableware, mostly from Italy and Portugal. W-S also sells foodstuffs and an expanding line of Williams-Sonoma cookbooks. **Numerous other locations**.

MEAT, POULTRY & SEAFOOD

ANCHOR OYSTER BAR & SEAFOOD MARKET

579 Castro St., Castro District 94114
415-431-3990, *Open daily*

Since 1977, Anchor has sent forth countless oysters on the half shell, icy cold and smelling of the ocean tide. At the back of the small café the owners sell those same oysters in the shell or shucked, along with fresh clams, mussels, shrimp and prawns. Whatever they bought for the lunch and dinner specials—maybe snapper, sole or ahi tuna—is for sale, too, usually at favorable prices, along with tartar sauce and salad dressing.

BRYAN'S QUALITY MEATS

3473 California St., Laurel Heights 94118
415-752-3430, *Open Mon.-Sat.*

Abundant quantities, a rich variety of cuts, and the freshest in meat, poultry and seafood make Bryan's a pleasure to visit. Beef is aged on the premises, with handsome steaks and roasts cut to order. This is one of the few places in the city to buy prime beef. The selection of poultry includes naturally raised chicken and turkey, Cornish hens and poussin. A variety of marinated meats are ready for the grill. In the front of the store the seafood and shellfish are displayed on ice.

DRAGON MARKET

1145 Stockton St., Chinatown 94133
415-433-0403, *Open daily*

Five big tanks hold live sea creatures, from sleek, whiskered catfish to crabs in season. The long, narrow center aisle may be flanked by a pile of eels, a heap of fish heads for stock, and a crate of live frogs. Step carefully: this market is always crowded.

GUERRA QUALITY MEATS

490 Taraval St., Outer Sunset 94116
415-564-0585, *Open Mon.-Sat.*

The Guerra family supplies premium meats and poultry cut to order by pros. Veal topini, boneless rolled veal breast, is one of half a dozen veal cuts. Flat-iron roast and Jewish filet from the shoulder are both good for a pot roast or stew. Freezer specials are a good way to get a cuts at yesterday's prices.

HING LUNG MEATS

1261 Stockton St., Chinatown 94133
415-397-5521, *Open daily*

On one side of the store, roasted and barbecued meats are chopped and sliced for takeout. This is the place to order a whole suckling pig or a flock of roasted ducks. In the remaining two-thirds of the store, pork cuts, beef and poultry are for sale. Prices are cook-friendly.

HARRIS'

2100 Van Ness Ave., Van Ness 94109
415-673-1888, *Open daily*

Prime-grade beef, dry-aged for three weeks, forms the backbone of this steakhouse's menu. During restaurant hours (beginning at 5:30 p.m. nightly) and from a counter just inside the door, you can buy the same meat that they serve in the restaurant. T-bone and New York cuts are popular.

ISRAEL & COHEN KOSHER MEAT & POULTRY

5621 Geary Blvd., Richmond District 94121
415-752-3064, *Open Sun.-Fri.*

Fresh and frozen kosher poultry and meats are joined by bargain-priced lox and caviar. Matzos, gefilte fish, honey-cake mixes and other kosher packaged goods are also on display.

LITTLE CITY MEATS

1400 Stockton St., North Beach 94133
415-986-2601, *Open Mon.-Sat.*

They call themselves "Home of the Sicilian Sausage," but that's just the beginning. Fresh sausage abounds, but fresh veal is also a specialty: dainty filets of just 12 to 16 ounces and boneless legs are waiting to be seasoned with olive oil, sherry, onion and herbs for a simple roast. Veal shanks for osso buco, scaloppine for saltimbocca or veal Milanese, veal shoulder for stew—all are available along with printed recipes.

SUPER KOYAMA

1790 Sutter St., Japantown 94115
415-921-6529, *Open daily*

In this pristine Japanese supermarket, the fishmonger cuts sushi-grade tuna and salmon, exquisitely fresh squid and other seafood to order while you pick up the fixings for a Japanese meal. The produce counter features daikon, petite bok choy, peppery radish sprouts, shiitake mushrooms and napa cabbage. The selections of dashi (fish stock) and dried noodles for making a miso soup or shabu-shabu are extensive.

SWAN OYSTER DEPOT

1517 Polk St., Polk Gulch 94109
415-673-1101, *Open Mon.-Sat.*

Fresh cherrystone clams, bluepoint oysters and West Coast little necks destined for the oyster bar's patrons can be purchased for home consumption too. Since 1912 the friendly staff at this café and fish market have accommodated home cooks by sharing the impeccably fresh seafood, which may include squid, swordfish or whole red snapper.

WINE, BEER & SPIRITS

CALIFORNIA WINE MERCHANT

3237 Pierce St., Marina 94123
415-567-0646, *Open daily*

Proprietor Greg O'Flynn is particular about what he sells, so you won't find a bad bottle of wine in this modest shop (though you may find an empty bin from time to time). True to its name, the shop represents mostly small California producers but occasionally offers something extraordinary from Oregon or Washington.

CASTRO VILLAGE WINE CO.

4121 19th St., Castro 94114
415-864-4411, *Open daily*

Wandering the aisles of this hugely appealing shop, you're likely to encounter more labels that you don't know than ones you do. Boyd Swartz has packed more than 500 fine California wines from small-case producers (and a handful of imported vintages) into this tidy space, and he's delighted to introduce customers to every one of them. The selection of grappa, port and brandy features world-class California spirits.

COIT LIQUORS

585 Columbus Ave., North Beach 94133
415-986-4036, *Open daily*

Yes, Tony Giovanzana does carry excellent California and French wines among his personal picks. But the Italian wine selection is the best in the city and has some of the best bargains. Pick up a case of bright, fruity Dolcetto D'Alba (Beaujolais' Italian cousin) to imbibe while you cellar the weighty Barolo. Knowledgeable staff people are always on hand to give guidance; plus, the store is open until midnight.

JOHN WALKER & CO.

175 Sutter St., Union Square 94104
415-986-2707, *Open Mon.-Sat.*

No fewer than three dozen single-malt scotch whiskeys are carried in this oak-paneled shop reminiscent of a gentleman's club from days gone by. To help customers find their way through the collection of fine old red wines from Burgundy or Bordeaux and the strictly edited group of California wines, the shop has a shelf of the best in wine reference books.

THE JUG SHOP

1567 Pacific Ave., Polk Gulch 94109
415-885-2922, *Open daily*

Once an unassuming liquor store, the Jug Shop has grown up into a shop with an active tasting bar and events at least twice a month. The values and selection are best in the under-$10 range, full of many California and Italian bottles.

PLUMPJACK WINES

3201 Fillmore St., Marina 94123
415-346-9870, *Open daily*

This trendy wine shop features very informed service in the high-price range and what may be the best collection of half bottles in the city. You'll find a good selection of California sparkling wines and locally packaged Tsar Nicoulai caviar.

WINE CLUB SAN FRANCISCO

953 Harrison St., SoMa 94107
415-512-9086, *Open daily*

A quest for the best wines at the lowest prices brings people to this warehouse space, where wines are stacked on the floor in random order. All the producing countries are represented: Australia, Chile, Spain, wherever the buyers find good value for the price. Consequently, the Wine Club's offerings change more than most as bargains come and go.

THE WINE HOUSE

535 Bryant St., SoMa 94107
415-495-8486, *Open Mon.-Sat.*

The exposed brick walls enclosing case upon case of fine French Burgundies and white and red Bordeaux make you feel you've just entered owner John Carpenter's personal wine cellar. In one sense, you have. The rare and noble is a specialty here. Even the California vintages are restricted to the lesser-known vineyards. The knowledgeable and enthusiastic service is an amateur oenophile's dream, while the generous case discount helps take the sting out of building a cellar.

Marin County

MAP OF MARIN COUNTY

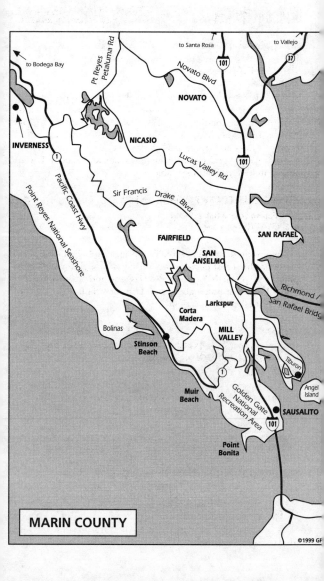

to Bodega Bay

to Santa Rosa

to Vallejo

101

37

Pt Reyes Petaluma Rd

Novato Blvd

NOVATO

INVERNESS

1

NICASIO

Lucas Valley Rd

101

Pacific Coast Hwy

Point Reyes National Seashore

Sir Francis Drake Blvd

FAIRFIELD

SAN RAFAEL

SAN ANSELMO

Richmond / San Rafael Bridge

Larkspur

Bolinas

Corta Madera

MILL VALLEY

Stinson Beach

1

Tiburon

Muir Beach

Golden Gate National Recreation Area

Angel Island

101

SAUSALITO

Point Bonita

MARIN COUNTY

©1999 GF

INTRODUCTION

In Marin County, just north across the Golden Gate Bridge from San Francisco, older and newer towns plus expanding suburbs coexist with tourist attractions. **San Rafael,** the largest city, has a host of economic levels, while **Mill Valley** is home to many movers and shakers in the entertainment and creative fields. **Tiburon, Larkspur** and **Sausalito** overlook the water, and towns like **Inverness** retain their rural character. All have restaurants that are worth the drive.

RESTAURANTS

A.G. FERRARI FOODS   ITALIAN   ¢

107 Corte Madera Town Center, Corte Madera 94925
415-927-4347, *Open daily*

Dozens of varieties of imported dried pasta, olive oil, balsamic vinegar and a large selection of Italian wines make this place an Italian foodie heaven. Breads from many of the Bay Area's finest bakeries are delivered fresh daily. The deli counter offers everything from ham 'n' cheese on sourdough to fresh cannelloni, ravioli, frittatas, salads and sauces. Eat at several indoor and outdoor table.

AMICI'S EAST COAST PIZZERIA   PIZZA   ¢

1242 Fourth St., San Rafael 94901
415-455-9777, *Open daily*

In a room done up to look like an upscale Italian caffè, you get good thin-crust pizzas with a variety of straightforward toppings, a surprisingly light and tasty lasagne and passable pastas. The salads are a notch above standard pizzeria fare, as are the desserts. Best of all, they deliver.

ATRIUM   CHINESE   12/20

Village Shopping Center, 1546 Redwood Hwy., Corte Madera 94925
415-927-8889, *Lunch & Dinner daily, $$*

This upscale pan-Asian (primarily multi-regional Chinese) restaurant is light and airy with ultramodern decor, floor-to-ceiling windows, lots of greenery, marble accents and ceiling fans. We recommend the Chinese lettuce "tacos" but not the too-thick "crustacean fantasy" soup crowned with puff pastry. The Singapore vermicelli in a light curry has nice spice to it.

THE AVENUE GRILL   AMERICAN   11/20

44 E. Blithedale Ave., Mill Valley 94941
415-388-6003, *Dinner nightly, $$$*

If it weren't for the maddening inconsistency in the food, we'd be happy to give the Avenue Grill a higher rating. But the

147

ambience is fun and fast-paced, and the good dishes outnumber the indifferent ones. You might be seduced by cornmeal-dusted fried rock shrimp, plump and juicy barbecued oysters and lamb sirloin served with roasted-garlic bread pudding. Then your palate might be sorely disappointed by clunkers such as pork chops grilled to the texture of hardwood.

BISTRO ALSACIENNE FRENCH 13/20

655 Redwood Hwy., Mill Valley 94941
415-389-0921, *Dinner Tues.-Sun.*, $$$
☎ 🖥️ ⟳

The hearty, soul-satisfying cuisine of Alsace-defined "comfort food"—choucroute, coq au vin and beef bourguignon—are all big in flavor and portion. Industry professional Fritz Frankel adds a little formality to the dining room, a welcome aspect in casual Marin.

BOLERO SPANISH 11/20

125 E. Sir Francis Drake Blvd., Larkspur 94939
415-925-9391, *Lunch & Dinner daily*, $$$
☎ 🚗 🛩️ 🍷 ⟳

Bolero may not have great food, but it certainly has an exotic, romantic decor. The restaurant occupies the actual kiln—a long, gently curving tube with 11-foot-thick brick walls—in which most of the bricks used to rebuild San Francisco after the 1906 earthquake were fired. Bolero features both a tapas bar and a more formal dining room. Main courses like a lusty zarzuela and garlicky grilled lamb chops are successful, but the overcooked paella failed to impress us.

BUBBA'S DINER AMERICAN 14/20

566 San Anselmo Ave., San Anselmo 94960
415-459-6862, *Breakfast, Lunch & Dinner Wed.-Mon.*, $$
♥ 👫

After many years of working with Bradley Ogden at Lark Creek Inn and One Market, Steve Simmons may seem an unlikely candidate to be cooking up meatloaf, pork chops and chicken pot pie in a retro diner. On the other hand, Simmons loves cooking simple food and actually seeing his customers, who line up for seats at the counter. And if you just can't live without those big, overflowing California salads, Simmons does those, too. Bubba's home-style pies are also a big plus—enormous portions at old-fashioned prices.

BUCKEYE ROADHOUSE AMERICAN 14/20

15 Shoreline Hwy., Mill Valley 94941
415-331-2600, *Lunch Mon.-Sat., Dinner nightly, Brunch Sun.*, $$$
☎ 👫 ⟳

New-fashioned American food with a California twist combined with a snappy, energetic ambience have made this upscale roadhouse one of the North Bay's most popular restaurants. Smoky barbecue is one of the house signature dishes, as is a playful take on oysters Rockefeller, here called oysters Bingo. The roast chicken and mashers are top-notch. Desserts are generally rich and luscious.

THE CAPRICE   CALIFORNIA   12/20

2000 Paradise Dr., Tiburon 94921
415-435-3400, *Dinner nightly, $$$*

For years the Caprice was the Cadillac of Marin restaurants––prestigious, upscale and pretty dull except for the fabulous Bay view. But the old-fashioned menu, formal service and location make it a favorite of conservative and/or romantic diners. Caesar salad and rack of lamb appear on the menu alongside modern dishes like seared sea scallops with a soy-porcini sauce. The limited wine list is strong in moderately priced varietals.

CASA MAÑANA   MEXICAN   ¢

711 D St., San Rafael 94901
415-456-7345, *Open daily*

This tiny restaurant in a hard-to-find courtyard can compete with the best Mexican eateries in SF's Mission District. The menu lists all the standard dishes—tacos, burritos, enchiladas—but they're distinguished by their bold flavors, good-quality ingredients and careful preparation. This is not typical suburban Cal-Mex food. The chiles rellenos are light and flavorful, as is the Salvadoran tamale. The chicken mole is great.

CENTO STELLE   ITALIAN   12/20

901 Lincoln Ave., San Rafael 94901
415-485-4422, *Lunch Mon.-Fri., Dinner nightly, $$*

Cento Stelle is something of a formula restaurant. But it's a pretty good formula. It starts with a convenient location and bare-bones decor: cans of tomato sauce, boxes of pasta and cases of wine are stacked around the dining room. It continues with big servings of hearty, home-style Italian food and inexpensive Italian wines, and ends with prices on the saintly side of moderate. **Also in San Francisco & the East Bay.**

CHRISTOPHE   FRENCH   12/20

1919 Bridgeway Blvd., Sausalito 94965
415-332-9244, *Dinner Tues.-Sun., $$$*

Christophe offers moderately priced French country cuisine in a dollhouse of a restaurant with stained-glass windows, art nouveau accents, Villeroy & Boch china and all the cozy, romantic atmosphere you could want. Creamy duck-liver mousse is a comforting old friend, as is the beef tartare. The kitchen has a way with duck and lamb dishes, and the signature profiteroles are delectable.

THE CLUB AT MCGINNIS   CALIFORNIA   12/20

350 Smith Ranch Rd., San Rafael 94901
415-491-5959, *Lunch & Dinner daily, Breakfast & Brunch Sat.-Sun.,* $$$

Golf and good food aren't often associated with each other, but at the restaurant in San Rafael's McInnis Park Golf Center, you'll find both. If you can forgive the dining room opening onto the pro shop and the fashion-challenged wardrobe of most golfers, you'll be happy here. The California fare has an Italian flourish, with such dishes as crisply fried rock shrimp in a large radicchio "cup," brassy spaghetti alla puttanesca, and grilled salmon with an earthy tomato-mushroom ragoût.

CUCINA JACKSON FILLMORE   ITALIAN   14/20

337 San Anselmo Ave., San Anselmo, 94960
415-454-2942, *Dinner Tues.-Sun.,* $$

An offshoot of a lively San Francisco, this upbeat spot features yellow walls, a stone floor and stained-glass light fixtures. Everyone starts with complimentary bruschetta with basil, tomato and olive oil. Linguine with prawns is a real winner, and we adored the perfectly grilled 16-ounce veal chop. The scrumptious tiramisu comes in generous portions. Friendly and efficient service is an added attraction.

DAVID'S FINEST TAQUERÍA   MEXICAN   ¢

425 Corte Madera Town Center, Corte Madera 94925
415-927-6572, *Open daily*

David's Finest Taquería makes perfect use of the fresh vegetables available at David's Finest Produce, which is ceded a small alcove off to one side of the taqueria's kitchen and counter. The taqueria fare is more authentic than you might expect, given its shopping-mall location. You'll find good burritos, quesadillas, roasted chicken, vegetarian dishes and salsas.

EL PASEO   CONTEMPORARY   13/20

17 Throckmorton Ave., Mill Valley 94941
415-388-0741, *Dinner nightly,* $$$

A perennial choice for one of the Bay Area's most romantic restaurants, El Paseo features decent food in its lavishly decorated dining rooms. Best bets are the rack of lamb or salmon, which go well with wines chosen from the excellent list.

EVER RAIN   CHINESE   13/20

7089 Redwood Blvd., Novato 94947
415-892-6563, *Lunch Tues.-Fri., Dinner Tues.-Sun.,* $

Although Novato is fairly bereft of fine-dining opportunities, the Taiwanese food here can compete with many of its citified counterparts. The prawns with candied walnuts are given a refined treatment; the sea scallops in a tart, chile-spiked sauce probably won't be found in many other local Chinese eateries.

FILOU   FRENCH   NO RATING

198 Sir Francis Drake Blvd., San Anselmo 94960
415-256-2436, *Lunch Mon.-Fri., Dinner Tues.-Sun.*, $$

The menu at this new spot is firmly planted in the current rage—French bistro food. Starters include smoked trout, chicken liver pâté and veal sweetbreads, here on a potato-and-carrot pancake. Main courses we'd like to try include the coquilles St. Jacques perched on lime-flavored mashed potatoes. The desserts range from crème brûlée to lemon tart.

THE FLATIRON   AMERICAN   ¢

724 B St., San Rafael 94901
415-257-4320. *Open daily*

At times nothing can satisfy like a great big, juicy burger. On that score this sports bar delivers. A good choice for the non-carnivore is the grilled-vegetable sandwich with Provolone and pesto sauce. Fish and chips are excellent with a frosty beer and a 49ers game. Desserts tend toward gooey but good.

FRANTOIO   ITALIAN   12/20

152 Shoreline Hwy., Mill Valley 94941
415-289-5777, *Lunch Mon.-Sat., & Dinner daily*, $$$

"Frantoio" translates as olive press, and it's more than just a catchy name. Behind a huge glass wall at the back of this lively restaurant is a massive, state-of-the-art olive press. It's a real crowd-pleaser, as is the light authentically Italian cuisine. Some examples: mussels roasted in Frantoio's oak-fired oven, decadent risotto with fresh asparagus and crisp pizzas. The list of California and Italian wines is lengthy.

GIRA POLLI   ITALIAN   12/20

590 E. Blithedale Ave., Mill Valley 94941
415-383-6040, *Dinner nightly*, $

Herb- and citrus-perfumed chickens turn on 18 spits over an almond-wood fire in the $50,000 imported Italian rotisserie. The result: chicken with golden, crispy skin and moist, tender meat. Not everything else on the menu is up to the birds' standard, though we've sampled some good pastas and salads.

GUAYMAS   MEXICAN   12/20

5 Main St., Tiburon 94920
415-435-6300, *Lunch & Dinner daily*, $$

Guaymas' food is only part of the restaurant's immense local appeal; its sleek California-Mexican decor, thriving bar scene and ideal waterfront location make it a prime destination. Seasonings are often applied with a timid hand; the salsas, however, deliver real flavor, and you'll need them to goose many of the dishes. Among our favorites are roasted duck with pumpkin-seed sauce and prawns cooked on rock salt.

HALF DAY CAFÉ   CALIFORNIA   13/20

848 College Ave., Kentfield 94904
415-459-0291, *Breakfast, Lunch & Dinner daily, $$*

At first glance, Half Day Café tries to do way too much. Open daily for breakfast, lunch and dinner, its menu is a multicultural tour that begins in California and winds its way around the globe. Dinner shows the restaurant's creativity: you can get anything from jerk-marinated baby back ribs or pork quesadillas to a near-perfect roasted chicken and diet-busting bread pudding. The patio makes for idyllic outdoor dining.

HOUSE OF LEE   CHINESE   12/20

885-887 Fourth St., San Rafael 94901
415-457-9977, *Lunch & Dinner daily, $*

There's nothing out of the ordinary about Lee's lengthy menu: it's the expected roster of Cantonese, Szechuan and Hunanese dishes. But they're prepared with greater skill than in most local restaurants and yet priced the same. Of particular note are salt-and-pepper fried prawns and tea-smoked duck. House of Lee also serves good dim sum on weekends.

IL DAVIDE   ITALIAN   12/20

901 A St., San Rafael 94901
415-454-8080, *Lunch Tues.-Sat., Dinner Tues.-Sun., Brunch Sun., $$$*

A colorful, Italian-countryside mural fills an entire wall of this popular restaurant, adding character to what could be a rather sterile environment. There's lots of flavor in the fried calamari with spicy aïoli, fettuccine frutti di mare, chicken cooked under a hot brick and the tiramisu. They offer small flights of reasonably priced wines to sample with dinner.

IL FORNAIO   ITALIAN   13/20

223 Corte Madera Town Center Corte Madera 94925
415-927-4400, *Lunch & Dinner daily, $$*

See review in PENINSULA chapter.

INDIA VILLAGE   INDIAN   14/20

555 E. Francisco Blvd., San Rafael 94901
415-456-2411, *Lunch Mon.-Sat., Dinner nightly, $*

Some of the best Indian cuisine in the the Bay Area can be found at this cozy eatery hidden in a nondescript shopping center. Ask for one of the many semi-private booths and order as much of a variety of Indian dishes as your appetite and wallet will allow. You won't be disappointed with the samosas, the chicken tikka masala, the creamy-textured eggplant and the tandoori dishes.

INSALATA'S   MEDITERRANEAN   14/20

120 Sir Francis Drake Blvd., San Anselmo 94960
415-457-7700, *Lunch Mon.-Sat., Dinner nightly, Brunch Sun.,* $$

Chef-owner Heidi Krahling has created one of the best restaurants in Marin, if not the entire Bay Area. Delightful paintings of vegetables dominate the large open room. One of the tastiest starters is a wonderful trio of dips (an eggplant caviar is one), served with pita triangles and olives. Entrées we've liked include a center-cut pork chop and a Catalan-style salmon grilled in a grape leaf. Sides include hummus, onion rings and shoestring potatoes. We also love the fromage blanc panna cotta with fresh strawberries, but then again there's the warm apple tarte tatin. The well-chosen wine list is divided between California and Europe.

JHAN THONG   THAI   ¢

5835 Northgate Mall, San Rafael 94901
415-499-3501, *Open daily*

In a shopping-mall food court surrounded by fast-food purveyors, this amazingly good Thai eatery is a favorite of North Bay chefs and foodies because of its long hours and quick turnover. Our favorites are satays and savory curries.

JOE'S TACO LOUNGE & SALSARIA   MEXICAN   ¢

382 Miller Ave., Mill Valley 94941
415-383-8164, *Open daily*

Joe's blends your basic taqueria food with a California attitude to satisfy your desire for cheap, fun and not-too-caloric dining. The brightly painted room is a jumble of wacky decorations, from dozens of bottles of hot sauce to ceramic Madonnas to a mounted fish. The food is timidly seasoned, but Joe's makes several piquant salsas that can inject life. Best bets are fish tacos, rock-shrimp tostadas and roasted chicken.

KASBAH MOROCCAN RESTAURANT   MOROCCAN   14/20

200 Merrydale Rd., San Rafael 94903
415-472-6666, *Lunch Mon.-Fri., Dinner nightly,* $$$

This opulent dining room brings the atmosphere of Marrakesh to the Bay Area. Diner sit at low brass tables and eat their food with their hands, most nights watching a floor show of sensual belly dancing. We recommend the lamb with prunes, rabbit tagine and lamb brochettes served over couscous. The fixed-price meal is a bargain. Forks are supplied for those who want them. Cookies and mint tea make a great ending to a fun dining experience.

LARK CREEK INN CONTEMPORARY 15/20

234 Magnolia Ave., Larkspur 94939
415-924-7766, *Lunch Mon.-Fri., Dinner nightly, Brunch Sun.,* $$$$

This country-style yet elegant restaurant gets better and better. Chef Bradley Ogden and partner Michael Dellar now divide their time among other restaurants, One Market in San Francisco and the Lark Creek Cafés around the Bay Area. Still the food, service and ambience remain tops. The yellow-and-white wood-frame building, nestled in a grove of redwood trees, has a timeless American feel, while the menu features the best available local ingredients prepared with skill and creativity. Signature dishes like the Caesar salad, Yankee pot roast and ravioli made with ham hocks, are consistently soul-satisfying. Having the Inn's Sunday brunch outdoors in balmy weather gives real meaning to the phrase "Marvelous Marin." Sample the house-baked breads and pastries, followed perhaps by scrambled eggs with asparagus, smoked salmon and chèvre. The all-American wine list is well-chosen and pricey. The bar menu, which can be ordered anywhere in the restaurant, allows you to visit repeatedly without damaging your wallet.

LEFT BANK FRENCH 14/20

507 Magnolia Ave., Larkspur 94939
415-927-3331, *Lunch & Dinner daily,* $$

See review in PENINSULA chapter.

MANKA'S INVERNESS LODGE CALIFORNIA NO RATING

Calendar Way at Argyle, Inverness 94937
415-669-1034, *Breakfast daily, Dinner hours vary during the year,* $$$

This former hunting lodge sprawled across a hill overlooking Tomales Bay is loaded with rustic atmosphere and charm; it's the perfect place to get away from the rat race, whether for dinner or overnight. At press time the owner had redone the kitchen, but the chef had left and the current menu was unavailable.

MARIN JOE'S ITALIAN/STEAKS 12/20

1585 Casa Buena Dr., Corte Madera 94925
415-924-2081, *Lunch Mon.-Fri., Dinner nightly,* $$

Joe's is a longtime favorite with locals who enjoy the old-time atmosphere, the Italian American food, good steaks and moderate prices. The Caesar salad, pastas and cheesecake are all good.

MIKAYLA   CALIFORNIA   13/20

Casa Madrona Inn, 801 Bridgeway Blvd., Sausalito 94965
415-331-5888, *Dinner nightly, Brunch Sun.*, $$$$

A new name, a new look, a new menu and new-and-improved service have given life to the restaurant perched atop this charming toney inn. A couple of new chefs have neither hurt nor vastly improved the food, and the view of the Bay and the Sausalito yacht harbor remains among the most panoramic in the Bay Area. Some of the memorable dishes are the crab salad, a fork-tender rack of lamb and a luscious crème brûlée.

MULBERRY STREET PIZZERIA   PIZZA   ¢

101 Smith Ranch Rd., San Rafael 94903
415-472-7272, *Lunch Mon.-Fri., Dinner nightly*

Now that Mulberry Street has settled in across the street from a massive theater complex, you no longer have to wait interminably at the front door to get a taste of owner Ted Rowe's hearty, generously topped pizzas. The Caesar salad is better than many of those offered by upscale restaurants, and the dome-shaped calzone may be the North Bay's best.

NORTH SEA VILLAGE   CHINESE   13/20

300 Turney Ave., Sausalito 94965
415-331-3300, *Lunch & Dinner daily*, $$

The arrival of this Hong Kong–style Chinese restaurant has been welcomed by Marin diners. In addition to the sophisticated seafood dishes for which Hong Kong is known, this stylish and elegant restaurant offers some of the finest and most delicate dim sum in the Bay Area, served daily. At dinner, check out the dried scallop soup or spicy salt-baked prawns.

PACIFIC CAFÉ   SEAFOOD   13/20

850 College Ave., Kentfield 94904
415-456-3898, *Dinner nightly*, $$

Simple, fresh fish has been the draw here since 1975. Little known outside the immediate area, it's a terrific find if you're in the neighborhood. Moist, quickly sautéed sand dabs are better than at most San Francisco grills; while a couple of other fish, depending on availability, are deep-fried to perfection.

PING'S   CHINESE   13/20

817 W. Francisco Blvd., San Rafael 94901
415-492-1638, *Lunch & Dinner daily*, $

You'll find reliable regional Chinese cuisine in a room decorated with Asian artifacts and art works. We've enjoyed the chicken in lettuce cups, and the deep-flavored sizzling rice soup. Other good choices are the meaty, barbecued spare ribs, tasty prawns with lobster sauce and cashew chicken.

THE RICE TABLE   INDONESIAN   13/20

1617 Fourth St., San Rafael 94901
415-456-1801, *Dinner Wed.-Sun.,* $$

One of the first Indonesian restaurants in the Bay Area is still the best. The rijstaffel ("rice table") of a dozen or so small dishes make up an exotic grazing feast priced at $16.95 or $19.95. The sambals—creamy peanut, tart cilantro and incendiary chile—are very good, as are the Indonesian-style egg rolls and prawns cooked in a tangy butter-tamarind sauce. Salads are fresh and the long-simmered curries are savory. Even the omnipresent fried banana is a treat.

ROBATA GRILL & SUSHI   JAPANESE/SUSHI   13/20

591 Redwood Hwy., Mill Valley 94941
415-381-8400, *Lunch Mon.-Fri., Dinner nightly,* $$

The attractive dining room has high ceilings with large, floating, colorful fabric hangings. Start with some edamame (salty, cooked soy beans) and a fine California roll. Make sure to taste the soup with soba (buckwheat noodle soup with chicken). Also enjoyable is the tempura prawn rolled in rice and seaweed, topped with grilled freshwater eel. Service is gracious.

ROSSETTI OSTERIA ROMANA   ITALIAN   13/20

510 San Anselmo Ave., San Anselmo 94960
415-459-7937, *Lunch & Dinner Tues.-Sun., Brunch Sun.,* $$

The focus here is on house-made pastas and pizzas baked in a wood-fired oven. However, it's the crusts—thin, crisp, chewy and faintly smoky—that make Rossetti's pies some of the best around. Pastas and specials aren't quite up to that standard, but they're solid osteria fare.

SUSHI TO DAI FOR   JAPANESE/SUSHI   13/20

869 Fourth St., San Rafael 94901
415-721-0392, *Lunch Mon.-Sat., Dinner nightly,* $$

The name of this wildly popular spot is a play on the name of its owner, Dai Takeda, whose high-caliber sushi shows careful preparation. Takeda's forte is offbeat "designer" sushi, like the Harley-Davidson roll, a blend of deep-fried yellowtail, avocado, cucumber and sprouts. Try the donburi, small bowls of rice topped with meat, fish or vegetables.

THEP LELA   THAI   13/20

411 Strawberry Village, Mill Valley 94941
415-383-3444, *Lunch Mon.-Sat., Dinner nightly,* $

Despite the restaurant's generic location in a shopping center, proprietors Natalie and Sak Kamloonwasaraj have made sure that the ambience and service equal the caliber of the food coming out of their tiny kitchen. The restaurant is filled with ornate Thai artworks and a primitive-style mural of Thailand. The Thai salads, the rich and creamy coconut-milk curries and the pad Thai, exhibit the fine balance of flavors and textures that makes this cuisine so popular.

YAHIRO SUSHI BAR & RESTAURANT   JAPANESE/JAPANESE 12/20

69 Center Blvd., San Anselmo 94960
415-459-1504, *Tues.-Sun.*, $$

This unassuming purveyor of fresh, well-made sushi, is tucked away in a tiny building partially hidden from the street. Beyond the quality of its raw fish, Yahiro's chief asset is its neighborly atmosphere. All the usual nigiri and maki sushi are represented. A few other traditional dishes like sukiyaki and teriyaki are also offered, but skip the tempura.

YES BURGERS & MALTS   ¢

5035 Northgate Mall, San Rafael 94901
415-472-6235, *Open daily*

For just a couple of bucks more than you would pay for a limp, tasteless meal at a franchise joint, you can get a one-third-pound burger cooked to order, along with a malted as thick as the ones in the days when cars had tail fins.

YET WAH   CHINESE   13/20

2019 Larkspur Landing Cir., Larkspur 94939
415-461-3631, *Lunch & Dinner daily*, $

Located in the Larkspur Landing Shopping Center, this is a great place to savor dim sum at lunch: barbecued pork, foil-wrapped chicken, deep fried prawns, steamed vegetable crêpes, barbecued pork buns and pot stickers. The prawns with mushrooms are delectable; so is the three-princess chicken.

GOURMET SHOPS & MORE

BAKERIES: BREAD & PASTRIES

HOUSE OF BAGELS & NY STYLE DELI

640 Fourth St., San Rafael 94901
415-454-5348, *Open daily*

The owner, a transplanted New Yorker, not only makes all manner of bagels—even some California-type flavors—but also flies in pastrami and corned beef from the Big Apple. Salads are made in-house.

MARIN BAGELS

1560 Fourth St., San Rafael 94901
415-457-8127, *Open Mon.-Sat.*

Now distributed throughout the Bay Area, Marin bagels are made in some wacky flavors, which any self-respecting bagel lover would shun. But anyone will enjoy the onion, garlic, sesame and poppyseed varieties as well as the plain. The bagels are chewy and don't turn stale after one day.

PASTICCERIA RULLI

464 Magnolia Ave., Larkspur 94939
415-924-7478, *Open daily*

Gary Rulli is a pâtissier extraordinaire, fanatically devoted to producing the finest Italian pastries, cakes, candies and gelati in his handsome shop in downtown Larkspur. You'll always find special breads and pastries to complement holidays. You can enjoy a light snack and cup of espresso in the adjacent café. See also Whole Foods Market, in this chapter, whose in-house bakery produces a variety of breads.

PÂTISSERIE LAMBERT

457 Miller Ave., Mill Valley 94941
415-389-1977, *Open Mon.-Sat.*

Chef-owner Sarah Lambert is quite a rising-star chef. A visit to her high-tech style shop reveals a few savory items like classic quiche, but its real focus is French pastries. The store closes at 2 p.m. on Monday and Tuesday and 6 p.m. Wednesday through Saturday, so arrive early to pick up tonight's dessert.

CHEESE

TOMALES BAY FOODS

80 Fourth St., Point Reyes Station 94938
415-663-8153, *Open Wed.-Sun.*

Former Chez Panisse chef Peggy Smith has created a terrific take-out emporium in this cute little town. The mostly Mediterranean menu features salads and sandwiches. Partner

Sue Conley spotlights local produce and artisanal cheeses, including Smith and Conley's own from their Cowgirl Creamery, adjacent to the store.

CHOCOLATE & CANDY

LYLA'S CHOCOLATES

417 Miller Ave., Mill Valley 94941
415-383-8887, *Open Mon.-Sat.*

Handmade chocolates that look as good as they taste have made this shop a favorite of North Bay chocoholics. Any type of chocolate can be made into any type of shape—they have 1,000 molds—but must be special-ordered. The house-made truffles and boxed chocolates are legendary.

COFFEE & TEA

CHAI OF LARKSPUR

25 Ward St., Larkspur 94939
415-945-7161, *Open daily*

Now that upscale espresso bars are as common in Marin as SUVs, it's time for tea. Or at least that's the theory behind this cozy, Victorian-style tea salon. More than 70 imported teas and tea paraphernalia are on sale here. Chai also serves afternoon and evening tea with a variety of sweet and savory snacks. Afternoon tea for kids can be a special treat.

GRAFFEO COFFEE ROASTING CO.

1314 Fourth St., San Rafael 94901
415-457-5131, *Open Mon.-Sat.*

See review in SAN FRANCISCO chapter.

PEET'S COFFEE & TEA

88 Throckmorton Ave., Mill Valley 94941
415-381-8227, *Open daily*

See review in SAN FRANCISCO chapter. **Also in Greenbrae (276 Bon Air Shopping Center, 415-461-2695).**

DELIS

A.G. FERRARI FOODS

107 Corte Madera Town Center, Corte Madera 94925
415-927-4347, *Open daily*

See review in Marin Restaurants.

LET'S EAT

1 Blackfield Dr., Cove Shopping Center, Tiburon 94920
415-383-3663, *Open daily*

This tiny shop seems perpetually jammed with both products and customers. It offers classy and sophisticated food to go that's miles beyond standard deli fare. Particularly popular are the Chinese chicken salad, curried turkey and fruit salad, and sandwich number eight: poached chicken on focaccia, with fresh basil, aïoli, and roasted red peppers. For Thanksgiving and other holidays, you can put together a complete guest-worthy dinner from the dishes prepared here.

See also House of Bagels under Bakeries above.

ETHNIC MARKETS

AZTECA MARKET NO. 2   MEXICAN

802 Fourth St., San Rafael 94901
415-457-2518, *Open daily*

You'll find just about everything you'll need for a complete Mexican meal at this small market in downtown San Rafael. The emphasis is on canned and bottled goods, but there's also a limited selection of fresh produce and pastries, along with a variety of dried Mexican chiles in barrels, all reasonably priced.

ASIAN MARKET   ASIAN

5 Mary St., San Rafael 94901
415-459-7133, *Open Mon.-Sat.*

Besides all manner of Asian canned goods, dry noodles and huge bags of rice, this little store also has its own meat and seafood department, making it a one-stop destination for anyone hankering to stir-fry dinner.

FARMERS' MARKET

MARIN FARMERS' MARKET

Marin County Civic Center, Hwy. 101 & San Pedro Rd., San Rafael 94903
No phone, *Open Thurs. & Sun. year-round*

A small forest of white tents in a parking lot behind Marin County's Frank Lloyd Wright-designed Civic Center marks the twice-weekly farmers' market, open from 8 a.m. to 1 p.m. During Marin's usually warm and sunny spring and summer days, the market is as much a crafts bazaar and meeting place for moms with kids as it is a place to buy high-quality fruits and vegetables from local growers.

GOURMET MARKETS

MILL VALLEY MARKET

12 Corte Madera Ave., Mill Valley 94941
415-388-3222, *Open daily*

Mill Valley Market is to your garden-variety supermarket what a race-tuned Ferrari is to a Chevy station wagon. Seemingly every gourmet product known competes for space in this compact store. You'll find an excellent fresh seafood counter, more handmade sausages than you ever thought existed and a separate wine and cheese shop whose selection is even more amazing.

MOLLY STONE'S

270 Bel Air, Greenbrae 94901
415-461-1164, *Open daily*

See review in SAN FRANCISCO. **Also in Sausalito (100 Harbor Drive, Sausalito 415-331-6900).**

TRADER JOE'S

337 Third St., San Rafael 94901
415-454-9530, *Open daily*

A WalMart for the foodie set, Trader Joe's crams this barn-like, bare-bones room with a staggering array of food and wine products, from convenience foods like frozen burritos to gourmet items like vintage French Champagnes. Prices are low, but service is minimal and the place has all the ambience of an auto parts warehouse. Good deals abound, although you may have to look carefully to find them.

WHOLE FOODS MARKET

414 Miller Ave., Mill Valley 94941
415-381-1200, *Open daily*

See listing in SAN FRANCISCO chapter. **Also in San Rafael (340 Third St., 415-451-6333).**

HEALTH FOODS

MILL VALLEY HEALTH FOODS

11 E. Blithedale Ave., Mill Valley 94941
415-388-7434, *Open daily*

This is a great place to buy herbs, supplements, vitamins and to relax with a made-to-order carrot juice at the Juice Bar.

WHOLE FOODS MARKET

414 Miller Ave., Mill Valley 94941
415-381-1200, *Open daily*

See review above.

ICE CREAM

See Pasticceria Rulli in Bakeries above.

KITCHEN EQUIPMENT

HOMECHEF COOKING SCHOOL & KITCHEN STORE

329 Corte Madera Town Center, Corte Madera 94925
415-927-3191, *Open daily*

An upscale purveyor of professional cookware and gourmet food products, HomeChef's jam-packed shop is just the place to find that specialized piece of equipment you can't find anywhere else. At the demonstration kitchen in back of the store, cooking classes are taught by local chefs and food authorities.

MEAT, POULTRY & SEAFOOD

CARUSO'S

Foot of Harbor St., Sausalito 94965
415-332-1015, *Open daily*

At the end of the pier facing the yacht harbor and Richardson Bay, Caruso's has been dispensing boating and fishing supplies and fresh seafood since 1957. There's a small café where you can get burgers—salmon, calamari and ham—as well as soups, salads, sandwiches and seafood cocktails. The retail selection is limited, but fish and shellfish are sparkling and smell fresh from the sea.

FOR GAYOT'S UPDATED SAN FRANCISCO RESTAURANT REVIEWS, GO TO:

Digitalcity.com/sanfrancisco/dining

ROCKY'S QUALITY MEATS

71 San Pablo Ave., San Rafael 94903
415-479-2131, *Open Mon.-Sat.*

This old-fashioned butcher shop can properly prepare a rack of lamb or a crown roast and bone out a turkey breast—services missing in mega-supermarkets. Grill-ready steaks come in either prime or choice cuts.

PRODUCE

DAVID'S FINEST PRODUCE

Corte Madera Town Center, 341 Corte Madera 94925
415-927-2431, *Open daily*

From humble beginnings in a converted gas station, David Findlay's small produce stand has expanded to a spacious, colorfully painted room in Corte Madera Town Center, a local shopping mall that's making a concerted effort to bring in high-quality restaurants and food purveyors. David's focuses on what's in season, and in spring and summer it overflows with lusciously ripe fruits and vegetables.

WINE, BEER & SPIRITS

BEVERAGES, 'N MORE

760 W. Francisco Blvd., San Rafael 94901
415-456-8367, *Open daily*

No false advertising here: the Marin Beverages, 'n More is a warehouse-size room packed with good things to eat and drink, from sparkling water and vintage French Champagnes to dozens of salsas and fresh caviar priced at about half of what it would cost anyplace else in the Bay Area. The roster of California wines can be overwhelming; the selection of French, Italian, German, Australian and South American wines is less so. A counter is devoted to the display of fine stogies.

MICHAEL'S WINE CELLAR

207 Corte Madera Ave., Corte Madera 94925
415-927-7029, *Open Tues.-Sun.*

Proprietor Michael Boyd offers the kind of personalized service that's rare in any business nowadays. His cramped shop is full of hard-to-find wines from small and obscure producers, as well as a few carefully chosen "value" wines. It has a wine bar, where five days a week Boyd offers flights of still and sparkling wines, in addition to fortified wines such as sherry and port.

"Gault Millau is provocative and frank."
—*Los Angeles Times*

"You will enjoy their prose."
—*US News & World Report*

"Gault Millau is the toque of the town."
—*San Francisco Examiner*

321/99

East Bay

MAP OF THE EAST BAY

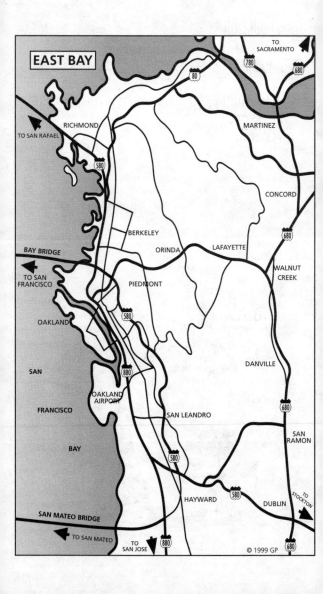

INTRODUCTION

The East Bay encompasses everything from gritty, multi-cultural Oakland, home to a rainbow of ethnic restaurants, to the rolling hills of Walnut Creek, a former bedroom community with a burgeoning population of two-income households seeking fine dining and gourmet shops. Berkeley, site of the University of California, not only produced Chez Panisse, the restaurant that spurred a fresh-food revolution in restaurants 25 years ago, but also hosts many artisanal food producers, bakers and entrepreneurs meeting the demands of sophisticated East Bay palates. Other major towns with good restaurants are Alameda, Concord, Danville, Emeryville, Lafayette, Orinda, Piedmont and San Ramon.

RESTAURANTS

AJANTA
REGIONAL INDIAN   14/20

1888 Solano Ave., Berkeley 94707
510-526-4373, *Lunch & Dinner daily, $*

Chef-owner Lachu Moorjani offers an Indian dining experience a cut above most, with attentive service and a selection of regional Indian specialties. Even the look is sophisticated: Buddhist cave paintings cover the ceiling and murals of Indian life warm the walls. The full dinner is a bargain, as it includes pappadum, appetizers like tandoori chicken wings, a choice of three entrées, basmati rice, tandoori bread, a vegetable, a trio of pickles and chutneys and a sweet ending. The badal jaam—pan-fried slices of eggplant topped with a fragrant tomato sauce and served with garlic-laced yogurt—is outstanding.

AMFORA FINO
MEDITERRANEAN   13/20

65 Moraga Way, Orinda 94563
925-253-1322, *Lunch Mon.-Fri., Dinner Tues.-Sun, $$*

Owner Alexander Gailas combines a Greek background with experience in Italian restaurants. Your eyes are not deceiving you: the appetizer menu really does include bruschetta, dolmadakia, spanakopita and calamari fritti. The Greek Athenese spinach salad with a sherry-orange dressing is just as tasty as the Italian Fantasia with romaine, endive, Gorgonzola, pears and walnuts. The pasta, pizza, calzone crowd is kept happy with many choices. We also recommend the cannelloni or the 16-ounce veal chop. Desserts include a to-die-for Italian zabaglione cake.

ARCO-IRIS
FUSION   13/20

1332-C Park St., Alameda 94501
510-521-4747, *Lunch Mon.-Fri., Dinner nightly, $$*

What a delightful surprise to find this sublime, romantic restaurant in a courtyard off busy Park Street. Each of the two elegant dining rooms has only six tables. Plush chairs and abstract art add to the decor. Here you can enjoy flavors from around the world, ranging from a soba noodle cake immersed in a curried court bouillon and covered with shellfish, and a grilled pork chop glazed with saké, orange juice and ancho chiles, to halibut steamed in jasmine tea. If the soup of the day is grilled corn with scallops and shrimp, be sure to order it. Desserts run the gamut from tiramisu to a rich dark-chocolate sabayon.

AUTUMN MOON CAFÉ   CALIFORNIA   13/20

3909 Grand Ave., Oakland 94611
510-595-3200, *Breakfast & Lunch Wed.-Fri., Brunch Sat.-Sun., Dinner nightly*, $-$$

This is a quintessential neighborhood restaurant—note the stack of coloring books for the kids. Weekend brunch runs from lox and bagels to huevos rancheros. At dinner, the old-fashioned iceberg-lettuce salad is napped with creamy blue-cheese dressing, the grilled skirt steak comes with red-chile onion rings, clouds of garlic mashed potatoes and blanched vegetables. Hearty desserts include warm bread pudding with hot fudge sauce.

BATTAMBANG   CAMBODIAN   13/20

850 Broadway, Oakland 94607
510-839-8815, *Lunch & Dinner daily*, $

This modest little eatery on the ground floor of a high-rise condominium complex in downtown Oakland, is the best Cambodian restaurant in the Bay Area. Sample a cross-section of Cambodian dishes via the inexpensive "special combo," which includes shredded chicken breast in a lime-freshened cabbage salad, red lemon-grass soup with pineapple, chiles and chicken chunks, a plate of grilled meat items with dipping sauce, plus rice and fried rice noodles.

BAY WOLF   MEDITERRANEAN   15/20

3853 Piedmont Ave., Oakland 94611
510-655-6004, *Lunch Mon.-Fri., Dinner nightly*, $$$

In 1995, owners Michael Wild and Larry Goldman celebrated the 20th anniversary of this well-loved, unpretentious restaurant, often described as the Chez Panisse of Oakland. The menu changes often to highlight the cuisines of a wide variety of regions. Appetizers include a silky duck flan paired with duck rillettes and smoked duck breast, grilled sardines and a perfect Caesar. Appealing entrées include grilled swordfish with lentils, Liberty Ranch duck panzanella with grapes and lamb shanks with polenta.

BETTE'S OCEANVIEW DINER   AMERICAN   ¢

1807 Fourth St., Berkeley 94710
510-644-3230, *Breakfast & Lunch daily*

Don't miss Bette's soufflé pancake filled with fresh fruit or chocolate, the corned beef hash with poached eggs or the omelets, especially with cheese and herbs. You finds lots of good shopping on the burgeoning Fourth Street corridor after breakfast.

BIGHORN GRILL   AMERICAN   14/20

2410 San Ramon Valley Blvd., San Ramon 94583
510-838-5678, *Lunch & Dinner daily, $$$*

Though new, Bighorn Grill is a big ol' restaurant. It serves big ol' plates of big-flavored, stomach-filling, all-American food. It serves big ol' martinis in glasses that could double as birdbaths, and it plays to big crowds because the prices aren't quite as big as everything else. Partner and designer Pat Kuleto gave the shopping-center restaurant an upscale mountain-cabin look, complete with bighorn sheep motifs. We loved the savory spit-roasted prime rib, the massive pork chops and, for dessert, the big slab of blackstrap molasses gingerbread with vanilla ice cream, caramel sauce and spiced pecans.

BLACKHAWK GRILL   MEDITERRANEAN   12/20

3540 Blackhawk Plaza Cir., Danville 94506
925-736-4295, *Lunch & Dinner daily, Brunch Sun., $$$*

The focus at this upscale shopping-center restaurant is on pizza and other small plates kissed by the Mediterranean. Main dishes include seafood from the wood-fired oven and hearty meats from the grill and rotisserie. The most stunning meal is brunch at an outside table overlooking the beautiful pond while a jazz combo plays. If the Meyer lemon tart is on the menu, go for it.

BRAZIO   ITALIAN   15/20

3412 Blackhawk Plaza, Danville 94506
925-736-3000, *Lunch & Dinner daily, $$$*

The newest of Napa chef Fred Halpert's restaurants, Brazio is a stunning Tuscan restaurant with an open kitchen that runs the entire length of one dining room. Food is served on colorful pottery plates or in deep bowls. The warm bread comes with butter and a pungent olive oil. Steaks, including a double-cut T-bone for two, are house specialties. An outstanding appetizer, generous enough to be shared by two or even three, is the seasonal vegetable antipasti. Save room for the mocha mousse cake with chocolate.

BRIDGES RESTAURANT & BAR   FUSION   14/20

44 Church St., Danville 94526
925-820-7200, *Lunch Fri., Dinner nightly, $$$*

☎ 💻 🎎 🍷 🍸 ⟨⟩

   Locally, Bridges is probably most famous for its appearance in the movie Mrs. Doubtfire, though it really deserves fame for its first-rate cuisine, some of it with a pronounced Asian influence. Chef Kevin Gin is equally adept preparing a salmon and scallop mousse wrapped in rice paper and drizzled with lemon beurre blanc, or a hearty roast leg of lamb with garlic mashed potatoes. For dessert, the profiteroles are delicious.

BUCCI'S   CALIFORNIA/ITALIAN   13/20

6121 Hollis St., Emeryville 94608
510-547-4725, *Lunch Mon.-Fri., Dinner Mon.-Sat., $$*

☎ 🎎 🍸

   In the morning, this place is an espresso bar for the locals. Lunch and dinner may surprise you. Although the menu is simple—pizzas, pastas, salads and chicken or fish—the food is thoughtfully prepared, and the ingredients of the highest quality. The high-ceiling restaurant with lots of windows provide an airy setting. Wines are mostly from California with a few nice selections from Italy and France.

CACTUS TAQUERIA   MEXICAN   ¢

5525 College Ave., Oakland 94618
510-547-1305, *Lunch & Dinner daily*

🎎

   Cactus offers generous, flavorful burritos, tacos, tamales, tortas and enchiladas. You order at the counter from a long list of fillings that include pollo asado, red or green mole, shrimp, carnitas, and the lighter but equally delicious vegetables asados, a combination of grilled squash and seasonal vegetables marinated in garlic and red wine. The tortillas are lard free, the chips are fried in safflower oil, and the pork and beef are from high-quality purveyor Niman Schell. Also in Berkeley (1881 Solano Ave., 510-528-1881).

CAFÉ AT CHEZ PANISSE   CONTEMPORARY   15/20

1517 Shattuck Ave., Berkeley 94709
510-548-5525, *Lunch & Dinner Mon.-Sat., $$*

☎

   You can shut your eyes, point at the menu and be assured of receiving an array of finely tuned flavors. Unlike the Chez Panisse dining room downstairs (see below), the Café, with its comfortable interior of wood, copper and brick, is open for both lunch and dinner, and it offers more choices. The simple dishes are divine: baby lettuces with baked goat cheese (the dish has become almost a cliché, but not here, where they not only invented but also perfected it); a pizza tart with goat cheese, mozzarella, herbs and prosciutto; or grilled fish. You'll usually find seven salads to choose from, four or five entrées, plus a nice selection of wines by the glass.

CAFÉ FANNY   AMERICAN/BREAKFAST   ¢

1603 San Pablo Ave., Berkeley 94702
510-524-5447, *Breakfast Mon.-Sat.*

This tiny stand-up bar with a few outdoor seats was founded by Alice Waters of Chez Panisse fame. It has only a toaster and egg steamer, so don't expect eggs over easy and home fries. Instead, enjoy a bowl of cappuccino, poached eggs, great toast made with Acme bread, or the signature granola with fruit.

CAFÉ FOUR-ELEVEN   CALIFORNIA/ITALIAN   12/20

411 Hartz Ave., Danville 94526
925-552-5821, *Lunch & Dinner Tues.-Sat.,* $$

Formerly the Wine Sellars Bistro, Café Four-Eleven recently changed its name and menu. It's still a cozy restaurant with most of the seating in a glassed-in dining room, and everything looks the same, right down to the chairs with their distinctive wine-print upholstery. Start with gnocchi or one of several pasta dishes, then move on to a New York steak with a Jack Daniels green-peppercorn sauce, or Tuscan chicken. The wine list reflects the wide variety sold at the restaurant's nearby wine shop.

CAFÉ ROUGE   CONTEMPORARY   12/20

1782 Fourth St., Berkeley 94710
510-525-1440, *Lunch & Dinner daily,* $$$

A welcome addition to the East Bay, Café Rouge reminds us of San Francisco's Zuni Café. Patrons can slurp up five or six varieties of oysters, sample any number of lovely salads or a good charcuterie plate, then settle on such satisfying main courses as a grilled steak with red wine butter, leg of lamb, spaghetti with mussels or a delicious spit-roasted chicken. On one visit rude service marred a nice dinner.

CAFÉ RUSTICA   MEDITERRANEAN   12/20

5422 College Ave., Oakland 94618
510-654-1601, *Dinner Tues.-Sun.,* $$

Café Rustica satisfies hungry diners in two ways. One, it loads its huge pizzas with an array of interesting toppings. Two, it serves well-portioned tapas in the lively upstairs dining room. The pizzas are good, but we come for tapas like the tortilla español studded with chunks of potato, onion, eggplant and mushrooms, and the marinated chicken wings with tomato-cucumber salad.

CAFFÈ DELLE STELLE   ITALIAN   12/20

1532 N. Main St., Walnut Creek 94525
925-943-2393, *Lunch & Dinner daily,* $$

Don't look for subtlety and sophistication here—look for soulful satisfaction at reasonable. Skip the dessert-sweet starter of Chianti-braised pears and head for the ricotta-filled roast eggplant with pizziola sauce, or the pasta rustica, a winning combination of orecchiette with roasted red potatoes, pancetta, sage, Fontina and truffle oil. The tiramisu is more hearty than elegant, but it's pretty good.

CAFFÈ 817   ITALIAN   11/20

817 Washington St., Oakland 94607
510-271-7965 *Breakfast & Lunch Mon.-Sat., $*

Concrete, mahogany and metal blend with style in this Italianate café. The line at lunch is for the sandwiches such as eggplant, sun-dried tomato and feta on a baguette, or grilled prosciutto and mozzarella on focaccia. The accompanying small salad of organic greens dressed in a heavy-handed balsamic vinaigrette is a bit too punchy to eat on its own but terrific when tucked into the sandwich.

CASA ORINDA   AMERICAN   12/20

20 Bryant Way, Orinda 94563
925-254-2981, *Dinner nightly, $$$*

Casa Orinda is a delightful throwback to a time when gastronomic correctness wasn't even a gleam in its advocates' eyes. Customers in the impossibly packed dining room chow down on tire-size onion rings with a blue-cheese and sour-cream dip, huge pieces of fried chicken with plenty of rich cream gravy, and towering, old-fashioned ice cream sundaes drenched in chocolate sauce.

CESAR   SPANISH   14/20

1515 Shattuck Ave., Berkeley 94709
510-883-0222, *Open daily 3 p.m.-midnight, $$*

This self-described "bar with food" has been packed since it opened its doors, offering Berkeleyites a truly Spanish-style café for drinking and grazing. What could be more fun than the opportunity to explore 19 rums or 17 vodkas, not to mention flights of Cognacs, single-malt scotches, whiskeys and grappas as well as a reasonably priced wine list with good Iberian offerings? A broad array of piquant tapas such as piquillo peppers and fresh cheese, fried potatoes with tomato and aïoli, pungent salt cod and potato purée, and the not-to-be-missed batter-fried scallions with romesco sauce add up to a lively evening of dining. The place can get loud as the evening progresses (the attractive tiled walls and handmade white-oak benches don't absorb much sound), but don't be put off by the crowd, as the tables turn quickly.

CHEESE BOARD   PIZZA   ¢

1512 Shattuck Ave., Berkeley 94709
510-549-3045, *Lunch Tues.-Thurs. & Sat.*

This minimalist pizzeria is operated by the neighboring Cheese Board Collective cheese store and bakery. The pizzas feature a chewy, sourdough crust and cheeses selected from the vast variety available a few doors away. A recent favorite was topped with onion, garlic, cilantro and tomato, with feta and mozzarella and a bright sprinkling of lemon zest.

CHEZ PANISSE   CONTEMPORARY   16/20

1517 Shattuck Ave., Berkeley 94709
510-548-5525, *Dinner Mon.-Sat.,* $$$$

After more than 25 years of business in Berkeley's "gourmet ghetto," Alice Waters' groundbreaking restaurant remains one of the standards by which other restaurants are judged. Waters' passion for procuring only the finest and freshest raw materials is legendary. First-time diners may be surprised at the simplicity of the menu, which changes daily and is served to the entire dining room (meaning you have no choices). Devotees know that even an elemental-sounding dish like a Maine lobster-chanterelle salad will be brought to new levels by the orange-oil dressing. You'll savor every bite of dishes that make the most of the bounteous local produce, such as a black-turnip confit with foie gras salad and balsamic vinegar. Despite its reputation as a temple to gastronomy, Chez Panisse's ambience is surprisingly informal, but the service is as impeccable as the food. A few things are worth noting: the prix-fixe menu is posted each Saturday for the coming week, but you will need to make reservations well in advance. Also, a 15 percent gratuity is added to your bill in the European manner.

COMMODORE'S WATERFRONT CAFÉ   CREOLE   12/20

2402 Mariner Island Dr., Alameda 94501
510-523-3474, *Lunch & Dinner daily,* $$

Adjacent to the original Chevys on the quaint island of Alameda, executive chef Michael Richards, who did stints with Wolfgang Puck and New Orleans chef Paul Prudhomme, turns out lobster bisque, oysters Bienville, crabcakes and shrimp Creole. Non-southern faves include a 14-ounce rib-eye. Save room for the ten-layer chocolate-bourbon cake.

DOUG'S   BARBECUE   13/20

3600 San Pablo Ave., Emeryville 94608
510-655-9048, *Lunch & Dinner daily* $

Located in a neighborhood that makes you glad to see police cars periodically cruising by, Doug's produces fiery, intensely smoky, thoroughly addictive barbecue. Strictly take-out, Doug's usually has a long line. The chicken is very good, the beef and pork ribs are terrific, and if you want barbecued goat, Doug's has that too. Baked beans, potato salad, coleslaw and sweet-potato pie are all worth carting home.

GARIBALDI'S ON COLLEGE MEDITERRANEAN 13/20

5356 College Ave., Oakland 94618
510-595-4000, *Lunch Mon.-Fri., Dinner daily, Brunch Sun.,* $$

See listing in SAN FRANCISCO chapter.

GEOFFREY'S INNER CIRCLE AMERICAN 12/20

410 14th St., Oakland 94607
510-839-4644, *free appetizers nightly, Brunch Sun.,* $

Geoffrey's is primarily a bar, but every night between 5:30 and 8:30 p.m., a spread including lasagne, bread, salad and pan-fried chicken wings is set out for the taking. Sunday Brunch, occasionally a gospel brunch, is yummy and great fun.

GIGLIO ITALIAN 12/20

5427 College Ave., Oakland 94618
510-594-0798, *Dinner nightly,* $

This is not a mock-up of an authentic Italian restaurant—this is the real thing. The lightly cured salmon carpaccio is a good start. Of the seven pizzas, the one with mushrooms, mozzarella, tomato sauce and truffle oil was the most compelling. Rosemary roasted chicken and braised veal shank with soft polenta are here. But it is the pastas—rich, cheesy, comfortingly gooey—that satisfy your soul. The house-made desserts include a stellar tiramisu.

GINGER ISLAND AMERICAN 13/20

1820 Fourth St., Berkeley 94710
510-644-0444, *Lunch & Dinner daily, Brunch Sat.-Sun.,* $$

The fresh ginger ale, the mix of fries (yellow potatoes, yams and taro) and some of the noodles have remained, but Ginger Island has morphed from a fusion restaurant into a very good American one. The most popular dinner entrées are the grilled guava-glazed pork chops, baby back ribs and roast chicken with mashers. Don't miss the ginger cake with orange cream.

GREEN GARDEN CHINESE/DIM SUM 12/20

1101 Civic Dr., Walnut Creek 94563
925-938-8878, *Open daily,* $

Traditional dim sum, steamed, fried, pan-fried, stir-fried and baked, is the draw here weekdays at lunch—and big time on weekends. Our favorites are the juicy har gow (shrimp dumplings), sui mai (pork in a noodle dumpling) and pan-fried flat-leaf chive dumplings, washed down with jasmine tea.

IL PORCELLINO   ITALIAN   12/20

6111 La Salle Ave., Oakland 94611
510-339-2144, *Lunch Mon.-Sat., Dinner nightly, $*
☎ 🏃

The colorfully stained cement floor and partially glazed exposed brick wall are reminiscent of rustic Italy. Against a background of Italian pop music, the Florentine owner greets everyone like a returning friend. Start with the fritto misto, an array of deep-fried calamari, shrimp, artichokes and lemon. The Caesar salad is swathed in a creamy, lemon-spiked, Parmesan-rich dressing best suited for those who lack affection for anchovy and garlic. The light potato gnocchi in a cream-enriched rosemary-tomato sauce are luscious, as is the chicken piccata.

KATHMANDU   NEPALESE/TIBETAN   13/20

1410 Solano Ave., Albany 94706
510-526-3222, *Dinner nightly, $$*
☎ 🏃

Dining at Kathmandu is like dining in an art gallery; the Nepalese owners also own East Bay gift shops. The simply prepared char-grilled lamb marinated in spices, and the room-temperature smoked lamb marinated in a spicy sauce with onions, are good examples of the cuisine. Vegetarian diners will enjoy a thick curry made with 19 varieties of beans in a garlic-kissed tomato sauce. Start your meal with the traditional Tibetan thukpa, ginger and garlic soup, or chatamari, a soft rice-flour bread stuffed with spicy chicken.

KOREA PALACE   KOREAN   12/20

4436 Clayton Rd., Concord 94521
925-674-0180, *Lunch & Dinner daily, $$*
☎ 👯

Beyond Korea Palace's almost monolithic facade is a charming dining room that includes a small indoor waterfall and a "stream" spanned by an arching wooden bridge. The restaurant's location on a multi-lane suburban highway belies the rigorously authentic cuisine. The familiar Korean dish of marinated and charbroiled steak is very good here, as are the tempura-style fried prawns.

LA BAYOU CAJUN & CREOLE CAFÉ   CAJUN/CREOLE 12/20

3278 Adeline St., Berkeley 94703
510-594-9302, *Lunch & Early Dinner Tues.-Sat., $*
☎ 👯

Not every Cajun/Creole restaurant offers smoked turkey-apricot sausage as one of the choices in its sausage po'-boy sandwiches. Traditionalists will opt for the Louisiana hot or mild sausage or, perhaps, choose a fresh seafood po'-boy made with Mississippi catfish or oysters. Tasty as the sandwiches may be, it's the chicken-sausage gumbo or the jambalaya that brings home the complexity of seasonings in Cajun/Creole cuisine. Seasonal specials include crawfish etouffée, dirty rice and deep-fried turkey. End your meal with a slice of sweet-potato pie and a steaming cup of chicory coffee. (Dinner until 7 p.m. except on Friday until 9 p.m.)

LALIME'S   MEDITERRANEAN   14/20

1329 Gilman St., Berkeley 94706
510-527-9838, *Dinner nightly, $$*

Lalime's serves California-inspired Mediterranean fare to a loyal following in a warm, two-level dining room. Although prices have crept up over time, the prix-fixe menus remain good values. One night the adventure began with a risotto with scallops, well paired with a glass of 1994 Vermentino de Gallura; a grilled rack of lamb marinated with pomegranate and herbs was paired with a 1993 Solitude; and "chocolate silk" cake was paired with an Italian Muscatelli. Vegetarians will enjoy the artichoke stuffed with winter vegetables and chanterelles on a richly spiced bed of couscous.

LA MAISON   FRENCH   12/20

3774 Castro Valley Blvd., Castro Valley 94546
510-733-2780, *Dinner Tues.-Sat., $-$$*

Located in a little white house ringed with twinkling lights and surrounded by gardens, La Maison is a welcome sight in Castro Valley. Since the chef grows his own sorrel, don't miss the soup he makes with it. Other classic dishes include frogs' legs, sautéed prawns and scallops in a rich lobster-Cognac sauce and saddle of rabbit enlivened with Dijon mustard. For dessert, we love the floating island, mounds of ethereal meringue gliding on a sea of crème anglaise. The wine list is small but adequate.

LA NOTE   FRENCH   13/20

2377 Shattuck Ave., Berkeley 94704
510-843-1535, *Breakfast & Lunch Mon.-Fri., Dinner Fri.-Sat., Brunch Sat.-Sun., $$-$$$*

La Note is a breath of Provence in the middle of downtown Berkeley. Inside the tiny storefront you will find yourself engulfed in warm cheerful colors as you dine off handmade Provençal pottery, which is also offered for sale. Salads, served in deep glass bowls, comprise an array of colors and flavors. We've enjoyed the bouillabaisse and the ravioli filled with pears, arugula and smoked goat cheese. We sometimes stop at La Note just for a dessert of lavender crème brûlée.

LARK CREEK CAFÉ   CONTEMPORARY/AMERICAN   13/20

1360 Locust St., Walnut Creek 94593
925-256-1234, *Lunch & Dinner daily, $$*

This more casual version of chef Bradley Ogden's tony Lark Creek Inn (see the MARIN chapter) opened to huge crowds giddy that one of the country's foremost celebrity chefs chose to settle in their town. And they had plenty to be excited: the elegantly rustic, contemporary American fare Ogden serves at the Inn translates wonderfully into a simpler, lower-priced and less complex idiom. The Caesar salad is textbook perfect, as are onion rings with a blue-cheese dipping sauce. You might consider dishes like roast duck breast with wild-rice croquettes and grilled salmon with a Yukon-gold potato cake. In season, you can dig into a luscious strawberry shortcake. Also in San Mateo.

LE CHEVAL   VIETNAMESE   13/20
1007 Clay St., Oakland 94612
510-763-8495, *Lunch Mon.-Sat., Dinner nightly, $*

Le Cheval serves mouthwatering Vietnamese cuisine in a huge, open, bustling room. The restaurant has no trouble keeping the space brimming with diners seeking generous portions of tasty food at reasonable prices. Good bets are the rice vermicelli with chicken shish-kebabs and the large bowls of beef-noodle soup called pho. Wherever possible, entrées are prepared with your choice of beef, chicken or tofu. Try the rich Vietnamese iced coffee.

LE MARQUIS   FRENCH   14/20
3524-B Mt. Diablo Blvd., Lafayette 94549
925-284-4422, *Dinner Tues.-Sat., $$$*

Le Marquis bucks the current trend of informal, casual dining. It's not pretentious or stuffy, mind you, and no one will raise an eyebrow if a gent shows up without a tie, but still, it's a more formal spot than most. Chef Robert Guerguy's cooking is on the conservative side, leavened with imaginative touches. House-smoked salmon gets squiggles of pungent horseradish cream; ahi tuna gets a zippy coating of crushed black peppercorns and coriander seed. The crème brûlée is its requisite creamy-crispy self.

LOS PAISANOS DE COLARINA   MEXICAN   ¢
2293 E. International Blvd., Oakland 94601
510-261-2472, *Lunch & dinner daily*

With humble beginnings as one of Oakland's many taco trucks, Colarina now enjoys an equally inelegant incarnation in a tiny storefront. But ambience is not why you go to a taqueria. In this case it's the fabulous tacos filled with pork al pastor, butter-tender tongue or juicy chicken. The fillings are also available in burritos and tortas, but they're best appreciated in the tacos, where nothing distracts from the meat but chopped onion and cilantro. Order three of these little wonders along with an aqua fresca.

MADRAS INDIAN 12/20

2217 San Ramon Valley Blvd., San Ramon 94507
925-838-9090, *Lunch & Dinner daily, $$*

Pakoras (chickpea batter encasing vegetables or chicken and chiles) or samosas (lamb turnovers) are perfect starters here. Ten meatless choices for vegetarians make this place particularly good: be sure to try the eggplant curry. Dishes from the tandoor oven, like chicken, prawns or lamb, will also satisfy you. The restaurant is plain, but the staff is extremely gracious.

MAZZINI TRATTORIA ITALIAN 15/20

2826 Telegraph Ave., Berkeley 94705
510-848-5599, *Lunch & Dinner daily, $$*

Laura Maser and her co-owner husband, Jim, are involved with two other successful Berkeley restaurants, Café Fanny and Picante Cocina Mexicana. Here, start with a few shared appetizers including crostini al cavolfiore, a creative mix of cauliflower, capers, anchovy and olive oil atop toasted thin slices of whole-grain bread. The orecchiette with turnip greens, garlic and a touch of hot pepper is our idea of Italian comfort food. We also like the Tuscan fish stew and the tagliata, thinly sliced New York strip steak served with arugula, shaved Parmigiano-Reggiano and french fries. The all-Italian wine list, with many selections rarely found in restaurants, complements the menu. Our favorite dessert is the panna cotta, a slightly sweet, thickened cream garnished with tiny pieces of candied orange and semisweet chocolate.

MILLIE'S KITCHEN AMERICAN 12/20

1018 Oakhill Rd., Lafayette 94549
925-283-2397, *Breakfast & Lunch daily, $*

In the 20-plus years since it opened, Millie's has become something of a local institution. There's nothing hip or fancy here, just big, filling omelets and egg dishes like huevos rancheros, along with remarkably light waffles and the typical lunchtime fare of burgers and sandwiches.

MONTECATINI ITALIAN 12/20

1528 Civic Dr., Walnut Creek 94596
925-943-6608, *Dinner Tues.-Sun., $$*

Montecatini is a neighborhood restaurant specializing in familiar northern Italian fare. It is distinguished from its competitors by the quality of its food and an unusually large, well-chosen and moderately priced wine list. Start with a simple salad, then move on to one of several hearty pastas such as the gnocchi with pesto, or a fine version of the classic "chicken under a brick." The so-so desserts offer inspiration to begin dieting.

NAN YANG ROCKRIDGE   BURMESE   12/20

6048 College Ave., Oakland 94618
510-655-3298, *Lunch & Dinner Tues.-Sun.,* **$$**

Even in the ethnically diverse Bay Area, Burmese cuisine has an air of the exotic, drawing upon the cooking of its neighbors: India, Thailand and China. Nan Yang looks like an ultramodern Italian caffè, with a black-and-gray color scheme and a wine list that goes far beyond the standard at casual Asian eateries. The food is a delight to the palate, especially the wonderfully varied Burmese salads with as many as 16 ingredients and are probably unlike any salads you've ever tasted. We also like the ethereal garlic noodles with curried spinach and tomatoes.

O CHAME   JAPANESE/FUSION   14/20

1830 Fourth St., Berkeley 94710
510-841-8783, *Lunch & Dinner Mon.-Sat.,* **$$**

Enter through a gate past a kiosk into a warm, Japanese-style room decorated with the works of artist Mayumi Oda, and you'll find yourself in a more peaceful world. Tea is the drink of choice here, and it is offered in so many varieties that you may need help in matching a tea to the delicious and artfully presented East/West starters. Sample a portobello mushroom, watercress and green-onion pancake, or soul-satisfying burdock root, carrot and tofu dumplings. Any of the meals in a bowl are definitely worth consideration: try, for example, wheat or buck-wheat noodles in a flavorful broth with a choice of salmon, pork tenderloin, smoked trout or grilled chicken breast.

OBELISQUE   CONTEMPORARY FRENCH   14/20

5421 College Ave., Oakland 94618
510-923-9691, *Dinner nightly,* **$$$**

In contrast to the many casual restaurants along Oakland's restaurant row, Obelisque is a sophisticated venue worthy of a special occasion. The comfortable banquettes and the gold and rich-brown tones of the décor add to the elegance. Classic French dishes are given a contemporary treatment: duck confit is served with braised ginger, pears and black risotto, and monkfish is wrapped in prosciutto. Early diners can enjoy a $20 prixe-fixe three-course menu Sunday through Thursday between 5 and 7 p.m. Ask to be seated on the mezzanine for more intimate dining.

OLIVETO   MEDITERRANEAN   14/20

5655 College Ave., Oakland 94618
510-547-5356, *Lunch Mon.-Fri., Dinner Mon.-Sat., Brunch Sun.,* **$$$**

Long the force in the kitchen at nearby Chez Panisse, Paul Bertolli is Oliveto's executive chef and partner. The menu changes with the seasons and what's best in the market, but we've enjoyed dishes like a lusty tagliolini with capers, olives, anchovies, chiles and meaty chunks of tuna confit; grilled quail with endive and potato gratin; and polenta pound cake draped in anise cream and paired with figs roasted in red wine.

OLIVETO CAFÉ   MEDITERRANEAN   ¢

5655 College Ave., Oakland 94618
510-547-4382, *Breakfast, Lunch & Dinner daily*

This casual yet sophisticated street-front café is a good place for a quick, tasty bite. A selection of little dishes are displayed behind the glass at the counter, where you order your repast: it could be a panini of sautéed leeks and goat cheese, or a plate of goat cheese and olives with a baguette. A glass of Chianti and the people-watching at the bustling Rockridge Market Hall could make you linger.

PASTA POMODORO   ITALIAN/PASTA   ¢

5500 College Ave., Oakland 94618
510-923-0900, *Open daily*

See listing in the SAN FRANCISCO chapter.

PICANTE COCINA MEXICANA   MEXICAN   ¢

1328 Sixth St., Berkeley 94710
510-525-3121, *Lunch & Dinner daily*

The menu and atmosphere of this busy---and sometimes noisy---taqueria have been updated with splendid results. Wonderful fresh tamales are filled with either pork braised in ancho chile sauce or butternut squash and roasted poblano chiles. Tostadas, served on a choice of a crispy corn or flour tortilla, are topped with black or pinto beans, Mexican cheese and an array of vegetables.

POSTINO   ITALIAN   14/20

3565 Mt. Diablo Blvd., Lafayette 94549
925-299-8700, *Dinner nightly, $$$*

Postino occupies a vine-covered brick building that dates back to 1937, and was at one time the Lafayette post office. Postino can be relied on for creative, well-prepared dishes. The panzanella con mozzarella al peperone, bread salad with roasted peppers, tomatoes, capers and house-made mozzarella, is a tasty starter. The Caesar salad, its romaine leaves standing upright in a bowl with garlic breadsticks, invites diners to eat with their hands. The sautéed swordfish with almonds and golden raisins, the rabbit risotto and the sautéed pork loin are popular main dishes. The bomboloni di mela, a free-form apple tart with cinnamon ice cream, may be one of the best pastries in all of Contra Costa County. The wine list features several bottles of moderately priced Italian wines, a refreshing change from the pricey wine lists at many restaurants of this caliber.

PRIMA TRATTORIA ITALIAN 14/20

1522 N. Main St., Walnut Creek 94596
925-935-7780, *Lunch Mon.-Sat., Dinner nightly, $$$*

Since its beginnings in 1977 as a wine-and-cheese shop that served informal meals, Prima has been an East Bay favorite. It still has a wine shop at the back of one dining room, from which diners can choose a wine right off the shelf for a modest corkage charge; there are weekly wine tastings, and all wines served by the glass are available by the taste—great if you just want a sip or two at lunch. Such hearty dishes as osso buco, Italian sausage and grilled chicken—all with gnocchi—are favorites. Save room for a slice of warm caramelized green-apple tart, baked in the wood-burning oven, for dessert. A jazz piano player comes in Wednesday through Saturday evenings.

PYRAMID ALEHOUSE BREWPUB ¢

901 Gilman St., Berkeley 94709
510-528-9880, *Lunch & Dinner daily*

A rainbow of brews are the draw at this humongous industrial-looking brewpub. When it comes to food, pizzas, smoked chicken and baby back ribs are good tastes. Try a hearty stout instead of the forgettable desserts. Brewery tours are held daily.

RESTAURANT PEONY CHINESE/DIM SUM 13/20

388 Ninth St., Oakland 94607
510-286-8866, *Lunch & Dinner daily, $$*

This is simply the best place in Oakland to eat dim sum. We especially appreciate the nearly greaseless egg rolls and other fried items. At night the dim sum is replaced by typical Hong Kong fare, with the focus on simply prepared seafood.

RICK & ANN'S AMERICAN 12/20

2922 Domingo Ave., Berkeley 94705
510-649-8538, *Breakfast, Lunch & Dinner daily, $$*

Rick & Ann's has been serving the homey foods of childhood to packed audiences since 1989. There's often a wait for a table, and you may be asked to share a section of the long table down the middle of the room. Breakfasts include all the basics, as well as specialties like potato-cheese pancakes with sour cream, chives and applesauce. The memories will begin with Solomon's onion soup, served with croutons and melted cheese, or with the house-smoked pork chops with sweet-pota-to biscuits. For that real touch of nostalgia, finish with a milk-shake.

RIVOLI RESTAURANT   MEDITERRANEAN   14/20

1539 Solano Ave., Berkeley 94707
510-526-2542, *Dinner nightly, $$*

The unassuming exterior of this little treasure on the Berkeley/Albany border belies the enticing aromas and flavors that await inside. At the back of this small restaurant is a wall of glass that looks out on an enclosed garden. As for the menu, they can't change certain items without enduring a slew of complaints from regulars; one dish is the portobello mushroom fritters served with lemon aïoli. Other favorite starters are the house-smoked salmon tart and the Caesar salad. The best entrées are the duck cooked two ways, the pot roast and the juniper-cured pork loin. Temptations like a hot fudge sundae are hard to resist.

ROSCOE'S CHICKEN AND WAFFLES   SOUTHERN/SOUL   ¢

336 Grand Ave., Oakland 94610
510-444-5705, *Breakfast & Dinner Tues.-Sun., Lunch Mon.-Sun.*

Chicken and waffles seem like a surprising combination to some, but fans of Roscoe's continue to flock to its new location near Lake Merritt for a succulent piece of chicken and a waffle or two. You can go the more traditional soul-food route with chicken smothered in gravy and onions. If you come for breakfast, add an egg to that chicken combination, or simply indulge in a platter of waffles made with Roscoe's special mix. Come in as late as midnight on Saturdays and Sundays.

SALUTE RISTORANTE   ITALIAN   13/20

1900 Esplanade Dr., Richmond 94804
510-215-0803, *Lunch & Dinner daily, $$*

Hidden behind a warehouse area of Richmond, Salute surprises diners when they come upon its New England yacht-club-like building on the Richmond Marina. Its glassed-in dining veranda makes Salute the best place for view dining in the East Bay. Chef Diogenes Chavez's menu can be relied on for well-executed classic Italian dishes. Veal scaloppine, sautéed calamari with soft polenta, braised lamb shank and grilled salmon are popular main courses.

SANTA FE BAR & GRILL   CALIFORNIA   14/20

1310 University Ave., Berkeley 94702
510-841-4740, *Lunch Mon.-Fri., Dinner nightly, $$$*

We lament that the name "Santa Fe" might put off those who fear a blue-corn-happy Southwestern menu. There's no such thing here—the restaurant is so named because it was once the Santa Fe Pacific Railroad stationhouse. Today, owner-chef Ahmed Behjati is happy to take diners on a tour of the adjacent 4,000 square-foot garden, where he grows much of the organic bounty that goes into his oft-changing contemporary California menu, including many rare herbs and vegetables imported from his native Iran and elsewhere. One day he might pluck golden beets and endive and dress them in a Champagne-lemon vinaigrette; for an entrée he'll pick sweet peas to stuff into the ravioli that accompany the roasted Cornish game hen. On warm evenings, it's delightful to sit on the sprawling patio among the gardens, finishing dinner with, say, a Meyer-lemon cake topped with gingered strawberry compote and whipped cream.

SANTA FE BISTRO   CALIFORNIA   ¢

2142 Center St., Berkeley 94702
510-841-4047, *Lunch Mon.-Fri., Dinner Mon.-Sat.*
☎

A casual spinoff of the noteworthy Santa Fe Bar & Grill, this little sister bistro is best at lunch, when the place transforms into a cafeteria-style do-it-yourself affair in the open kitchen, and the prices are remarkably low. At any time, the dishes feature fresh regional ingredients, many from owner Ahmed Behjati's own organic garden. Translation: roast asparagus soup; a tangy salad of arugula and blood orange slices; roast chicken with Caesar salad. Dinner is less of a bargain, but you'll find everything from spit-roasted leg of lamb to Atlantic salmon with Kalamata olive tapenade. The interior features suspended mini-halogen lights and sleek dark-wood tabletops.

SHEN HUA   CHINESE   13/20

2914 College Ave., Berkeley 94705
510-883-1777, *Lunch Mon.-Sat., Dinner nightly, $*
☎ 👫 🍾

Berkeley locals pack this large modern restaurant just as much to be seen as for the northern Chinese dishes. The freshest ingredients are used, whether in such classics as hot and sour soup and mu shu pork or in more exotic dishes such as chien pi chicken with sun-dried orange peel and roasted red-hot peppers. The stir-fried black mushrooms, water chestnuts and fresh snow peas is good as an accompaniment for other dishes or by itself. A tea menu is a nice touch.

SOIZIC   FUSION   13/20

300 Broadway, Oakland 94607
510-251-8100, *Lunch Mon.-Fri., Dinner Thurs.-Sat., $$$*
☎ 👫 🍸

The menu in this relaxed, artsy restaurant, a stone's throw from Jack London Square, is influenced by Italian and Asian culinary traditions: you'll find dishes such as a smoked-trout salad with Belgian endive, pears, hazelnuts and capers, served with a dill cream sauce. Desserts include a rich chocolate torte and a creamy ginger custard. The wine list offers selections from Italy and France, several by the glass, to match the menu.

SPIEDINI   ITALIAN   12/20

101 Ygnacio Valley Rd., Walnut Creek 94596
925-939-2100, *Lunch & Dinner Mon.-Fri., Dinner Sat.-Sun.,* $$$

The specialties at this sleekly modern restaurant, set in an office building, are the spit-roasted meats. We've even been known to call ahead to reserve our very own duck or rabbit. Pastas, pizza from the wood-fired oven, and grilled meats and fish round out the menu. The well-priced wine list is chock-full of California and Italian favorites.

TAPAS SEVILLA   SPANISH   13/20

267 Hartz Ave., Danville 94526
925-837-2355, *Lunch & Dinner daily,* $$

Order tapas—we suggest two per person—to share with the table. Or order a few tapas as starters and follow them with one or more platos especiales. A single serving of Valenciana-style paella is generous enough for two or three to share after tapas. Other platos especiales include the rabo de toro estafado, an oxtail stew casserole, and the boneless pork medallions with grapes, parsley, brandy and mashed potatoes. For dessert, we recommend the strawberry shortcake.

TOWNHOUSE BAR & GRILL   CALIFORNIA   13/20

5872 Doyle St., Emeryville 94608
510-652-6151, *Lunch & Dinner Mon.-Sat.,* $$

Here you can apply the line from the movie Field of Dreams: "If you build it, they will come." For years, there wasn't anything in Emeryville. This lovingly restored restaurant used to be a speakeasy decorated in the Old West motif. The garlic fries are addicting, as is the fried-calamari appetizer. The large salads, pastas such as the ravioli or linguine, and the fish dishes are notable. For dessert, go straight for the crème brûlée.

UNCLE YU'S   CHINESE   14/20

999 Oak Hill Rd., Lafayette 94549
925-283-1688, *Lunch & Dinner daily,* $$

Uncle Yu's is hardly the typical suburban Chinese restaurant. It boasts excellent service and a coolly contemporary dining room with glass-block room dividers, stressed concrete pillars and luxurious furnishings. It also boasts a wine list brimming with fine selections from California and France, as well as a menu that goes well beyond the usual Chinese dishes. The real strength of Uncle Yu's kitchen lies in such dishes as pan-fried baby lobster tails with a scattering of scallion and jalapeño rings; roasted quail with a tart-spicy sauce and wilted spinach; five-spice marinated quail; and an elegant tea-smoked duck. Forget the fortune cookies; there's chocolate mousse for dessert.

UZEN   JAPANESE   13/20

5415 College Ave., Oakland 94618
510-654-7753, *Lunch & Dinner Mon.-Sat., $$*
☎

This teeny restaurant—eight tables, plus eight seats at the sushi bar—offers good food and lots of atmosphere. The lunch and dinner menus feature a selection of perfectly fresh and artfully presented sushi and sashimi, tempura, teriyaki and other dishes. Especially satisfying is the Uzen udon, with chicken, shiitake mushrooms, shrimp and vegetable tempura. Another good choice is the sashimi platter with miso soup, rice, good green tea and a salad. The dinner menu, priced slightly higher, adds appetizers and a few specials.

VOULEZ-VOUS   FRENCH   NO RATING

2930 College Ave., Oakland 94618
510-548-4708, *Lunch & Dinner daily, $$*
☎ 🍷 🍶

This new kid on the block reinforces recent Bay Area trends; that is to say, French food is back in a big way. Located in the busy Elmwood District, Voulez-Vous hits the right marks with a menu of crêpes, quiche, soups and a plat du jour.

VULCAN CAFÉ   THAI   11/20

915 45th Ave., Oakland 94601
510-536-6303, *Breakfast, Lunch & early Dinner (until 8:30) Mon.-Sat., $*
🍴 👫

Hidden away in an industrial district that boasts many artists' studios, the Vulcan Café features an extensive menu of Thai dishes. Those who are part of this neighborhood treat the café like their home away from home. Some good choices include pra-rahm-long-song (a mix of steamed spinach and cabbage with chicken, pork, or beef topped with peanut sauce) and the flavorful red curry made with beef or chicken. Those who judge a Thai restaurant by its pad Thai will be pleased with the Vulcan Café's rendition.

WALKER'S RESTAURANT & PIE SHOP   AMERICAN   12/20

1491 Solano Ave., Albany 94707
510-525-4647, *Breakfast & Lunch Tues.-Sat., Dinner Tues.-Sun., $*
☎ 👫

This restaurant is comfortable and reassuring in a world of fusion food and exotic cuisine. Most of the fare is coffee-shop friendly. Dinner revolves around prime rib, steak, fried chicken and roast leg of lamb. A slice of the delicious house-baked pies is included in the price of dinner.

WENTE VINEYARDS RESTAURANT   CONTEMPORARY   14/20

5050 Arroyo Rd., Livermore 94550
925-456-2400, *Lunch & Dinner daily, $$$*
☎ 📷 👫 🍷 🍶 🚗 ⟳

Overlooking the vineyards of one of the oldest wineries in the state, this is the epitome of a California restaurant: it has casually elegant surroundings, delicious food and a great wine list. Longtime chef Kimball Jones grounds his menu in the basics. Start with an eggplant bruschetta, the house-cured salmon or Hog Island oysters with a Wente sparkling-wine mignonette. Grilled beef is paired with a potato-chanterelle gratin, while pan-seared swordfish gets a green-olive and herb garnish. For dessert, the chocolate-bourbon pecan torte won our hearts. The wine list carries the winery's offerings along with other Chardonnays and Cabernets.

ZACHARY'S CHICAGO PIZZA   PIZZA   ¢

1853 Solano Ave., Berkeley 94706
510-525-5950, *Lunch & Dinner daily*

Handling a perennial crowd hovering in the entryway and a line out the door, Zachary's serves up hearty Chicago-style double-crust pizzas, stuffed and topped with a variety of traditional and innovative ingredients. If you don't want to wait in line, you can pick up a half-baked pie and finish it at home. A favorite is the version chock-full of spinach and mushrooms. The same toppings are offered on a thin-crust pizza, which is also available by the slice at lunch. Also in Oakland (5801 College Ave., 510-655-6385).

GOURMET SHOPS & MORE

BAKERIES: BREAD & PASTRY

ACME BREAD COMPANY

1601 San Pablo Ave., Berkeley 94702
Open Mon.-Sat.

This award-winning bakery, established in 1983, supplies loaves to many of the Bay Area's finest restaurants. Acme's baguettes, sweet or sourdough, are sought after, but the bakery makes more than 20 other bread varieties. The exceptional Upstairs Bread is named for the Chez Panisse Café, whose long-standing relationship with Acme has contributed to the bakery's success. Although you can purchase Acme breads at many supermarkets and other retail locations, you get the best selection here—especially if you arrive early.

ARIZMENDI

3265 Lakeshore Ave., Oakland 94610
510-268-8849. *Open Mon.-Sat., 7 a.m.-7 p.m.*

✕

Former members of the Cheese Board collective in Berkeley opened this bakery a couple of years ago, in a neighborhood that needed one. Bread choices include potato, Asiago, sesame-sunflower, corn-oat molasses, Provolone-olive, corn-cheddar and multigrain. Treats include scones and even pizzas.

BOOGIE WOOGIE BAGEL BOY

1227 Park St., Alameda 94501
510-523-8979, *Open Mon.-Sat.*

This small shop makes the expected bagel flavors as well as a delicious green-olive bagel on the weekends, a doughnut-like bagel with sugar and cinnamon baked onto the outside, and an Asiago-cheese variety.

GRACE BAKING

5655 College Ave., Oakland 94618
510-428-2662, *Open daily*

Who can resist Grace Baking's luscious focaccia topped with artichokes and tomato pieces? Grace also makes a great and sturdy walnut bread, an olive bread and ciabatta. The breads are also available in Bay Area supermarkets. Also in Albany (1127 Solano Ave., 510-559-4564).

KATRINA ROZELLE

5931 College Ave., Oakland 94618
510-655-3209, *Open daily*

Katrina Rozelle creates incredibly beautiful and tasty homemade cookies and cakes. They also make cakes for any occasion; the wedding cakes are spectacular. Also in Alamo (215-B Alamo Plaza, 925-837-6337).

LA FARINE

6323 College Ave., Oakland 94618
510-654-0338, *Open Tues.-Sun.*

✕

This bakery, which translates in French as "flour," makes more than 20 kinds of cakes, fresh-fruit tarts, cookies, biscotti, bread and morning pastries like scones and buns. The cinnamon buns alone make La Farine worth seeking out.

MONTCLAIR BAKING

2220 Mountain Blvd. Ste. 140, Oakland 94611
510-530-8052, *Open Mon.-Sat.*

✕

This bakery features morning items such as danishes, scones and muffins, plus cookies, an assortment of cakes and individual pastries—all scrumptious and handmade. The wedding and special-order cakes are beautiful, especially those made with fruit.

NOAH'S NEW YORK BAGELS

3170 College Ave., Berkeley 94705
510-654-0944, *Open daily*

Noah's, which started locally at the College Avenue shop in Berkeley, is now based in San Leandro, where the bagel dough is prepared and delivered to their numerous stores and wholesale clients. As always, some will love the 14 varieties of extra-large bagels, while others will continue to find them inauthentic: they're steamed before being baked, rather than boiled in the New York tradition. Also at Noah's you will find a variety of cream cheese schmears (some low-fat), along with pickles, smoked fish, knishes, drinks and other delicacies.

CHEESE

THE CHEESE BOARD COLLECTIVE

1504 Shattuck Ave., Berkeley 94709
510-549-3183, *Open Mon.-Sat.*

One of the last true collective businesses, the Cheese Board offers an astounding variety of cheeses along with olives, fresh butter and great baked goods. If you're in a hurry, a few of the most common selections are available wrapped in the refrigerator. But it's far more fun to take a playing card (which determines your order in line) and purchase your cheese from the 200 or so varieties at the counter. A member of the collective will help you make your pick by tasting each variety with you. In addition, the Cheese Board bakes about a dozen varieties of breads, scones and rolls each day, including scrumptious cheese-filled loaves.

COFFEE & TEA

FAR LEAVES TEAS

2979 College Ave.. Berkeley 94705
510-665-9409, *Open Mon.-Sat.*

Besides its three dozen teas, this cute and new shop also sells books on tea, teapots and serving sets. The tea itself may be from single-estate harvests from the far corners of the globe.

PEABERRY'S COFFEE & TEA

Rockridge Market Hall, 5655 College Ave., Oakland 94618
510-653-0405, *Open daily*

Located in the wonderful Market Hall complex, Peaberry's sells a good selection of coffees, teas, chocolates, and coffee and tea drinks.

PEET'S COFFEE

2124 Vine St., Berkeley 94709
510-841-0564, *Open daily*

Peet's was around even before Starbucks; in fact, the first outlet was right here. Since Starbucks has taken over the world, Peet's outlets have grown too, with locations throughout the Bay Area now. See review in SAN FRANCISCO chapter.

DELIS

A.G. FERRARI

4001 Piedmont Ave., Oakland 94611
510-547-7222, *Open daily*

This Italian-style delicatessen carries fresh foods and gourmet ingredients, breads from local bakeries, imported oils and vinegars, house-made desserts, wines and other essentials of the Italian kitchen. The deli counter offers panini sandwiches, fritatte, focaccia and side dishes, as well as soups, sliced meats, cheeses and pasta sauces. Ultra Lucca also offers catering and party trays. Also in Berkeley (2905 College Ave., 510-547-7222), Montclair, the Elmwood District of Berkeley & in Marin County.

RICK & ANN'S PANTRY

2922 Domingo Ave., Berkeley 94705
510-649-0869, *Open daily*

Next door to Rick & Ann's Restaurant, this shop offers the same taste of Americana to go: you'll find some produce, grocery and gourmet items, as well as soups, salads and sandwiches. "Breakfast Bags" hold frittata and fruit salad, granola with fruit and milk, fruit and yogurt with a muffin or scone, or a bagel with cream cheese, tomato, onion, cucumber and fruit. Platters serving up to 24 are also available.

VASILIO'S KITCHEN AT ANDRONICO'S

1550 Shattuck Ave., Berkeley 94709
510-841-7946, *Open daily*

Grocery prices at Andronico's tend to be slightly higher than at other supermarkets, but the selection is good and the produce is usually top-notch. Vasilio's Kitchen is the store's deli department. Here you will find an assortment of marinated olives (which you can sample before you choose), breads from the Bay Area's best purveyors, sandwiches, soups, salads, smoked fish, cakes and pastries, and prepared foods like eggplant Parmesan, hummus, spicy tofu and roast chicken. Also at 2655 Telegraph Ave., 510-845-1280; 1414 University Ave., 510-548-7061; 1850 Solano Ave., 510-524-0513, & in San Francisco (1200 Irving St., 415-753-0403).

FARMERS' MARKETS

BERKELEY:

Derby St. & Martin Luther King Jr. Way
Open Open Tues. 2 p.m.-7 p.m. year-round; 1 p.m.-dusk in summer
510-548-3333,

CENTER ST. & MARTIN LUTHER KING JR. WAY

Open Sat. 10 a.m.-2 p.m. year-round
510-548-3333

OAKLAND:

Broadway & Embarcadero
Sun. 10 a.m.-2 p.m.
800-949-FARM

And in almost every other community in the East Bay.

GOURMET MARKETS

RATTO & CO. INTERNATIONAL GROCERS

821 Washington St., Oakland 94607
510-832-6503, *Open Mon.-Sat.*

This vintage Italian market stocks a great mélange of Italian and other international (mostly Middle Eastern) products, including hard-to-find items such as Machaalany (a Lebanese date syrup scented with rose water) or riso superfino carnaroli, reputed to be the best type of rice for making risotto. There's a variety of imported olive oils and balsamic vinegars, meats and pâtés, cheeses, pastas, bulk spices and dried legumes and a small collection of cooking paraphernalia. The store opens up into a self-service café offering an Italian menu of soups, salads, hot and cold sandwiches, daily pastas and other specials at lunchtime.

ROCKRIDGE MARKET HALL

5655 College Ave., Oakland 94618
510-655-7748, *Open daily*
Card policies vary

This urban market with a European feel in Oakland's Rockridge District boasts a pasta shop, a bakery, a coffee and tea bar, a wine shop, produce, meat and fish markets, and a lovely little flower stand, along with Oliveto (the restaurant and café). Pasta Shop Fine Foods peddles fresh pastas and sauces, plus olives, cheeses, gourmet groceries, sweets, fresh and frozen prepared foods, and a variety of gift boxes and baskets ranging from $14 to $95. The same shop holds classes highlighting many of their products (such as "The Great Olive Oils of the World"). Grace Baking makes a variety of breads and pastries, including some of the best focaccia around.

TRADER JOE'S

5700 Christie Ave., Emeryville 94608
510-658-8091, *Open daily*

See listing in SAN FRANCISCO chapter. Numerous locations in Northern California

HEALTH FOOD & ORGANIC MARKETS

THE FOOD MILL

3033 MacArthur Blvd., Oakland 94602
510-482-3848, *Open Mon.-Sat.*

This truly old-fashioned neighborhood market has been "serving health in Oakland since 1933." Here you'll find apron-wearing grocers who go to the back of the store to measure your flour or spices—this is real, personal service. In addition to organic produce, vitamins, bulk items and ready-to-eat snacks, the Food Mill boasts the largest assortment of esoteric health food items that you're likely to find anywhere: four types of nutritional yeast, three kinds of textured vegetable protein, honey-sweetened, old-fashioned bakery products, and canned meat substitutes like links, sausages, patties and meatballs.

JUCY'S

5701 College Ave., Oakland 94618
510-428-2100, *Open daily*

This mostly take-out juice bar (there's one large table inside and a couple more on the street) presses a variety of fresh fruits and vegetables to order. Most fun are the big 20-ounce smoothies, with names like Rhythm & Blues (blueberry, banana and nonfat frozen yogurt blended with apple juice) and Copabanana (strawberry, blueberry and banana blended with pineapple juice). Vitamin C, lecithin, spirulina, protein powder, ginseng or bee pollen can be added to boost the nutritional barometer.

WHOLE FOODS MARKET

3000 Telegraph Ave., Berkeley 94705
Open daily

See listing in PENINSULA chapter. Numerous locations in the Bay Area.

WILD OATS COMMUNITY MARKET

1581 University Ave., Berkeley 94703
510-549-1714, *Open daily*

Formerly Living Foods, this popular Berkeley natural-food market was purchased in 1995 by Wild Oats, a Boulder, Colorado, company with two dozen stores in six western states.

In addition to organic and locally grown produce, Wild Oats offers a deli with homemade soups, sandwiches, salads and other sweets and savories, a meat and fish counter, a "juice and java" bar, vitamins, cosmetics, and other health products.

KITCHEN EQUIPMENT

SUR LA TABLE

1806 Fourth St., Berkeley 94710
510-849-2252, *Open daily*

Sur La Table, with a flagship store in Seattle, has 5,000 square feet of everything for the home cook from molds to pots to pans to books. The store holds product demonstrations, book signings and cooking classes for children and adults. Sur La Table also has a mail-order catalog. Also in San Francisco (77 Maiden Lane, 415-732-7900).

PRODUCE

MAD RIVER PRODUCE

1788 Fourth St., Berkeley 94710
510-528-9800, *Open daily*

This new little produce store is just part of a major expansion of Berkeley's Fourth Street "gourmet ghetto." Located in a small complex just off the street, Mad River joins Sur La Table and Peet's Coffee in a neighborhood replete with culinary opportunities. Mad River features a full line of organic produce and groceries in addition to a salad bar featuring a daily vegetarian soup. A few tables are available on the patio.

WINES & SPIRITS

KERMIT LYNCH

1605 San Pablo Ave., Berkeley 94702
510-524-1524, *Open Tues.-Sat.*

Kermit Lynch made a name and a business for himself when he became the premier importer of French wines to the Bay Area. He has gems from Spain, Italy and Germany also. The staff is very knowledgeable, and browsing in the store is a pleasure. You can make an outing of it: Acme Bakery is just next door, as is Café Fanny.

PAUL MARCUS WINES

5655 College Ave. in the Rockridge Market Hall, Oakland 94618
Open daily

An expertly stocked little wine shop in Rockridge's bustling shopping center, Marcus is a good place to look for the best from California, Italy and France. You'll also find a good selection of Spanish wines, and wine collections from estate sales or private auctions that occasionally include marvelous old California bottles.

Wine Country

WINE COUNTRY
MAP

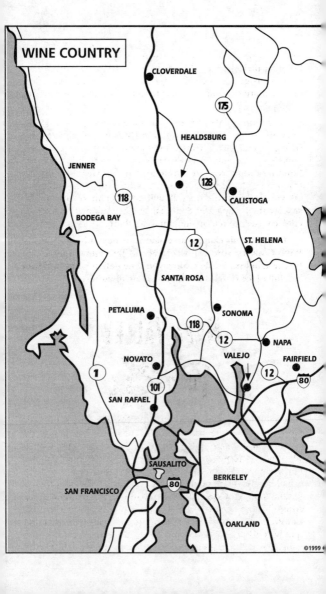

WINE COUNTRY

CLOVERDALE

175

HEALDSBURG

JENNER

118

CALISTOGA

BODEGA BAY

128

12

ST. HELENA

SANTA ROSA

PETALUMA

SONOMA

118

12

NAPA

VALEJO

FAIRFIELD

NOVATO

1

80

12

101

SAN RAFAEL

SAUSALITO

80

BERKELEY

SAN FRANCISCO

OAKLAND

©1999

AMONG THE VINES

You'll find wineries nearly everywhere in the state of California, but it is a bucolic area north of San Francisco that has captured the undisputed title of Wine Country. Climate and soil conditions in Napa, Sonoma and Mendocino counties, similar to those in the great grape-growing regions of France and Italy, have rendered this part of the state the premier wine region in the country. Many of the winery owners bought defunct wineries or founded their own in the 1960s, a time of renaissance in both valleys. They came from diverse backgrounds: science, business and finance. Most were not born agriculturists, but rather amateur winemakers who became gentleman farmers.

With the boom of California wines, Europeans interested in a sophisticated but bucolic lifestyle emigrated to the region, bringing their own sensibilities to the New World. For tourists, this means good wine, good food, lovely lodgings and shopping that are of a quality rarely found in primarily agricultural regions.

If Napa is all about wine, Sonoma is a mix of agricultural pursuits. It has its share of vineyards, but you'll also find a strong vegetable-and-fruit-growing component as well as cattle and sheep ranching. And where Napa draws world-class chefs, Sonoma enjoys unique home-grown eateries. Mendocino County, two hundred miles north of San Francisco, has about 40 wineries and less than 20,000 acres planted to wine. It's smaller than Napa and Sonoma, but its untamed beauty and choice wines are reason enough to go there.

Dive into this chapter and plan your next adventure in the Wine Country. And call weeks ahead for reservations in the best restaurants. While dining, you'll be delighted to find wine lists full of local labels you may not find elsewhere.

NAPA VALLEY

Established, popular and affluent, Napa county is home to more than 225 wineries and some of the best restaurants in the country. Nearly all of them can be accessed from Highway 29. The town of **Napa** marks the south end of the wine country. Further north, **Yountville, Oakville** and **Rutherford** have established themselves not only as wine producers but also as tourist destinations. **St. Helena**, further north still, boasts some of the county's best dining. And at Napa's northernmost border, **Calistoga** effervesces with natural geothermal springs, hotel-spas and a flock of restaurants to suit every taste and pocketbook. The rolling hills and verdant valleys, dotted nearly everywhere with vines, make Napa a delight to visit in the fall, when the light is golden and the air is filled with the perfume of crushed grapes.

RESTAURANTS

ALL SEASONS CAFÉ & WINE SHOP   CALIFORNIA 12/20
1400 Lincoln Ave., Calistoga 94515
707-942-9111, *Lunch Thurs.-Tues., Dinner nightly, $$*

The food here can be a bit on and off, but the rich tomato-basil soup with thin slices of pear and shredded smoked chicken is reliably restorative. The All Seasons BLT is a good one—pancetta, watercress and arugula, dressed with a tangy aïoli. This charming little place also contains one of the area's best wine shops, with more than 800 selections. You can purchase a bottle (at retail!) to accompany your meal.

ANA'S CANTINA   MEXICAN   ¢
1205 Main St., St. Helena 94574
707-963-4921, *Open daily*

Imaginative tacos, burritos and other Mexican dishes are all made with fresh ingredients here. You'll also find a wide range of sandwiches and other "gringo" treats. The selection of beers is better than average, but margaritas are the real specialty. On weekends patrons enjoy live music and karaoke, and the pool table is always a big draw.

ATLAS PEAK GRILL   ITALIAN/STEAKHOUSE   13/20
3342 Vichy Ave., Napa 94558
707-253-1455, *Dinner Wed.-Sun., $$$*

The owner is Al Petri, who also owns the wonderful Alfred's Steakhouse in San Francisco, so it's no surprise that steaks are the heart of the menu. All the cuts are prime and perfectly grilled. We recommend the bistecca alla Fiorentina, a T-bone marinated in olive and rosemary, plus the filet mignon and the peppered New York steak. The appetizers are Italian favorites. Atlas has a very good wine list and a nice selection of well-priced single-malt scotches.

AUBERGE DU SOLEIL   CALIFORNIA/FUSION 14/20
Rutherford Hill Rd., Rutherford 94573
707-967-3111, *Breakfast, Lunch & Dinner daily, $$$*

Perhaps the most romantic restaurant in the wine country, Auberge du Soleil has one of the most incredible views as well. To look out over the fabled vineyards at sunset while sipping a wine from those very vines is a heady experience. The menu supports the experience adequately–often with brilliance. Executive chef Andrew Sutton offers a seasonally changing menu with a sometimes surprising selection of dishes. Many appetizers have an Asian twist, such as the tempura'd ahi-salmon sashimi, but you'll also find more traditional seared sea scallops with a caviar-Champagne sauce. Entrées include lamb medallions with roasted garlic paired with a luscious truffled Saint André risotto, and a lovely three-course vegetarian tasting. Desserts are sublime, and change according to the fruits in season for crisps, sorbets and tarts. The wine list is first-rate.

BERGMAN'S   AMERICAN   13/20

1234 Main St., St. Helena 94574
707-963-1063, *Lunch & Dinner Mon.-Sat.,* $$

Owners Bryan Bergman, his wife Alexis and brother Andy, describe their menu as anti-Napa. In a sea of high-concept, pricey restaurants, Bergman's is refreshing—and it serves until 1 a.m. from May through September. The daily blue-plate special might feature Salisbury steak. Other entrées we like are the meatloaf, baked peppers stuffed with vegetables, and roast chicken. Vegetarians can enjoy five of the many side dishes for only $10. Napa Valley restaurants hate diners who bring their own wines (although many of these patrons make wine and feel they should be allowed to BYOB). To combat that, restaurants typically charge a high corkage fee. But not Bergman's. The corkage fee is . . . a taste of the wine for the house!

THE BIG DIPPER   ICE CREAM PARLOR   ¢

1336-A Oak Ave., St. Helena 94574
707-963-2616, *Open daily*

If you like kids (an elementary school is across the street), soda fountain memorabilia and goopy ice cream creations, this is the place for you. Besides a full menu of sundaes, ice cream sodas and frozen yogurt, the Big Dipper also features snacks such as nachos, hot dogs, soft pretzels and bulk candy.

BISTRO DON GIOVANNI   MEDITERRANEAN   14/20

4110 St. Helena Hwy. (Hwy. 29), Napa 94558
707-224-3300, *Lunch & Dinner daily,* $$

This restaurant, lying at the gateway to the part of the Napa devoted almost exclusively to grape growing, is your first good opportunity when driving north to dine well. It has been through a number of recent changes: the owners added outdoor dining, remodeled the dining room, and installed a new fountain and fireplace, all of which creates a very welcoming ambience. Best of all, the food has improved. The menu leans heavily on wood-oven pizzas and pastas such as pappardelle with braised duck. The braised rabbit and pancetta and the braised lamb shanks with a Tuscan bean ragoût are both winners. At lunch, focaccia sandwiches are a real treat. The wine list is solid and reasonably priced.

BISTRO JEANTY   FRENCH   15/20

6510 Washington St., Yountville 94599
707-944-0103, *Lunch & Dinner daily, $$$*

Lacy café curtains, a snappy striped awning, and Pernod and Maurice Chevalier posters make it clear that you've been transported to the French countryside. You'll be seated at tables topped with white linen and butcher paper, either in the main dining area or in the bar. A chalkboard lists the day's specials, as they do in every bistro in France. The concept is dear to the heart of Philippe Jeanty, who has realized his dream here after making Domaine Chandon one of Napa's foremost restaurants for 20 years. This is the place to go when you want bistro food: pâté, escargots, lamb's tongue, cassoulet, beet salad, sweetbread ragoût, salade niçoise, crisp fried smelts and haricots verts. If you order the tomato soup en croûte, you won't want to share even a teaspoon of it. The cassoulet arrives with a chicken leg poking out, as if beckoning you to the duck confit, sausage and white beans within. The coq au vin is equally hearty. On a lighter note, the petrale sole meunière is redolent of butter and parsley with a whiff of lemon. The wine list features many half bottles, a treat for adventurous wine lovers.

BOUCHON   FRENCH   15/20

6534 Washington St., Yountville 94599
707-944-8037, *Lunch & Dinner daily, $$$*

In the fall of 1998, chef Thomas Keller of French Laundry fame and his brother Joseph opened a classic brasserie nearby. If Bouchon's snazzy décor—lots of mirrors, glistening crystal, a zinc bar, white walls topped by a white-on-white frieze—was designed by Adam Tihany, who did Le Cirque 2000 in New York. A lot of tables are jammed into the space, and the noise can rise to ear-splitting levels. Bouchon could survive solely on turn-aways from the French Laundry, but it need not depend on its older sibling. Anyone with doubts should start with the beignets of cod brandade, a smooth, deep-fried mixture of fish and mashed potatoes. Classic appetizers like a charcuterie plate, chilled leeks and a perfect Bibb lettuce salad, are all satisfying, as is the cheese course. Get down to business with a pan-seared sole meunière that could serve as the poster dish for brasserie food. Mussels meunière are accompanied by a little Eiffel Tower of crisp fries. Another plus: Bouchon is the only place around serving food until 2 a.m.

BRANNAN'S GRILL   AMERICAN   13/20

1374 Lincoln Ave., Calistoga 94515
707-942-2233, *Lunch & Dinner daily, $$*

This newish addition to the town of Calistoga looks spectacular. The owners have remodeled the interior of this 1906 structure to preserve the Old West flavor but have given it modern touches such as skylights, a new stone fireplace and windows that open to the street on warm days. In the dining room, a mural of Napa Valley's pioneer days forms an attractive backdrop. The food is rib-sticking American: baby back ribs, Yankee pot roast, rotisserie chicken with a lavender-honey glaze, and the pulled-pork sandwich hit the spot. If the lemon pudding cake is on the menu, don't hesitate. The wine list offers many lower-priced bottles.

BRAVA TERRACE   CALIFORNIA/FRENCH 14/20

3010 St. Helena Hwy. (Hwy. 29), St. Helena 94574
707-963-9300, *Lunch & Dinner daily (May-Oct.), Thurs.-Tues. (Nov.-Apr.),* $$

One of Napa Valley's most pleasant sites for dining is Fred Halpert's wood-frame restaurant, replete with arresting art and a massive fireplace. An even better spot is Halpert's terrace overlooking the herb garden, where, surrounded by flowers, you'll have a view of the nearby vineyards. The menu is typically California eclectic. So while the menu includes dishes like half a chicken with roasted herbed potatoes and a breathtakingly garlicky Caesar salad, it also boasts such deftly executed dishes as a savory cassoulet, osso buco and creamy risotti. Complex fresh salads and creative sandwiches fill the bill at lunch. A well-priced wine list also beckons.

BRIX   FUSION/SEAFOOD   15/20

7331 St. Helena Hwy. (Hwy. 29), Napa 94558
707-944-2749, *Lunch & Dinner daily,* $$$

Chef Tod Michael Kawachi taps into his Japanese-Chinese heritage as well as classical French technique. His eclectic menu tilts toward seafood, with starters that include a seafood risotto and a seared tuna with wasabi aïoli. For dinner, we recommend the macadamia nut–crusted ono with a roasted-pepper coconut sauce, and the herbed maple-glazed rotisserie chicken with caramelized onion jus. You'll love the New York steak, which gets a roasted garlic demi-glace and a wedge of blue cheese, and the Dayboat scallops with mandarin-orange beurre blanc. Desserts are fanciful, and the airy space has great vineyard views.

CALISTOGA INN RESTAURANT & BREWERY   ECLECTIC   12/20

1250 Lincoln Ave., Calistoga 94515
707-942-4104, *Open daily,* $$

If you 've had your fill of wine, check out the Calistoga Inn Restaurant and Brewery. In the summer the patio offers a pleasant place to rest, sip a wheat ale and snack on the house black-bean chile, crabcakes or refreshing Caesar salad. The dining room–bar area, which looks as if it's been transported from Gunsmoke, has a vintage bar, a display of antique plates and lots of old-timey touches. Entrées range from all over the world, from jerk chicken to a nice grilled steak. Desserts, like the chocolate brownie with ice cream, are gooey and simple.

CANTINETTA AT TRA VIGNE ITALIAN ¢

1050 Charter Oak Ave., St. Helena 94574
707-963-8888, *Open daily (until 5:30 p.m.)*

The Cantinetta at Tra Vigne is the quintessential wine-country deli and an ideal spot for the chefs at Tra Vigne next door to sell their homemade cheeses and sausages, the house-cured prosciutto, and an array of infused oils and vinegars. It also stocks a limited but well-chosen selection of Napa Valley wines and a large number of gourmet foods from other local producers. Prepared items include an excellent garlicky Caesar salad and slices of focaccia pizza, along with overstuffed sandwiches and a tangy lemon-garlic roasted chicken. Dine outdoors on Tra Vigne's sun-drenched patio, which brings to mind scenes from an Italian piazza.

CATAHOULA CALIFORNIA/SOUTHERN 15/20

Mount View Hotel, 1457 Lincoln Ave., Calistoga 94515
707-942-2275, *Lunch & Dinner Wed.-Mon.*, $$$

The Catahoula is the state dog of Louisiana, which doesn't make much sense for the name of a restaurant in Calistoga's elegant, art deco Mount View Hotel—until you realize that chef-proprietor Jan Birnbaum is a native of that Gulf Coast state. His cooking reflects both the gutsy, soul-satisfying character of Paul Prudhomme's Cajun/Creole cookery and the style and refinement of the dishes he prepared as a chef at San Francisco's Campton Place Hotel before he migrated to the wine country. Somehow it all works, whether it's a spicy rooster gumbo or pan-fried, pecan-crusted jalapeño catfish with griddled hominy cakes. Anything from the wood-fired oven is terrific, including the thin-crust pizzas. In the adjacent bar, you can snack on tasty bites. Food also can be enjoyed poolside. Desserts, like the beignets, are appealing.

CHANTERELLE CALIFORNIA 12/20

804 First St., Napa 94559
707-253-7300, *Lunch Mon.-Sat., Dinner daily, Brunch Sun.*, $$

A satisfying mix of eclectic dishes awaits you in a room with floor-to-ceiling windows overlooking a serene private garden. Crisp and tender fried calamari, poached salmon with a fines herbes Champagne sauce, and a pan-seared venison highlighted with a rich bordelaise sauce and accompanied by a goat-cheese corn soufflé exemplify the cuisine. The prix-fixe menu gives you an appetizer, soup or salad, entrée, dessert and beverage for $34. The wine list is weighted toward Napa.

COMPADRES MEXICAN BAR & GRILL MEXICAN 12/20

Vintage Estate Mall, 6539 Washington St., Yountville 94599
707-944-2406, *Breakfast, Lunch & Dinner daily*, $$

Set in a historic building that was the home of 19th-century winemaker Gottlieb Groezinger, this stylish chain has an outdoor patio that's perfect for cocktails and snacking on tacos, wilted spinach salad or barbecued ribs. On the main menu you'll find fajitas, burritos and enchiladas, as well as meat, poultry and fish entrées made with Mexican flavors. The fiesta rice and black beans are prepared without lard. The margaritas come in several sizes and flavors. **Also in Palo Alto and Hawaii.**

THE DINER   AMERICAN/BREAKFAST   ¢

6476 Washington St., Yountville 94599
707-944-2626, Breakfast, Lunch & Dinner Tues.-Sun.

This is one of the most popular breakfast spots in the wine country, with long waits routine on weekends. Morning eaters line up for the satisfying waffles, pancakes, omelets, and house-made chorizo and eggs. The rest of the day, tuna sandwiches, burgers and Cal-Mex specialties like burritos and tacos fill out the menu. Tired of Cabernet? Have a malted instead.

DOMAINE CHANDON   CALIFORNIA/FRENCH 15/20

1 California Dr. (at Hwy. 29), Yountville 94599
707-944-2892, Lunch daily, Dinner Wed.-Sun. (Apr.-Oct.); Lunch & Dinner Wed.-Sun. (Nov.-Mar.), $$$

The revered restaurant at Domaine Chandon, the first winery in Napa to build a top-flight dining establishment on its premises, remains one of the best known in the valley. The setting, which overlooks slow-growing vines and a pretty pond, is as magnificent, and the dining room has gained a certain elegance with time. Chef Philippe Jeanty left to open his bistro nearby; his longtime sous chef, Robert Curry, is now at the helm. The kitchen is still finding its way after 20 years of Jeanty's guidance. We can recommend the black-mussel potato salad and the house-smoked rainbow trout as starters. Entrées we liked were the seared yellowfin tuna with a foie gras sauce and the pan-seared Atlantic salmon. The menu also features properly rare squab with sweet caramelized onion jus, as well as a rack of lamb accompanied by potato gnocchi that float off the plate. For dessert, indulge in the intense lemon tart or the warm chocolate soufflé. The wine list has bargains on Domain Chandon wines—big surprise—but prices generally run high.

DOWNTOWN JOE'S   AMERICAN/BREWPUB   ¢

902 Main St., Napa 94558
707-258-2337, Breakfast, Lunch & Dinner daily

Near the Napa River, which makes for a nice setting, Downtown Joe's brews 210 gallons of beer several times a week. The most popular, especially with winery workers, who say it takes a lot of beer to make good wine, is the Joe's Dancin' Feet Red Ale. A lager, a couple of ales and a stout are also made and on tap here. The food is pretty straightforward and involves Italian specialties, burgers and addictive garlic fries.

FOOTHILL CAFÉ   CALIFORNIA   14/20

2766 Old Sonoma Rd., Napa 94559
707-252-6178, *Dinner Wed.-Sun.*, $$

Diners wanting glamour opt for the high-profile restaurants in St. Helena or Yountville, but the town of Napa has seen an explosion of small, moderately priced restaurants that are chef owned. Although Foothill is located in an older shopping center, its warm atmosphere, first-rate food and small but intriguing wine list draw hungry travelers from all over the Bay Area. If you're not in the mood for chef-owner Jerry Shaffer's stylish California cuisine, such as his mussels and clams in a white wine broth, try the prime rib. Service is down-home friendly.

THE FRENCH LAUNDRY   FRENCH/CALIFORNIA   18/20

6640 Washington St., Yountville 94599
707-944-2380, *Lunch Fri.-Sun.*, *Dinner nightly*, $$$$

For 15 years, the restaurant in this rustic stone building on a quiet street in Yountville was a Bay Area institution under proprietors Sally and Don Schmitt. But the couple eventually got tired of the daily grind, and in 1994 a new French Laundry was born when chef-owner Thomas Keller arrived from L.A. With Keller in the kitchen, the food has soared to stratospheric heights, yet the restaurant has stayed true to its rural, wine-country roots. There's no big-city glitz or attitude, just impeccably prepared and artfully presented cuisine that few restaurants in the U.S. can match. Keller also has a refreshing sense of humor about his cooking, unusual in a chef operating at such rarefied culinary levels. A case in point: the fetchingly named "tongue in cheek," buttery beef cheeks paired with slices of veal tongue, pencil-thin baby leeks and horseradish cream. Or take his coffee and doughnut: an espresso mousse encircled by puff pastry. Keller's restaurant boasts smoothly professional service and an extensive wine list, with many choices available by the half bottle. Reserve well in advance for a dinner here. Enjoying the multi-course prix-fixe meal can take about four hours, so —you're in nirvana.

GORDON'S   AMERICAN   13/20

6770 Washington St., Yountville 94599
707-944-8246, *Breakfast & Lunch Tues.-Sun.*, *Dinner Fri.*, $

Yountville is a small town and Sally Gordon has a small café, so sometimes it looks as if the entire population has stopped for coffee and the house-baked morning pastries. One taste of the raspberry muffins will persuade you to stop by when you're in the neighborhood, too. We also recommend the made-from-scratch daily soups, sandwiches—chicken, arugula and pesto for one—and the gigantic house-baked cookies. The small wine bar is fun in the late afternoon. The shop sells food to go, plus prepared and bottled products and wine. On Friday night a $29.50 prix fixe draws the locals and savvy tourists. A recent menu included the opportunity to buy wine at retail.

THE GRILL AT MEADOWOOD   AMERICAN   13/20

Meadowood Resort, 900 Meadowood Ln., St. Helena 94574
707-963-3646 x307, Breakfast, Lunch & Dinner daily, $$

Less formal than the Restaurant at the Meadowood Resort (see review below), this pretty bistro serves simple food in an airy ambience, American classics such as grilled salmon, rib-eye steak and crabcakes. The Grill is one of the few wine-country restaurants to present a spa menu, with five choices daily.

LA BOUCANE   FRENCH   13/20

1778 Second St., Napa 94559
707-253-1177, Dinner Mon.-Sat., $$$

In a region where easygoing California cuisine predominates, this restaurant, with its elaborately constructed classic French dishes, is a bit of an oddity. But Algerian-born chef-owner Jacques Mokrani is a colorful character and his food has plenty of personality. Mokrani's best starters include escargots in garlic butter and prawns Provençal. Standout entrées include the sweetbreads with port and the veal with applejack. Subtle essences are distinctively combined in the creamed vegetable soups. For dessert, a couple of real winners are the chocolate and hazelnut mousses. Served in a pleasant, remodeled Victorian house, dinners include soup, salad and dessert.

LA TOQUE   FRENCH   16/20

1140 Rutherford Rd., Rutherford 94573
707-963-9770, Lunch Sun., Dinner Wed.-Sat., $$$$

Before arriving in Napa in 1998, Ken Frank was a ground-breaking chef in Los Angeles. Here, Frank prepares what he wants when he wants, and guests are invited to come along for the ride. The rustic yet elegant restaurant is an adjunct to the Rancho Caymus Inn: Thirteen well-spaced tables are arranged around a giant floral centerpiece in the ochre-walled dining room featuring antique beams, a stone fireplace and soft lighting. Guests may choose to sample selected dishes across the hall in the comfy bar-lounge, rather than sign on for the multi-course prix-fixe dinners served with an optional wine pairing. First courses may include a game consommé with tender ravioli of chestnuts and rabbit, braised chanterelles and buttery brioche toast. A good candidate from the limited bar menu is the seared foie gras with fresh corn polenta and, in season, black truffles, which Frank uses lavishly (he makes terrific truffle ice cream). Rabbit prepared three ways, and a cannellini-cranberry bean ragoût with sugar snap peas, are examples of the later courses. Frank puts teeth in his cheese courses, and after all this, you might yet be tempted by the chocolate concorde, a complex arrangement of mousse ringed with chimneys of meringue.

LIVEFIRE GRILL & SMOKEHOUSE   AMERICAN   13/20

5518 Washington St., Yountville 94599
707-944-1500, *Lunch & Dinner daily, $$$*

As the name implies, Livefire is a hot, even toasty, restaurant. Earth tones, combined with the warmth of the wait staff, make it a cozy yet chic retreat. Armed with a French rotisserie, a Chinese smoker and wood that's augmented with California Chardonnay and Zinfandel barrel staves, the kitchen cooks your meat, fish and poultry just about any way you like it. Start off with zippy stuffed pasilla peppers. Options then include superb barbecued baby back ribs that have been rubbed with cumin, mustard, and 20 other herbs and spices and allowed to rest for 24 hours before they're soaked in house-made barbecue sauce. Cool off with a fruit cobbler à la mode.

MUSTARDS GRILL   CALIFORNIA   14/20

7399 St. Helena Hwy. (Hwy. 29), Napa 94558
707-944-2424, *Lunch & Dinner daily, $$*

A favorite stop on Highway 29 for many years now, this restaurant is the province of chef-owner Cindy Pawlcyn. Her California cuisine includes fare such as smoked Peking duck with "100 almond-onion" sauce, barbecued baby back ribs with corn pudding and slaw, and always popular fresh-fish specials, many of which are grilled. One universal favorite is the crisp tangle of deep-fried onion threads. The menu runs the gamut from hamburgers and sandwiches to starters such as curried-chicken skewers with grilled eggplant and sweet-onion relish, and seared rare ahi tuna with wasabi cream on sesame crackers. The nice choice of wines by the glass makes it easy to sample two or three varietals with dinner. Those who still have room should try the vanilla-bean angel-food cake.

NAPA VALLEY GRILLE   CALIFORNIA   13/20

6795 Washington St., Yountville 94599
Lunch Mon.-Sat., Dinner nightly, Brunch Sun., $$

In this bold, brash, huge dining room and patio, with a bustling wait staff, grill food means steak, fried potatoes and home-baked breads. But the broader menu also includes such creations as game hen served with caramelized onion–infused mashed potatoes, spicy linguine with jumbo prawns, and one pasta dish for which the restaurant is famous: black spaghetti with seafood in white wine, soy sauce and garlic. Side dishes include crispy potato pie and herbed french fries. The carefully chosen wine list starts with two dozen wines by the glass.

NAPA VALLEY WINE TRAIN   AMERICAN   12/20

1275 McKinstry St., Napa 94559
707-253-2111. *Departs daily for lunch, $$$*

OK, it's politically incorrect in the company of some Napa winemakers even to mention the Wine Train, but like many other touristy things, it can be fun. The food is straightforward—grills of chicken, salmon or red meat—and the wood-paneled cars are a piece of history. Service is excellent. After lunch, you'll be ushered into the car that houses the wine bar, to taste wines by the glass.

OAKVILLE GROCERY CAFÉ   MEDITERRANEAN   14/20

7848 St. Helena Hwy. (Hwy. 29), Oakville 94562
707-944-8802, *Breakfast & Lunch daily, $$*

Maybe Jeremiah Tower, of Stars fame in San Francisco, couldn't make a go of his café here, but the owner of the nearby Oakville Grocery knows what locals want. Folks down the valley stop by here for their breakfast favorites: two eggs with the works, chicken hash with poached eggs, and brioche french toast. At lunch you'll find roasted mussels and crabcakes, along with tasty sandwiches and pizzas.

PACIFIC BLUES CAFÉ   AMERICAN   ¢

6526 Washington St., Yountville 94599
707-944-4455, *Breakfast, Lunch & Dinner daily, $$*

This is the only blues restaurant in the Napa Valley. The rub is that the music kicks in only on Saturday night. But it's a lively place anytime to grab a burger and sit on the patio sipping a beer—ten brews are on tap. We liked the traditional buffalo drumettes and the beer-battered rock shrimp and calamari. The Cobb salad is a good light choice, but most of the menu relies on hearty all-American fare: St. Louis ribs, red-hot chile and fried chicken. The desserts are just OK.

PACIFICO MEXICAN RESTAURANT   MEXICAN   ¢

1237 Lincoln Ave., Calistoga 94515
707-942-4400, *Open daily*

The Mexican fare is tasty, and the surroundings—brick walls and colorful banners—and terrific margaritas make this a fun place. One nice touch: the still-warm tortilla chips come with pico de gallo, a vegetable relish. Combination plates, including a huge plate with all the specialties—chile relleno, taco, enchilada and tamale—cost less than $15.

PAIRS PARKSIDE   CALIFORNIA/FUSION   13/20

1420 Main St., St. Helena 94574
707-963-7566, *Lunch & Dinner Wed.-Mon., $$*

Pairs is a delightful spot for lunch or dinner. Yellow sponged walls and splashes of greenery near the wooden bar, where patrons also dine, soothe the eye. The prices are reasonable for the quality, and the food shows imagination. Start with the tasty Meyer-lemon oyster stew. The main dishes include chile-spiced sea bass with an artichoke-lentil gumbo; honey-cider roast suckling pig with pomegranate-pear chutney; and a host of other goodies. The wine list is well chosen, with a recommended wine for each item on the menu.

PASTA PREGO TRATTORIA ITALIAN 11/20

Grapeyard Shopping Center, 3206 Jefferson St., Napa 98445
707-224-9011, *Lunch Mon.-Fri, Dinner nightly*, $

Yet another Cal-Italian with an open kitchen and a lively ambience redolent of garlic. You'll find tasty pizzas, pastas and other trattoria standards—good for a quick family dinner.

PEARL CALIFORNIA 13/20

1339 Pearl St. #104, Napa 94559
707-224-9161, *Lunch & Dinner Tues.-Sat.*, $$

Peter and Nickie Zeller's first Napa eatery, Brown Street Grill—now closed—was a hit from day one, and its successor Pearl (in a different location) has now expanded its hours beyond lunch to include dinner service. At lunch you'll be happy with the soft tacos filled with ginger flank steak and chiles; smoked-chicken salad with Danish blue cheese, apples and toasted pecans; and a seared ahi sandwich. We love the barbecued oysters, the whole-leaf Caesar, and the triple double pork chop and New York steak poivre.

PIATTI RISTORANTE ITALIAN 12/20

6480 Washington St., Yountville 94599
707-944-2070, *Lunch & Dinner daily*, $$

Piattis are everywhere but in San Francisco, a conscious choice by restaurateur Claude Rouas, proprietor of the fancy Auberge du Soleil, and partner Bob Harmon. Who needs San Francisco if you have 16 venues in the surrounding suburbs? The Piattis have clearly come up with a winning formula: a little pizza, a little pasta, some grilled specialties—all served in the sort of warm, unpretentious trattoria setting that makes Italian food feel so, well, Italian. What to order? The antipasti, cheese-stuffed pizza, grilled radicchio wrapped in pancetta, any of the "rotisseried" items and the tiny roasted potatoes. The wine list combines wine-country favorites with selected Italian bottlings.

PINOT BLANC FRENCH/CALIFORNIA 15/20

641 Main St., St. Helena 94574
707-963-6191, *Lunch & Dinner daily*, $$$

Los Angeles chef Joachim Splichal has a flock of restaurants in Southern California, but his style didn't translate to the valley when Pinot Blanc opened three years ago. In a resort area where summer temperatures can hit the 90s, the look of the place--heavy velvet drapes, dark paneling--was stifling even with air conditioning. A recent remodeling changed all that. Now the walls open up in good weather, the paneling is white, and all the fabrics are lighter and brighter. And instead of the previously fussy food, the tastes of Provence infuse appetizers such as salmon rillettes, herbed fromage blanc, eggplant caviar, tapenade and foie gras with a Riesling-poached pear. The menu changes seasonally, but for dinner, we like the pork chop, steak frites, risotto and venison when it's available. Desserts are not up to the quality of the rest of the menu. The wine list has some rare local wines. We predict even more good things at Pinot Blanc in the future.

THE RESTAURANT AT MEADOWOOD   CALIFORNIA 15/20

Meadowood Resort, 900 Meadowood Ln., St. Helena 94574
707-963-3646 x303, *Dinner nightly, Brunch Sun.*, $$$

By the time you wind your way up the scenic Silverado Trail and then along the bucolic Meadowood Lane to the luxurious Meadowood Resort, you are reminded that some things are worth every penny they cost. Chef Pilar Sanchez has brought a fresh approach to a menu that was formerly overly French for the Napa Valley. It shows in her exquisitely wrought dishes, like the California Bunderfleisch, air-dried beef served with olive oil, lemon and shaved Parmesan. A rich, creamy mushroom soup is garnished with luscious fried Brie and a shower of black truffles. A goat-cheese risotto pairs with a tender veal chop. This is a dress-up kind of restaurant that feels like a grand lodge catering to well-heeled wine country gentry. The wine list offers an exhaustive collection of Napa Valley bottlings.

ROADHOUSE 29   AMERICAN/BARBECUE   12/20

1065 Main St., St. Helena 94574
707-967-9997, *Lunch Wed.-Sun., Dinner Tues.-Sun.*, $$

When it's time to eat—really eat, not dine—this roadside wonder fills the bill with hearty fare and lots of it. But given that it's in the Napa Valley, it stuffs the rib-eye with sautéed onions, mushrooms and a wedge of Brie. Owner Greg Perez, who ran a successful restaurant in St. Louis before opening this bare-wood-and-ceiling-fans joint, pays homage to local sensibilities in other ways. Most main courses are as substantial as half a smoked duck or an aromatic rosemary-smoked rack of lamb, but starters can be as elegant as sautéed local foie gras. Accompanied by any of the nearly 80 wines and topped off by chocolate-bourbon pecan pie, dinner here will really stick to your ribs.

RUTHERFORD GRILL   AMERICAN   11/20

1180 Rutherford Rd., Rutherford 94573
707-963-1792, *Lunch & Dinner daily*, $$

When this chain restaurant (part of Houston's) opened, it wasn't bad. The service was amateurish, but the ribs and rotisserie chicken were quite good. As time went on, though, the food went decidedly downhill. The ribs and chicken were cooked to a fare-thee-well and the service, rather than improving, got more fast-food-like. But locals patronize it, though we don't see how they can put up with the long waits. It must be because they can have cocktails on the patio or near the fireplace; a house-loaned beeper summons them to be seated.

SHOWLEY'S   CALIFORNIA   13/20

1327 Railroad Ave., St. Helena 94574
707-963-1200, *Lunch & Dinner Tues.-Sun.*, $$$

Southern California restaurateur Grant Showley took over the former Miramonte and has made it his own. Though the food isn't as impressive as it is at many similar local eateries, it's hearty, well-made fare that, with the excellent service and relaxed, comfortable atmosphere, makes Showley's worth a visit. Fine starters are the house-made duck rillettes and veal-pistachio pâté. The coq au vin and osso buco are winning presentations. For dessert, don't attempt the awfully sweet, chocolatey desserts. A piano player entertains on Friday and Saturday nights, and the best seating on a warm evening is under the sprawling fig tree on the back patio. Showley's cat sometimes slinks down the tree to check out the fare.

TERRA   CALIFORNIA   15/20

1345 Railroad Ave., St. Helena 94574
707-963-8931, *Dinner Wed.-Mon.*, $$$$

Terra has attracted a solid following, and for good reason. The extraordinary menu is filled with unusual dishes that stretch the definition of California cuisine. Chef Hiro Sone and Lissa Doumani, his wife and pastry chef, both worked for Wolfgang Puck at Spago. They've occupied this beautifully restored 1880s-vintage stone structure for several years now, turning out daringly sophisticated food. The tiled floors, flickering candles, cushy banquettes and wooden beams make this one of the most romantic restaurants in the valley. Sone draws on many countries for inspiration. A Thai-influenced grilled salmon comes enrobed in a kicky red curry sauce. His spicy tripe with spaghetti is heavenly for the adventurous, but so is his foie gras terrine; and a grilled quail sits atop wild-rice risotto. Doumani's desserts are a treat, especially her tiramisu. The wine list has all the Napa boutique varieties, plus nice wines from all over the world, listed as "foreign invaders."

TOMATINA   PIZZA   ¢

1016 Main St., St. Helena 94574
707-967-9999, *Open daily*

This offshoot of Tra Vigne is a good fast-food alternative for visitors to the valley, especially those with hungry kids along. You order a pizza at the counter, and a runner brings it to you when it's ready. Lots of long tables mean that groups are easily accommodated. Many of the choices are constructed of a pizza—your choice of topping—with a salad plopped on top. Pizza purists may not like it, but it is a meal-in-one.

TRA VIGNE ITALIAN 15/20

1050 Charter Oak Ave., St. Helena 94574
707-963-4444, *Lunch & Dinner daily, $$$*

Entering the grounds under the trellised archway, you feel as if you're on vacation in some part of Italy. You pass through the patio first, where tables are generously spaced apart for warm-weather dining. When you go through the heavy door, you encounter a spacious restaurant with tall ceilings, a bar, an open kitchen that faces the dining room, and delicious smells from grilled items, herbs and bread. Chef Michael Chiarello's food is generally delicious, but on occasion a dish may be completely off the mark. Part of the inconsistency is due to the high numbers of people this restaurant serves. You'll enjoy any of the pizzas or the house-cured duck prosciutto. Grilled items shine, particularly the salmon and the roasted chicken. The desserts and wine list have an Italian accent.

UVA TRATTORIA ITALIANA ITALIAN NO RATING

1040 Clinton St., Napa 94559
707-255-6646, *Lunch & Dinner daily, $$*

Chef-owner Candido Di Terlizzi is a newcomer to Napa but not to the Bay Area. He has owned restaurants in Berkeley since emigrating from his native Bari. When the popular Brown Street Grill moved to bigger quarters and reopened as Pearl, Di Terlizzi seized the opportunity to open in the town of Napa. The menu at Uva covers all the basics: pastas, risotto, gnocchi, pizza and traditional preparations of meat, poultry and seafood. At lunch the bill of fare includes panini, soups and salads. One nice touch is that pastas are offered in both appetizer and meal-sized portions. The small wine list ranges from Napa Valley varietals to selections from Italian producers.

VINTNERS COURT AMERICAN 12/20

Silverado Country Club, 1600 Atlas Peak Rd., Napa 94558
707-257-0200, *Dinner nightly, $$$*

The genteel surroundings perfectly match a solid menu of American classics and fresh New American dishes. Traditionalists can order Dungeness crabcakes, Caesar salad and filet mignon. Foodies can find carpaccio in truffle oil and fried herbs; house-smoked salmon on a potato crisp with horseradish cream; and pork chops in an achiote-lime marinade.

WAPPO BAR BISTRO CALIFORNIA 12/20

1226-B Washington St., Calistoga 94515
707-942-4712, *Lunch Wed.-Mon., Dinner Thurs.-Mon., $$*

Wappo is fine for an informal dinner, especially if you get to sit on the brick-paved patio, surrounded by rose bushes and

an arbor. In cool weather, the dark wood-panneled front dining room is cozy. The eclectic menu encompasses world
cuisines to sometimes less-than-satisfying results. But you have
to give the restaurant credit for attempting everything from
Greek to Indian cuisine. Wappo is such a homey-looking place
that it's a surprise when the service is curt. The good wine list
concentrates on Napa bottles priced under $30.

THE WINE SPECTATOR RESTAURANT   CONTEMPORARY NO RATING

Greystone, Culinary Institute of America
2555 Main St., St. Helena 94574
707-967-1010, *Lunch & Dinner Wed.-Mon.*, $$$

☎ 🏕 🍷 🍶

Taking over the historic Greystone Winery, the Culinary
Institute of America—the famed cooking school of Hyde Park,
New York—spent nearly $14 million to turn the sprawling,
dilapidated structure into a showplace academy and restau-
rant. *The Wine Spectator Magazine* contributed $1 million, so the
official name of this place is a confusing merger of all three
entities. Cooking at the Greystone is done by professionals, so
you don't wind up eating students' mistakes. A new chef, the
esteemed Todd Humphries, uses wild herbs and little-known
flavorings to enhance his market cuisine. His stewardship can
only mean good things for the restaurant. You'll dine in nou-
veau rustic splendor, in a room with 22-inch-thick volcanic
stone walls, punctuated by copper wall sconces and modern
metal sculptures. The wine list has come up to speed since the
opening and is fun to explore at the pleasant wine bar.

GOURMET SHOPS & MORE

BAKERIES: BREAD & PASTRY

MODEL BAKERY

1357 Main St., St. Helena 94574
707-963-8192, *Open Tues.-Sun.*

Former home-baker Karen Mitchell bought the Model
Bakery in 1984. Over its 70-year history, the various owners
have concentrated on either bread or pastries. While Mitchell
doesn't do wedding cakes and the like, she bakes simple pas-

tries and spectacular breads. Her workers produce lovely morning buns, scones, English muffins and bagels. Lured by these offerings, locals and visitors fill the café part of the bakery. The sourdough bread is made with a starter derived from wine-grape yeasts, while the pain au vin is a whole-wheat version. For lunch, you can get pizzas with inventive toppings.

NAPA VALLEY OVENS

1353 Lincoln St., Calistoga 94515
707-942-0777, *Open Thurs.-Tues.*

Fred Halpert, the chef-proprietor of Brava Terrace in nearby St. Helena, opened this stylish bakery/retail store on Calistoga's quaint main drag. Freshly baked breads, muffins, cookies, cakes and pastries are temptingly arrayed, along with luncheon items such as quiche, savory flatbreads, pizzas and meat-filled pies. Of course, a full selection of coffee drinks is available, as is homemade ice cream.

SCIAMBRA FRENCH BAKERY

685 S. Freeway Dr., Napa 94558
707-252-3072, *Open Mon.-Sat.*

Loaves of chewy sourdough, dark raisin-walnut, black-olive, honey-wheat and classic French country breads emerge from old-world brick ovens at this decades-old Italian-owned bakery. In addition to supplying Bay Area restaurants and distributing to local stores, the Sciambra family sells its loaves out of this storefront to locals and picnickers. Don't miss the heavenly array of cookies, cream puffs, lemon bars and napoleons.

CHEESE

See **Dean & DeLuca**, **Oakville Grocery** and **V. Sattui** under Delis/Gourmet Markets.

CHOCOLATE & CANDY

See Dean & DeLuca, Oakville Grocery and V. Sattui under Delis/Gourmet.

COFFEE & TEA

NAPA VALLEY COFFEE ROASTING COMPANY

1400 Oak Ave., St. Helena 94574
707-963-4293, *Open daily*

Located off the main drag on a sunny corner, this is one of the most popular hangouts in St. Helena. In the winter, with its tall windows looking out on a residential street, it's a cozy spot for a muffin, a coffee or tea drink, or for getting a pound of java beans to go. In summer, the draw is the outdoor tables, where pet dogs lounge around and their owners read newspapers with a cup of joe. The scones and bagels could be better.

DELIS/GOURMET MARKETS

DEAN & DELUCA MARKET

607 S. St. Helena Hwy. (Hwy. 29), St. Helena 94574
707-967-9980, *Open daily*

Tourists and local foodies who never look at prices will be happy here. This is the first West Coast branch of the esteemed Manhattan food and wine emporium. Prices are astronomical for simple foods like beans or produce. A section of all-California wines is impressive, but one savvy wine geek said that he found the same bottle of vintage Mondavi both here and at Keller's Market. At D & D it was priced at more than $250; at Keller's it was $70. The most attractive feature of the store is the excellent cheese selection and the cheese-aging room. All manner of fresh, bottled, packaged, bulk and frozen foods are handsomely displayed. One novelty, sold in the past, is the selection of giant cookies with the likenesses of Monica, Bill and Hillary. Monica was the most expensive at $20.

PALISADES MARKET

1506 Lincoln Ave., Calistoga 94515
707-942-9549, *Open daily*

Six years ago, Cary Gott, the senior executive vice president of wineries and vineyards for Seagram Wine Classics (he still works there), and his family bought this market and revamped it. The Gotts expanded the fresh deli section, introduced a much better wine selection, added gourmet condiments and olive oils, and brought in really good produce from area growers. Locals are happy, and visitors now have a good place "up valley" to buy picnic supplies and sandwiches.

OAKVILLE GROCERY

7856 St. Helena Hwy. (Hwy. 29), Oakville 94562
707-944-8802, *Open daily*

Joseph Phelps, the founder of Phelps Winery, had the foresight to open the Oakville Grocery many years ago so that city folks passing through the valley could stock up on well-made local products and good imported foodstuffs for a wine-country picnic. Oakville Grocery sells a variety of pâtés, cheeses, olive oils, imported cookies and local artisan breads. The house-cured olives are irresistible. The helpful counter people will make you a sandwich and there's an attractive selection of wines, sodas and beers to go with your lunch. If you're not planning a picnic, stop here on the way home for locally made goodies to-go. Warning: on a sunny Saturday or Sunday, the Oakville is likely to have a line out the door.

Also see **Oakville Café** under "Dining".

V. SATTUI WINERY

Hwy. 29 & White Ln., St. Helena 94574
707-963-7774, *Open daily*

When owner-winemaker Daryl Sattui opened this modest winery more than 20 years ago, he was cash poor, so he opened a deli to generate income and bring people in. Over the years, his wines have gotten better; his prepared foods and salads, sandwiches and baked goods have gone up several notches in quality; and he still maintains one of the nicest picnic areas in the valley. We especially like the cheese selection. Desserts and candies fill out the bill of fare. Best of all? No charge for the wine tasting, and shaded grounds on which to picnic.

ETHNIC MARKETS

LA LUNA MARKET

1153 Rutherford Rd., Rutherford 94573
707-963-3211, *Open daily*
ATM accepted.

If you ask a Hispanic vineyard worker or a couple of local cooks where they and their families shop for all things Latino, only one name comes up continuously: La Luna. Need a piñata, a video or kids' clothes? This is the spot. Want to pick up a good taco or burrito for lunch? La Luna again. Shoppers can find thin-sliced beef for carne asada, cuts of pork, fresh produce, and all manner of bottled, canned and frozen Mexican foodstuffs. We highly recommend the tamales, filled with savory pork and warm from the steamer. Está bueno!

FARMERS' MARKETS

ST. HELENA FARMERS' MARKET

Railroad Ave. at Pine St., St. Helena
No phone. *Open Fri. May-Nov.*

What a joy this market is! The products and produce come not only from the surrounding area but also from Santa Rosa and Sonoma county. You'll find identifiable local and branded cheeses such as Bellwether Farms' and Laura Chenel's. The most delicious vine-ripened tomatoes, baby lettuces, Santa Rosa plums, and corn bursting with sweetness are just some of the lovely and yummy produce items. Jams, vinegars and olive oils and even lamb can be had at a good price.

ICE CREAM

See the **Big Dipper** in "Dining".

MEAT, POULTRY & SEAFOOD

Gerhard's Sausages: see **Vallerga's Silverado Market** below.

KELLER'S MARKET

1320 Main St., St. Helena 94574
707-963-2114, *Open daily*

If you have children who have only been to mega-supermarkets, Keller's is a good example of a small old-time supermarket. All of life's necessities are here. And an independently owned butcher shop has pork, beef and lamb cuts, plus prepared meat entrées ready to be cooked or grilled: meat and vegetables on skewers, pork tenderloin wrapped in pancetta, or marinated cuts. The several kinds of house-made sausages are all terrific. They also stock well-priced wines.

OMEGA 3 SEAFOOD MARKET

1732 Yajome St., Napa 94559
707-257-3474, Open Tues.-Sat.

Workers from this market drive every day to Pier 45 in San Francisco to pick up fresh fish and seafood. Omega 3 sells up to 25 kinds of fish, including sushi-grade tuna, big-eye or yellowfin tuna for grilling; Hawaiian and Fijian fish and the ever popular Chilean sea bass. They carry fresh spot prawns from Monterey when they can get them in season, plus Dungeness crab and mussels and clams.

VALLERGA'S SILVERADO MARKET

426 First St., Napa 94558
707-253-1666, Open daily

One draw at this nice market is that you can buy Gerhard's sausages, which are made in an industrial part of Napa. Sales at the plant are wholesale only. Valleraga's carries just about all of Gerhard's line. The chicken sausages come in apple, Thai (with ginger), apricot, and jalapeño and tequila. Gerhard's also produces a smoked duck sausage, a smoked pork variety called andouille, and Italian sweet and hot sausages made with pork. Their wines are discounted (see review in "Wine, Brews & Spirits" below).

WINE, BREWS & SPIRITS

All wineries that are open to the public for touring and/or tasting sell their wines, though you won't get a discount unless you buy a case. Napa's gourmet grocery stores also carry a broad selection of local and international wines. (See review of Dean & DeLuca Market above for a report of outrageously wine pricing.)

ALL SEASONS CAFÉ & WINE SHOP

1400 Lincoln Ave., Calistoga 94515
707-942-6828, Open Thurs.-Tues.

The owners are wine connoisseurs of the first order. Looking for a little-known French or California wine? You may very well find it here, and you can have lunch in the café. The prices are fair.

NAPA ALE WORKS

110 Camino Oruga, Napa 94559
707-257-8381, Tours by appointment

John Wright, who co-founded Domaine Chandon more than 20 years ago, is never short of creative ideas. His latest is ale. With a couple of partners he founded the Ale Works five years ago. They produce Napa Red Ale, Napa Wheat Ale and Napa Oatmeal Stout. Their line of brews is served around the valley and sold in many local stores. A tour of the brewery can be a nice respite from winery hopping.

J.V. WAREHOUSE

Vallerga's Silverado Market, 426 First St., Napa 94558
707-253-1666, *Open daily*

Many local wine-industry people shop here, where a savvy buyer can get real bargains in good vintage wine. Set up like the Wine Club, everything is on the shelves: beer, spirits and wine.

WINE TOURING

For detailed maps and additional information about touring wineries in **Napa Valley, contact the Napa Valley Vintners Association** (900 Meadowood Ln., St. Helena 94574; 707-963-0148),

NAPA VALLEY HOLIDAYS

707-255-1050
$30 per person, reservations required
Very friendly and knowledgeable Eli and Laura Glick will pick you up at the Embassy Suites or Marriott hotel (both in the town of Napa) and take you in a comfortable bus to three Napa wineries and a lunch stop. The cost does not include lunch.

WINE & DINE TOURS

P.O. Box 513
St. Helena 94574
707-963-8930
Call for reservations & prices
If you'd like to see a few Napa or Sonoma wineries that are not open to the public and be treated to lunch and sparkling wine (perhaps in a wine cave?), this company will handle all the details, including your ground and air transportation, accommodations and spa treatments. A tour of three wineries plus lunch runs about $145.

WINERIES OPEN TO THE PUBLIC:

ACACIA WINERY

2750 Las Amigas Ln., Napa 94559
707-226-9991

BEAULIEU VINEYARD

1960 St. Helena Hwy. (P.O. Box 219)
Rutherford 94573
707-963-2411

BEAUCANON

1695 St. Helena Hwy. S., St. Helena 94574
707-967-5230 *(By Appt. Only)*

BERINGER VINEYARDS
2000 Main St. (P.O. Box 111),
St. Helena 94574
707-963-7115

CAKEBREAD CELLARS
8300 St. Helena Hwy., Rutherford 94573
707-963-5221

CAYMUS VINEYARDS
8700 Conn Creek Road
Rutherford 94573
707-963-4204 *(By Appt. Only)*

CHARLES KRUG WINERY
2800 Main St., St. Helena 94574
707-967-2201

CHATEAU MONTELENA
1429 Tubbs Ln., Calistoga 94515
707-942-5105

CHATEAU POTELLE WINERY
3875 Mt. Vedeer Road
Napa 94558
707-255-9440

CHÂTEAU WOLTNER
150 S. White Cottage Rd.
Angwin 95408
707-963-1744 *(By Appt. Only)*

CHIMNEY ROCK WINERY
5350 Silverado Trail, Napa 94559
707-257-2641

CLOS DU VAL WINERY
5330 Silverado Trail
Napa 94558
707-259-2225

CLOS PEGASE
1060 Dunaweal Ln., Calistoga 94515
707-942-4981

CODORNIU NAPA
1345 Henry Rd., Napa 94558
707-224-1668

CUVAISON WINERY
4550 Silverado Trail (P.O. Box 384)
Calistoga 94515
707-942-6266

DOMAINE CARNEROS
1240 Duhig Rd.
Napa 94581
707-257-0101, Fax 707-257-3020

DOMAINE CHANDON
   1 California Dr. (P.O. Box 2470)
   Yountville 94599
   707-944-8844

DOMAINE NAPA
   1155 Mee Ln.
   St. Helena 94574
   707-963-1666

DUCKHORN VINEYARDS
1000 Lodi Ln., St. Helena 94573
707-963-7108

FLORA SPRINGS WINERY
1978 W. Zinfandel Ln., St. Helena 94573
677 St. Helena Hwy. S. 94573 (tasting room)
707-967-8032

FOLIE À DEUX WINERY
   3070 St. Helena Hwy. (29)
   St. Helena 94574
   707-963-1160

FRANCISCAN ESTATES
   1178 Galleron Road
   Rutherford 94574
   707-963-7112

FREEMARK ABBEY
   3022 St. Helena Hwy. (P.O. Box 410)
   St. Helena 94574
   707-963-0554

FROG'S LEAP
   8815 Conn Creek Rd.
   Rutherford 94573
   707-963-4704

GRGICH HILLS CELLAR
   1829 St. Helena Hwy.
   Rutherford, CA 94573
   707-963-2784

GROTH VINEYARDS & WINERY
   750 Oakville Cross Rd. (P.O. Box 390)
   Oakville 94562
   707-944-0290

HAKUSAN SAKE GARDENS
One Executive Wy., Napa 94558
707-258-6160

HEITZ CELLARS
436 Hwy. 29, St. Helena 94573
707-963-3542

THE HESS COLLECTION WINERY
4411 Redwood Road
Napa 94558
707-255-1144

JOSEPH PHELPS VINEYARDS
200 Taplin Rd. (P.O. Box 1031)
St. Helena 94574
707-963-2745

LOUIS M. MARTINI
254 S. St. Helena Hwy. (P.O. Box 112)
St. Helena 94574
707-963-2736

MARKHAM VINEYARDS
2812 St. Helena Hwy. North
St. Helena 94574
707-963-5292

MERRYVALE VINEYARDS
1000 Main St.
St. Helena 94574
707-963-2225

MUMM NAPA VALLEY
8445 Silverado Trail (P.O. Drawer 50)
Rutherford 94573
707-942-3300

NIEBAUM-COPPOLA ESTATE
1991 St. Helena Hwy. (29)
Rutherford 94573
707-963-9435

PINE RIDGE WINERY
5901 Silverado Trail
Napa 94558
707-253-7500

PRAGER WINERY AND PORT WORKS
1281 Lewelling Ln.
St. Helena 94574
707-963-3720

RAYMOND VINEYARD
849 Zinfandel Ln., St. Helena 94573
707-963-3141

ROBERT MONDAVI WINERY
7801 St. Helena Hwy. (P.O. Box 106)
Oakville 94562
707-963-9611

ROBERT PEPI WINERY
7585 St. Helena Hwy.
Oakville 94562
707-944-2807

ROMBAUER VINEYARDS
   3522 Silverado Trail
   St. Helena 94574
   707-963-5170

RUTHERFORD HILL WINERY
   200 Rutherford Hill Rd.
   Rutherford 94573
   707-963-7194

S. ANDERSON WINERY
1473 Yountville Crossroads, Yountville 94599
707-944-8642

ST. SUPÉRY VINEYARDS & WINERY
   8440 St. Helena Hwy.
   Rutherford 94573
   800-942-0809 or 707-963-4507

SCHRAMSBERG VINEYARDS
   1400 Schramsberg Rd.
   Calistoga 95415
   707-942-4558

SILVER OAK WINE CELLARS
   915 Oakville Cross Rd. (P.O. Box 414)
   Oakville 94562
   707-944-8808

STAG'S LEAP WINE CELLARS
   5766 Silverado Trail
   Napa 94558
   707-944-2020

STERLING VINEYARDS
   1111 Dunaweal Ln. (P.O. Box 365)
   Calistoga 95415
   707-942-3300

SUTTER HOME WINERY
   277 St. Helena Hwy. South
   St. Helena 94574
   707-963-3104

TREFETHEN VINEYARDS
   1160 Oak Knoll Ave. (P.O. Box 2460)
   Napa 94558
   707-255-7700

V. SATTUI WINERY
Corner Hwy. 29 and White Ln., St. Helena 94574
707-963-7774

WHITEHALL LANE WINERY
1563 St. Helena Hwy. S., St. Helena 94574
707-963-9454

SONOMA COUNTY

Sonoma Valley spreads out to the west of Napa, and the pace of life here is decidedly quieter and more relaxed. Nevertheless, it has come into its own as a wine producing region and can no longer be considered second best. The picturesque town of Sonoma marks the south boundary of the valley. As you head north, you'll pass through the towns of Kenwood and Glen Ellen. Santa Rosa is the largest city and the business center of the county. Further north, Healdsburg, Geyserville and Cloverdale each have numerous small wineries. Sonoma is also renowned for its bounty: vegetables and fruits, cheeses, ducks and rabbits (indeed, game of all kinds) can be found in local restaurants and gourmet food shops.

RESTAURANTS

APPLEWOOD INN & RESTAURANT CALIFORNIA/FRENCH 15/20
13555 Hwy. 116, Guerneville 95446
707-869-9093, Dinner Tues.-Sat., $$-$$$

Located in the Russian River Valley, this quiet and very appealing off-the-beaten-path country inn artfully blends small-town friendliness with the attentive service you can expect in big-city hotels. At press time, owners Jim Caron and Darryl Notter were about to move their restaurant to a new setting across the courtyard, with two rock fireplaces, lofty beamed ceilings, an elegant curved copper bar and views of the garden and redwood trees. David Frakes, the chef, is taking the à la carte and six-course prix-fixe menus in a Mediterranean direction with offerings such as Chardonnay-poached prawns and arugula salad, pan-fried soft-shell crab with a baby leek and olive nage, and a delicate lavender crème brûlée. Selections from the award-wining wine list can be paired with the six-course feast for an extra charge.

BABETTE'S CALIFORNIA/FRENCH 15/20
464 First St. E., Sonoma 95476
707-939-8921, Dinner Tues.-Sat., $$-$$$$

Babette's is the creation of a charming young couple, Daniel Patterson and Elizabeth Ramsey. Although Patterson lacks formal culinary schooling, he makes up for it with prodigious talent and an artist's eye for detail and presentation. Ramsey is the quintessentially gracious hostess. A block off the Sonoma Plaza, Babette's is actually two restaurants in one: a casual French bistro and wine bar in the front, and the Feast Room to the rear, where the chef offers exquisite multi-course menus. These prix-fixe dinners, made up of many small dishes, may begin with Sonoma foie gras with cherries, hazelnuts and chervil, followed by lobster-corn soufflé, smoked and pan-fried

Muscovy duck breast and a delectable walnut-chèvre tart.

BAYVIEW RESTAURANT   AMERICAN   13/20

Inn at the Tides, 835 Pacific Coast Hwy. (Hwy. 1), Bodega Bay 94923
707-875-2751, *Dinner Wed.-Sun.*, $$$

The menu here concentrates on seafood, with a sprinkling of meat and poultry dishes. The monthly winemaker dinners are a good opportunity to meet the local stars of the wine industry. A carpaccio of smoked duck is a nice non-seafood appetizer, but the Dungeness crabcakes with basil aïoli are truly memorable. The menu is eclectic. A filet mignon served atop a béarnaise sauce is named for Alfred Hitchcock, who filmed The Birds on location at the inn. Other choices include a wild-mushroom-encrusted rack of lamb and shrimp.

BIG THREE FOUNTAIN   AMERICAN   ¢

Sonoma Mission Inn, 18140 Sonoma Hwy. (Hwy. 12)
Boyes Hot Springs 95476
707-938-9000, *Breakfast, Lunch & Dinner daily*

Here you can get the greatest chocolate malts. Good lunch bets include cheeseburgers and sandwiches as well as home-made pizzas and hearty pastas. Oenophiles can order off the Grille's extensive wine list.

BISTRO RALPH   CALIFORNIA   14/20

109 Plaza St., Healdsburg 95448
707-433-1380, *Lunch Mon.-Fri., Dinner nightly*, $$$

This narrow sliver of a restaurant is almost unnoticeable among the small storefronts that line Healdsburg's charming, park-like town plaza. Chef-proprietor Ralph Tingle melds culinary sophistication with back-country neighborliness—an inviting and thoroughly satisfying combination. The menu consists mostly of hearty and popular Cal-Med dishes—grilled polenta with a mushroom ragoût, or the local C-K leg of lamb—with occasional nods to Asian cuisine, like the Szechuan-peppered calamari with ginger-soy dipping sauce, or the seared-rare ahi with a salad of green papaya and glass noodles. Dessert might be an ethereal chocolate soufflé.

CA' BIANCA RESTAURANT   ITALIAN   14/20

825 Second St., Santa Rosa 95404
707-542-5800, *Lunch Mon.-Fri., Dinner nightly*, $$

This stately white Victorian with a wraparound veranda and a shaded patio is a striking and comfortable former home. The owners have done a spectacular job remodeling the interior. Pale gray murals of Italy decorate the wall spaces framed with wood moldings. The menu does not have the Italian-American focus of most of the other local Italian eateries. We like the polenta topped with Gorgonzola and sautéed mushrooms for a starter; the pasta dishes are some of the best around and include light spinach gnocchi, spaghettini with clam sauce, and ravioli stuffed with salmon and Mascarpone. We loved the roasted lamb, breast of duck and pork sauté. Save room for the chocolate terrine or the poached pear with Mascarpone. The selections of port, grappa and wine are excellent.

CAFÉ CITTI — ITALIAN — 12/20

9049 Sonoma Hwy. (Hwy. 12), Kenwood 95452
707-833-2690, *Lunch & Dinner daily, $$*

It looks like another roadside eatery, but when you enter Café Citti, you're struck by the handsome deli case stocked with freshly made salads, cold cuts and cheeses, and by the bronze chickens twirling on the rotisserie. Locals love this place and tourists stop for picnic supplies. The outdoor deck is a pleasant area for tucking into a garlic-strewn pasta dish.

CAFÉ DA VERO — CALIFORNIA/ITALIAN — 12/20

7531 Healdsburg Ave., Sebastopol 95472
707-823-1531, *Lunch Mon.-Fri., Dinner nightly, $$*

The chef-owner here prepares a pretty straightforward Italian menu, with more than a dozen pastas. The smaller list of entrées featuring meat, poultry and seafood, ranges from veal Parmigiano to pollo Portofino, in which a tender half chicken breast is sautéed in butter with white wine, capers and prawns. At lunch, the soup and salad combos are popular.

CAFÉ LA HAYE — CONTEMPORARY — 14/20

140 E. Napa St., Sonoma 95476
707-935-5994, *Dinner Tues.-Sat., Brunch Sat.-Sun., $$*

This casual spot off the plaza depends on simple-sounding entrées that often incorporate one or two surprise ingredients. It also depends on the amazing dexterity of cooks who turn out half a dozen main courses working in a kitchen smaller than a ship's galley. What sounds simple—say, a filet of beef—is seared in black pepper and lavender and served with Gorgonzola potato gratin. A grilled pork chop gets a hot-sweet mustard vinaigrette and a warm cabbage salad that seems born to the role. We give brunch extra points for the divine white Cheddar grits and grilled ham. The high-ceilinged storefront room is split level, which gives it a bit of visual interest and allows half the diners to see what the other half is eating.

CAFÉ LOLO — CALIFORNIA — 14/20

620 Fifth St., Santa Rosa 95404
707-576-7822, *Lunch Mon.-Fri., Dinner Mon.-Sat., $$*

A tiny jewel of a restaurant in downtown Santa Rosa, Café Lolo melds the laid-back spirit of the wine country with exciting food. The pleasure here is dining on chef-owner Michael

Quigley's finely crafted, boldly flavorful creations, such as crispy sweetbreads with fava beans, smoked bacon and white truffle oil, and a duck confit and wild mushroom lasagne. Entrées such as the grilled lamb T-bone and the baked Alaskan halibut enrobed in an herb crust are both memorable.

THE CAFÉ AT CHÂTEAU SOUVERAIN   CALIFORNIA/FRENCH   ¢

400 Souverain Rd., Geyserville 95441
707-433-3141, *Lunch daily, Dinner Fri.-Sun.*

Once an elegant restaurant, this venue has been downscaled to an airy café that serves fresh, excellent French/California fare. It's a good place to pair a lunch or dinner with the winery's fine Chardonnays or Zinfandels.

DEUCE   CONTEMPORARY   14/20

691 Broadway, Sonoma 95476
707-933-3823, *Lunch & Dinner daily, $$*

Art nouveau touches and carved wood finishings on doors and arches left by former tenants distinguish the interior of this downtown Sonoma restaurant. Veteran valley restaurateurs Peter and Kirstin Stewart, who met chef Richard Whipple at Masa's, wisely promote local products like sea bass, wild mushrooms, duck and produce. It's rare to find the perfect fried calamari, but here they are: tangy, crunchy and tender, accompanied by a low-key Key lime aïoli. The top dishes are a sweet breast of roast duck served with potato risotto and an ultra-fresh halibut roasted with cilantro-lime butter. Diners seeking simpler fare will find a dry-aged club steak. We're crazy about pastry chef Christopher Dever's chocolate mousse tower.

EQUUS   CALIFORNIA/MEDITERRANEAN   12/20

Fountain Grove Inn, 101 Fountain Grove Pkwy., Santa Rosa 95403
707-578-6101, *Lunch Mon.-Fri., Dinner nightly, Brunch Sun., $$*

Local duck figures largely on the menu here: you'll find a Sonoma duck antipasto plate, a barbecued duck leg, a slow-cooked duck breast with a zucchini-tomato concassé. Other satisfying offerings include the lobster bisque and the filet mignon with wild-mushroom risotto.

FELIX & LOUIE'S   ITALIAN/AMERICAN   12/20

106 Matheson St., Healdsburg 95448
707-433-6966, *Lunch & Dinner daily, $$*

In 1998, Ralph Tingle, of Bistro Ralph, opened his second restaurant across the plaza from his first, and it's a total departure from the bistro's chic Sonoma cuisine. The order of the day here is hearty Italianate fare, from bruschetta to wood-fired pizza to fish and baby back ribs, plus a sumptuous lasagne that defies its pallid description as vegetarian. And the pizzas, cooked in full view in a back corner oven, are inspired: rock shrimp nestles in pesto and goat cheese on one; on another, red onion spikes up smoked salmon set off with crème fraîche. The full bar somewhat compensates for an unimpressive wine list that offers only a couple of by-the-glass choices.

GARY CHU'S   CHINESE   12/20

611 Fifth St., Santa Rosa 95402
707-526-5840, *Lunch & Dinner Tues.-Sun, $$*

One of the best Chinese restaurant in Sonoma County, Gary Chu's aims for the highest quality but doesn't exceed the bounds of traditional cooking. The vast menu includes spicy chicken with sweet basil and snow peas (piquant but not hot); walnut prawns are served in a sweet, creamy apple dressing. Seasonal items might include crispy chicken salad in a ginger-vinegar dressing, or pine-nut chicken in lettuce cups served with a delicate hoisin sauce. The handsome jade-and-black decor is peaceful, and the seating very comfortable. The small wine list is reasonably priced and well chosen.

THE GENERAL'S DAUGHTER CALIFORNIA   11/20

400 Spain St., Sonoma 95476
707-938-4004, *Lunch & Dinner daily, $$$*

In the 19th century, this beautifully restored Victorian was the residence of the daughter of General Mariano Vallejo, the last Spanish governor of California. The decor by the designer-owner has whimsical touches like the prints of cow's hooves climbing up a wall and into a realistic painting of—what else?—cows. The setting is beautiful, but the food and service have never equaled it. Start with a Caesar salad and then try the tender Sonoma lamb or grilled rib-eye steak.

GIRL & THE FIG   FRENCH/CALIFORNIA   14/20

13690 Arnold Dr., Glen Ellen 95442
707-938-3634, *Dinner nightly, $$*

This restaurant has captured the imagination of locals and visitors alike. The way the menu describes the food is as whimsical as the name of the restaurant itself. Soups are described as "from the garden to the stockpot." The restaurant takes advantage of the local artisanal cheeses, with its nightly cheese plates: one with aged sausage and olives, another with fresh fruit and nuts. Another sampler concentrates solely on goat cheeses. We like the pork tenderloin, the lamb with mustard sauce and the fat and juicy burger. The excellent wine list hits French varietals heavily—with 16 Viogniers and lots of other Rhone bottlings, for example—mostly from California.

GLEN ELLEN INN RESTAURANT CALIFORNIA 14/20

13670 Arnold Dr., Glen Ellen 95442
707-996-6409, *Dinner nightly*, $$

Christian and Karen Bertrand, who opened this restaurant in 1993, recently added an outdoor seating area, a new dining room and an exhibition kitchen. The menu now includes a chef's tasting menu priced between $35 and $50, which can be paired with selected glasses of wines. On the regular menu expect starters like the fire-and-ice salad: field greens, apples, pears, Laura Chenel goat cheese, sweet pecans and a kick from jalapeño essence. Main courses include a smoked Gouda-artichoke and a filet mignon. The exclusively Sonoma wine list has quite a few gems.

THE GRILLE AT SONOMA MISSION INN CALIFORNIA 13/20

Sonoma Mission Inn, 18140 Sonoma Hwy. (Hwy. 12)
Boyes Hot Springs 95476
707-938-9000, *Dinner Mon.-Fri., Brunch Sun.*, $$$

Toni Robertson has breathed new life into the grill at this venerable spa, where many dishes carry a list of their calories, cholesterol and fat content. Robertson takes Laura Chenel goat cheese and makes it into a smooth and satiny flan. "Eat local lamb" could be the watchword. Chef Robertson prepares it simply, marinated in herbs and Dijon mustard and then grilled and served with a creamy risotto. A grilled duck breast is napped with mango sauce, and tender ostrich is paired with a corn salsa. Lunch at the Grille, at a table overlooking the pool on a sunny day, can be a treat. The wine list is deep in California wines, with a special emphasis on Sonoma County.

HEIRLOOM CALIFORNIA 14/20

110 West Spain St., Sonoma 95476
707-939-6955, *Lunch & Dinner daily*, $$

The baby spinach and frisée salad hints at the culinary talents of chef Michael Dotson, who serves up a winning combination with crunchy toasted almonds, paper-thin pear slices and Sonoma-made Bellwether Carmody cheese. The menu is short but promising, with starters like sweet-potato dumplings with truffled cheese. Dotson's idea, honed after three years at PlumpJack's in San Francisco and Squaw Valley, is to meld American dishes with French influences. That melding translates into, say, grilled free-range Argentine rib-eye with a cardoon-and-potato gratin or, perhaps, a roasted half chicken with sage and butternut squash. Heirloom opened in late 1998 at the historic Sonoma Hotel. The wine list is small and mostly Sonoma based.

JOHN ASH & CO. CALIFORNIA 13/20

4330 Barnes Rd., Santa Rosa 95403
707-527-7687, *Lunch Tues.-Sat., Dinner nightly, Brunch Sunday, $$$*

☎ ♥ 🖵 👥 🍸 ➡

When John Ash founded this restaurant 15 years or so ago, it was one of the first to serve a market-based menu—what came to be called California cuisine. Ash is now a consultant with the restaurant, having sold his interest a few years ago. Although the restaurant may no longer be on the cutting edge, the menu has a lot to like. We recommend the Sonoma onion soup with Gruyère, the sautéed Dungeness crabcakes, and the salmon grilled Japanese style, as well as the pan-seared pepper-coated ahi tuna. But a reduction sauce of Cabernet and sun-dried cherries, or a side dish of pears and yams, leave us cold.

KENWOOD RESTAURANT & BAR CALIFORNIA 13/20

Sonoma Hwy. (Hwy. 12), Kenwood 95452
707-833-6326, *Lunch & Dinner Wed.-Sun., $$$*

☎ 🖵 🚶 👥 🍷

At this light and airy Sonoma Valley restaurant you are likely to see local winemakers at the next table. The bar is popular with other locals, too. Fresh Sonoma County ingredients are shown to advantage in such dishes as roast Petaluma duck served with house-made ravioli filled with lamb, mushrooms and herbs and napped with a red-wine reduction sauce. Starters are filling (try the baked polenta with goat cheese, tomatoes and herbs from the restaurant's garden), as are the entrées. Desserts, like the delightful chocolate-walnut tart, are homey. The wine list, too, features locally grown bottlings.

LASALETTE PORTUGUESE/BRAZILIAN 14/20

18625 Hwy. 12, Sonoma 95476
707-938-1927, *Lunch & Dinner Tues.-Sun., $$*

☎ 🖵 👥 ➡

A native of the Azores, Manny Azevedo worked at the Kenwood Restaurant before finally getting back to his roots. LaSalette, named for his mother, is the only place in the wine country you're likely to encounter Portuguese food, let alone dishes inspired by African and Brazilian cuisines. The menu ranges from an elegant stuffed squid to cataplana, a fragrant stew of tomatoes and mussels served peasant style with bread slices to sop up the broth. Other specialties include Mozambique prawns that maintain their integrity in a mélange of tomatoes and grilled plantains. Paintings and sculpture enliven the off-white walls in this small, upbeat restaurant.

LISA HEMENWAY BISTRO CALIFORNIA NO RATING

710 Village Court Mall, Farmer's Lane, Santa Rosa 95401
707-526-5111, *Lunch & Dinner Mon.-Sat., Tea Mon.-Fri., Brunch Sun., $$*

☎ 👥 🍷

In Santa Rosa, Lisa Hemenway, the popular restaurateur and caterer, has reorganized her business in the Montgomery

Village shopping center, closing her large eponymously named restaurant in December and creating a bistro in what used to be her nearby take-out venue. Now called Lisa Hemenway Bistro, her entire operation, including takeout and catering, is in one space. The chef-owner has put together an eclectic menu based on Sonoma County products. Look for the familiar charcuterie plate, eggplant rouladin and coq au vin. The wine list contains a number of high-quality selections.

LO SPUNTINO: AN ITALIAN TASTE   CALIFORNIA/ITALIAN   ¢

400 First St. E., Sonoma 95476
707-935-5656, *Lunch to 6 p.m. Sun.-Thurs., Lunch & Dinner Fri.-Sat.*

Several years ago, Vicki and Sam Sebastiani, of the Sonoma winemaking family, established the Viansa Winery and Italian Marketplace in the Carneros region. So it was natural to do a branch in the town of Sonoma. The chefs make all manner of salads, panini, and roasted meats. Lo Spuntino, like Viansa, is a great place to buy Sam Sebastiani's wines—mostly Italian varietals—and picnic supplies for a snack or light dinner.

MADRONA MANOR   CALIFORNIA   13/20

1001 Westside Rd., Healdsburg 95448
707-433-4231, *Dinner nightly, $$$*

Chef Todd Muir established the style of the food in the dining room of this lovely 19th-century mansion at the edge of the Dry Creek Valley. Muir is now the culinary consultant, and the chef de cuisine, Chris Mazzanti, continues Muir's focus on California cuisine. Like Muir, he draws on top local ingredients. It's clear from recent visits that the food is less fussy these days. Seared Day Boat scallops, for example, are paired with a sugar-pumpkin truffle sauce, while a foie gras terrine is married with a grilled pear and candied cashews. The mesquite-grilled beef or Dijon pistachio-encrusted lamb will satisfy meat lovers. Finishing touches include a luscious banana mousse.

MARY'S PIZZA SHACK   PIZZA   ¢

452 First St. E., Sonoma 95476
707-938-8300, *Open daily*

Some "best-kept secrets" should be kept when it comes to local restaurants, but the venerable pizza chain Mary's is not one of them. Mary's is terrific: you can choose regular thin or thick crust, regular pizza tomato sauce or basil and tomato. Toppings number an astounding two dozen. Pastas, hamburgers, salads and Italian casserole dishes round out the menu. But everyone comes here for the pizza. **Also in Sonoma, Napa, the East Bay & Marin.**

MES TROIS FILLES   FUSION   12/20

13648 Arnold Dr., Glen Ellen 95442
707-938-4844, *Dinner Wed.-Sun., $$*

Chef Len Moriyama has three daughters—thus the name of the restaurant. The chef fuses French technique, Japanese flavors and local ingredients into a personalized cuisine that sometimes hits and sometimes misses. Wine sauces appear in many dishes—the rack of lamb with a Merlot sauce is particularly good. The room is pale pink, and flowers grace each table.

MISTRAL   MEDITERRANEAN   13/20

1229 N. Dutton Ave., Santa Rosa 95401
707-578-4511, *Lunch & Dinner daily*, $$

Michael Hirschberg is a trailblazing Sonoma restaurateur. He opened Siena and the delightful Mescolanza bakery. Siena, an Italian concept, morphed excitingly into Mistral. Hirschberg's Mediterranean menu features some of the pasta dishes of Siena, alongside Greek spinach salad, house-cured salmon, ahi tuna grilled rare with olive-caper aïoli and breast of chicken stuffed with ham and Gruyère cheese. The mainly local wine list is astoundingly well priced and is supplemented by esoteric Italian wines. You can enjoy the lovely patio as well.

MIXX   CONTEMPORARY   15/20

135 Fourth St., Santa Rosa 95402
707-573-1344, *Lunch Mon.-Fri., Dinner Mon.-Sat.*, $$

This is among the best restaurants in wine country. Chef Dan Berman's chicken pie is not à la Swanson's: it has large chunks of chicken breast and fresh, still-crunchy vegetables (such as haricots verts) in a Marsala-cream sauce. A deceptively straightforward-sounding grilled venison flank steak is paired with a relish of sun-dried cherries and pecans, plus roasted sweet potatoes and ginger green beans. Start with the smoked seafood platter, and don't miss soups such as the guajillo chile and smoked chicken. Wines are almost all local and fairly priced, with a by-the-glass program with of 20 selections. Dan's wife, Kathleen, creates first-class desserts, including a frozen Caribbean Key lime torte.

MIXX PASTRY & ACCESSORIES   CONTEMPORARY   ¢

135 Fourth St., Santa Rosa 95402
707-573-1344, *Lunch Tues.-Sat.*

Kathleen and Dan Berman, the owners of Mixx, have transformed Mixx Express into a pastry shop that also offers a limited menu of quick lunches and chocolate. They also sell coffee beans and coffee and tea drinks.

101 MAIN BISTRO & WINE BAR   CALIFORNIA/FRENCH   15/20

101 S. Main St., Sebastopol 95472
707-829-3212, *Dinner Tues.-Sun., Brunch Sun.*, $$$

This 40-seat jewel of the Russian River wine region, deserves its popularity. The breadth of the wine list would be exceptional even for a restaurant three times its size: it has 125

regional offerings, 30 by the glass, and many hard-to-find vintages. The creative renovation of the elegant 1907 bank building—30-foot ceilings draped with woven bronze fabric, rich terra-cotta walls, and a hand-forged wrought iron bar with twinkling lights—shows a refined sensibility. The chef's salad of chopped beets, cucumber, smoked shrimp and avocado is molded and garnished with chive sprigs. Roasted escolar sits on a pool of delicate mango sauce. A dish celebrating the local lamb comes with locally foraged wild mushroom. Dessert finales include a poached-pear goat-cheese tart.

PIATTI RISTORANTE   ITALIAN   12/20

504 First St.W., Sonoma 95476
707-996-2351, *Lunch & Dinner daily, $$$*

☎ 🖥

See the review under "Napa Valley Restaurants" in this chapter.

RASTA DWIGHT'S BARBECUE   BARBECUE   13/20

Grapevine Shopping Center, 7981 Old Redwood Hwy., Cotati 94931
707-794-1268, *Open Tues.-Sun., $*

👫

Previously known for its rock 'n' roll bars and annual accordion festival, Cotati now sports some of the best barbecue north of Oakland, thanks to restaurateur-chef Rasta Dwight Jones. The fanciful Caribbean-inspired murals that line the walls of the take-out counter and back dining room set the tone for Jones' attention to detail and the fresh ingredients. He slow-smokes his jerk pork, spareribs and brisket for 13 hours and mixes all his own spices, throwing in a little bit of Texas, a smidgen of St. Louis and a whole lot of his own preferences. Sonoma locals have learned to call ahead to reserve the "Burn Your Face" hot links & chicken before they sell out. The side dishes change daily.

RAVENOUS   CALIFORNIA   ¢

117 North St., Healdsburg 95448
707-431-1770, *Lunch & Dinner Wed.-Sun.*

✂ 👫

This tiny hole-in-the-wall, off the lobby of the wonderful Raven movie and performance theater, has surprisingly sophisticated food for its size. Expect toothsome quail, good sandwiches, freshly made soups and delicate salads. This café is convenient, affordable and very good before or after a film.

ROB'S RIB SHACK   AMERICAN   ¢

18709 Arnold Dr., Sonoma 95476
707-938-8520, *Lunch & Dinner daily*

🖥 🍴 👫

Chef-owner Rob Larman brings years of experience heading the kitchens of upscale Bay Area restaurants to this fun and funky roadhouse. There's live music on summer nights, a driving range in back, and a dining room set with picnic tables and strung with bright red lights in the shape of hot chiles. Larman built the wood-fired smoker that delivers up lip-smacking baby back ribs, savory chicken and meltingly tender pork butt. Burgers, salads and sandwiches are also available.

TIDES WHARF RESTAURANT   AMERICAN   12/20

The Inn at the Tides, 835 Pacific Coast Hwy. (Hwy. 1), Bodega Bay 94923
707-875-2777, Breakfast, Lunch & Dinner daily, $$

It's great family-vacation fun to sit in this rustic wharfside setting off the beaten path in the rugged Sonoma Coast hills and watch fishing boats unloading their day's catch. Inside, you'll be eating the day's catch, from oysters and clams to cracked Dungeness crab and grilled salmon. Dishes come with chowder or salad, and hunks of sourdough.

TWISTED VINES   CALIFORNIA   12/20

16 Kentucky St., Petaluma 94952
707-766-8162, Lunch & Dinner Tues.-Sat., $$

This wine bar, café and wine shop in the Landmark building is popular with the locals, who no doubt appreciate the hearty fare and the wine sold at retail prices plus a $5 corkage. Many of the vegetarian offerings—such as the rosemary polenta rounds with pesto—are among the best bets. Roasted chicken prepared in a variety of ways, and a beef bourguignon are all reliable comfort fare. The ever changing retail wine list provides excellent value. The wine-bar menu offers inexpensive tastes as well as 30 wines by the glass.

WILLOWSIDE CAFÉ   CALIFORNIA   15/20

3535 Guerneville Rd., Santa Rosa 95401
707-523-4814, Dinner Wed.-Sun., $$

The plain red building, six miles west of downtown, houses a happy local crowd that trusts chef Richard Allen's creativity with fresh ingredients. Examples of Allen's handiwork include a spicy red-lentil soup with blood-orange cream, and duck with a macadamia crespelle. On a recent visit, thyme perfumed the three-cheese ravioli. The menu, with never more than five entrées (always including a steak or lamb dish), is kept manageable so that quality is maintained. Wine is reasonably priced and features bottles from Russian River wineries.

GOURMET SHOPS & MORE

BAKERIES:BREAD & PASTRIES

DOWNTOWN BAKERY & CREAMERY

308-A Center St., Healdsburg 95448
707-431-2719, *Open daily*

    Incredibly delicious cakes, cookies, pastries, pies—enough to satiate the most demanding sweet tooth—are all baked on the premises of this unassuming little shop. Prime material for savory picnics are Downtown's traditional crusty sourdough loaf and stellar focaccia flavored with blue cheese, sun-dried tomatoes, Kalamata olives or Fontina. Ice cream and sherbet, made at the store, are the perfect treats for a warm afternoon as you stroll around the central plaza.

CHEESE

SONOMA CHEESE FACTORY

2 W. Spain St., Sonoma 95476
707-996-1931, *Open daily*

    In the heat of the summer tourist season, this local institution really does seem like a factory, besieged by hordes of visitors clamoring for a drink or a sandwich or buying jars of fancy, flavored mustard. Despite the sometimes impossible crush of customers and general commotion, have a little patience and the Factory's efficient staff will get you fed and on your way. A few tables are provided for on-premises picnicking, but we prefer to cross the street to the park, where you can sit under a gnarled tree and eat in peace.

VELLA CHEESE CO.

315 Second St. E., Sonoma 95476
707-938-3232, *Open daily*

    An artisanal cheesemaking operation that's been around since long before such craftsmanship was considered trendy, Ignacio Vella's modest shop is a few steps off the well-trod tourist path on Sonoma's town square. It's worth visiting for a taste of Vella's excellent Jack, flavorful Dry Jack and blue-veined cheeses.

CHOCOLATE

PETER RABBIT'S CHOCOLATE FACTORY

2489 Guerneville Rd., Santa Rosa 95403
707-575-7110, *Open Mon.-Sat.*

This tiny hole-in-the-wall is a magical place, populated (in season) by chocolate Easter bunnies, truffles, barks, peanut brittle and fudge. All the chocolate and other offerings are prepared the old-fashioned way in copper kettles, stirred with wooden sticks, and then worked on marble slabs.

COFFEE & TEA

BARKING DOG ROASTERS

17999 Sonoma Hwy., Sonoma 95476
707-939-1905, *Open daily*

Music blaring, beans roasting (on the premises) and pastries and bagels sold all day long make this a coffeehouse worth locating. Just follow your nose.

FLYING GOAT COFFEE

324 Center St., Healdsburg 95448
707-433-3599, *Open daily*

This roastery gets its name from an old-world legend: A sheepherder saw his goat eat some coffee berries. As the goat began to dance around (not fly), the shepherd thought the goat might have had something there, and that is how coffee (and its effects) were discovered. At this handsome roastery, they specialize in organic blends and single-origin or estate-grown coffees. Patrons can buy beans or ground coffee, coffee and tea drinks, and fresh-baked goods. **Also in Santa Rosa.**

DELI/GOURMET MARKETS

FOOD FOR THOUGHT MARKET & DELI

621 E. Washington St., Petaluma 94952
707-762-9352, *Open daily*

This store, like the trailblazing Whole Foods chain, is a combination health-food store and fresh-food store stocking everything from organic produce to hormone-free meats and poultry. Look for the array of supplements, bulk foods, herbs and cosmetics. The in-store deli produces salads, sliced meats to order, and sandwiches, including some new grilled panini. The in-house pâtisserie produces croissants and sweet treats. Tables placed inside and out allow snackers to enjoy coffee drinks, sandwiches or pastries at the store.

JIMTOWN STORE

6706 Hwy. 128, Healdsburg 95448
707-433-1212, *Open daily*

Carrie Brown and John Werner fled New York for the peace, quiet and relative isolation of Sonoma's Alexander Valley. The pair's ramshackle deli/grocery store has been part of local lore since it was established in 1893. They work hard to serve locals and prevent it from becoming yet another precious wine country boutique. However, the food—from the house-roasted turkey sandwiches to full-scale dinner entrées—is a lot better than you'd find at most stores off the beaten track.

PEARSON & COMPANY

2749 Fourth St., Santa Rosa 95405
707-541-3868, *Open Mon.-Sat.*

This stylish store offers restaurant-quality meals to go. The highest-rated to-go item is a delicious meatloaf. In addition we recommend the salads, pastries and desserts. If you're too hungry to wait till you get home, you'll have a pleasant spot to enjoy your repast, as there is seating inside and out.

SONOMA MARKET

520 W. Napa St., Sonoma 95476
707-996-3411, *Open daily*

All the locals swear by this store. Established in 1985, it is a specialty market with an old-fashioned butcher shop, a produce department with organically grown fruits and vegetables; a counter of fresh fish trucked up from San Francisco; a deli with entrées to go plus salads and sandwiches; and an in-house bakery. The wine department carries local labels at fair prices.

TRAVERSO'S MARKET

Third & B Sts., Santa Rosa 95401
707-542-2530, *Open Mon.-Sat.*

This deli/food/wine shop is well stocked with the best items from local purveyors and winemakers. It's run by a family that infuses every sale with small-town friendliness. It's a good place to stock up on drinks, cheeses and sandwiches for a picnic, or to pick up a good bottle of wine and some frozen ravioli or pasta for dinner. You'll also find an extensive selection of oils, vinegars and other gourmet food products.

ETHNIC MARKETS

G & G MARKET

1211 W. College Ave., Santa Rosa 95401
707-546-6877, *Open daily*

Need a 100-pound bag of jasmine rice? Five gallons of peanut oil? This is the place to get it. With 60,000 square feet of selling space this international market goes beyond its original, solely Asian concept. It has a huge Latino food-products section, as well as fresh meat, seafood and vegetables. The produce ranges from vine-ripened tomatoes to gai lan and other Chinese greens.

FARMERS' MARKETS

SANTA ROSA

The east parking lot at the Veteran's Memorial Bldg., off Hwy. 12, across from the fairgrounds.
707-522-8629, *Open Wed. and Sat. mornings only, year-round*

HEALDSBURG

The parking lot to the west of the plaza, off Healdsburg Ave.
707-431-1956, *Open Sat. morning only, May through early Dec.*

SONOMA

The parking lot in front of the Depot Museum on First St. W.
Open Fri. morning only, April through Oct.

ICE CREAM

See Downtown Bakery & Creamery, under Bakeries.

WINE & SPIRITS

WINE EXCHANGE OF SONOMA

452 First St. E. #C, Sonoma 95476
707-938-1794, *Open daily*

The owners stock all the Sonoma wines they consider fit to drink. The clerk says a few are missing, but he won't say which ones. Really good wines from Napa, Santa Barbara, Oregon and Washington are also on hand. There's not much interest in "invaders" from Europe except for some choice ports and sherries. But the owners do search for good wines priced under $8. Bravo!

Also see Traverso's & Sonoma Market under Deli/Gourmet Markets.

WINE TOURING SONOMA

For detailed information and maps for touring wineries in Sonoma Valley, contact the **Sonoma County Vintners Association** (7675 Conde Ln., Windsor 95492; 707-838-6678); **Sonoma Valley Vintners & Growers Alliance** (9 E. Napa St., Sonoma 95476; 707-935-0803).

CALIFORNIA WINE TOURS
22455 Broadway, Sonoma 95476
800-294-6386 or 707-939-722
www.californiawinetours.com

This 20-year-old company has all manner of transportation to accommodate a personalized tour of wineries: limo, maxi-van, mini-coach and luxury coach. They offer three wine-oriented limo tours from Napa, Sonoma and San Francisco to the wine country. Call for current rates and schedule.

WINERIES OPEN TO THE PUBLIC:

ARROWOOD VINEYARDS & WINERY
14347 Sonoma Hwy. 12, Glen Ellen 95442
707-938-5168

BENZIGER WINERY
1883 London Ranch Road
Glen Ellen 95442
800-989-8890

BUENA VISTA WINERY
1800 Old Winery Rd., P.O. Box 1842, Sonoma 95476
707-938-1266, 707-252-7117

CHÂTEAU SOUVERAIN
400 Souverain Rd., P.O. Box 528, Geyserville 95441
707-433-8281

DE LOACH VINEYARDS
1791 Olivet Ln., Santa Rosa 95401
707-526-9111

FERRARI-CARANO VINEYARDS & WINERY
8761 Dry Creek Rd., P.O. Box 1549, Healdsburg 95448
707-433-6700

FERRARI-CARANO VINEYARDS
8761 Dry Creek Rd. (P.O. Box 1549)
Healdsburg 95448
707-433-6700

GEYSER PEAK WINERY
22281 Chianti Rd. (P.O. Box 25)
Geyserville 95441
707-857-9463

GLORIA FERRER CHAMPAGNE CAVES
23555 Hwy. 121 (P.O. Box 1427)
Sonoma 95476
707-996-7256

GUNDLACH-BUNDSCHU
2000 Denmark St., Sonoma 95476
707-938-5277

KENDALL JACKSON VINEYARDS & WINERY
337 Healdsburg Ave., Healdsburg 95448
707-433-7102

KENWOOD VINEYARDS
9592 Sonoma Hwy. (12) (P.O. Box 447)
Kenwood 95452
707-883-5891

KUNDE ESTATE WINERY
10155 Sonoma Hwy.
Kenwood 95452
707-833-5501

LANDMARK VINEYARDS
101 Adobe Canyon Rd., Kenwood 95452
707-833-0053

MATANZAS CREEK WINERY
6097 Bennett Valley Rd., Santa Rosa 95401
707-528-6464

MURPHY-GOODE
4001 Hwy. 128, Geyserville 95441
707-431-7644

PARADISE RIDGE WINERY
4545 Thomas Lake Harris Drive
Santa Rosa 95403
707-528-9463

PIPER SONOMA
11447 Old Redwood Hwy. (P.O. Box 309)
Healdsburg 95448
707-433-8843

ROCHIOLI
6192 Westside Rd., Healdsburg 95448
707-433-2305

RAVENSWOOD WINERY
18071 Gehricke Rd.
Sonoma 94576
707-938-1960

RODNEY STRONG VINEYARDS
11455 Old Redwood Hwy. (Healdsburg) (P.O. Box 368) Windsor 95492
707-431-1533

SEBASTIANI VINEYARDS
389 Fourth St. East
Sonoma 95476
707-938-5532

STONE CREEK
9380 Sonoma Hwy.
Kenwood 95452
707-833-5070

VIANSA WINERY & ITALIAN MARKETPLACE
25200 Arnold Dr.
Sonoma 95476
707-935-4700

WINDSOR VINEYARDS
308 B Center St.
Healdsburg 95448
800-204-9463

MENDOCINO COUNTY

After the indigenous peoples, loggers, mostly from New England, were the first settlers of Mendocino's rough and beautiful coast, exploiting great stands of redwoods. Today, besides the tourist and timber industries, agriculture, that is orchards left over from the Prohibition era, and wineries are important to the economy. The most beautiful route through Mendocino is Highway 128, where wineries may specialize in sparkling wines, Chardonnay and Gewurztraminer.

Many of the best cafés and restaurants can be found in the bed-and-breakfasts and lodges that dot the landscape, in picturesque towns like Boonville, Mendocino and Little River. And because Mendocino is a slow-growth area, restaurants that do a good job last, and trendy restaurants just don't open. Maybe because temperatures are lower in Mendocino County, perched as it is on the Pacific Ocean, or maybe because many locals work with their hands, the restaurants here serve larger portions than their Bay Area counterparts.

RESTAURANTS

BOONVILLE HOTEL   CALIFORNIA/MEXICAN   13/20

14150 Hwy. 128, Boonville 95415
707-895-2210, *Lunch Wed.-Sun., Dinner Wed.-Mon.*

The town of Boonville, located halfway down beautiful Highway 128 when you're driving west from Sonoma County to the ocean, was at one point in its history as about as remote as you could get in these part. By the late 1970s, however, the Boonville Hotel was on the cutting edge of California cuisine. Today, owner-chef John Schmitt appeals to the employees of the wineries scattered along this winding highway, along with visitors to the hotel and day-trippers. At lunch, sous chef Libby Favela prepares Mexican specialties, and at night Schmitt presents his personalized cuisine based on fresh, local ingredients.

BUCKHORN SALOON   AMERICAN/BREWPUB   ¢

14081 Hwy. 128, Boonville 95415
707-895-3369, *Open five to seven days a week, depending on the season*

The draw at this rustic brewpub is the down-home grub, burgers and chicken, and the beers made on-site at the Anderson Valley Brewing Company. Choose from a pack of ales, including an award-winning Boont amber, plus the Indian Pale ale, Extra Special Bitter ale and Oatmeal stout.

CAFÉ BEAUJOLAIS   CALIFORNIA   14/20

961 Ukiah St., Mendocino 95460
707-937-5614, *Dinner nightly, $$*

This romantic country spot, established by cookbook author and chef Margaret Fox and her chef husband, Chris

Kump, emphasizes fresh, organic ingredients on a seasonally changing menu. Start with a glass of local sparkling wine, and then dig in to homegrown dishes such as a goat cheese-bacon salad on dressed greens, or the roast free-range chicken with kumquat sauce. A broiled Niman Ranch pork rib chop is flavored with a Calvados-cider sauce. For dessert, the profiteroles, brioche bread pudding and lemon charlotte are some of our favorites. You'll find a fine selection of brut rosés and sparkling wines on a very tempting list of local vintages.

HORN OF ZEESE   AMERICAN   ¢

14025 Hwy. 128, Boonville 95415
707-895-3525, *Open six or seven days a week, depending on the season; closed Tues. off-season*

In the local patois, horn of zeese means a cup of coffee. We recommend stopping at this plain-Jane coffeeshop to get a cup of Joe and eavesdrop on the locals. In the morning you can tuck into some eggs with a never empty cup of zeese and lots of local gossip.

MENDOCINO BAKERY & CAFÉ   CAFÉ   ¢

10483 Lansing St., Mendocino 95460
707-937-0836, *Open daily*

The folks from Thanksgiving Coffee own this small café. You can buy their environmentally friendly, organically shade-grown beans—no trees died for your cup of Joe. Locals and tourists flock here for coffee, pastries and sandwiches. Yummy pizzas are added at night.

MENDOCINO SHOWPLACE RESTAURANT   AMERICAN 12/20

Mendocino Hotel, 45080 Main St., Mendocino 95460
707-937-0511, *Breakfast, Lunch & Dinner daily, $$*

The Victorian setting at this venerable hotel is worth the price of admission. The dining room, topped with a stained-glass dome, is graced with beautiful Persian rugs and a massive mahogany bar. The garden room, used for breakfast and lunch, is overflowing with plants and is lighter in style. Trendy dishes don't make it on this traditional menu, but look for an excellent French onion soup and a New England-style clam chowder. At dinner we like the roast chicken with fluffy potato dumplings and the double pork chop with apple relish. A prix-fixe menu for $32 includes a glass of wine, appetizer, entrée and dessert—such a deal, and all that Victoriana to boot.

STEVENSWOOD LODGE & RESTAURANT   CALIFORNIA 13/20

8211 Hwy. 1, Little River 95456
707-937-2810, *Breakfast daily, Dinner nightly, Brunch Sat.-Sun., $$*

Stevenswood is a little bit of heaven on the Mendocino Coast nestled in a stand of redwoods. The lodge is comfortable, and the restaurant noteworthy. Chef Marc Dym presents a free-ranging menu that hits on many well-known tastes of California: cured gravlax napoleon, a meld of beef carpaccio and steak tartare, and entrées that spring from the river and the sea. The swordfish poached in olive oil is alluring, and the bouillabaisse sounds almost perfect. From the forest and the range, we can try a dry-aged New York steak or a duck-confit pasta. Desserts are listed "from the soul" and sound that way: a Mission fig Linzertorte, and a Tuaca and espresso crème brûlée, for example, will call to you. Whoever put together the wine list has an eye and palate for taste and value.

GOURMET SHOPS & MORE

FARMERS' MARKETS

BOONVILLE FARMERS' MARKET
Boonville Hotel Parking Lot
Open Sat. 9 a.m.-noon, May-Oct.

MENDOCINO FARMERS' MARKET
Howard & Main Sts.
Open Fri. Noon-2 p.m., May-Oct.

HEALTHY/ORGANIC

CORNER OF THE MOUTH
45015 Ukiah, Mendocino 95460
707-937-5345, *Open daily*

Located in a former church, this collectively owned new-age store carries supplements, all organic produce, locally for-aged seaweed, smoked fish, bulk foods and herbs, and baked goods. From Boonville they get Bruce Bread, a local favorite.

MENDOCINO WINE TOURING

For detailed maps and information about touring wineries in Mendocino Country, contact the **Mendocino County Vintners Association** (P.O. Box 1409, Ukiah 95482; 707-1363).

WINERIES OPEN TO THE PUBLIC:

FETZER VINEYARDS
45070 Main St., Mendocino 95465
707-937-6191

HANDLEY CELLARS
3151 Hwy. 128, Philo 95466
707-895-2190

HUSCH VINEYARDS
4900 Hwy. 128, Philo 95466
707-895-3216

ROEDERER ESTATE
4501 Hwy. 128, P.O. Box 67
707-895-2288

PENINSULA

PENINSULA MAP

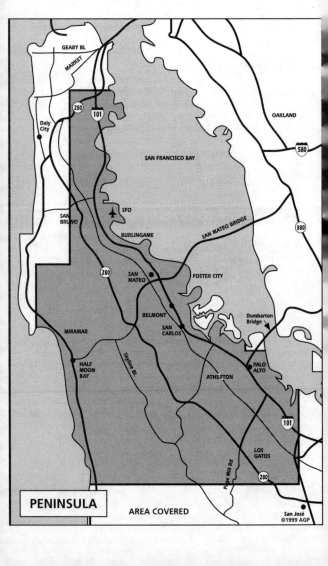

SOUTH TO SILICON VALLEY

San Francisco came into its own during the Gold Rush, but except for Redwood City and Palo Alto, the peninsula just to the south didn't take off until another boom: the postwar years of the late 1940s and early 1950s. The lumber industry—they didn't call it Redwood City for nothing—fueled the growth of that waterfront city during the 1850s. A little later, education helped attract newcomers to Palo Alto, the home of Stanford University.

The Bay Area Peninsula encompasses **Burlingame, Campbell, Cupertino, Half Moon Bay, Los Altos, Los Gatos, Menlo Park, Millbrae, Moss Beach, Palo Alto, Pescadero, Princeton by the Sea, San Carlos, San Mateo, Saratoga, South San Francisco, Sunnyvale** and **Woodside.** We've given San Jose, at the southernmost point of the Bay, is now the largest city in Northern California, so we've given it its own chapter.

Primarily an agricultural area, with groves of prunes, apricots and cherries stretching for miles, the Peninsula was essentially a bedroom community for San Francisco commuters until the rise of the high-tech businesses of Silicon Valley. These days Peninsula commuters are as likely to be bound for Cupertino or San Jose as downtown San Francisco. A number of San Francisco restaurateurs, realizing that hard-working techies and affluent commuters, like most other people, are more comfortable dining out in their own back yard, have opened branches in places like Palo Alto, Burlingame, Menlo Park and San Mateo. And, some of the Peninsula's own home-grown dining venues have opened branches in San Francisco.

RESTAURANTS

AMBER INDIAN RESTAURANT   INDIAN   14/20
2290 El Camino Real, Mountain View 94041
650-968-7511, *Lunch & Dinner daily, Brunch Sun.,* **$$**

Discriminating diners consistently rank this one of the best Indian restaurants in the Bay Area. The refined interior features classic Indian artwork and luxurious serving pieces, and the menu features many specialties unavailable at more cookie-cutter Indian venues. The dishes on the reasonably priced Indian buffet lunch (and Sunday brunch) are refreshed often, and the dinner menu offers light and oil-free appetizers such as chicken, fish, vegetable or cheese pakoras, along with Amber's Special, a melange of potatoes and paneer, fresh farmers' cheese. In addition to tandoori meats and breads, you'll find vegetarian specialties from baingan bharta (tandoor-roasted eggplant) to spicy okra.

AMELIA'S   SALVADORAN   ¢
2042 Broadway, Redwood City 94063
650-368-1390, *Lunch & Dinner daily*

Amelia's prepares Mexican food, but savvy diners opt for such Salvadoran specialties as the hand-patted pupusas, griddled corn masa filled with chicken, pork, cheese or beans. The traditional way to eat these snacks is to spoon on some curtido, a spicy cabbage slaw. Platters of beef salad (salpicón) or chicken encebollado, onions and grilled chicken in sauce, are accompanied by fried yucca, the starch of choice in Central America, plus sautéed plantain—a nonsweet cooking banana—and of course beans and rice.

BARBARA'S FISH TRAP   SEAFOOD   12/20

281 Capistrano Rd., Princeton by the Sea 94038
1-650-728-7049, *Lunch & Dinner daily, $*

Perched on pilings and adjoining the Princeton pier, this fisherman's diner, built in 1929, is the real thing: it's both funky and homey, with good, straightforward food. Lunch is our meal of choice because of the incredible sunlit view. We recommend the greaseless calamari, fish and chips, or any of the daily fish specials.

THE BASIN   CALIFORNIA   NO RATING

14572 Big Basin Way, Saratoga 95070
408-867-1906, *Dinner nightly, $$*

Two ex-Netscapers, a chef and a GM, opened this grill restaurant in a peaked-roof building in downtown Saratoga. The menu has twists on the classics: horseradish and spicy mustard flavor the Caesar salad, while a Niman Ranch hot dog is transformed into a high-class corn dog. Other starters include seared tuna with Manchego cheese and olives, and cracker-thin pizzas with appropriately hip toppings such as roasted potatoes, pancetta or wild mushrooms. "Main grub," as it is listed on the menu, includes a whole Dungeness crab that is interestingly said to be lightly smoked; chicken.

BELLA VISTA RESTAURANT   CONTINENTAL   13/20

13451 Skyline Blvd., Woodside 94062
650-851-1229, *Dinner Mon.-Sat., $$$*

A roaring fire and sweeping panoramic views of the Bay and the East Bay hills set the scene for this Continental venue. Classic starters include escargots, oysters Rockefeller or Kilpatrick or, from the cold side, sparkling Blue Point oysters on the half shell or prosciutto with melon. The food here is not groundbreaking, but it is well executed. The chateaubriand for two is cooked to perfection and served with "fancy" swirls of mashed potatoes, turned vegetables and a béarnaise sauce. Other good choices include filet of sole Florentine and veal saltimbocca. Caesar salads are freshly made at the table; even better is the toss of warm spinach and pancetta. Soufflés are the dessert of choice; they are light and not overly sweet. Another plus is that the restaurant is open until midnight daily.

BIRK'S   AMERICAN   12/20

3955 Freedom Cir., Santa Clara 95054
408-980-6400, *Lunch Mon.-Fri., Dinner nightly, $$*

☎ ♈ ☺

Birk's is a long-time magnet for Silicon Valley singles and couples. The simple menu centers on steaks, chops and seafood. In early evening the bar rocks with techies seeking techies. To aid their search and to warm them up, Birk's has myriad single-malt scotches and tasty microbrews. Opt for the smoky meats from the rotisserie, main-plate salads (the cobb is very good), or pastas.

BRAVO FONO   ITALIAN/FRENCH   13/20

99 Stanford Shopping Center, Palo Alto 94304
650-322-4664, *Lunch & Dinner daily, $$*

☎ ⚰ ▮

The owners had the Paprika Fono Hungarian restaurant at San Francisco's Ghirardelli Square before coming to Palo Alto in the 1980s. An outside wall of glass bricks lends a glow to the dining room, further enhanced at night by candlelight, white tablecloths and brightly colored paintings by the restaurateur's daughter. Favorites at lunch are the light salads and the seafood melange in puff pastry with a sherry sauce. At night, lovers opt for the bouillabaisse, braised lamb shank or tender mussels sautéed in a wine-perfumed sauce. Desserts are rich.

BUCA DI BEPPO   ITALIAN   11/20

643 Emerson Ave., Palo Alto 94301
650-329-0665, *Dinner daily, $$*

♙ ☺

The first venue opened by a midwestern chain, BdiB is a theme restaurant capitalizing on everyone's love of old-fashioned Italian American culture. The icons are here: Frank Sinatra, Dean Martin, even the pope. Background music is likely to be That's Amore. The kitsch on the walls is amusing but looks store-bought. The front door leads directly through the kitchen to the dining room. Wooden booths, red-checked tablecloths and ebullient waiters all set the stage. Unfortunately, the large portions are only that. Plates overflow with pastas, meatballs and salads, but most of it is molto mediocre. Sinatra, the Chairman of the Board, would not be pleased. **Also in San Francisco**

BUCK'S RESTAURANT   AMERICAN   ¢

3062 Woodside Rd., Woodside 94062
650-851-8010, *Breakfast, Lunch & Dinner daily*

♙

Much has been made of the venture-capitalist clientele that frequents Buck's Restaurant, a carnival of a coffee shop in rural Woodside. But to borrow an overused Silicon Valley catchphrase: At the end of the day, is a meal at Buck's a smart investment? Well, you can't go wrong with the power-breakfast buckwheat hotcakes, and Buck's makes a fine omelet. But when the kitchen tries anything as complicated as pot roast or barbecued ribs, the results are uneven. For a safe lunch or dinner investment, order a burger and a hot-fudge sundae.

BUFFALO GRILL   AMERICAN   13/20

66 Hillsdale Mall, San Mateo 94403
650-358-8777, *Lunch Mon.-Sat., Dinner daily, $$*

All the versions of classic comfort food and familiar yet upscale environments have been updated here. Braised brisket in rich brown gravy with horseradish mashed potatoes, maple-cured double-cut pork chops with corn spoon bread or baked macaroni and cheese—here with sharp Cheddar—sound familiar but are tastier. Even desserts, such as the peanut butter cookies sandwiched with fresh banana ice cream and two sauces, get the same treatment. Service is comforting.

CAFÉ LA SCALA   ITALIAN   13/20

1219 Burlingame Ave., Burlingame 94010
650-347-3035, *Lunch & Dinner daily, $$*

From the frescoed walls to the warmth of the maître d's greeting, this narrow, busy trattoria provides an authentically Italian experience. The menu is limited, but the food is good. Start with a balsamic-dressed green salad with goat cheese; follow it with the house fettuccine, tossed with mushrooms, sundried tomatoes and cream sauce. "La Scala," a scaloppine of thin medallions of veal prepared with eggplant, tomato and mozzarella, transports you to Florence. Another dish brought to new heights is the house lasagne, made here with layers of ground veal, spinach, cheeses and a creamy tomato sauce—served only at lunch. Standouts among the desserts are the house-made ice creams in a variety of flavors, including a luxurious strawberry and chocolate torta.

CARPACCIO   ITALIAN   12/20

1120 Crane St., Menlo Park 94025
650-322-1211, *Open daily, $$*

When it opened several years ago, Carpaccio was a hot ticket, one of the first modern-style Italian trattorias on the Peninsula. Now the menu seems boilerplate Italian—salads, pizzas, pastas—but the food is consistently good, especially the pastas and veal. Have the capellini with tomatoes, basil and garlic, or the gnocchi with meat sauce. One intriguing antipasto includes smoked mozzarella served with roasted eggplant and sun-dried tomatoes. An especially well-done entrée is the grilled salmon served with a pleasant lemon risotto and sautéed Swiss chard. There's a handsome bar and a decent wine list. Ask to be seated by the front windows, which are flung wide open in good weather.

CHEF CHU'S   CHINESE/DIM SUM   11/20

1067 N. San Antonio Rd., Los Altos 94022
650-948-2696, *Lunch & Dinner daily, $*

This popular long-standing restaurant is a mixed bag.
Dishes such as the mu shu pork with unusually tasty pancakes,
the dry-braised seafood or the Mandarin specialties can be
superb. For a special dinner, order the Peking duck a day in
advance: wrapped in tender pancakes slathered with hoisin
sauce, it's worth the cost. There's a full bar but a limited wine
list.

CHICKEN! CHICKEN!   CARIBBEAN   ¢

234 Primrose Rd., Burlingame 94010
650-344-4436, *Lunch & Dinner daily*

Owners Cliff and Susan Woods do a great job at their
brightly decorated chicken emporium. And as if a delicious
whole roast chicken for $9.95 weren't enough, they've added a
Caribbean twist. As in fast-food places, patrons can order chick-
en pieces for a song, or a whole meal for a bit more. But unlike
the big chains, Chicken! Chicken! marinates their birds in
herbs and lemon or rub them with a hot jerk seasoning, and
you get them fresh off the rotisserie. Among the sides are a
selection of salads, including new-potato salad and jicama
coleslaw, West Indian rice, garlic potatoes and buttermilk
mashed potatoes, along with the spicy house-made cornbread.
Desserts, which run to coconut-caramel brownies and chocolate chip cookies, are just okay. You'll find a nice selection of
beers and ales, including Red Stripe from Jamaica.

CREOLA—A NEW ORLEANS BISTRO   CREOLE/CAJUN   13/20

344 El Camino Real, San Carlos 94070
650-654-0882, *Lunch Wed., Dinner Tues.-Sat., $$*

Tucked away in a small off-street shopping area, CreoLa
flies in ingredients a couple of times a week from the Big Easy.
Posters of New Orleans in the small narrow room are the back-
ground for some pretty tasty food. We favor the the greaseless
and flavorful crayfish hush puppies, the corn fritters encasing
tender crayfish tails and served with a rémoulade sauce and
the addictive Cajun popcorn, cornmeal-battered crayfish tails
served with a satiny sherry-tomato aïoli. Rarely seen in the Bay
Area, the alligator piccata is just ok. Don't miss the softshell-
crab dishes paired with crayfish etouffée. One or two entrées
show an incongruous Asian or California bent like the salmon
with Creole seasonings and a soy glaze, better ignored. Stick
with Creole and Cajun dishes and finish off dinner with sturdy
New Orleans–style bread pudding.

DUARTE'S TAVERN   AMERICAN   11/20

202 Stage Rd., Pescadero 94060
650-879-0464, *Breakfast, Lunch & Dinner daily, $$*

When you see this restaurant, housed in an Old West-style
wood-and-stucco building near Pescadero's general store,

you'll feel as if you've traveled back in time. Duarte's (pronounced doo-arts) is still owned and operated by the family that built it in 1894. The fourth generation serves dishes that Bay Area natives travel down the coast for. Artichokes, from the nearby fields are steamed and served with garlic-mayonnaise, and in omelets, and in a delicious cream soup. Keeping with its down-home character and Portuguese heritage, the menu offers eggs with linguica sausage or in a sandwich, fried smelt, and tripe with fries. More traditional entrées include a huge New York steak, fish and chips, mussels marinara and deep-fried prawns. Portions are huge, but leave room for some delicious fruit pie, another tradition started by Grandma Emma and continued today.

ELBE　　　　　　　　GERMAN　　14/20　

117 University Ave., Palo Alto 94301
650-321-3319, *Dinner nightly, $$*

The music may be Mozart, but the menu is solidly late-twentieth century. The appetizers will delight those tired of olives and sun-dried tomatoes—especially the shredded carrot and red cabbage salad, the sausage sampler or the venison ragout with sun-dried cherries. Indulge in thin, crisp Wiener Schnitzel, or try the rich and savory wild-boar stew with Black Forest mushrooms served with parsley Spätzle and braised red cabbage. Because the chef has so successfully updated the entrées, the desserts are a disappointment. The German chocolate layer cake is just as heavy as you would expect. Those who want a lighter finish would do better with the warm, flaky apple strudel. Lagers, Pilseners, ales, porters and hard cider are joined by good German wines—perfect partners for this food.

EMPIRE GRILL & TAP ROOM　　AMERICAN　　13/20　

651 Emerson St., Palo Alto 94301
650-321-3030, *Lunch Mon.-Fri., Dinner nightly, Brunch Sat.-Sun., $$*

This is a popular place for outdoor dining, under the ivy-covered trellises at lunch and under the stars on balmy nights, the glow of candles adding a romantic feel. Deep-fried calamari, crab cakes or steamed mussels start the meal on a high note. The house-smoked pork chop at dinner is delicious; a sandwich version is offered at lunch. We recommend the burger made with Niman-Schell beef. You can also order pizzas, sandwiches or pastas, and there's a good wine list. The weekend brunch features many favorites: Belgian waffles, omelets, fresh fruit. We're fans of the apple pie with cinnamon sauce à la mode.

EVVIA ESTIATORIO　　　　GREEK　　12/20

420 Emerson St., Palo Alto 94301
650-326-0983, *Lunch Mon.-Fri., Dinner daily, $$*

When this Greek restaurant opened three years ago, it was distinctive, because if there is one missing cuisine in the Bay

Area, it's Greek. Now the owners have opened a more luxurious location in San Francisco–Kokkari. You could say Evvia was their practice for that more ambitious project. It's casual yet pretty, with an open kitchen and multicolored bottles decorating the back wall. As soon as you enter, you can smell the wood-fire oven where the lamb, chicken and fish are roasted. The food, however, can be inconsistent. The appetizer plate is lovely, especially the selection of spreads: roasted eggplant, yogurt-cucumber, cod roe purée, served with stuffed grape leaves and crispy pita bread for dipping. The grilled items like tuna or striped bass are done well, and the salads—classic Greek, tossed greens or, better yet, the grilled octopus with olives and peppers—go well with the entrées. On the downside, the souvlaki was dry and the spanakopita (spinach-feta pie) was soggy on our last visit. The good phyllo desserts are bathed in honey, or you can finish with a nice brandy. The wine list is pedestrian, and the Greek wines are unexplained. **Also in San Francisco: See Kokkari**

FAZ RESTAURANT & CATERING   MEDITERRANEAN 12/20

1108 N. Matilda Ave., Sunnyvale 94087
408-752-8000, *Lunch & Dinner daily, $$*
☎ 🖳 🍴 ⟳

With restaurants in San Francisco, Concord and Danville, Faz Poursohi replicates his Mediterranean and Middle Eastern menus wherever he opens. There's nothing wrong with that idea. His casual, stylish restaurants may not stand up to the best in San Francisco, but they do well in the 'burbs. Our two favorite appetizers are the Mediterranean plate with a selection of dips like hummus and eggplant purée, plus tabouli salad and the silky house-smoked salmon napped with a cucumber-cream sauce and capers. Pizzas here are great, especially the chicken pesto. Pastas are good, but a better option is almost anything from the grill: pork chops, steak and the burger with the works. Desserts are typical American fare, gooey and on the heavy side. **Also in San Francisco & the East Bay.**

THE FISH MARKET   SEAFOOD   11/20

3150 El Camino Real, Palo Alto 94306
650-493-9188, *Lunch & Dinner daily, $$*
♥ 🍴

The owners of these chain eateries maintain their own fishery, two boats, and an interest in a Puget Sound oyster farm. Salmon is smoked and cured at the fishery, and the oysters are fresh from the Northwest. They're hitting all the bases with a menu that obviously wants to appeal to everyone: the seafood is mesquite grilled, Japanese pankoed, baked and Cajun-ed. But wait, there's also sashimi and pasta, Italian fish dishes, a variety of smoked fish, and two kinds of clam chowder. Dieters will find the steamed clams, mussels oysters and salads appealing. For the best meal, stick with a simple grilled fish steak and fries. The ambience is casual and has the look of a thrown-together warehouse full of nautical kitsch. The wine list is an insult to seafood. **Also in San Jose (1007 Blossom Hill Rd., 408-**

269-3474), Santa Clara (3775 El Camino Real, 408-246-3474) &
San Mateo (1855 S. Norfolk Ave., 650-349-3474).

FLEA ST. CAFÉ   CALIFORNIA   12/20

3607 Alameda de las Pulgas, Menlo Park 94025
650-854-2145, *Lunch Tues.-Fri., Dinner Tues.-Sun., Brunch Sun., $$*

Strolling through the warren of rooms that make up this
restaurant you can feel the exuberant nature of the owner.
Victorian-era lace, florals and subtle decorative touches lend
an air of romance. Chef-owner Jesse Cool's menu, however, is
anything but quaint: organic produce and vegetarian choices
abound, and the dishes are spunky, latter-day inventions that
sometimes work and sometimes don't. One of the heartier and
more popular dishes is the "Wild, Wild pasta," fettuccine with
wild mushrooms, wild rice, sun-dried tomatoes and feta in a
garlic sauce. The grilled salmon, another favorite, is perched
on lovely mashed potatoes. The omelets, melanges of vegeta-
bles and fluffy eggs, are the big draw at Sunday brunch.

FOOK YUEN   CHINESE   13/20

195 El Camino Real, Millbrae 94030
650-692-2833, *Lunch & Dinner daily, $$*

Sandwiched between the two Flower Lounge restaurants,
Fook Yuen should not be overlooked. The dim sum is a good
deal, served from trays at lunch, but as it is at many other
Hong Kong-style restaurants, the sparkling fresh seafood is the
star attraction. There's a fried whole flounder, crispy catfish,
steamed prawns with garlic, and fat, juicy oysters steamed with
a variety of sauces. Good bets are the barbecued meats and the
very respectable Peking duck. The servers, some of whom do
not speak much English, can be curt.

GAMBARDELLA'S   ITALIAN   12/20

561 Oak Grove Ave., Menlo Park 94025
650-325-6989, *Lunch Tues.-Fri., Dinner Tues.-Sun., $$*

This small restaurant could have been designed in North
Beach and air-lifted here. You can rely on simple southern
Italian food, hearty and flavorful. The pine-walled room is
lined with empty wine bottles signed by inspired customers,
which serve as a wine list. The pastas are good, the service very
friendly. Try the penne with fennel sausage and sweet peppers
in a cream sauce, the fettuccine with artichoke hearts, roasted
peppers, spinach, onions, garlic and tomatoes, or the seafood-
stuffed ravioli. A toothsome grand finale is the meltingly good
warm chocolate cake.

GORDON BIERSCH   AMERICAN/BREW PUB   12/20

640 Emerson St., Palo Alto 94301
650-323-7723, *Lunch & Dinner daily, $$*

When partners Dan Gordon—he's the brewmaster—and
Dean Biersch got together, they were adamant that pub grub

would have no place in their brewery-restaurants. The high ceilings and exposed ductwork look like familiar brewpub decor, but the menu shows care in dishes like a savory seafood stew; roast chicken redolent of rosemary and sage; and individual pizzas with toppings such as andouille sausage, four cheeses, and roast chicken and artichoke hearts. Our fave is the garlic-rubbed hanger steak with the horseradish-spiked "smashed" potatoes. Forget the wine and opt for the house brews: from light to dark, they are Pilsener, Export, Märzen and Dunkles. It's usually hard to have a conversation, especially on Friday nights and weekends, when there's quite a scene. **Also in San Francisco & San Jose.**

HIGASHI WEST   PACIFIC RIM/SUSHI   13/20
636 Emerson St., Palo Alto 94301
650-323-9378, *Lunch Mon.-Fri., Dinner Mon.-Sat.,* $$$
☎

Sushi purists will hate creations like the ELT: an eel-lettuce-tomato sushi roll with cream cheese, or the Higashi West roll, smoked salmon wrapped around a tiger prawn and baked. Innovation in sushi can only go so far, and the best offerings here may be the traditional choices, sparkling fresh fish and shellfish simply prepared. Smaller dishes, called tsumami, include steamed shrimp dumplings with ponzu sauce; a garlic-crusted pork chop with a mixed-mushroom demi-glace and marinated cabbage; a soba noodle salad with hearts of palm and a rice vinaigrette; and a salad of baby napa cabbage and grilled chicken breast in a peanut-ginger dressing. Those with fusion-phobia can try the excellent grilled salmon or teriyaki dishes. A tinkling indoor waterfall and plantings of bamboo set a serene stage.

HONG KONG FLOWER LOUNGE   CHINESE   13/20
1671 El Camino Real, Millbrae 94030
650-588-9972, *Lunch & Dinner daily,* $$
☎ 📷 🏃 🍸 🔄

The El Camino Real branch is a huge temple to Hong Kong cuisine, from its tiled roof with traditional upturned corners to the floor-to-ceiling windows. The bilevel restaurant plays frequent host to large banquets and family parties of all sizes. Well-seasoned Cantonese dinner specialties include minced squab in lettuce cups, shark's-fin soup and many seasonal seafood dishes. The daily dim sum menu features baked or steamed barbecued-pork buns (bao), braised bean curd and shrimp dumplings. Finish with warm, mildly sweet egg-custard tarts. The food is reliable, but service can be impersonal and rushed; large tables get more attention than duos. The first location is a 200-seater on Millbrae Ave. Also in Millbrae (51 Millbrae Ave., 650-878-8108) & Palo Alto (560 Waverly St., 650-326-3830) where the decor turns its back on traditional Chinese and has a refined look in shades of burgundy, green and gold. One new dish to look for is the Aberdeen prawns with deep-fried garlic. **Also in San Francisco.**

IL FORNAIO ITALIAN 13/20

520 Cowper St., Palo Alto 94301
Breakfast & Lunch Mon.-Fri., Dinner daily, Brunch Sat.-Sun., $$

Il Fornaio once monopolized the restaurant scene in Palo Alto, being among the first to venture from San Francisco to open a branch on the Peninsula. It's busy most of the time, and the din can be exasperating—it's not the place for a quiet business lunch. Il Fornaio makes excellent crusty breads, hearty mushroom polenta, competent grilled dishes and delicious pastas. Two standouts are the rotisseried rabbit with polenta and the lobster-filled ravioli in a cream sauce topped with shrimp. The regional Italian dinners are also done well. The wine list is well paired with the food, especially by region. **Also in San Francisco, Marin, the East Bay & San Jose.**

JOANN'S CAFÉ AMERICAN/BREAKFAST ¢

1131 El Camino Real, South San Francisco 94080
650-872-2810, *Breakfast & Lunch daily*

If breakfast is the most important meal of the day, then JoAnn's is the most important restaurant on the Peninsula. JoAnn di Lorenzo makes terrific french toast from homemade orange bread topped with orange slices and glazed with maple syrup; the huevos rancheros Don Pasqual come with black bean salsa, green chile salsa, feta cheese and a side of cinnamon-flecked sautéed bananas. Portions are generous. At lunch time, leave room for the homemade desserts.

KABUL AFGHAN 12/20

135 El Camino Real, San Carlos 94070
650-594-2840, *Lunch Mon.-Fri., Dinner nightly, $*

Afghan cuisine combines the flavors of Turkey, Greece and India and adds its own spices. The results, as you'll learn from dining at Kabul, are interesting. Consider an appetizer such as pakawra e badenjan, chunks of eggplant dipped in a light batter, then sautéed to crispness and garnished with the contrasting tastes of yogurt and meat sauce. The lamb and chicken entrées are reminiscent of Indian-style tandoori cookery: tender meat seared on the outside, moist and delicate within. Kebabs, especially lamb, are tender and cooked to order. Vegetarians will revel in the wealth of choices, including a stew of spinach, garlic and onions, and pumpkin dumplings in yogurt. Both locations have comfortable dining rooms and efficient service, but the wine lists are rather weak. **Also in Sunnyvale (833 W. El Camino Real, 408-245-4350).**

KATHMANDU WEST NEPALESE 11/20

20916 Homestead Rd., Cupertino 95014
408-996-0940, *Lunch Mon.-Fri., Dinner nightly, $*

You might think "Indian" walking into this restaurant, but you'd be wrong. The food here is Nepalese, which shares some of the ingredients of South Asian cooking, but it's prepared differently. The national dish is dhal bhat, lentils cooked in a brothy dhal and served with rice. Ginger enlivens a stir fry of chicken, while grilled marinated meats are done to a turn. Vegetarians will find lots to like on this menu.

KULETO'S TRATTORIA   CALIFORNIA/ITALIAN   13/20

1095 Rollins Rd., Burlingame 94010
650-342-4922, *Lunch Mon.-Fri., Dinner daily, $$*

The excitement begins when you round the corner just inside Kuleto's entrance to face an immense brick oven and open kitchen. Cooks turn out several roasted appetizers: prawns, radicchio, clams paired with mussels. Pizzas are fine, thin-crusted and not over-dressed. Fresh pasta dishes vie for the diner's attention with succulent fried calamari served with garlicky aïoli or peppery Romesco sauce. Main courses of fresh fish, lamb sirloin or chicken paillard wrapped in pancetta are frequently served with vegetable-and-herb sauces for a light presentation. California wines dominate the wine list. **Also in San Francisco.**

L'AMIE DONIA   FRENCH   15/20

530 Bryant St., Palo Alto 94301
650-323-7614, *Lunch & Dinner Tues.-Sat., $$*

Chef-owner Donia Bijan won early acclaim at San Francisco's Sherman House and Brasserie Savoy before transforming a former luncheonette into her eponymous Peninsula restaurant. We love her French bistro specialties, such as earthy classic onion soup or a salad of gathered greens dressed with a simple wine-friendly lemonette and enlivened with Roquefort croutons. A lemon sole poached in Chablis is superbly paired in a salad with wedges of pink grapefruit, blood oranges and fennel. Some entrées, such as a pan-roasted Alaska halibut with crab and potato griddle cakes, lean toward California cuisine, while a New York steak with a mushroom bordelaise sauce is accompanied by pommes frites. Two desserts—the tarte tatin and Sachertorte—are standouts. Service has improved since our last visit, and we're impressed by the California and French wine list.

LATE FOR THE TRAIN   VEGETARIAN   ¢

150 Middlefield Rd., Menlo Park 94025
650-321-6124, *Breakfast & Lunch daily, Dinner Tues.-Sat.*

The look is French country, but the food is healthy California. You'll find luscious omelets, buttermilk pancakes and even quiche. The owners grow some of the produce and feature it in delightfully fresh salads. Sitting on the patio on a warm day, surrounded by potted plants, will indeed make you late for the train.

LE MOUTON NOIR   FRENCH   14/20

14560 Big Basin Way, Saratoga 95070
408-867-7017, *Dinner nightly, $$$*

Recently this French country-style restaurant got a facelift. It's still romantic, but it has fresh paint and a fresher look. The food is still very French with subtle Asian touches, with the emphasis on skillfully cooked duck, lamb and game (prepared differently every night), as well as an extensive wine selection. A starter of smoked goose breast is wrapped in a thin crêpe and garnished with a salsa of tomatoes, chiles and avocado. Scallops are crusted with sesame seeds, seared and served with a sauce of tropical fruits and a garnish of paper-thin lotus chips. Desserts are deluxe.

LEFT AT ALBUQUERQUE   SOUTHWESTERN   11/20

445 Emerson St., Palo Alto 94301
650-326-1011, *Lunch & Dinner daily, $*

On weekend nights, you can find this place by the line out the door. The students pile in presumably for the tequilas, which total more than a hundred. The food is overpriced, Californian-ized Southwestern fare, but who's listening to us? Any of the burritos are worth ordering as are the specials. The appetizers—such as the Southwestern gravlax with lime and onions, the poblano chiles on a flour tortilla, or the Gulf Coast cocktail with poached shrimp and scallops in a spicy broth—are much more tantalizing than the entrées. **Also in San Francisco.**

LEFT BANK   FRENCH   15/20

635 Santa Cruz Ave., Menlo Park 94025
650-473-6543, *Lunch & Dinner daily, $$*

If it's possible, this branch of Roland Passot's venue for grand-mère's cuisine is even better than the original in Larkspur. It has an open kitchen and high ceilings, so when it's busy, the noise level can soar. Many favorite bistro dishes are here: mussels steamed in wine (great with crispy shoestring potatoes), rotisserie chicken, bouillabaisse, salmon and scallop quenelles, grilled salmon with a tapenade crust, and a lovely crisp duck from the spit with oranges and rice. Don't leave without sampling the warm tarte tatin with vanilla ice cream or the lemon tart with raspberry coulis. The wine list, with lots of French and California choices, is priced to go with the food. Service is crisp and professional without being snooty. **Also in Marin County.**

MACARTHUR PARK   AMERICAN   11/20

27 University Ave., Palo Alto 94301
650-321-9990, *Lunch Mon.-Fri., Dinner nightly, Brunch Sun., $$*

Housed in a landmark craftsman-style building designed during World War I by Julia Morgan, MacArthur Park is a big, welcoming place, and is now livlier than the original in San Francisco, which has lost some of its luster since other restaurants have opened nearby. The special appetizer is addictive–a heaping plate of crisp, delicate fried onion strings. The restaurant is also known for its lean barbecued baby back ribs and chicken served with the house sauce. Unfortunately, on our last visit the ribs seemed to have been boiled tender and tasteless, then loaded with the sweetish sauce. If you're in the mood for something different, try the quail, catfish or vegetarian dishes. The flourless chocolate cake and seasonal fruit crisps are good, and the wine list and beer selection are sophisticated. Also in San Francisco.

MANGO CAFÉ   CARIBBEAN   ¢

435 Hamilton Ave., Palo Alto 94301
650-325-3229, *Lunch Fri., Dinner Mon.-Sat.*

This funky little place serves the cuisine of Jamaica, Trinidad and Tobago. Like they say, they have the real "ting" here with such exotic dishes as hot curried goat over rice—and it's served with the best salad accompaniment we've ever had (dressed with Dijon vinaigrette)—and spicy jerked joints. The vegetarian dishes are appropriately Rastafarian-inspired: pigeon peas, black-eyed peas or red beans covering sliced cho-cho (a member of the squash family) on a bed of white rice. You can also get sides of plantains, rice and peas, mango chutney and huge smoothies. For dessert, we like the sweet potato pudding. The Jamaican beer and ginger beer are pluses. This is a fun place with good food, reggae music and informal service.

MAX'S OPERA CAFÉ   DELI   ¢

711 Stanford Shopping Center, Palo Alto 94304
650-323-6297, *Lunch & Dinner daily*

MAX'S BAKERY & KITCHEN   DELI   ¢

111 E. Fourth Ave., San Mateo 94402
650-344-1997, *Lunch & Dinner daily*

Max's has many restaurants and a central commissary, and it tries to be a New York deli. The sandwiches are a several inches high, but the pastrami or corned beef cannot come close to what is available elsewhere in the Bay Area, and it's certainly not as good as what you can get in New York. The daily blue plate special features homestyle dishes of dubious merit, like meatloaf and mashed potatoes; there are also grilled steaks, chicken and fish. The service is rushed and can be quite chummy. **At the Opera Café**, a server, cook or host may break out into song at the drop of a knish. The desserts, like everything else, are huge and mediocre. **Also in numerous other locations around the Bay Area, including San Francisco and the East Bay.**

MING'S — CHINESE/DIM SUM — 12/20

1700 Embarcadero Rd., Palo Alto 94301
650-856-7700, *Lunch & Dinner daily, $$*

This large restaurant with two huge dining rooms is always bustling, quite an accomplishment for a restaurant established in 1956. It's a good place for dim sum because you don't have to flag down the carts. Pork dumplings are the best. The chicken salad (shredded iceberg lettuce, Chinese mustard and crispy fried chicken) and the sautéed cod with black bean sauce are distinctive. At lunch there are several vegetarian lunch boxes—a dim sum combo, Hunan eggplant and curry vegetables, all served with a gluten salad and meat-free fried rice—priced at $8.25 to $8.75. The $22.95 dinner for two features a nice selection of the house specialties.

MIRAMAR BEACH RESTAURANT — SEAFOOD — 11/20

131 Mirada Rd., Half Moon Bay 94019
650-726-9053, *Lunch & Dinner daily, Brunch Sun., $$*

Only a narrow frontage road separates the window tables from dramatic vistas of the Pacific at this low-key eatery. Preparations of fresh seafood dominate the menu with appetizers like crab cakes, oysters Rockefeller, shrimp tempura and a prawn cocktail. A chilled artichoke with spicy aïoli sauce is de rigueur on menus in this seaport farm community. The menu has been updated in recent years, and a Caesar salad has debuted, as well as a very good spinach salad with a raspberry vinaigrette, chopped egg and bacon. You'll find many pastas, but the prices—over $15—are steep. Besides the local catch, the salmon en croute and the steamed clams, the menu features three steak dishes. Since the Miramar was once a speakeasy, lots of vintage photos add interest.

MIYAKE — JAPANESE/SUSHI — 13/20

140 University Ave., Palo Alto 94301
650-323-9449, *Lunch & Dinner daily, $*

It's tempting to dismiss Miyake. The sushi menu features too many too-cute homages to Apple, IBM and Hewlett-Packard. There's even a salmon-and-asparagus hand roll named after Stanford's own Chelsea Clinton. On most nights Japanese pop music blares, disco lights spin, and an intermittent fog machine does its inexplicable thing. But gimmicks aside, Miyake is just about the best sushi bar on the Peninsula. The orange roughy nigiri is almost ethereal—eating it is more like breathing than eating. Kurumi ume is a delightful combination of walnuts and plum sauce, and the sweet black mushrooms and soft avocado in the cat's roll are perfect foils to the crunchy cucumber. **The Cupertino branch (10650 S. Dianza Blvd., 408-253-2668) is not quite as noisy.**

MOSS BEACH DISTILLERY AMERICAN 11/20

Beach Way & Ocean Blvd., Moss Beach 94038
650-728-5595, *Lunch & Dinner daily, Brunch Sun., $$*

This restaurant is housed in a 1920s building that was a retreat for Hollywood types in its early days and a haven for bootleggers during Prohibition. Enjoy the great view and stick with the simpler dishes. Appetizers like the cheesy garlic bread are addictive, while on some nights oysters on the half shell are inexpertly opened. But we have found the eight- or ten-ounce filet mignon charbroiled to perfection, served with mashed potatoes and a green peppercorn sauce. Most of the dinner entrées are seafood including our favorites: garlic prawns and the fresh fish of the day, straight from fishermen on the nearby Pillar Point Harbor. The Sunday brunch is popular, with a fixed-price entrée that includes a bottomless glass of sparkling wine, seasonal fruit, muffins, home fries and coffee or tea; children under 12 are half price.

THE OASIS AMERICAN ¢

241 El Camino Real, Menlo Park 94025
650-326-8896, *Lunch & Dinner daily*

This is a fun, noisy place that serves burgers and more burgers and some pizzas. There are pinball machines, plus a TV over the bar. It's funky and greasy but a popular hangout for all ages, particularly the Stanford crowd. Sports fans arrive early to watch the Big Game against the University of California at Berkeley. There's a good long list of beers.

OSHO JAPANESE/SUSHI 13/20

102 S. El Camino Real, Millbrae 94030
650-692-7787, *Lunch Mon.-Fri., Dinner Mon.-Sat., $*

It is easy for a family to dine casually and affordably at Osho. It is also easy to reserve a tatami room and dine lavishly on a 12-course gourmet Japanese dinner. Finely cut sushi flows from the sushi bar, which features abalone, sea urchin, roe and other seafood as well as fish. The agemono (fried dishes) such as tempura, pork cutlet and oysters, are light and succulent. Seasonal specialties of stewed yellowtail tuna and crab steamed in saké are worth waiting for all year. Beer, green tea, and hot or cold saké are the preferred beverages.

THE PALACE CALIFORNIA 11/20

146 S. Murphy Ave., Sunnyvale 94086
408-739-5179, *Dinner Tues.-Sat., $$$*

A popular entertainment venue for the under-35 crowd, this former movie palace with art deco design elements was remodeled several years ago and transformed into a nightclub-restaurant. The food has gotten more formal in recent years;

the $35 four-course tasting menu is popular. Appetizers, from spicy pork and green chile empanadas to prosciutto with grilled asparagus and goat cheese, are inspired by cuisines from all over the world. Try the pan-roasted spearfish steak, tamarind-glazed game hen, or the rack of lamb with savory balsamic-roasted onions and a fennel-roasted-pepper risotto. Vegetarians may feel left out, although the kitchen will create something on the spot. Desserts are good, and you can dance off the calories to live music after dinner.

PARKSIDE GRILLE   AMERICAN   13/20

884 Portola Rd., Portola Valley 94028
650-529-9007, *Lunch Tues.-Fri., Dinner Tues.-Sun., Brunch Sun., $$*

Nestled in redwoods, this restaurant has a mountain feel, with high ceilings, an open kitchen and lots of windows. The grilled items are best, including the pizzas from a wood-burning oven. One starter we'd go back for is the roasted corn and sweet-potato chowder; another is the warm spinach salad with seared scallops and pancetta. You'll find a Spago-like smoked salmon pizza, a four-cheese version and a simple margherita. The main courses hit the right notes with a horseradish-coated salmon, a smoked pork chop and delicious baby back ribs. Vegetarians will like the oven-roasted veggies in a goat-cheese strudel. The wine list features mostly California wines, including some local bottlings.

PASTA?   ITALIAN   ¢

326 University Ave., Palo Alto 94301
650-328-4585, *Lunch & Dinner daily*

Most people refer to this spot as "that pasta-question-mark place on University." But if its name presents a challenge, its cuisine does not. The delicious ravioli della casa is stuffed with spinach and bathed in a pink nutmeg-tinged cream sauce. The mussels appetizer is also elegant, although it is too delicately seasoned, as are many of the other dishes at Pasta? The spaghetti pomodoro, for example, could do with more basil and garlic, and the rigatoni with bolognese sauce would be helped by even a whiff of wine. Still the prices are right, and the narrow room feels friendly rather than cramped. The tiramisu is satiny and rum rich, easily consumed with a nice espresso.

PENINSULA FOUNTAIN & GRILL   AMERICAN   ¢

566 Emerson St., Palo Alto 94301
650-323-3131, *Breakfast, Lunch & Dinner daily*

This classic soda fountain (circa 1923) evokes the simple pleasures of yesteryear. The place has genuine old-time decor and serves soda-fountain standards at old-fashioned prices. There are burgers, pancakes, meatloaf, fried chicken, banana splits, fruit pies and milkshakes.

PIATTI RISTORANTE   ITALIAN   13/20

2 Stanford Shopping Center, Palo Alto 94304
650-324-9733, *Open daily, $$*

A big draw to this Piatti, part of an extensive chain, is the welcoming patio. Within the warm, seashell-neutral walls is an exhibition kitchen and a large wraparound bar that's a good place to wait for your table. Any of the pasta dishes are winners, especially the cheese-filled ravioli in a lemon-cream sauce. The orecchiette would be good just with broccoli, but here the dish is overloaded with artichokes, fennel, toasted garlic and Fontina. Salads are fresh and not overdressed. One of the best dishes is the chicken cooked under a brick, served with garlic mashed potatoes and oven-roasted vegetables. A hearty entrée is the slow-braised lamb shank with a delightful sun-dried tomato demi-glace. **Also in Marin, Napa, Sonoma & Carmel.**

PLUTO'S   CAFETERIA   ¢

482 University Ave., Palo Alto 94301
650-853-1556, *Open daily*

In keeping with an outer-space theme, one wall carries the names of astronauts, although we haven't gone to Pluto yet. This is a New Age cafeteria, with made-to-order salads; there's also a veggie counter, where a baked potato or grilled eggplant could be the heart of your meal. At the next station grilled flank steak or roasted turkey can complete a plate. Sandwiches from the freshly carved meats are generous and good. This place is popular with students, who add to the din. Also in San Francisco.

RANGOON   BURMESE/CHINESE   12/20

565 Bryant St., Palo Alto 94301
650-325-8146, *Lunch & Dinner Mon.-Sat., $*
No codes

The cream-colored walls and Southeast Asian motifs create a serene atmosphere for the Chinese-Burmese menu here. Stick with the Burmese specialties--with curries, potatoes, crunchy bean sprouts and lentils--for a taste treat. We like the several noodle dishes, including one with curried noodles and veggies. The soups, some made with coconut milk, are good, especially the chicken noodle. The samosas are a good way to start your adventure.

RESTAURANT SENT SOVI   FRENCH   15/20

14583 Big Basin Way, Saratoga 95070
408-867-3110, *Dinner Tues.-Sun., $$*

This restaurant paved the way for more modern French food in this area, long the center of classic French venues. David Kinch, a chef whose credits include the now closed

Ernie's in San Francisco, starts everyone with an amuse-gueule —a touch of caviar, a bite of something delicious, to excite the palate. We recommend the sumptuous lobster salad with fava beans; another salad pairs baby leeks with beef tongue. On a California note, ahi tuna tartare melds with avocado and a black truffle vinaigrette. Entrées feature wild striped bass, lamb shank and braised rabbit. A tasting menu is served with or without wine, but unfortunately must be ordered by the entire table. The wine list nicely highlights nearby Santa Cruz wineries.

RESTAURANT ZIBIBBO   MEDITERRANEAN   14/20

430 Kipling St., Palo Alto 94301
650-328-6722, *Lunch Mon.-Fri., Dinner nightly, Brunch Sat.-Sun.*, $$

The design of this restaurant warrants an essay in itself. Architect Cass Calder Smith tied together a Victorian house and an adjacent structure to create a venue with two patio dining areas, seating near the wood-fired oven, quiet nooks for lovers, a mezzanine and a comfortable bar area. Jody Denton, a veteran of San Francisco's Restaurant LuLu, brought that wildly successful formula to the Peninsula. This place has rocked since the day it opened. And why not? Almost everyone loves wood-baked pizzas, mussels and meats. One favorite appetizer is the Manchego cheese, cured ham and Medjool dates, a perfect trio to kick off a meal. Another is the house-cured anchovies with roasted gypsy peppers. But you really haven't dined here if you haven't had the baked mussels, perfumed with smoke from the oven. One lovely entrée transported from Restaurant LuLu is the quail glazed with white-truffle honey. The partners have a line of house-made products, including this sinful honey, that are available here for purchase. Another product, an award-winner, is the fig-balsamic vinegar. For something not from the wood ovens, try the sparkling fresh oysters, grilled steak and, for dessert, the delightfully runny warm chocolate cake.

SCALA MIA HOUSE OF GARLIC   ITALIAN   11/20

820 Santa Cruz Ave., Menlo Park 94025
650-323-3665, *Lunch & Dinner daily*, $$

Located on what is becoming Menlo Park's restaurant row, Scala Mia does a straightforward job but breaks no new ground. Good starters include the stuffed and steamed artichoke and the mussels or clams sautéed in a white wine-lemon sauce. The pastas star: linguine with clams or calamari, fettuccine primavera or tender gnocchi with pesto. We like their huge salads, fresh and dressed lightly, and such secondi piatti as the polenta with sausage or the chicken sauté with artichokes. Finish your dinner with the light lemon cheesecake or the luscious tiramisu.

SPAGO PALO ALTO   CALIFORNIA   15/20

265 Lytton Ave., Palo Alto 94301
650-833-1000, *Lunch Mon.-Fri., Dinner nightly, $$$*

When Jeremiah Tower faltered with his Palo Alto branch of Stars, who should scoop up this property, a lovely restaurant with several dining areas, inside and out, but superchef Wolfgang Puck. He brought chef Michael French from his Postrio in San Francisco and flew in Manhattan designer (Le Cirque 2000) Adam Tihany to bring comfort and bright colors to the low-ceilinged space. The bar area, called the Pavilion—on warm nights the ceiling rolls back—is a delightful place to snack on one of Wolf's signature smoked salmon pizza while enjoying a cocktail. Good appetizers include steak tartare inventively paired with a raw oyster and tuna sashimi. Pastas are also a good choice, especially the feather-light sweet-potato gnocchi with prosciutto. The main courses, most priced over over $20, feature such favorites of ours as roasted veal loin with sweetbreads and cipollini onions, Columbia River quail with a bright-tasting pancetta-oyster stuffing, and squab bathed in a bit of wild honey and paired with apples and butternut-squash ravioli. The dessert sampler should be your dessert of choice. One problem for sophisticated restaurants in the suburbs has been getting professional waiters. They worked hard on the problem here and it shows—the service is seamless.

STRAITS CAFÉ   SINGAPOREAN   12/20

3295 El Camino Real, Palo Alto 94306
650-494-7168, *Lunch Mon.-Fri., Dinner nightly, $$*

Americans may not be familiar with the food of Singapore, but they should be. One dish not to miss is the signature whole crab sautéed in a sweet and hot sauce—it's finger-licking good. Appetizers are also tasty, whether they're grilled oysters with a ginger marmalade; an Indian-style bread, filled or not, served with a curry dipping sauce; or satay skewers of grilled chicken or lamb with one of the best peanut sauces around. Among the noodle and rice dishes are nasi goreng, the national dish of spicy coconut rice with prawns and vegetables. Another national dish is gado gado, assorted vegetables napped with a sweet and spicy peanut sauce. The desserts are okay, but a better choice would be to have a second appetizer instead. **Also in San Francisco.**

SUE'S INDIAN CUISINE   INDIAN   12/20

216 Castro St., Mountain View 94042
650-969-1112, *Lunch & Dinner daily, $*

Two can eat like kings at Sue's Indian Cuisine. Begin with onion masala dosa, a light and spongy pancake that's folded in half and filled with sweet sautéed onions, aromatic cilantro, fiery chiles and soothing partially mashed potatoes, streaked carrot-orange thanks to a liberal shower of turmeric. For dinner, order the chicken korma and soak up every drop of the dish's golden-colored nut sauce with the fresh-baked naan. A side order of mint chutney will seal the marriage of flavors. The lamb vindaloo, in a tomato-based tamarind curry sauce, is also excellent, and it packs serious heat. Raita accompanies every meal to cool things off, or you can refresh yourself with an icy bottle of Taj Mahal beer.

TAQUERIA LA CUMBRE   MEXICAN   ¢

28 North B St., San Mateo 94401
650-344-8989, *Open daily*

This branch of one of the best taquerías in San Francisco's Mission District serves a dizzying variety of burritos. Nothing fancy here. You see everything that goes into your burrito right from the counter as you choose the combination you want. All the meats for the superior burritos—pork, carne asada, chile colorado, grilled or stewed chicken—are also available on dinner plates or in small tacos. Vegetarians won't feel left out: there's a super deluxe with cheese, rice, beans, sour cream, guacamole, lettuce and tomatoes. Fish tacos, popular around the Bay Area, were recently added to the menu. Also in San Francisco.

THAI BASIL #2   THAI   ¢

210 Town & Country Village, Sunnyvale 94086
408-774-9090, *Lunch & Dinner Mon.-Sat.*

Even though Thai Basil #2 lacks the pleasantly funky lived-in feel of the nearby original on South Murphy, the food is just as good. Start with a skewered satay, or a variation called train kai yang. The salad-like larb is refreshing and fiery, ample for two, and a good change of pace from pad thai, though Thai Basil does that well, too. For dinner, go for the kweaw wan, a lovely coconut-tinged green curry, or the peppery angel dance, which features a generous catch of prawns. Also at 101 S. Murphy Ave., 408-773-1098

231 ELLSWORTH   CALIFORNIAN   14/20

231 S. Ellsworth Ave., San Mateo 94402
650-347-7231, *Lunch Mon.-Fri., Dinner Mon.-Sat., $$$*

This restaurant has the same exterior as a dry cleaner's tucked in a strip mall. But inside, the understated surroundings are casually elegant and change your mood immediately. Both the wait staff and the kitchen crew are first-rate. The menu changes every few months, but you can expect such exquisite dishes as a crayfish soufflé with black winter truffles or veal sweetbreads with truffled risotto cake, napped with a port reduction. Main courses include a rack of lamb with a strange-sounding but yummy cucumber-cashew napoleon. A venison filet pairs well with chestnuts, apple and endive. The selection of cheeses is very good, but it's hard to pass up pastry chef Phil Oglela's creations. The extensive wine list of California and French selections is outstanding.

THE VILLAGE PUB   CALIFORNIA   13/20

1969 Woodside Rd., Woodside 94062
650-851-1294, *Lunch Mon.-Fri., Dinner daily, $$$*

Woodside has always been estate country and horse country, and members of San Francisco society weekend here still. The Village Pub suits the community perfectly: the atmosphere is cushy yet welcoming and unpretentious; the fare is fresh and sophisticated. Dinner brings entrées such as roast duck paired with ancho chiles and mango, a Louisiana-style etouffée of scallops and crayfish accompanied by the traditional dirty rice, or sweet-and-spicy braised lamb shanks with Moroccan couscous. The well-rounded, exclusively California wine list includes many hard-to-find excellent vintages, some from wineries just around the bend.

VIOGNIER   CALIFORNIA   NO RATING

222 E. Fourth Ave., San Mateo 94401
650-685-3727, *Lunch Mon.-Fri., Dinner nightly, Brunch Sat.-Sun., $$$*

Chef Gary Danko left the Ritz-Carlton in San Francisco to open this casually elegant restaurant. Attractive watercolors grace the walls of this airy second-floor space, interestingly located atop Draeger's Marketplace, an upscale grocery that's long been a Peninsula favorite. Recently, Danko left as the executive chef to pursue his own restaurant in San Francisco, but he vows that the staff will continue to produce the high quality that fans of this restaurant have come to expect—and he's staying on as a consultant. Look for lovely starters such as a chilled asparagus soup with lemon crème fraîche and mint, or glazed oysters with zucchini pearls, leeks and sevruga caviar. The menu features thin-crust pizzas, one especially good version features the roasted red peppers with feta cheese. Sturdy main courses include a rotisserie duck with Fuji apples and cider sauce; a soy-mustard-napped filet of beef; and fettuccine with venison and goat cheese. The trio of crèmes brûlées is a big draw when dessert rolls around.

WHOLE FOODS   AMERICAN   ¢

774 Emerson St., Palo Alto 94301
650-326-8676, *Open daily*

For a quick bite, Whole Foods has a snack area in each store that could rival any deli. There are fresh soups, prepared entrées, a very good salad bar—be sure to try the cashew-pineapple salad dressing—plus smoothies, coffee and sodas. Nearby, baked goods can be bought to go, like the prepared food, or munched at one of the simple seating areas. Whole Foods makes everything from Thai noodle salad to burritos to grilled chicken. Service is cafeteria style, and you're expected to bus your own table. **Also in Campbell (1690 S. Bascom Ave. 408-371-5000), Cupertino (20830 Stevens Creek Blvd., 408-257-7000), & Los Gatos (15980 Los Gatos Blvd., 408-358-4434), as well as in San Francisco, the East Bay, Marin and Monterey.**

ZAO NOODLE BAR   ASIAN NOODLES   ¢

261 University, Palo Alto 94301
650-328-1988, *Open daily*

Owner Adam Wilner is committed to bringing affordable, authentic noodle dishes to the masses. The concrete walls in the Palo Alto store are softened with bright banners of wild animals, but the noise level can rise when this small place is hopping. Snacks include crunchy shrimp chips, seasoned soybeans and roasted wasabi peas. Satays (skewers) of vegetable and meat come with a spicy-sweet peanut sauce or a soothing yakitori sauce. Other starters include crispy imperial rolls, Vegas summer rolls, and meat dumplings. But the heart of the menu lives in its noodles: room-temperature chicken and ramen noodles are a great salad, as is the seared-beef salad à la Thailand. Bowls of steaming noodles appear in a traditional Japanese soba bowl. **Also in San Francisco.**

GOURMET SHOPS & MORE

BAKERIES/PASTRIES

MOONSIDE BAKERY & CAFÉ

604 Main St., Half Moon Bay 94019
650-726-9070, *Open daily*

Thomas Grauke, who owns this enticing bakery with his wife, Barbara, is a German-trained master baker, which explains the flaky strudels, danish pastry and almond-studded bear claws. But what accounts for Moonside's tasty and creative variety of cookies? You'll find Italian biscotti, macaroons and the shop's own half-moons, a shortbread pastry filled with marzipan and apricot marmalade dipped in chocolate. Breads here are also worth noting, including German rye, rosemary-garlic and sourdough.

SOUZA BAKERY

2079 El Camino Real, Santa Clara 95051
408-243-5443, *Open Mon.-Sat.*

For an early morning treat, stop at Souza—it opens at 5 a.m. Some unique goodies here are the chewy Portuguese doughnuts called malasadas, glazed with chocolate or sprinkled with powdered sugar; and the Portuguese sweet bread, not sugary, but not a sourdough either. They also sell all sorts of berry and fruit pies, cookies, and American and European-style breads, including cracked wheat, French and butter-top loaves. The special-occasion cakes—especially wedding cakes—are uniquely designed and personalized.

SUGAR 'N' SPICE

2965 Junipero Serra
Daly City 94015, Open daily

Jeanné Lutz is the doyenne of cake decorators in the Bay Area. In the last two decades she has taught legions in cake decorating, candymaking and other pastry arts. All the tools for the various decorative techniques are here to buy: brushes, spatulas, paste and spray colors, invert sugar, meringue powder, decors in a dozen shapes and colors, nonpareil seeds and silver dragées. Custom wedding ornaments can be ordered. Lutz's classes are taken by both professional bakers and hobbyists.

CHEESE

CHEESE PLEASE

299 California Dr., Burlingame 94010
650-348-5040, *Open daily*

The basics—Cheddar, Emmental and mozzarella—are here, along with imported cheeses from Italy, France and Holland, plus locally made fresh chèvre. Chunky country pâtés and smooth mousses, prepared salads, and an extended selection of wines and Champagne are available to round out a cocktail party or fill a picnic basket for a drive to the coast.

VILLAGE CHEESE HOUSE

157 Town & Country Village, Palo Alto 94301
650-326-9251, *Open Mon.-Sat.*

Romano, grated Pecorino, creamy Port-Salut, crumbly aged Cheddars and regal Roquefort are just a few of the finds at Village Cheese House. They've been catering to Palo Alto's cosmopolitan clientele for years, and it's hard to think of a popular cheese they don't carry. They also have candies, chocolates, teas, crackers, pâtés and other accompaniments, plus huge sandwiches (each literally made with three slices of bread). To carry it all, there's a nice selection of picnic baskets that you can fill with a variety of other gourmet foodstuffs for a special gift or for an afternoon of leisure. **Also in all the Gourmet Markets.**

CHOCOLATE & CANDY

AIDA OPERA CANDIES

1375 Burlingame Ave., Burlingame 94010
650-344-3333 Open daily

You might pass by this lovely shop, thinking it must carry only very expensive chocolates. You would be depriving yourself of a great treat. A large array of gift boxes, bags, baskets, flowerpots and such, many of them well priced, are waiting to be filled with a supply of English toffee, malt balls, lemon drops or Rocky Road for some lucky recipient. New tastes include a white chocolate bark with lemon drops and a chocolate bark with peanut brittle melded in. **Also in Village Cheese House.**

ETHNIC MARKETS

BRITISH FOOD CENTRES

1800 W. Campbell Ave., Campbell 95008
408-374-7770, Open daily

British cuisine may seem an oxymoron to some, but the three British Food Centres in California (Campbell, San Carlos and Solano Beach farther south) carry appealing imported British foods. The owners, Bill Fredlund, a retired air force colonel, and his Yorkshire-born wife, Betty, ran an antique business, importing furniture from England. Friends were always asking them to bring back specialty foods from England, and the British Food Centres evolved from these requests. Popular items include Branston pickles, traditionally served on a ploughman's plate; real frozen kippers; and, of course, a large selection of teas. Some of the more exotic items are Batchelors mushy peas, haggis (a Scottish dish of sheep's innards and oatmeal cooked like a sausage) and frozen cakes such as spotted dick. **Also in San Carlos (1652 El Camino Real, 650-595-0630).**

MARINA FOOD

2992 S. Norfolk St., San Mateo 94403
650-345-6911, Open daily

Delicious roast duck, barbecued pork and dumplings are available to go at this Asian supermarket. It carries every imaginable Asian produce, whole fish and spices. The staff is very patient with "curious" customers.

SOUTH SEAS MARKET/GLOBAL FOODS

612 San Mateo Ave., San Bruno 94066
650-873-2813, Open daily

When this store was established 23 years ago, the owners concentrated on Polynesian foodstuffs and Hispanic ingredients. But they've forged a new road, remodeled the store—it's cleaner and brighter—and now feature Indian, British, Caribbean, South African, Swedish, German and Greek foods for these communities on the Peninsula. Shopping at South

Seas is like taking a world tour. Canned corned beef is a big seller, especially with Pacific Islanders who acquired a taste for it back home (it reached Samoa from New Zealand). The hot sauces alone take up half a shelf.

TAKAHASHI CO.

221 S. Claremont St., San Mateo 94401
650-343-0394, *Open Mon.-Sat.*

Takahashi is one of the oldest retail establishments in San Mateo, dating from 1906. Starting out as a dry-goods store, the family business became a food store in the mid-1950s, when more Asians moved to the Peninsula. Takahashi carries all kinds of Asian groceries, including sushi-grade fish, sukiyaki beef, fresh vegetables and Ani's Hawaiian Bread, flown in weekly from Honolulu. Jack Takahashi makes his pickles every week. Called kyuri zuke in Japanese, they're Japanese cucumbers, marinated in two vinegars, chile flakes, sesame seed oil, garlic and salt.

VALLEY PRODUCE MARKET

3380 Middlefield Rd., Menlo Park 94025
650-368-9226, *Open daily*

The smell of roasting peanuts welcomes you to this produce market, where you can pick up many of the ingredients to make Mexican, Caribbean and Polynesian dishes. In addition to the serrano and jalapeño chiles, Mexican limes, coconuts in the husk and green plantains, there are corn husks for making tamales, soft queso fresco (fresh cheese) and salty aged queso cotijo (another Mexican cheese), mole poblano to sauce a roast chicken, and jamaica flower and tamarind fruit syrups for desserts and drinks.

FARMER'S MARKETS

MENLO PARK

Santa Cruz & Chestnut Sts.
408-461-9557, *Open Sun. 10 a.m.-2 p.m.*

PALO ALTO

Hamilton & Gilman Sts.
650-325-2088 *Open Fri.- 8 a.m.-noon, May through Dec.*

SAN MATEO

College of San Mateo parking lot
408-461-9557, *Open Wed. & Sat. 9 a.m.-1 p.m.*

GOURMET MARKETS

ANDRONICO'S

690 Los Ranchos Shopping Center, Los Altos 94024
650-948-6648, *Open daily*

From the immaculate produce to the assortment of baked goods, from the pristine fish to the lean cuts of meat, you could spend literally hours in this place, not to mention a fortune. One nice touch is the showy metal racks for packaged goods, rather than wooden shelves, lending an open look to the many aisles of goodies. Don't miss the extensive deli, with all manner of prepared dinners and deli fare. Andronico's also carries everything from toilet paper to aspirin, even liquor, beer and wine. It's a very organized store, and the staff is professional and knowledgeable. **Also in San Francisco and the East Bay**

COSENTINO'S

3521 Homestead Rd., Santa Clara 95051
408-243-9005, *Open daily*

These are venerable carriage-trade stores and full-service groceries with a loyal following. There's a good deli, a bakery, meat and seafood, and outstanding fresh produce. The reheatable entrées, freshly made salads and party trays are particularly attractive.

DRAEGER'S

342 First St., Los Altos 94022
650-948-4425, *Open daily*

It's hard to know where to start in Draeger's, a complete gourmet market under one roof. In the meat department, tray after tray proffers naturally raised chicken and turkey, fresh house-made sausages, plus roasts, steaks and chops of every description. The bakery publishes a 20-page booklet to describe the delights found there, from the best crusty sweet French rolls to Boston cream pie to brown-butter pear tart. The produce department is a bounty of fresh fruits and vegetables—baby artichokes, shiitake mushrooms, crimson strawberries, organically grown kiwi fruit—purchased from local farmers, as well as out-of-season items from around the world. The wine department is extensive, largely French and California, and very pricey. Cookbooks, tabletop wares and cooking classes by well-known chefs are offered at the **Menlo Park (1010 University Dr., 650-688-0686) and San Mateo (222 E. Fourth Ave., 650-685-3700) locations.**

OAKVILLE GROCERY

715 Stanford Shopping Center, Palo Alto 94304
650-328-9000, *Open daily*

This is ground zero for specialty foods, but no grocery items are carried. Packaged gourmet goods beckon from attractively arranged displays. Imported pastas made of all-semolina flour are cut with traditional brass dies. Salad dressings range from a light vinaigrette to creamy ranch and blue cheese. You'll find pastes in tubes of anchovy, tomato, onion and garlic for adding just a touch of flavor to a sauce, along with a selection of cheeses and cured meats like pancetta (unsmoked Italian bacon) for dicing into spaghetti alla carbonara. Need olive oil? They stock thirty brands, both domestic and imported. **Also in Los Gatos, Napa and the East Bay.**

ROBERT'S MARKET

3015 Woodside Rd., Woodside 94062
650-851-1511, *Open daily*

The bulletin boards outside this old Spanish-style building advertise summer homes and horsemen, which foreshadows the chichi market inside. This places sells only the best. The produce is squeaky clean. The meats are so organized that they stand at attention. And olive oils get their own special display. For convenience, Robert's also sells laundry detergent and such, and it has recently added espresso, soup and smoothie bars—all items prepared to go.

HEALTH FOODS

WHOLE FOODS

774 Emerson St., Palo Alto 94301
650-326-8676, *Open daily*

This Texas-based chain took the Bay Area by storm with its New Age-influenced grocery stores. You'll find crystals, incense and massage oil; books on vegetarianism along with every tofu product ever made; and more traditional foods, groceries, meats, fish and poultry. An in-house bakery does superior breads, rolls, cakes, cookies and pastries. But produce displays are stupendous, beautiful enough to tempt the most rabid carnivore to switch to a veggie diet. Every vegetable and fruit display is labeled: organic, transitional or conventional; the last term means that the product may have been sprayed with pesticides. In addition, Whole Foods, with numerous locations in the Bay Area, carries many chemical-free, minimally processed foods plus an abundance of vitamins and other health-oriented products. Even the canned pet food is the healthy kind. **Also in Campbell (1690 S. Bascom Ave., 408-371-5000) and Los Gatos (15980 Los Gatos Blvd., 408-358-4434), and in San Francisco, the East Bay, Marin and Monterey.**

ICE CREAM & MORE

ROMOLO'S ICE CREAM & CANNOLI FACTORY

81 37th Ave., San Mateo 94403
650-574-0625, *Open Tues.-Sat.*

Romolo's looks like a modest ice cream parlor but there is more to it than meets the casual eye. Husband-and-wife team Angela and Romolo Cappello have been making cannoli here since 1975, producing 60,000 a year for the wholesale and retail market. And what delicious cannoli! For the traditional version, they start with sheep's-milk ricotta from Wisconsin, then mix it with glazed fruit and chocolate chips. Other varieties are filled with house-made chocolate chip or spumoni ice creams. Their tiramisu includes their own handmade Mascarpone, and they also carry an extensive selection of Italian specialty cakes and ice cream creations.

MEAT, POULTRY & SEAFOOD

PACIFIC SEAS FISH MARKET

3360 Middlefield Rd., Menlo Park 94025
650-368-4628, *Open daily*

✂

Most fish are advertised by their melodious Fijian or Samoan names: malo lelei, kuku, tuitui, kanahe. You'll recognize shrimp, snapper, shark and the like. Ask at the counter (although not everyone speaks English) for young, tender lamb and the oft-neglected baby goat, when they can get it. Patrons often order these meats ahead for special holidays.

WINES & SPIRITS

BELTRAMO'S WINE & LIQUOR

1540 El Camino Real, Menlo Park 94025
650-325-2806, *Open daily*

This is a huge store with a strong selection of good wines (especially imports), beer and liquor. The knowledgeable staff will go out of their way to help you. The shop is priced competitively with clubs, and it ships nationwide. It also carries wine glasses, gift baskets, wine boxes and party supplies such as snacks and napkins. Beltramo's offers tastings and classes, too. It's so nice to buy from experts.

VIN VINO

437 California Ave., Palo Alto 94306
650-324-4903, *Open Tues.-Sat.*

If you're looking for imported French wines, this is the place. It even carries wines imported by Kermit Lynch, which is convenient if you don't feel like driving to Berkeley. The other half of the store houses Italian and California wines. The staff is very knowledgeable and helpful. Inquire about the classes offered in the newly remodeled upstairs.

THE WINE STOP

1300 Burlingame Ave., Burlingame 94010
650-342-5858, *Open daily*

More than a thousand wine selections line the spacious aisles at this welcoming shop. Avtar Johal will guide you to an affordable California Zinfandel or a French Burgundy ready for cellaring, and he'll do it with humor and charm. The selection is excellent, the prices are favorable, and the service can't be faulted.

SAN JOSE

INTRODUCTION

San Franciscans may not want to hear it, but San Jose is now the largest city in Northern California. Born of the high-tech revolution and the information age, San Jose has stepped out from San Francisco's shadow and established itself in world trade, technology and finance, and has established its own particular lifestyle. Formerly there were miles of orchards. Now, San Jose sprawls for miles with housing developments and business- and light-industrial parks. Suburban homes coexist with an older downtown area that is a gathering point for immigrants, especially from Asia and Central America.

Redevelopment around Market and San Carlos streets, the building of the San Jose Arena (a venue for big-name stars from the entertainment world and for the beloved Sharks hockey team), a newish light-rail system, and a well-booked convention center have all contributed to a resurgence of interest in downtown. New watering holes and swanky grills have blossomed. Several San Francisco restaurants have opened branches, while high-tech money has backed some homegrown eateries.

RESTAURANTS

AGENDA RESTAURANT　　CALIFORNIA　13/20

399 S. First St., San Jose 95113
408-287-3991, *Dinner Tues.-Sat.*, $$

Located in a turn-of-the-century building, Agenda is part of the hot South First Street restaurant and bar scene. Its menu is drawn from around the globe: bruschetta with assorted toppings, seared ahi tuna, seafood spring rolls, and blue-corn quesadillas are just a few of the featured starters. Most of the entrées are well prepared on the grill, like the game hen perfumed with lemon and oregano, or the pork chop that has been marinated in Guinness. Chef Brad Kraten does a nice filet mignon with pâté de foie gras. Service is gracious.

A.P. STUMPS　　CALIFORNIA　15/20

163 W. Santa Clara Ave., San Jose 95113
408-292-9928, *Lunch & Dinner daily*, $$$

When Postrio opened almost ten years ago, it was the beginning of a new era in San Francisco, one of high-profile, stylish restaurants with ground-breaking food. A.P. Stumps is the Postrio of San Jose, a $5 million restaurant in an historic building, with a look that blends traditional elegance with contemporary character. The decor features pressed-tin ceilings, crown moldings and rich woodwork, and no expense has been spared on materials–etched glass, bird's-eye and heartwood cabinetry, and tortoise-shell blown-glass chandeliers. Talented chef-partner Jim Stump has a clear vision: Tuck into a typical

French salad with frisée, a quail egg and warm bacon vinai-grette, atypically garnished with crispy fried smelts. Stump smokes his own salmon, glazes pork chops with molasses and crusts venison with peppercorns. The wine list includes tanta-lizing choices by the glass, more than 20 sparklers and a huge selection of Chardonnays, Pinots Noirs and Cabernets. Service is excellent, and there's live jazz to boot.

BELLA MIA   ITALIAN/GRILL   13/20

58 S. First St., San Jose 95113
408-280-1993, *Open daily*, $$

The "bones" of an historic building—brick walls, aged wood—add to the romantic ambience. Service is friendly and attentive, and in nice weather many opt to sit outside on the comfortable patio. Especially popular at lunch with those on the run is the "dine and dash" offering: a half order of lasagne or linguini with bolognese sauce. At dinner, start with one of the yummy flatbreads or the toothsome mushroom tart. Entrées feature items from the grill, like the filet mignon with grilled prawns and a wild-mushroom sauce. Pastas include good salmon ravioli. Save room for the cappuccino mud pie.

BILL'S CAFÉ   AMERICAN/ECLECTIC   ¢

1115 Willow St., San Jose 95125
408-294-1125, *Open daily*

This family restaurant is busy morning till night, and one look at the menu tells you why: it has heart-healthy garden burgers, breakfast anytime, a kid's section, and pleasers like fried calamari, fettuccine, jumbo prawns and almost a dozen sandwiches. You'll also find such eclectic dishes as Greek spaghetti, Cajun snapper and Belgian waffles.

BLAKE'S STEAKHOUSE & BAR   STEAKHOUSE   12/20

17 N. San Pedro Sq., San Jose 95110
408-298-9221, *Lunch Mon.-Fri., Dinner nightly*, $$$

This downtown newcomer serves up steaks, from a 7-ounce petit filet mignon to a 22-ounce porterhouse, in a no-nonsense setting with a lively. A popular appetizer is a roasted Castroville artichoke served with a lemon-garlic aïoli. Oysters on the half shell, a huge prawn cocktail and crabcakes are also well-pre-pared starters. In a nod to retro dining, the wedge of iceberg lettuce is napped with blue-cheese dressing and bits of bacon; spinach salad is done classically, and so is the Caesar. The juicy prime ribs come with creamy horseradish sauce. Chicken, fish and pasta dishes round out the menu. Service is crisp.

CAFÉ PRIMA VERA   ITALIAN   ¢

1359 Lincoln Ave., San Jose 95125
408-297-7929, *Lunch & Dinner Mon.-Sat.*

Tucked away with an entrance literally off a parking lot, this tiny place does well at both lunch and dinner. At lunch, service is cafeteria style, but at dinner the faux-painted walls, tile floors and candlelit tables create a cozy atmosphere. House-made soups, salads, quiches and pasta are the draw here. Anything with the creamy pesto sauce is good, and the grilled chicken or salmon is always satisfying, followed by a fruit crisp.

CAMERA CAFÉ — AMERICAN CAFÉ — ¢

288 S. Second St. San Jose 95110
408-998-0932, *Open daily*

Going to the movies and sick of popcorn? This cute little café is adjacent to the Camera Three art theaters, so before the main feature you can stop in for soup, a sandwich, salad, or a combo. The sandwiches have cinema-friendly names like the Naked Lunch, with avocado, artichoke hearts and sprouts; the Rumble Fish turns out to be smoked salmon and a toasted bagel with the works.

EMILE'S — CONTINENTAL — 14/20

545 S. Second St., San Jose 95112
408-289-1960, *Dinner Tues.-Sat., $$$$*

For more than 25 years, Emile's has been a culinary destination for patrons from all over the South Bay. In recent years, the menu has been updated, but the touches that made the place popular are still here: generously spaced tables, flowers in vases and subtle lighting. The wine list is deep with labels from France and California. Among the many tempting starters are a napoleon of satiny house-cured gravlax, goat cheese and caviar and prawns bordelaise. Lobster appears in a thermidor; a tender breast of chicken comes coq au vin style; a grilled Muscovy duck breast lounges atop a sweet-potato galette. The elaborate desserts include a Grand Marnier or cappuccino soufflé. The crisply professional service, wine selection, ambience and retro—but good—food don't come cheap.

EULAPIA RESTAURANT & BAR — CALIFORNIA — 15/20

374 S. First St., San Jose 95112
408-280-6161, *Lunch Tues.-Fri., Dinner Tues.-Sun., $$*

Since its opening in 1977, Eulapia, named for a song on a jazz album, has brought a hip note to the San Jose dining scene. Upstairs is a lively bar. Downstairs, the brick walls, modern art, candles and white tablecloths set the stage for some tasty combinations. At lunch, try the moist Chinese pulled-pork sandwich with house-made potato chips. A sesame crust enrobes the grilled rare ahi tuna, while the spiciness of the blackened rib-eye steak is cooled by herb-roasted potatoes. We don't recommend the occasional—and unusual--entrée of grilled ostrich with prawns. The outstanding wine list concentrates on the best of California, and includes all the giants of the high-end Cabs.

THE FOUNTAIN AT THE FAIRMONT   AMERICAN   ¢

Fairmont Hotel, 170 S. Market St., San Jose 95113
408-998-1900, *Breakfast, Lunch & Dinner daily*

This casual restaurant at the Fairmont Hotel is a handy place for a quick bite, whether it's in the dining room or the attractive little ice cream parlor. You'll find Cobb and Caesar salads, and an $11.95 burger loaded with bacon, cheese and grilled onions. Main courses include meatloaf, beef stew and a good herb-roasted chicken. Friday nights, the $15.95 Italian buffet features pasta cooked to order, an antipasti bar, pizzas and a towering array of desserts. On Saturday nights for the same price, there's an all-American buffet with rib-sticking choices like prime rib, grilled chicken and gooey desserts.

GERMANIA RESTAURANT AT THE HOCHBURG   GERMAN   14/20

261 N. Second St., San Jose 95112
408-295-4484, *Dinner Tues.-Sun.,* $$

Even when it's not Oktoberfest, Germania features lively entertainment and ballroom dancing along with its German food. Bring a hearty appetite and kick off your meal with the grilled sausage sampler, the crispy light potato pancakes or the marinated herring with sour cream, onions and apples. The Wiener Schnitzel is revamped with a lemon beurre blanc, but the Sauerbraten is classic. The apple strudel will transport you to Berlin, and the Black Forest cake will make you want to stay—at Germania.

GORDON BIERSCH   AMERICAN/BREWPUB   12/20

33 E. San Fernando St., San Jose 95113
408-294-6785, *Lunch & Dinner daily,* $$

See review in PENINSULA chapter.

THE GRILL ON THE ALLEY   AMERICAN/GRILL   12/20

The Fairmont Hotel, 172 S. Market St., San Jose 95113
408-294-2244, *Lunch Mon.-Sat., Dinner nightly,* $$$

The look of this stylish restaurant, a sibling of one in Beverly Hills, is retro and new at the same time. Dark-stained wood and lots of leather give masculine touches. The comfortable bar, showcasing vintage photos of San Jose, has become a magnet for downtown business people. Crabcakes, gravlax and huge salads are part of the starting lineup. Some old-time dishes are here also, like calf's liver and onions. The portions are enormous, especially the steaks. We find that the desserts have a made-somewhere-else taste and look.

HENRY'S WORLD FAMOUS HI-LIFE   BARBECUE   12/20

301 W. Saint John St., San Jose 95110
408-295-5414, *Lunch Tues.-Fri., Dinner nightly,* $$

For almost 40 years, Henry's Hi-Life has been taking care of the barbecue needs of San Joseans. Located in an old roadhouse, its walls covered with memorabilia, Henry's is known by everyone. The menu also features steaks, a couple of pastas, plus fish and chicken dishes. All the entrées come with salad and a baked potato—a 16-ounce wonder, but there are no desserts. The service is weird: upon entering you take a number in the bar area and place your order. You are seated when your table is ready, and your salad will be waiting.

HOBEE'S — AMERICAN — ¢

920 Town and Country Village, San Jose 95128
408-244-5212, *Breakfast & Lunch daily*

The Hobee's chain, spread far and wide through the Silicon Valley, is a top breakfast and brunch destination for single techies and families. The look is country kitchen with wood tables and flouncy curtains. A pot of coffee or tea appears as soon as you're seated. Breakfasts consist of blueberry coffeecake and omelets. For lunch, you'll find sandwiches, quesadillas, a salad and soup bar, and black-bean chili with the works. **Also at 680 River Oaks Plaza at Montague Expressway, 408-232-0190, and in Cupertino, Mountain View & Palo Alto.**

IL FORNAIO — ITALIAN — 13/20

The Hyatt St. Claire, 302 S. Market St., San Jose, 95113
408-271-3366, *Breakfast, Lunch & Dinner daily, $-$$*

See review in PENINSULA chapter.

JOHNNY ROCKETS — AMERICAN — ¢

150 S. First St., San Jose 95112
408-977-1414, *Open daily*

In the good ole 1950s, a diner would have burgers, fries, milkshakes and a good jukebox—that's it. All of the above can be experienced at these chain outlets, but today you can also get a vegie burger. Every Johnny Rockets has a U-shaped counter and booths equipped with small jukeboxes. All the fare is good, especially the hot-fudge sundaes and malts. **Also at 840 Blossom Hill Rd., 408-229-1414, and in Campbell, Milpitas, Saratoga & other locations in the Bay Area.**

KHANH'S GARDEN RESTAURANT — VIETNAMESE — 12/20

618 Town and Country Village, San Jose 95128
408-241-4940, *Lunch & Dinner daily, $*

In a city with a large Vietnamese population, this is one of the more attractively decorated Vietnamese restaurants. The open, airy room has lots of wood, tiles and plants. Among the many familiar dishes is a good "fresh roll," an assemblage of cooked pork and shrimp rolled in a rice crêpe. The soups, like pho, are hearty. Khanh's desserts are French inspired.

LE PAPILLON   FRENCH   13/20

410 Saratoga Ave., San Jose 95129
408-296-3730, *Lunch Mon.-Fri., Dinner daily, $$$*

This well-established French restaurant seats guests in elegantly upholstered chairs as its cozy dining room flickers with candles on white tablecloths. The waiters are highly professional, and the food, consistently extravagant, has lately acquired some Asian flavors. The à la carte and changing tasting menus feature dishes such as a lobster brandade, ginger-glazed salmon with a kumquat glace, and grilled venison chops. The five-course prix-fixe dinner is a good buy, especially when paired with the suggested accompanying wines.

MIO VINCINO   ITALIAN   12/20

1140-8 Lincoln Ave., San Jose 95125
408-286-6027, *Lunch & Dinner daily, $$*

One of a friendly, family-owned Italian restaurant chain, Mio Vincino serves such lusty appetizers as grilled radicchio wrapped in pancetta and finished with a touch of goat cheese. The irresistible pizzas sport inventive toppings: try one with prosciutto, apples, Gorgonzola cheese and toasted pine nuts. Don't miss Mama Rose's sauce of artichokes, sun-dried tomatoes and cream over fresh pasta. Cioppino, pork chops and veal complete the menu, but the wine list is sadly deficient. **Also in Campbell & Santa Clara.**

MENARA MOROCCAN RESTAURANT   MOROCCAN   13/20

41 E. Gish Rd., San Jose 95112
408-453-1983, *Dinner nightly, $$*

This whimsical place near the Convention Center has been around for nearly 20 years, and provides a good break from the Cal-Ital places that abound. You know the Moroccan drill: seating is on pillowed couches; eating with your fingers is encouraged; and swirling belly dancers, sumptuous rugs and silver serving pieces complete the stage set for the various set menus. On the Diner Menara, enjoy a Moroccan salad, b'stilla, chicken with lemon, lamb with honey and a vegetable couscous. A serving of flaky baklava and mint tea conclude the feast. Service is warm and accommodating.

ORIGINAL JOE'S   ITALIAN   12/20

301 S. First St., San Jose 95113
408-292-7030, *Breakfast, Lunch & Dinner daily, $$*

So many Original Joe's can be found in the Bay Area that it's hard to know which one is the real "original." Order the famous Joe's Special, eggs scrambled with spinach, hamburger and onions, a dish, according to legend, that was created for a musician one late night from what was on hand. Lunch specials include lasagne, Swiss steak, osso buco and meatloaf. At dinner, hearty dishes like prime rib, calf's liver and several veal dishes are served with potatoes, spaghetti or ravioli. Service is friendly and quick, and they serve until 1:30 a.m. daily.

PAOLO'S — ITALIAN — 14/20

333 W. San Carlos St., San Jose 95114
408-294-2558, *Breakfast, Lunch & Dinner Mon.-Sat.,* $$

Paolo's is pretty much San Jose's celeb hangout, counting as former patrons President Ronald Reagan and the late Joe DiMaggio. Breakfast is simple—freshly squeezed juice, flaky pastries and strong espresso—but that doesn't mean it isn't good. At lunch, sandwiches, soups and salads make up the bulk of the menu. Most guests opt for the antipasto misto plate at dinner, a selection of perhaps house-made duck prosciutto, tuna carpaccio and rice croquettes. Try the potato gnocchi with white truffle butter, or osso buco with saffron rice and gremolata. Service is well rehearsed yet friendly.

RED SEA RESTAURANT — ETHIOPIAN — 12/20

684 N. First St., San Jose 95112
408-993-1990, *Lunch & Dinner daily,* $

Ethiopian food, mostly mild curry stews, is authentically served on top of a spongy crêpe called injera. One of the best dishes is tender strips of chicken sautéed with onions, tomato and spices, ordered extra spicy or mild. The food is eaten by tearing off a piece of the crêpe and scooping up some of the stew or stir fry. Taj, Ethiopian-style honey wine is a good accompaniment, but beer will cool the fiery food as well. And if the kids won't try the food, they can order spaghetti.

RUE DE PARIS — CONTINENTAL — 13/20

19 N. Market St., San Jose 95114
408-298-0713, *Lunch Mon.-Fri., Dinner daily,* $$$

In San Francisco, continental-style restaurants have pretty much had their day, but in San Jose, the idea of an upscale restaurant offering both classic Italian and French dishes is still popular. Rue de Paris, with its cutsey French country lace curtains, shutters and flower boxes, is one of the most successful. The usual suspects are here: escargots de Bourgogne, pâté de foie gras, rack of lamb and even beef Wellington. Chocolate mousse, and an array of soufflés are just part of the extensive and delicious dessert offerings. The wine list abounds with good French selections, and the port choices are exemplary, with vintages going back to 1896.

SCOTT'S SEAFOOD — SEAFOOD — 13/20

185 Park Ave., Sixth Floor, San Jose 95115
408-971-1700, *Lunch Mon.-Fri., Dinner daily,* $$

Scott's serves fresh seafood in big portions. Order oysters raw on the half shell or baked in oysters Rockefeller. Large prawns appear in a cocktail, in a huge mixed-seafood salad with scallops and bay shrimp, in a garlic sauté, or grilled. A good choice is the fisherman's stew, with all manner of seafood in a tasty broth, and almost large enough for two. You'll also find a decent New York steak, plus top sirloin and chicken. Desserts are pretty forgettable, though the pecan pie is not bad. **Also in Palo Alto and other Bay Area locations.**

71 SAINT PETER   MEDITERRANEAN   13/20

71 N. San Pedro St., San Jose 95115
408-971-8523, *Lunch Mon.-Fri., Dinner Mon.-Sat.*, $$

Part of the new wave of San Jose restaurants, 71 Saint Peter has an intimate and sophisticated atmosphere. Try to snare a table in the arbor. The interior has a loft look, with exposed brick walls, softened by fresh flowers on the tables and an inside arbor covered with ivy. The short menu features such appetizers as peppered seared ahi tuna, and a light roasted pepper-eggplant terrine with goat cheese. Zesty entrées include Parmesan-encrusted chicken breast stuffed with spinach and smoked mozzarella, a somewhat strange maple-glazed top sirloin, and good roasted duck and grilled salmon. The sour-cream fudge cake is moist and delicious.

SPIEDO RISTORANTE   ITALIAN/GRILL   11/20

151 W. Santa Clara Ave., San Jose 95115
408-971-6096, *Lunch & Dinner daily*, $$

This bilevel restaurant is sharp and comfortable. The focaccia, sprinkled with rosemary-perfumed olive oil, is some of the best in San Jose. Duck and rabbit both appeared to suffer from overcooking. Filled pastas and ravioli are a better way to go here, as is the satiny panna cotta for dessert. We've encountered confused or untrained servers. **Also in San Mateo.**

STRATTA GRILL & CAFÉ   MEDITERRANEAN   13/20

71 E. San Fernando St., San Jose 95113
408-293-1121, *Lunch & Dinner Tues.-Sat.*, $$

Softly faux-painted walls, hardwood floors, tiles and a welcoming wine bar all add to the European feel. Stratta has scored high with locals since it opened because of its straightforward food and warm atmosphere. The Caesar salad is excellent, while the seafood pasta melange is bright tasting and chock-full of scallops, calamari and prawns. The menu changes often, but patrons can count on the grilled steak, salmon or chicken, served with mashed potatoes.

TAIWAN   CHINESE   11/20

1306 Lincoln Ave., San Jose 95125
408-289-8800, *Lunch & Dinner daily*, $

Taiwan has been around for a long time because the food is familiar and affordable. The graceful interior has half-mir-

rored walls, large flower arrangements, and red tablecloths on
the mahogany-stained tables. All the popular Chinese restaurant favorites are here: lemon chicken, mu shu pork, meat and
vegetable stir fries, and fried rice and noodle dishes.

WHITE LOTUS RESTAURANT   VEGETARIAN   12/20

80 N. Market St., San Jose 95113
408-977-0540, *Lunch & Dinner Mon.-Sat., $*

Vegans, vegetarians and health-conscious diners flock to
White Lotus. The dishes are meatless, eggless and delicious.
The secret is the chef's knowledge of the spices and herbs that
enhance the tofu, gluten and vegetables prepared here. The
spring rolls are Vietnamese style but without the meat. Stuffed
tofu is one of the best dishes, and the soups are hearty.

WILLOW STREET WOOD-FIRED PIZZA   PIZZA   12/20

1072 Willow St., San Jose 95125
408-971-7080, *Lunch & Dinner daily, $*

Willow Street is one of a new breed of places that might be
called designer pizza emporiums. You can have a simple pizza
topped with tomato sauce and cheese, or one with chicken and
Brie, pesto and sun-dried tomatoes, barbecued chicken, or
goat cheese and pancetta? Pastas and salads are other menu
choices. The beer and wine list pairs well with the food. **Also in
Los Gatos & Marin.**

GOURMET SHOPS & MORE

COFFEE & TEA...281
DELIS 281
ETHNIC MARKETS..282
FARMERS' MARKET...282
FLEA MARKET..283
GOURMET MARKETS..283
HEALTH FOOD...283
MEAT & SEAFOOD...284
WINES & SPIRITS..284

BAKERIES: BREAD & PASTRIES

AMBROSIA BAKERY

2347 McKee Rd., San Jose 95116
408-258-9888, *Open daily*

The specialty at this cute little shop are Chinese and
Vietnamese buns, custard cups and small savory treats to con-

sume with tea. It also makes a full line of cakes for birthdays and special occasions.

ARAM BAKERY

5837 Camden Ave. # IA, San Jose 95124
408-448-3019, *Open daily*

This is a good place to buy Persian pastries, freshly made lavash bread, pita bread and pita chips. The baklava is especially good.

BAGEL BASKET

3255 S. White Rd., San Jose 95132
408-274-0876, *Open daily*

All sorts of bagels—20 flavors in all—are the draw here. The most popular for purists is the plain; then there are the herb-cheese, jalapeño and raisin. The bakery also produces bialys, scones and cinnamon rolls.

IL FORNAIO PANETTERIA BAKERY

Hyatt St. Claire Hotel, 302 S. Market St., San Jose 95113
408-271-3399, *Open daily*

Award-winning bread from Il Fornaio can be purchased here. Chipatta, the Italian "slipper bread," is tender and tasty, as is the rich olive bread. Another fave is the rosemary bread. For breakfast the raisin loaf or walnut loaf makes great toast. Mini-rolls are good for sandwiches, or you can buy the sturdy focaccia in green onion. A full line of pastries, including bear claws, flavored croissants and danishes, satisfies any sweet tooth.

COFFEE & TEA

MOULIN ROUGE COFFEE ROASTING

628 Town and Country Village, San Jose 95128
408-247-4611, *Open daily*

Kona is the most popular coffee sold at this upscale coffee roastery and coffeehouse. But if that pricey bean is not in the budget, you can choose from 20 other roasts and blends, plus a great array of teas. Coffee and tea drinks paired with a snack or cookie make this a popular hangout in the Town and Country shopping center.

Teas at the British Food Centres, under Ethnic Markets.

DELIS

ANTIPASTO'S BY DE ROSE GOURMET

3454 McKee Rd., San Jose 95127
408-251-5647, *Open Mon.-Sat.*

This store has freshly cooked Dungeness crab, in season, and the deli has the usual salads, cold cuts, roasted meats and olives. But by far the most popular reason for shopping here is the to-go entrées, which change daily. Friday night it's cioppino; Saturday, luscious baby back ribs. There are even slabs of tender prime rib with side dishes on Thursdays. For other delis see Andronico's, Draeger's, Lunardi's, Cosentino's and Oakville Grocery.

ETHNIC MARKETS

DOBASHI MARKET

240 Jackson St., San Jose 95112
408-295-7794, Open daily

This well-established San Jose market carries bottled, frozen and packaged Japanese foodstuffs: lots of crackers, snacks, flavored vinegars, noodles and rice. There are fresh vegetables and seafood but no fresh meat.

MI PUEBLO

235 Julian St., San Jose 95112
408-292-3177, Open daily

This is a popular venue for just about every ingredient needed in Mexican cuisine: fresh meat and fish, produce, spices, canned goods, baked goods and delicious sweet rolls and pastries. Knowing how to speak a little Spanish goes far in this authentic emporium.

YAOHAN MARKET

675 Saratoga Ave., San Jose 95129
408-255-6690, Open daily

This is the largest grocery store specializing in Asian groceries in Northern California. Established almost 11 years ago, it is a branch of the Los Angeles supermarket. All manner of packaged, bottled and frozen ingredients, many imported from Japan, are sold here, as well as fresh seafood, meat and vegetables. To-go products, such as freshly prepared sushi and entrées from the deli counter, are attractively displayed. If you can't find it in this 20,000-square-foot store, it's probably not made.

FARMERS' MARKET

SAN JOSE DOWNTOWN

San Fernando & S. First Sts.
800-949-FARM, Open Thurs. 10 a.m.-2 p.m. May through Nov.

FLEA MARKET

SAN JOSE FLEA MARKET

1590 Berryessa Rd., San Jose 95133
408-453-1110, *Open Wed.-Sun.*

Some 2,300 vendors set up shop from dawn to dusk to peddle their wares—everything from brand-name juice drinks (you wonder where they come from) to tires and vacuum bags. However, your visit wouldn't be complete without a stroll through the produce "aisles," which are crammed with an amazing variety of fresh and packaged Mexican foodstuffs, nuts, produce, freshly blended exotic fruit drinks and homemade pastries. This is also a great place for knives, party supplies, kitchenware (like dish drains) and kitchen towels. Be sure to bargain; that's half the fun. The food sold in the conveniently located food stands is OK if you're starved from walking so much. Follow the aroma to the barbecues. Parking is easy and the bathrooms are spotless.

GOURMET MARKETS

COSENTINO'S

2666 S. Bascom Ave., San Jose 95124
408-377-6661, *Open daily*

These are venerable carriage-trade stores and full-service groceries with a loyal following. There's a good deli, a bakery, meat and seafood, and outstanding fresh produce. The reheatable entrées, freshly made salads and party trays are particularly attractive. **Also in Santa Clara (3521 Homestead Rd., 408-243-9005).**

LUNARDI'S MARKETS

4650 Meridian Ave., San Jose 95124
408-265-9101, *Open daily*

Locals love the old-fashioned butcher counter at this chain, where the butchers are only too happy to butterfly a leg of lamb or create a crown roast, they won't faint. The fish is fabulously fresh and well priced. Produce here is also a standout, although not much of it is organically grown. All the stores have grocery items, bakeries, delis, produce, meat, fish and poultry. **Also in Belmont, Los Gatos and San Bruno on the Peninsula, plus the East Bay.**

HEALTH FOODS

CAHALAN HEALTH FOODS

6067 Cahalan Ave., San Jose 95123
408-227-5453, *Open Mon.-Sat.*

This is a friendly health food store with a large array of vitamins, herbs and all manner of healthful potions. There's a nice selection of canned, packaged and frozen foods, free of antibiotics and chemicals, plus lots of bulk foods like grains, flours and even herbs. Many books are on sale to guide you to better nutrition.

MEAT & SEAFOOD

HONEY BAKED HAM

750 S. Winchester Blvd., San Jose 95128
408-247-1501, *Open daily*

At Easter and other major holidays, when putting out a good spread is important, patrons line up outside these chain stores for the prepared meats. The choices include an all-ham "grand-event platter"; turkey and roast beef combo platters; and sandwich, cheese or cocktail sandwich platters. The fare is fine, if not unique, and the platters are less expensive than hiring a caterer or ordering deli platters at some upscale markets. Also in Sunnyvale and a dozen other locations around the Bay Area.

SILVA SAUSAGE CO.

1266 E. Julian St., San Jose 95116
408-293-5437, *Open Mon.-Sat.*

Thirty years ago this sausage maker began by making linguica for the Portuguese community of San Jose. Today the company's 20 varieties of sausage are distributed around the Bay Area. In addition to the signature linguica, there's a mildly smoked andouille, plus hot and mild Italian sausages. Patrons can also buy sausages retail at the plant.

WINES & SPIRITS

BEVERAGES, & MORE

14800 Camden Ave. , San Jose 95124
408-369-0990, *Open daily*

This big chain carries all sorts of liquors, wines, beers, bar supplies and glasses. Prices here are attractive, and patrons can join the Beverages, & More buyers club for further savings. In numerous other locations, including San Francisco, Marin and the East Bay.

WINE TOURING

WINERIES OPEN TO THE PUBLIC:

J. LOHR WINERY

1000 Lenzen Ave., San Jose 95126
408-288-5057

MIRASSOU WINERY

300 Aborn Rd., San Jose 95135
408-274-4000

MIRASSOU CHAMPAGNE CELLARS

300 College Ave., Los Gatos 95031
408-395-3790 Tasting Wed.-Sun.

Monterey Carmel

MAP OF MONTEREY CARMEL

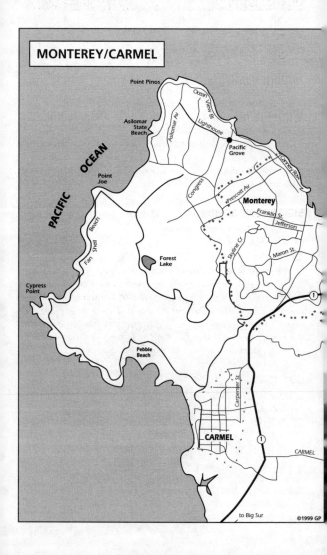

MONTEREY/CARMEL

Point Pinos

Asilomar State Beach

Point Joe

PACIFIC OCEAN

Cypress Point

Fan Shell Beach

Forest Lake

Pebble Beach

Ocean View Bl

Asilomar Av

Lighthouse

Pacific Grove

Cannery Row

Congress

Prescott Av

Monterey

Franklin St.

Jefferson

Skyline Cr

Maron St.

Carpenter St

CARMEL

CARMEL

to Big Sur

©1999 GP

INTRODUCTION

Located about two hours south of San Francisco, the Monterey-Carmel area encompasses panoramic stretches of the California coastline, verdant farmland, vineyards and several towns that have preserved landmarks from California's mission era. You'll also find plenty of recreational and culinary opportunities. The **Monterey Peninsula** encompasses **Carmel, Carmel Highlands, Monterey, Pacific Grove, Pebble Beach** and, further south, **Big Sur.**

RESTAURANTS

ANTON & MICHEL   CONTINENTAL   13/20

Mission St. between Ocean & Seventh Aves., Carmel 93921
831-624-2406, *Lunch & Dinner daily,* $$$

The salmon-hued dining room is hung with original oil paintings, and the patio is enhanced by fountains and a garden. We like the classic dishes such as rack of lamb, grilled veal medallions and poached salmon. Desserts include tiramisu and crème brûlée. The award-winning wine list concentrates on Napa and Monterey County wines, along with some from from Burgundy, Bordeaux and the Rhône Valley, but wines by the glass are few.

BUBBA GUMP SHRIMP CO.   AMERICAN   ¢

720 Cannery Row, Monterey 93940
831-373-1884, *Open daily*

We tread warily in theme restaurants—okay, so the kids like them, but will we find anything good to eat? At this Forest Gump-inspired joint, a joint venture of Paramount Pictures and the Rusty Pelican Restaurant chain, if you can get past the menu's cutesy references to the movie and survive the overdone interior, you'll find the food isn't bad. Try the peel-and-eat shrimp steamed in beer, served with two spicy dips.

CAFÉ FINA   ITALIAN   13/20

47 Fisherman's Wharf #1, Monterey 93940
831-372-5200, *Lunch & Dinner daily,* $$

A popular dining spot on Fisherman's Wharf, Café Fina is owned by the Mercurios, a third-generation Italian family. They produce their own pastas accented with fresh herb sauces, and bake authentic Italian pizzas in a wood-burning brick oven. The signature dish is the pasta Fina: baby shrimp, olives, tomatoes and green onions in a butter-clam sauce over linguine. House-made cannoli and crème brûlée top off the evening.

CASANOVA — MEDITERRANEAN 14/20

Fifth Ave. between San Carlos & Mission, Carmel 93921
831-625-0501, *Lunch & Dinner daily, Brunch Sun.,* $$$$

The three-course dinner begins with assorted appetizers, olives, cheese and bread; it continues with entrées such as broiled salmon with couscous and roasted duck perfumed with honey lavender. A warm chocolate cake with an oozing center is a perfect finale. Service is friendly and professional.

CIBO RISTORANTE ITALIANO — ITALIAN/SICILIAN 13/20

301 Alvarado St., Monterey 93940
Dinner nightly, $$

The Catalano family offers both Italian and Sicilian specialties at this downtown venue. A good starter is an artichoke stuffed with bread crumbs, currants, prosciutto and tomatoes. Main courses consist of pastas, pizzas and grilled items. Try the tangle of tagliatelle with tiger prawns in a sauce of white wine, saffron and butter. Round out the evening with the napoleon alla Cibo, a layered dessert of crisp phyllo rounds, creamy Mascarpone cheese, imported Amarena cherries and hazelnuts.

CLUB XIX INSPIRED BY H. KELLER — FRENCH/CONTEMP 16/20

The Lodge at Pebble Beach, 17 Mile Dr., Pebble Beach 93953
831-625-8519, *Lunch & Dinner daily,* $$$-$$$$

A few years ago, Hubert Keller of Fleur de Lys in San Francisco was hired as a consultant to revamp the menu here, working with Lisa Magadini, the chef de cuisine. Their collaboration has been a great success. Overlooking the 18th hole of the famed golf course, the covered patio is fun at lunch. Because of a loyal local following, the restaurant retained the popular club sandwich and the Cobb salad but added delights such as the sautéed soft-shell crabs. The luscious crab bisque contains a phyllo pillow filled with tender crab meat. At night the menu is more Kelleresque with dishes such as cassoulet of duck and lobster and a stuffed boneless quail. The wine list carries some lovely wines from California, Alsace and the rest of Europe. At night the setting is refined and romantic, even if the patrons can't see the ocean. Service is on the highest level.

THE COVEY AT QUAIL LODGE — CALIFORNIA 14/20

8205 Valley Greens Dr., Carmel 93923
831-624-1581, *Dinner nightly,* $$$$

In tranquil country surroundings, the restaurant features a view of a shining lake, fountains, lush gardens and the golfing greens. The daily changing menu of elegant fare includes fluffy shrimp- and-scallop quenelles and a Castroville artichoke steamed with lemongrass, both excellent starters. The rack of lamb and fresh-fish selections are consistently pleasing. Finish with the lemon meringue curd. The extensive wine list includes a good selection of Monterey County labels.

CYPRESS GROVE CALIFORNIA 13/20

663 Lighthouse Ave., Pacific Grove 93950
831-375-1743, *Lunch & Dinner Tues.-Sat., Brunch Sun., $$$*
☎

This eclectic California-cuisine eatery is a reincarnation of Melac's, with the same pleasant service and rustic atmosphere. Ahi tuna tartare with marinated cucumber, frizzled leeks and wasabi cream is a pleasant starter. The tasty quail with foie gras in puff pastry is wonderful when not overcooked. Desserts include seasonal fruit tarts and an orange-scented Mascarpone cheesecake.

FANDANGO MEDITERRANEAN 13/20

223 17th St., Pacific Grove 93950
831-372-3456, *Lunch Mon.-Sat., Dinner daily, Brunch Sunday, $$$*
☎ 🖥 🏃 ▮

Flowers, baskets of freshly baked breads and a crackling fire greet you in this cozy Mediterranean-style restaurant. In the rear, you'll find a more casual, glass-domed terrace. The menu features classics such as osso buco, duck a l'orange, seafood paella and simple pastas. For dessert, don't miss the frozen Grand Marnier soufflé for two. The wine list is outstanding, the service attentive without being intrusive.

FRESH CREAM FRENCH 15/20

99 Pacific St., Suite 100C, Monterey 93940
831-375-9798, *Dinner nightly, $$$$*
☎ 📷 🏃

Open since 1978, Fresh Cream remains, quite simply, one of the best restaurants on the Monterey Peninsula. The ambience measures up to the food, with glittering harbor views and a posh interior featuring gleaming blond woods and muted colors. We recommend the escargot appetizer and silky goose liver pâté. House specialties include a delectable Dover sole, ahi tuna, duck, lamb and filet mignon. The chocolate desserts are tempting, and the wine list pairs well with the food.

GRASING'S CALIFORNIA/SEAFOOD 14/20

6th & Mission Sts., Carmel 93921
408-624-6562, *Lunch & Dinner daily, $$$*
🖥 ▮

This sophisticated Carmel spot has a modern, fresh colorful décor, with flowers everywhere. We like the intriguing dishes as well. Starters include salmon cakes with cucumber relish, a three-onion tart with fennel sauce and a corn-flecked shrimp flan. There's a bounty of fresh seafood—grilled, broiled, herbcrusted, baked and even in a paella—as well as a few meat dishes. Desserts are heavenly, and wines, which come from partner

Narsai David's private cellar, include excellent bottlings at extraordinarily reasonable prices.

IL FORNAIO · ITALIAN · 12/20

Ocean Ave. at Monte Verde in the historic Pine Inn, Carmel 93921
831-622-5100, *Breakfast, Lunch & Dinner daily, $-$$*

As is the case with most of the restaurants in this Northern California chain, the flavors of Italy are well represented. You'll find wood-fired pizzas, rotisserie meats and fresh regional pastas. One favorite dish is the stuffed artichoke halves packed with garlic, bread crumbs, a touch of anchovy and crushed red-pepper flakes. The in-house bakery provides wonderful breads and morning pastries.

KINCAID'S BISTRO · FRENCH · 14/20

217 Crossroads Blvd., Crossroads Shopping Center, Carmel 93923
831-624-9626, *Lunch Mon.-Fri., Dinner nightly, $$$*

Chef-owner Robert Kincaid prepares classic bistro cuisine, with starters like pâté and escargots. His signature dishes include roasted duckling with wild-cherry sauce and rack of lamb enrobed in a mustard crust. The ambience is country French: graceful archways, an exposed wood-beam ceiling, a cozy fireplace with walls that look like weathered stone. Patrons almost forget that the restaurant is located in a sterile shopping center.

LA BOHÈME · MEDITERRANEAN · 13/20

Dolores between Ocean & Seventh Aves., Carmel 93921
831-624-7500, *Dinner nightly, $$*

La Bohème's decor is French country, and it offers a three-course, prix-fixe menu that changes daily. The family-style meal begins with a crisp salad; next come special soups, followed by entrées that range from a classic filet mignon with Roquefort to scampi served with a compote of fresh corn, roasted bell peppers, chile peppers, cilantro and black beans. Desserts such as a light lemon tart round out the dinner.

LA GONDOLA · ITALIAN · 13/20

3690 Barnyard Shopping Center, Carmel 93921
831-626-0430, *Lunch & Dinner daily, $$*

This reincarnation of Silver Jones and Michael's features the Venetian cuisine of Francesco Solda served in a charming dining room with white stucco walls, a beamed ceiling and louver shutters. Don't miss the generous portion of a scrumptious risotto tossed with artichoke bottoms and rock shrimp. On a recent visit, the mushroom pizza was tasty, but the crust was a bit soggy. Toothsome desserts included an Italian-inspired rice pudding.

MONDO'S TRATTORIA ITALIAN/FRENCH 13/20

Dolores between Ocean & Seventh Aves., Carmel 93921
831-624-8977, *Lunch & Dinner daily, $$*

For lovers of Italian food, the cozy European-inn atmosphere at Mondo's is welcoming. The light eater can choose from a variety of insalatas, bruschettas, antipasti and soups. Those with an appetite will find fantastic pastas combined with various sauces, homemade pizza, huge sandwiches and tempting specials. Italian wines, especially well-known Chiantis, are favored on the wine list, along with a good choice of French and California wines. Desserts include a heavenly tiramisu and crème brûlée.

MONTRIO CONTEMPORARY 14/20

414 Calle Principal, Monterey 93940
831-648-8880, *Lunch & Dinner daily, $$*

Montrio is located in a handsomely restored firehouse built in 1910. The frequently changing menu is influenced by the France, Italy and America. The chicken and Black Angus rib-eye are cooked to perfection on the wood-burning rotisserie. The garlic-mashed potatoes are a must. The house-made desserts include an innovative cannoli with raspberry coulis. Montrio has a wine list that features mainly domestic wines with a few French and Italian selections.

NEPENTHE AMERICAN 13/20

Pacific Coast Hwy. (Rte. 1, 29 miles south of Carmel), Big Sur 93920
831-667-2345, *Lunch & Dinner daily, Brunch Sun., $$*

Nepenthe is the name of an ancient drug purportedly used to forget sorrow. Today travelers from up and down the Big Sur coast experience that "high" by visiting this restaurant, perched dramatically high above the Pacific. In fact, we find it hard to think of a more inspiring "view" restaurant in all of California. But yes, you can eat at this hippie-era landmark too: the Ambrosia burger is served on a toasted French roll with a secret tomato sauce; Lolly's roasted chicken is stuffed with sage dressing. Reservations are available for parties of five or more. In good weather, the adjacent Café Kevah is open for breakfast and brunch. Time your visit so that you can catch a spectacular sunset.

PABLO'S MEXICAN RESTAURANT MEXICAN ¢

1184-H Forest Ave., Pacific Grove 93950
831-646-8888, *Lunch & Dinner daily*

Pablo's uses no animal fats, and the result is delicious, wholesome and moderately priced Mexican food. Servings are plentiful and the service is fast. You'll find daily specials along with tried-and-true combination plates. We love the red snapper tacos, seafood enchiladas and snapper Vera Cruz. For dessert, indulge in the rich, creamy house-made flan.

PACIFIC'S EDGE   CONTEMPORARY   NO RATING

Highlands Inn, Pacific Coast Hwy. (Rte. 1, 4 miles south of Carmel),
Carmel Highlands 93923
831-622-5445, *Lunch & Dinner daily, Brunch Sun.,* $$$

A longtime favorite of travelers along famed Highway 1, this historic restaurant is one of the most enchanting spots on the California coast. The innovative Californian cuisine is well suited to the breathtaking ocean views dotted by wind-blown cypress trees and a craggy coastline. Live music nightly, adds to the romance. Executive chef Cal Stamenov left at press time to begin another project, so we cannot give a review of the cuisine.

PETRA RESTAURANT   MIDDLE EASTERN   ¢

Lighthouse Ave. & 13th St., Pacific Grove 93950
831-649-2530, *Lunch & Dinner Mon.-Sat.*

This family-run establishment features favorites such as dolmadakia, split pea soup, baba ghanouj, gyros, falafel and kebabs. A plate of tabouli, falafel nuggets and baba ghanouj will satisfy vegetarians. A nice finish is a cup of strong Turkish coffee and baklava.

PIATTI   ITALIAN   12/20

Sixth and Junipero Serra, Carmel 93923
831-625-1766, *Lunch & Dinner daily,* $$

This outpost of the Northern California chain is dependable for middle-of-the-road Italian flavors. You'll find a spit-roasted chicken with garlic-mashed potatoes, myriad pasta dishes, antipasti (don't miss the fritto misto or carpaccio) and the white pizza with goat cheese, sliced tomatoes and a touch of pesto. The new rooftop patio dining is a wonderful way to while away a few hours in this quaint town.

RIO GRILL   CALIFORNIA/SOUTHWESTERN   12/20

101 Crossroads Blvd., Crossroads Shopping Center, Carmel 93923
831-625-5436, *Lunch & Dinner daily,* $$

The menu here reels between such California grill fare as wood-roasted chicken in chile butter, and Southwestern tastes like pork chops with red-eye gravy. One starter that we enjoyed was the rock-shrimp taco with guacamole.

ROSINE'S   AMERICAN   ¢

434 Alvarado St., Monterey 93940
831-375-1400, *Breakfast, Lunch & Dinner daily*

Rosine's son, James Cucasi, now runs this friendly family-style restaurant, which delivers heaping platters of comfort food from yesteryear: roast chicken with potatoes, pork chops, sliced roast turkey with cranberry sauce. The six-layer lemon-coconut cake is a finely executed extravagance.

ROY'S AT PEBBLE BEACH FUSION 15/20

The Inn at Spanish Bay, 2700 17 Mile Dr., Pebble Beach 93953
831-647-7423, *Breakfast, Lunch & Dinner daily, $$-$$$*

It's hard to decide which is more enchanting, the first-rate ocean view or the knowledge that you are dining at a Roy Yamaguchi restaurant without having to fly to Hawaii, his home base. On entering the high-ceilinged room accented with light woods, you'll inhale the tantalizing aromas wafting from the open kitchen. The blending of drizzled sauces in Roy's cuisine is what makes it so distinct. Good bets include the ravioli stuffed with shiitake, spinach and ricotta, the blackened ahi tuna and the lemon-grass-crusted swordfish. The service is friendly and accommodating. One caution: at peak times this is one of the noisiest dining rooms around.

SARDINE FACTORY RESTAURANT SEAFOOD/GRILL 13/20

765 Wave St., Monterey 93940
831-373-3775, *Dinner nightly, $$$*

For 30 years, visitors have flocked to this seafood eatery perched on a hill a couple of blocks from the beach. Of its four distinct dining areas, our favorite is the glass-domed conservatory overlooking lush greenery. The menu sticks with the classics and such specialties as abalone bisque, sand dabs and cioppino served with linguine. Prime-cut steaks round out the menu. The amazingly extensive 30,000-bottle wine cellar is deep in luscious French reds.

SIERRA MAR CONTEMPORARY 15/20

Post Ranch Inn, Pacific Coast Hwy. (Hwy. 1, 30 miles south of Carmel), Big Sur 93920
831-667-2800, *Dinner nightly, $$$$*

Post Ranch Inn guests would expect nothing less than this glassed-in dining room. After all, they are staying at one of the most exclusive hideaways in the West. Non-inn guests can dine here too, in an incomparably romantic, rustic cliff setting that lets in the night sky and Big Sur fog through numerous glass walls and skylights. The changing menu might offer seared sea scallops with figs and prosciutto, followed by sage-roasted duck breast with huckleberries. You can indulge or you can dine spa style. The wine list is massive and sophisticated.

STILLWATER BAR & GRILL PAN-ASIAN/SEAFOOD 13/20

The Lodge at Pebble Beach, 17-mile Drive, Pebble Beach 93953
831-625-8524, *Breakfast, Lunch & Dinner daily, $$$*

This is where sophisticated folks celebrate the good life when they're in a low-key mode. The posh Lodge golf resort has four restaurants, and this is the most casual, with a modern new-wavish style and a "resort casual" dress code. The menu is resort-casual too, featuring fresh oysters, clams, mussels and the like to start, along with colorful Pan-Asian entrées ranging from house-made lobster sausages with saffron sauerkraut to crispy cashew oysters in a soy-sesame sauce. Did we forget to mention the view? It's a killer, looking out onto the sparkling bay and Pebble Beach's legendary 18th green.

STOKES ADOBE   CONTEMPORARY   15/20

500 Hartnell St., Monterey 93940
831-373-1110, *Lunch Mon.-Sat., Dinner nightly,* $$

Kirk and Dorothea Probosco and chef Brandon Miller, who formerly worked in San Francisco's LuLu, have created one of the best restaurants on the Peninsula. The setting is a 160-year-old adobe house with a rustic bar, softly painted dining rooms overlooking the gardens, and an upstairs area for private parties. The veranda is a great place to wait for your table. The "small bites" include tapas like mussels salsa verde, fava bean crostini, and Basque veal meatballs flavored with allspice. The "large plates" range from chicken cooked under a brick to lamb shank to hanger steak. Desserts include a lemon-polenta pound cake and an open-face fresh-fruit strudel with an unnecessary caramel sauce.

TARPY'S ROADHOUSE   AMERICAN   12/20

2999 Monterey-Salinas Hwy., Monterey 93940
831-647-1444, *Lunch & Dinner daily,* $$

Hearty American fare is even more satisfying when enjoyed in this vine-covered stone building that was once a ranch house. The lunch menu offers unusual salads, sandwiches and innovative entrées. At dinner, you'll find such country favorites as honey-mustard rabbit with apples and thyme, and pecan barbecued duck. The American theme is carried through to desserts with a double-chocolate layer cake. The wine list is impressive, especially for a roadhouse.

TASTE CAFÉ & BISTRO   MEDITERRANEAN/CALIFORNIA   14/20

1199 Forest Ave., Pacific Grove 93950
831-655-0324, *Dinner Tues.-Sun.,* $$

Ask foodies on the Monterey Peninsula what their favorite restaurants are, and most of them will mention Taste. The food here is homey and bargain priced, and it's all made in-house from scratch. The salmon carpaccio, grilled rabbit with gnocchi in a green-peppercorn sauce and the herb-scented roast chicken will delight you. The modest shopping-center location is forgotten once you taste the food.

VENTANA — CALIFORNIA — 12/20

Ventana Inn, Pacific Coast Hwy. (Rte. 1, 28 miles south of Carmel), Big Sur 93920
831-624-4812, *Lunch & Dinner daily, $$*

Enjoy the famous Big Sur view and eclectic California cuisine at this internationally known Big Sur landmark. The menu features grilled items such as potato-wrapped quail with morels, and chestnut-crusted ahi tuna loin. There are also pastas, seafood, game and vegetarian dishes. The wine list of local and international wines offers many choices to complement the cuisine. For the perfect finish, try the chocolate espresso tart.

VILLAGE CORNER — AMERICAN/BREAKFAST — ¢

6th Ave. & Dolores St., Carmel 93923
831-624-3588, *Breakfast, Lunch & Dinner daily, $*

For 50 years, visitors and locals have been dining under the sun and stars on the heated patio of the Village Corner. The consistently good food encompasses light pasta dishes, meats, fresh fish and seafood. The chocolate espresso bread pudding with Amaretto cream is hard to pass up. The wine list features Monterey County wines.

VITO'S — ITALIAN/SICILIAN — 14/20

1180 Forest Ave., Pacific Grove 93950
831-375-3070, *Lunch & Dinner daily, $$*

When we first encountered Vito's, it was a funky little Sicilian restaurant hidden in the back of a strip mall. A couple of years ago, Vito's moved to the front of the mall and created a modern one-room restaurant with a wall-sized mural of Sicily. The light-as-air potato gnocchi in a creamy Gorgonzola sauce is one of the best dishes. The menu has some fish, meat and poultry, but stick to one of the 16 pastas and you'll be saying "Mama mia!" by the end of your meal.

ZIGZAG — CALIFORNIA/MEDITERRANEAN — 15/20

Mission and Fifth Sts., Carmel 93921
831-622-9949, *Dinner nightly, $$$*

This Post Ranch Inn venture with chef Wendy Little has reincarnated Giuliano's into an ultra-contemporary dining room with chartreuse walls, halogen lighting and green wooden chairs. The delicately dressed Tuscan bread and stewed tomato salad makes a delectable treat. Other suggested starters include seared rare albacore and a tart of goat cheese and caramelized onions. We loved the combination of duck risotto with baby artichokes and dried cherries. The barbecued short ribs go well with mashed potatoes, but not with the braised red cabbage and mustard glaze. The "market berry" tart is an almond tart with a strawberry-raspberry topping.

GOURMET SHOPS & MORE

BAKERIES: BREAD & PASTRIES

BAGEL BAKERY

201 Lighthouse Ave., Monterey 93940
831-649-1714, *Open daily*

With 15 flavors of bagels, this shop does a land-office business. The biggest sellers are the plain, sesame and the cinnamon-raisin. Coffee and tea drinks are also available. Also at 452 Alvarado St., Monterey, 831-372-5242.

PALERMO BAKERY

1620 Fremont Blvd., Seaside 93955
831-394-8212, *Open daily*

Two fellows from Sicily opened this bakery about five years ago and it's been popular from day one. Why? One taste of their wares will tell you. Try the ciabatta (Italian slipper bread) or the sweet French, semolina, focaccia and sourdough. They distribute to stores and restaurants in the area.

PÂTISSERIE BOISSIÈRE

Ocean & Seventh Aves., Carmel 93923
831-624-5008, *Open daily*

This cute little shop is known for its croissants, blueberry scones, brioche and cookies. But what has people lining up is the chocolate mousse cake with Bailey's Irish Cream liqueur.

CHOCOLATE & CANDY

COTTAGE OF SWEETS

Ocean Ave. & Monte Verde, Carmel 93923
831-624-5170, *Open daily*

The owners have their own line of chocolates and make at least half a dozen flavors of fudge, including a scrumptious

Rocky Road. You can also find a full line of British sweets, including Crunchies, Flakes and Maltesers. Unbelievable as it may sound, they also carry 50 kinds of black licorice.

CHEESE

THE CHEESE SHOP CARMEL

Carmel Plaza (Ocean & Junipero) P.O. Box 109, Carmel 93921
831-625-2272, Open daily

Tucked away in the Carmel Plaza, you will find John and Nancy McCormick's shrine to cheese and wine. The engineer-teacher (husband and wife) team has had this shop since 1974--now, that's consistency! Step in for a cheese-nutritional-value course, or hear all about Tony Coutini's jewel of a winery in Sonoma. The cheese-and-wine monks, Michael, Neil and Kent, will guide you through higher levels of Bacchus' world in a fun unpretentious atmosphere. These guys are great—in fact they are practically family, and they're always eager to add new members. And perhaps you might run into God Clint (Eastwood) buying some Epoise and a bottle of Romanee-Conti. You will definitely feel like a higher being on the way out, and their prices are much cheaper than the Church of Scientology.

COFFEE & TEA

CARMEL VALLEY COFFEE ROASTING

319 Mid Valley Center, Carmel 93923
831-624-5934, Open daily

This is the only in-house coffee roastery in the Carmel area. Every day they roast 40 kinds of beans, plus many blends. Flavored coffee beans are also available. All manner of coffee drinks and cold coffee concoctions are cheerfully served.

DELIS & ETHNIC MARKETS

ARONSON'S FINE FOOD

145 Crossroads Blvd., Carmel 93923
831-626-8778, Open daily

This shop, owned by a local caterer, carries gourmet food items and prepared frozen and ready-to-heat dishes such as lasagne. The six kinds of salads vary daily but might include spinach, couscous, Greek rice and chicken curry. You'll also find a selection of sandwiches and ready-made specialty items.

INTERNATIONAL MARKET & DELI

580 Lighthouse Ave., Monterey 93940
831-375-9451, *Open daily*

Such a variety of languages are heard in this market--
Russian, Italian, French--that you'll feel as though you've
entered the Tower of Babel. You'll find a good selection of
freshly made hummus, dolmadakia, vegetarian soup, caviar,
basmati rice and wine. Pick up some Middle Eastern food to
go.

FARMERS' MARKETS

MONTEREY FARMERS' MARKET

Monterey Peninsula College, 980 Fremont St., Monterey 93940
831-728-5060, *Thursday afternoons until 6 p.m.*

What better way to learn the bounty of this growing region
and get to meet the farmers that produce it?

GOURMET MARKETS

THE BOUNTIFUL BASKET

157 Crossroads Blvd., Carmel 93923
831-625-4457, *Open daily*

Savor the flavors of the Monterey Bay area long after your
return home: stop at the Bountiful Basket and pick up such
delicacies as Gil's Gourmet salsa, Pezzini Farms' artichoke
pesto and habañero garlic from the Pickled Garlic Company.
You'll also find flavored vinegars and oils, salad dressings, mari-
nades, sardines, coffee and tea. Like the idea, but don't want
to be hassled with carrying it home? Have your purchase delivered or shipped.

CORNUCOPIA COMMUNITY MARKET

26135 Carmel Rancho Blvd., Carmel 93923
831-625-1454, *Open daily*

A well-organized market with beautiful displays, this is a
favorite with those seeking wholesome foods. Cornucopia features a variety of fresh breads, including a delicious sour-
dough-olive. Other baked goods include mini ollalieberry,
blueberry and several vegetable pies. The market offers a large
variety of artfully arranged organic produce, fresh pastas, salads, sauces, juices, sandwiches, soups and entrées. It also carries gourmet cheeses, wines, specialty oils, vinegar, coffee and
tea.

5TH AVENUE DELI

5th Ave. between San Carlos & Dolores Sts., Carmel 93921
831-625-2688, *Open daily*

This popular deli features a wide variety of homemade specialty items, house-made soups, made-to-order sandwiches, imported cheeses, pâtés and a good selection of Monterey County wines. Don't miss the "death by chocolate" cake. For the ultimate in outdoor dining, order one of the all-inclusive gourmet picnic baskets and head for white-sand Carmel Beach.

MEDITERRANEAN MARKET

Ocean Ave. & Mission St., Carmel 93923
831-624-2022, *Open daily*

Many Carmel natives make this 48-year-old landmark a regular stop for its wonderful selection of spices, gourmet foods, coffee, chocolate and wine. For visitors, it's a first-class place to grab a picnic lunch of deli salads, made-to-order sandwiches, ready-to-eat hot foods, desserts and snacks.

A TASTE OF MONTEREY

700 Cannery Row, Monterey 93940
831-646-5446, *Open daily*

This unusual visitors' center offers information and a gourmet gift shop. It has the largest selection of Monterey-appellation wines on the Monterey Peninsula, which visitors are encouraged to taste. The showroom where winery maps and tour information are distributed boasts a panoramic ocean view. Tastings of locally grown produce are also held daily at this one-stop entry to Monterey County.

TRADER JOE'S

1170 Forest Ave., Pacific Grove 93950
831-656-0180, *Open daily*

Trader Joe's carries everything from frozen Alaska salmon and pâtés to French raspberry jam. Be warned, though: once you find that unbelievably low-priced delicacy, or a particularly good bottle of Burgundy, you might want to stock up. Because of its warehouse club orientation, Trader Joe's doesn't necessarily restock all its products.

HEALTH FOODS

CORNUCOPIA COMMUNITY MARKET

26135 Carmel Rancho Blvd., Carmel 93923
831-625-1454, *Open daily*

See review under Gourmet Markets above.

THE GRANARY MARKET

173 Central Ave., Pacific Grove 93950
831-647-2150, *Open daily*

This Pacific Grove landmark has been providing natural and organic groceries for more than 20 years. You'll find a wide selection of organic produce, bulk foods, health products, ready-to-eat gourmet deli items, sandwiches, juices and healthy snacks. The shop also sells fresh-baked breads that are delivered daily from local bakeries.

WHOLE FOODS MARKET

800 Del Monte Center, Monterey 93940
831-333-1600, *Open daily*

See review in PENINSULA chapter.

ICE CREAM

CARMEL BEACH CAFÉ

Ocean Ave. & Mission St., Carmel 93923
831-625-3122, *Open daily*

To the rear is an undistinguished Italian café serving breakfast, lunch and dinner. The main draws here are the Italian ice creams, tiramisu to go, and handmade chocolates and imported sweets.

KITCHEN EQUIPMENT

AMERICAN TIN CANNERY

125 Ocean View Blvd., Pacific Grove 93950
831-372-1442, *Open daily*

Shop at one of Cannery Row's most historic locations: a former sardine cannery, now a factory-direct shopping center. The housewares store is filled with every kitchen item you can think of and maybe some you haven't.

AT HOME IN CARMEL

5th Ave. between San Carlos, & Dolores Sts., Carmel 93921
831-624-7029, *Open daily*

This small shop features unique items for the home, including some gourmet foods. You'll find a number of spiced oils (such as basil, citrus and garlic) and flavored vinegars. Tea drinkers can enjoy the convenient flavored sticks of mulberry, raspberry, tropical and honey-lemon. A dazzling array of tableware in vivid colors is imported from France, Portugal and England.

PRODUCE

PEZZINI FARMS PRODUCE

102 Crossroads Blvd., Carmel 93923
831-626-2734, *Open daily*

If you are an artichoke lover, you'll delight in the freshly steamed artichokes from the Pezzini farm in Castroville. This market features a fresh and colorful selection of the best available produce from the farm. A variety of gourmet salad dressings, including artichoke pesto, are among the other ready-to-eat items.

WINE & SPIRITS

A TASTE OF MONTEREY

700 Cannery Row, Monterey 93940
831-646-5446, *Open daily*

See review in Gourmet Shops above.

THE CHEESE SHOP CARMEL

Carmel Plaza (Ocean & Junipero) P.O. Box 109, Carmel 93921
831-625-2272, *Open daily*

See review in "Cheese" above.

NIELSEN BROTHERS MARKET & WINE SHOP

Corner of Seventh Ave. & San Carlos St., Carmel 93921
831-624-9463, *Open daily*

The wine section of this market is the site of Carmel's only wine-tasting room. It has one of the Central Coast's broadest selections of California and European wines.

WINE TOURING

WINERIES OPEN TO THE PUBLIC:

BERNARDUS VINEYARDS AND WINERY
5 W. Carmel Valley Rd., Carmel Valley 93924
800-223-2533

BONNY DOON VINEYARD
10 Pine Flat Rd., Santa Cruz 95060
831-425-4518

DAVID BRUCE WINERY
21439 Bear Creek Rd., Los Gatos 95030
831-354-4214

CHATEAU JULIEN WINERY
8940 Carmel Valley Rd., Carmel 93923
831-624-2600

DURNEY VINEYARDS
18820 Cachagua Rd., Carmel Valley 93924
831-659-6220

GEORIS WINERY
2801 Cachagua Rd., Carmel Valley 93922
831-624-4310

JEKEL VINEYARDS
40155 Walnut Ave., Greenfield 93927
831-674-5522

JOULLIAN VINEYARDS
20300 Cachagua Rd., Carmel Valley 93924
831-659-2800

RAPAZZINI WINERY
4350 Hwy. 101, Gilroy 95021
831-842-5649

STORRS WINERY
303 Potrero St. Unit 35, Santa Cruz 95060
831-458-5030

ROBERT TALBOTT VINEYARDS
P.O. Box 776, Gonzales 93926
831-675-3000

VENTANA VINEYARDS
2999 Monterey-Salinas (Hwy. 68), Monterey 93940
831-237-8846

GLOSSARIES & RESTAURANT INDEXES

MENU SAVVY

A GUIDE TO INTERNATIONAL FOOD TERMS

FRENCH

Agneau: lamb

Aïoli: garlicky mayonnaise

Américaine: sauce of white wine, Cognac, tomatoes and butter

Andouille: smoked tripe sausage, usually served cold

Anglaise: boiled meats or vegetables

Béarnaise: sauce made of shallots, tarragon, vinegar and egg yolks, thickened with butter

Béchamel: sauce made of flour, butter and milk

Beurre blanc: sauce of wine and vinegar boiled down with minced shallots, then thickened with butter

Beurre noisette: lightly browned butter

Bisque: rich, velvety soup, usually made with crustaceans, flavored with white wine and Cognac

Blinis: small, thick crêpes made with eggs, milk and yeast

Boeuf bourguignon: beef stew with red wine, onions and lardons (Lardoon; larding fat cut into long strips and threaded through lean cuts of meat by a special larding needle in order to moisten the meat as it cooks).

Bombe glacée: molded ice cream dessert

Bordelaise: fairly thin brown sauce of shallots, red wine and tarragon

Borscht: thick Eastern European soup of beets and boiled beef, often garnished with a dollop of sour cream

Boudin noir: blood sausage

Bouillabaisse: various fish cooked in a soup of olive oil, tomatoes, garlic and saffron

Bourride: sort of bouillabaisse, usually made with large white fish, thickened with aïoli; served over slices of bread

Brie: cow's milk cheese with a soft, creamy inside and a thick crust, made in the shape of a disk and sliced like a pie

Brioche: a soft loaf or roll, often sweetened and used for pastries

Brochette: on a skewer

Canapé: small piece of bread topped with savory food

Canard: duck

Carbonnade: pieces of lean beef, first sautéed then stewed with onions and beer

Carré d'agneau: rack of lamb

Cèpes: prized wild mushroom, same family as the Italian porcini

Chanterelles: prized wild mushroom, trumpet-shaped

Charcutière: sauce of onions, white wine, beef stock and gherkins

Charlotte: dessert of flavored creams and/or fruit molded in a cylindrical dish lined with ladyfingers (if served cold) or strips of buttered bread (if served hot)

Chèvre: goat cheese

Choucroute: sauerkraut; often served with sausages, smoked bacon, pork loin and potatoes

Clafoutis: a dessert of fruit (usu. cherries) baked in an eggy batter

Confit: pork, goose, duck, turkey or other meat and sealed in its own fat

Coquilles St-Jacques: sea scallops

Coulis: thick sauce or purée, often of vegetables or fruit

Court-bouillon: stock in which fish, meat and poultry are cooked

Crème chantilly: sweetened whipped cream

Crêpe Suzette: crêpe stuffed with sweetened mixture of butter, Curaçao, tangerine juice and peel

Croque-monsieur: grilled ham and cheese sandwich

Croûte (en): in pastry crust

Crudités: raw vegetables

Daube: beef braised in red wine

Ecrevisses: crayfish

Entrecôte: "between the ribs"; steak cut from between the ribs

Epinards: spinach

Escalope: slice of meat or fish, flattened slightly and sautéed

Escargots (la bourguignonne): snails (with herbed garlic butter)

Financière: Madeira sauce enhanced with truffle juice

Florentine: with spinach

Foie gras: liver of a specially fattened goose or duck

Fondue: a bubbling pot of liquid into which which pieces of food are dipped—most commonly cheese and bread; can also be chocolate and fruit or various savory sauces and cubes of beef. Also, vegetables cooked at length in butter and thus reduced to pulp

Forestière: garnish of sautéed mushrooms and lardons (Lardon; larding fat cut into long strips and threaded through lean cuts of meat as it cooks).

Galantine: boned poultry or meat, stuffed and pressed into a symmetrical form, cooked in broth and coated with aspic

Galettes and crêpes (Brittany): galettes are thin pancakes made of buckwheat flour and are usually savory. Crêpes are made of wheat flour and are usually sweet

Gâteau: cake

Gelée (en): in aspic (gelatin usually flavored with meat, poultry or fish stock)

Génoise: sponge cake

Granité: lightly sweetened fruit ice

Gratin dauphinois: sliced potatoes baked in milk, sometimes with cream and/or grated Gruyère

Grenouille: frog (frogs' legs: cuisses de grenouilles)

Hollandaise: egg-based sauce thickened with butter and flavored with lemon

Jambon: ham

Julienne: vegetable soup made from a clear consommé, or any shredded food

Langoustine: saltwater crayfish

Lapin: rabbit

Limon: lime (also, citron vert)

Lotte: monkfish or anglerfish; sometimes called "poor man's lobster"

Madrilène (la): garnished with raw, peeled tomatoes

Magret (Maigret): breast of fattened duck, cooked with the skin on; usually grilled

Médaillon: food, usually meat, fish or foie gras, cut into small, round pieces

Moules marinière: mussels cooked in the shell with white wine, shallots and parsley

Noisettes: hazelnuts; also, small, round pieces of meat (especially lamb or veal)

Nougat: sweet made with roasted almonds, egg whites, honey and sugar

Oeufs: eggs

Pain: bread

Parfait: sweet or savory mousse; also a layered ice cream dessert

Parisienne: garnish of fried potato balls

Paupiettes: thin slices of meat stuffed with forcemeat and shaped into rolls

Pissaladière: tart with onions, black olives and anchovy filets

Pommes: apples

Pommes de terre: potatoes

Poulet: chicken

Profiteroles: small puffs of choux paste often filled with whipped cream of crème patissiere and piled high in a dish with chocolate sauce poured over

Provençale (' la): with garlic or tomato and garlic

Quiche: tart of eggs, cream and various fillings (such as ham, spinach or bacon)

Ratatouille: stew of eggplant, tomatoes, bell peppers, zucchini, onion and garlic, all sautéed in oil

Rémoulade: mayonnaise with capers, onions, parsley, gherkins and herbs

Rouille: sort of mayonnaise with pepper, garlic bread soaked in bouillon, olive oil and possibly saffron

Sabayon: fluffy, whipped egg yolks, sweetened and flavored with wine or liqueur; served warm

Saint-Pierre: John Dory, a white-fleshed fish

Salade niçoise: salad of tomatoes, hard-boiled egg, anchovy filets, tuna, sweet peppers, celery and olives (also can include green beans, potatoes, basil, onions and/or broad beans)

Sole meunière: sole dipped in flour and sautéed in butter with parsley and lemon

Sorbet: sherbet

Spätzle: round noodles, often made from eggs

Steak au poivre: pepper steak; steak covered in crushed peppercorns, browned in a frying pan, flambéed with Cognac; also sauce deglazed with cream

Tapenade: a paste of olives, capers and anchovies, crushed in a mortar with lemon juice and pepper

Tartare: cold sauce for meat or fish; mayonnaise with hard-boiled egg yolks,

onions and chopped
olives

Tarte: tart, round cake or
flan; can be sweet or
savory

Tarte tatin: upside-down
apple tart

Truffe: truffle; highly
esteemed subterranean
fungus, esp. from
Périgord

ITALIAN

Acciughe: anchovies

Aceto: vinegar

Aglio: garlic

Agnello: lamb

Agnolotti: crescent-shaped,
meat-filled pasta

Amaretti: crunchy almond
macaroons

Anguilla: eel

Aragosta: spiny lobster

Arrosto: roasted meat

Baccalo: dried salt cod

Bagna cauda: hot, savory
dip for raw vegetables

Bierra: beer

Biscotti: cookies

Bistecca (alla fiorentina):
charcoal-grilled T-bone
steak (seasoned with
pepper and olive oil)

Bolognese: pasta sauce with
tomatoes and meat

Bresaola: air-dried spiced
beef; usually thinly
sliced, served with olive
oil and lemon juice

Bruschetta: toasted garlic
bread topped with toma-
toes

Bucatini: hollow spaghetti

Calamari (calamaretti):
(baby) squid

Calzone: stuffed pizza-
dough turnover

Cannellini: white beans

Carbonara: pasta sauce with
ham, eggs, cream and
grated cheese

Carciofi (alla giudia): (flattened and deep-fried
baby) artichokes

Carpaccio: paper thin, raw
beef (or other meats)

Cassata: ice-cream bombe

Cipolla: onion

Conchiglie: shell-shaped
pasta

Coniglio: rabbit

Costoletta (alla milanese):
(breaded) veal chop

Cozze: mussels

Crespelle: crêpes

Crostata: tart

Fagioli: beans

Fagiolini: string beans

Farfalle: bow-tie pasta

Fegato alla veneziana: calf's
liver sautéed with
onions

Focaccia: crusty flat bread

Formaggio: cheese

Frittata: Italian omelet

Fritto misto: mixed fry of
meats or fish

Frutti di mare: seafood
(esp. shellfish)

Funghi (trifolati): mushrooms (sautéed with
garlic and parsley)

Fusilli: spiral-shaped pasta

Gamberi: shrimp

Gamberoni: prawns

Gelato: ice cream

Gnocchi: dumplings made
of cheese (di ricotta),
potatoes (di patate),
cheese and spinach
(verdi) or semolina (alla
romana)

Grana: hard grating cheese

Granita: sweetened, flavored grated ice

Griglia: grilled

Insalata: salad

Involtini: stuffed meat or
fish rolls

Maccheroni: macaroni pasta

Manzo: beef

Mela: apple

Melanzana: eggplant

Minestra: soup; pasta course

Minestrone: vegetable soup

Mortadella: large, mild
Bolognese pork sausage

Mozzarella di bufala: fresh
cheese made from
water-buffalo milk

Noce: walnut

Orecchiette: ear-shaped
pasta

Osso buco: braised veal shanks
Ostriche: oysters
Pane: bread
Panettone: brioche-like sweet bread
Panna: heavy cream
Pancetta: Italian bacon
Pappardelle: wide, flat pasta noodles
Pasticceria: pastry; pastry shop
Patate: potatoes
Pecorino: hard sheep's-milk cheese
Penne: hollow, ribbed pasta
Peperoncini: tiny, hot peppers
Pepperoni: green, red or yellow sweet peppers
Pesca: peach
Pesce: fish
Pesce spada: swordfish
Pesto: cold pasta sauce of crushed basil, garlic, pine nuts, parmesan cheese and olive oil
Piccata: thinly-sliced meat with a lemon or Marsala sauce
Pignoli: pine nuts
Polenta: cornmeal porridge
Pollo: chicken
Polipo: octopus
Pomodoro: tomato
Porcini: prized wild mushrooms, known also as boletus
Prosciutto: air-dried ham
Ragu: meat sauce
Ricotta: fresh sheep's-milk cheese
Rigatoni: large, hollow ribbed pasta
Risotto: braised rice with various savory items
Rucola: arugula
Salsa (verde): sauce (of parsley, capers, anchovies and lemon juice or vinegar
Saltimbocca: veal scallop with prosciutto and sage
Semifreddo: frozen dessert, usually ice cream, with or without cake
Spiedino: brochette; grilled on a skewer
Spumone: light, foamy ice cream
Tartufi: truffles
Tiramisu: creamy dessert of rum-spiked cake and triple-crème Mascarpone cheese
Tonno: tuna
Tortellini: ring-shaped dumplings stuffed with meat or cheese
Uovo (sodo): egg (hard-boiled)
Verdura: greens, vegetables
Vitello (Tonatto): veal (in a tuna and anchovy sauce)
Vongole: clams
Zabaglione: warm whipped egg yolks flavored with Marsala
Zucchero: sugar
Zucchine: zucchini
Zuppa: soup
Zuppa inglese: cake steeped in a rum-flavored custard sauce

SPANISH & LATIN AMERICAN

Because there are so many regional dialects in Spain and Latin America, the term for one food product might easily have four or five variations. We've chosen those ingredients and dishes most often found in Southern California restaurants.

Aceite: oil
Ajo: garlic
All-i-oli: aïoli; garlicky mayonnaise
Arroz: rice
Bacalao: dried, salted codfish
Burrito: soft, wheat-flour tortilla rolled and stuffed with meats, refried beans, cheese and vegetables
Caldo: broth
Camarones: shrimp
Carne: meat
Cerveza: beer

Ceviche: raw fish marinated in citrus juice

Chalupa: a small, thick corn tortilla folded into a boat shape, fried and filled with a mixture of shredded meat, cheese and/or vegetables

Chilequile: flat tortilla layered with beans, meat, cheese and tomato sauce

Chile relleno: large, mild chile pepper, stuffed with cheese and fried in an egg batter

Chorizo: spicy pork sausage flavored with garlic and spices

Empanada: pie or tart filled variously with meat, seafood or vegetables

Enchilada: a tortilla, fried and stuffed variously with meat, cheese and/or chiles

Entremeses: appetizers

Flan: a baked custard with a caramel coating (also crema caramela)

Frito (frita): fried

Gambas: shrimp

Garbanzo: chick pea

Gazpacho: Andalusian; a cold soup of fresh tomatoes, peppers, onions, cucumbers, olive oil, vinegar and garlic (also celery, breadcrumbs)

Guacamole: an avocado dip or filling, with mashed tomatoes, onions, chiles and citrus juice

Higado: liver

Huachinango: red snapper

Huevos: eggs

Huevos rancheros: tortillas topped with eggs and a hot, spicy salsa

Jalapeño: very common hot chile pepper, medium size

Jamón: ham

Licuado: fruit milkshake

Lima: lime

Limón: lemon

Mariscos: shellfish

Masa: cornmeal dough; essential for making tortillas

Menudo: a stew featuring tripe

Mole: sauce; most often a thick, dark sauce made with mild chiles and chocolate

Nachos: a snack dish of tortilla chips topped with melted cheese and chiles

Nopales: leaves of the prickly pear cactus; simmered and used in various dishes

Paella: a dish of saffron-flavored rice studded with meat (chicken, ham, sausages, pork), shellfish and vegetables

Papas: potatoes (also, patatas)

Papas fritas: literally "fried potatoes "; french fries

Parrillada: grilled

Pescado: fish

Pez espada: swordfish

Pimiento: red chile pepper; can be sweet or hot

Plátano: plantain; a starchy, mild-tasting variety of banana popular in Latin American; usu. cooked and served as a side dish

Pollo: chicken

Poblano: large, mild, dark green chile pepper; used for chile rellenos

Puerco: pig

Quesadilla: a soft, folded tortilla filled with cheese (and/or other savory stuffings) and toasted or fried

Queso: cheese

Salchicha: sausage

Salsa: sauce; also, an uncooked condiment employing fresh tomatoes, onions and chiles

Sangría: Spanish drink made with red wine, soda water, chopped fresh fruits and sugar, often with a touch of brandy; served on ice

Sopa: soup

Taco: a folded, fried tortilla filled with ground beef (or other meats or fish), refried beans, shredded lettuce, tomatoes, onion, cheese and salsa

Tamale: Corn dough made with lard, filled with a savory stuffing, wrapped up in a piece of corn husk, and steamed

Tapa: appetizer, Spanish in origin; usu. enjoyed with an apéritif such as dry sherry

Tortilla: a flat, unleavened bread made with cornmeal flour (masa) or wheat flour

Tostada: a fried tortilla topped with a saladlike mix of ground beef or chicken, beans, lettuce, tomato, guacamole

ASIAN

Chinese

Bao bun: dim sum item; small, steamed buns, white in color, stuffed with a variety of minced fillings (often chicken, shrimp, pork or lotus beans)

Bird's-nest soup: soup that has been thickened and flavored with the gelatinous product derived from soaking and cooking the nests of cliff-dwelling birds

Bok choy: Chinese white cabbage

Chop suey: strictly a Chinese American dish; meat or shrimp and vegetables (mushrooms, water chestnuts, bamboo shoots, bean sprouts) stir-fried together and served over rice

Chow mein: strictly a Chinese American dish; meat or shrimp and vegetables (mushrooms, water chestnuts, bamboo shoots, bean sprouts) stir-fried and served over crispy egg noodles

Dim sum: figuratively, "heart's delight"; a traditional meal featuring a variety of small dumplings, buns, rolls, balls, pastries and finger food, served with tea in the late morning or afternoon

Egg roll: thin wrapper stuffed with pork, cabbage or other vegetables, rolled up, and deep-fried or steamed

Fried rice: cooked, dried rice quickly fried in a wok with hot oil, various meats or vegetables and often an egg

Hoisin: a sweet, rich, dark brown sauce made from fermented soy beans; used as a base for other sauces

Lo mein: steamed wheat-flour noodles stir-fried with bean sprouts and scallions and either shrimp, pork, beef or vegetables

Lychee: small, round, fleshy fruit; used fresh, canned, preserved and dried

Mu shu: a delicate dish of stir-fried shredded pork and eggs rolled up in thin pancakes

Oyster sauce: a thick, dark sauce of oysters, soy and brine

Peking duck: an elaborate dish featuring duck that has been specially prepared, coated with honey and cooked until the skin is crisp and golden; served in pieces with thin pancakes or steamed buns, and hoisin

Pot sticker: dim sum item; dumpling stuffed with meat, seafood or vegetables, fried and then steamed

Shark's fin soup: soup thickened and flavored with the cartilage of shark's fins, which provides a protein-rich gelatin

Shu mai: dim sum item; delicate dumpling usu. filled minced pork and vegetables

Spring roll: a lighter version of the egg roll, with fillings such as shrimp or black mushrooms

Szechuan: cuisine in the style of the Szechuan province, often using the peppercorn-like black Chinese pepper to make hot, spicy dishes

Thousand-year-old eggs: chicken, duck or goose eggs preserved for 100 days in ashes, lime and salt (also, 100-year-old eggs)

Wonton: paper-thin, glutinous dough wrapper; also refers to the dumpling made with this wrapper, stuffed with minced meat, seafood or vegetables

Wonton soup: a clear broth in which wontons are cooked and served

Japanese

Amaebi: sweet shrimp
Awabi: abalone
Azuki: dried bean; azuki flour is often used for confections

Ebi: shrimp
Edamame: soy beans, served boiled and salted as an appetizer
Enoki (Enokitake): delicate mushrooms with long stems and small caps
Hamachi: yellowtail
Hibachi: small, open charcoal grill
Ikura: salmon roe
Kaiseki: Multicourse menu of luxury dishes reflecting the seasons with the use of seasonal foods and artistic dinnerware and presentation
Kappa: cucumber
Kobe beef: cattle raised in exclusive conditions (frequent massages and a diet featuring large quantities of beer), which results in an extraordinarily tender, very expensive beef
Konbu: dried kelp; used in soup stock, for sushi and as a condiment
Maguro: tuna
Maki: rolled
Mako: shark
Mirugai: giant clam
Miso (soup): soybean paste from which a savory broth is made, usu. served with cubes of tofu or strips of seaweed
Ono: wahoo fish; a relative of the mackerel often compared in taste to albacore
Ramen: soup noodles
Saba: mackerel
Sake: salmon
Saké: traditional rice wine served hot or cold
Sashimi: thinly sliced raw fish on rice, usually served with soy sauce and wasabi
Shabu shabu: similar to sukiyaki; beef and vegetables cooked tableside in a broth
Shiitake: Prized cultivated

311

mushroom, dark brown with a large cap

Shoya: soy sauce

Soba: buckwheat noodles

Sukiyaki: braised beef and vegetable dish with broth added after cooking

Sushi: Rounds of vinegared rice wrapped in dried seaweed with a center of raw fish or vegetables, served with wasabi and soy

Tako: octopus

Tamago: egg

Tamari: dark sauce similar in composition and taste to soy; often used for dipping

Tempura: deep-fried, batter-dipped fish or vegetables

Teriyaki: A marinade of soy and sweet saké, used on meats, fish and poultry

Tofu: bean curd, processed into a liquid and then molded into large cubes

Toro: fatty belly cut of tuna

Udon: wheat noodles

Uni: sea-urchin roe

Wasabi: a hot, spicy condiment made from the roots of Japanese horseradish, chartreuse in color

Yakitori: a dish of pieces of chicken and vegetables, marinated in a spicy sauce, skewered and grilled

Khao: rice

Khao suai: white rice

Khao phad: fried rice

King: ginger

Kung: prawns

Lab (or Larb): dish of minced meat with chilies and lime juice

Mu: pork

Nam: sauce

Nam pla: fish sauce

Nam phrik: a hot chili sauce

Nuea: beef

Ped: duck

Phad: fried

Phad king: fried with ginger

Phad phed: fried hot and spicy

Phad Thai: pan-fried rice noodles with chicken, shrimp, eggs, peanuts and bean sprouts

Phrik: chili pepper

Si racha (or Sri racha): spicy chili condiment

Tom kha kai: chicken coconut-cream soup flavored with lemongrass and chilies

Tom yam kung: hot-sour shrimp soup flavored with lemon grass, lime and chilies

Yam: flavored primarily with lime juice and chilies, resulting in a hot-sour taste; usually "salads" but can also be noodle dishes or soup

Yam pla: raw fish spiked with lime juice, chili, lemongrass, mint and fish sauce

Thai

Kaeng (or Gaeng): large and diverse category of dishes; loosely translates as "curry"

Kaeng massaman: a variety of coconut-milk curry

Kaeng phed: a red, coconut-cream curry

Kaeng som: a hot-sour curry

COFFEE SAVVY

THE ORIGINS OF THE COFFEE CRAZE

Nearly every culture in the world has a passion for coffee, and there are various stories about how it all started. One of our favorites has to do with a goat herder in ancient Abyssinia (Ethiopia) who one morning discovered his goats gleefully cavorting around a shiny, dark-leafed shrub with red berries. After nibbling a few of the red berries himself, the goat herder joined his goats in their spirited romp. Another story attributes the discovery to an Arabian dervish who, when exiled by enemies to the wildnerness, survived by making a broth from water and the berries he plucked from coffee trees.

Regardless of which story is true, botanical evidence indicates that coffea arabica actually originated on the high plateaus of what is now Ethiopia in Africa. Traders undoubtedly brought it across the Red Sea to what is now Yemen, where it was cultivated from the sixth century on. Though at first coffee was used as a medicine—and by dervishes readying for a spin—it soon became a popular social beverage, resulting in coffeehouses where men exchanged ideas and gossip while sipping cups of hot brew in cities from Cairo to Mecca.

Though the Arabs jealously guarded their discovery, a few sneaky coffee fanatics managed to smuggle seeds from Arabia into India and Java, where it was cultivated with great success. By the seventeenth century, the coffee culture had spread to Europe. Coffeehouses attracted politicians, seafarers, merchants, authors and scholars, who often used the premises for discussions, reading, musical performances and even duels. At a time when Europeans wealthy enough to afford exotic luxuries were enjoying their two, three or four cups a day, the greatest French lover of luxury, King Louis XIV, supposedly built the first greenhouse to house a coffee tree given him by the mayor of Amsterdam. It's said that from the Sun King's royal coffee tree, sprang billions of arabica trees, including those growing today in Central and South America.

THE COFFEEHOUSE FOR THE NINETIES

Cut, as they say in Hollywood, to Seattle, in the rainy Pacific Northwest. Here, the current coffee craze was born just over a decade ago with a—then tiny—coffee company named **Starbucks** (after the first mate in the classic novel, *Moby Dick*). Starbucks re-invented the coffeehouse for modern times, creating attractive, relaxed and congenial meeting places where men and women exchange ideas and gossip—or read, work or simply think—while enjoying a cup of coffee. And we're not just talking about *a cup of coffee*. The choices of specialty coffee drinks made with "specialty" coffee beans—those of the highest quality—are endless, which is why we've put together this brief primer on the vocabulary of specialty coffees:

THE WORLD OF COFFEE

Like wine grapes, specialty coffee beans get much of their distinctive flavor from the growing conditions and preparation methods of the regions in which they're produced. We can classify coffee flavor and aroma according to geographic origin:

CENTRAL & SOUTH AMERICAN COFFEES

The most popular origins in the U.S. market, these are usually light-to-medium bodied, with clean lively flavors. Their balance and consistency make them the foundation of good coffee blending as well. Among these are beans from Colombia, Costa Rica, Guatemala and Mexico. Kona, though geographically a product of the Pacific islands, falls within this Latin American range of taste and aroma.

EAST AFRICAN COFFEES

These unique beans—from Kenya, Ethiopia, Tanzania and Zimbabwe—often combine the sparkling acidity of the best Central Americans with unique floral or winy notes, and typically are medium-to-full bodied.

INDONESIAN COFFEES

Usually full-bodied and smooth, low in acidity, and often possessing earthy and exotic taste elements, coffee beans from Java, Sumatra, Papua New Guinea and Sulawesi are an important "anchor" component of choice blends.

DARK ROASTS

Coffees from varying geographic origins are dark-roasted to provide a specific range of flavors, from the caramel spice of Espresso, to the smoky tang of Italian Roast, to the pungent French Roast.

BLENDS

Typically, a blend might play off Central American acidity with Indonesian smoothness, or spice up a delicate origin with the tang of a dark roast. At its best, blending coffee is high art, offering a balance or diversity which few straight coffees can match.

DECAFFEINATED

Some coffee-drinkers find the effects of too much caffeine unpleasant; others are looking for a hot cup to enjoy before bedtime. For that reason, coffee beans from many geographic origins are put through a decaffeinating process.

GLOSSARY OF COFFEE TASTING TERMS

THE BASICS:

Flavor: the total impression of aroma, acidity and body.

Acidity: the sharp, lively quality characteristic of many high-grown coffees. Acid is not the same as bitter or sour. Acidity is the brisk, snappy, spicy quality which makes coffee refreshing and palate-cleansing.

Body: the tactile impression of the weight of the brewed beverage in the mouth. It may range from watery and thin, through light, medium and full, to buttery or even syrupy in the case of some Indonesian varieties.

OTHER USEFUL TERMS:

Aroma: the fragrance of brewed coffee. Terms used to describe aroma include: caramelly (candy or syrup-like), carbony (for dark roasts), chocolaty, fruity, floral, herbal, malty (cereal-like), rich (over-used), rounded, spicy.

Bitter: a basic taste perceived primarily at the back of the tongue. Dark roasts are intentionally bitter, but bitterness is more commonly caused by over extraction (too little coffee at too fine a grind).

Bland: the pale, insipid flavor often found in low-grown coffees. Under-extracted coffee (made with too little coffee or too coarse a grind) is also bland.

Briny: a salty sensation caused by application of excessive heat after brewing. (The familiar smell of "truck stop" coffee.)

Earthy: the spicy, "of the earth" taste of Indonesian coffees.

Exotic: coffee with unusual aromatic and flavor notes, such as floral, berry, and sweet spice-like qualities. Coffees from East Africa and Indonesia often have such characteristics.

Mellow: the term for well-balanced coffee of low-to-medium acidity.

Mild: a coffee with harmonious, delicate flavor. Fine, high-grown Latin American coffee is often described as mild.

Soft: low-acid coffees such as Indonesians, that may also be called mellow or sweet.

Sour: a primary taste perceived mainly on the posterior sides of the tongue, characteristic of light-roasted coffees.

Spicy: an aroma or flavor reminiscent of a particular spice. Some Indonesian arabicas, especially aged coffees, evoke an association with sweet spices like cardomom. Others, such as Guatemala Antiqua, are almost peppery.

Strong: technically the relative proportion of coffee solubles to water in a given brew.

Sweet: a general term for smooth, palatable coffee, free from defects and harsh flavors

Tangy: a darting sourness, almost fruit-like in nature, related to wininess. A fine high-grown Costa Rican coffee is frequently tangy.

Wild: a coffee with extreme flavor characteristics; it can be a defect or a positive attribute, and denotes odd, racy nuances of flavor and aroma. Arabian Mocha Sanani nearly always exhibits such flavors.

Winy: a desirable flavor reminiscent of fine red wine; the contrast between fruit-like acidity and smooth body creates flavor interest. Kenyan coffees are examples of winy coffee flavor.

GLOSSARY OF SPECIALTY COFFEE DRINKS

made by a **Barista**, an expert at preparing espresso drinks

Espresso: A small but intense shot of coffee produced by forcing hot water under pressure through tightly packed coffee, one cup at a time.

Espresso Con Panna: A shot of espresso with a dollop of whipped cream.

Espresso Macchiato: Espresso lightly "marked" with foamed milk.

Caffè Americano: A shot of espresso diluted with hot, purified water, to produce a full-flavored but still mild cup of coffee.

Caffè Latte: A shot of espresso plus steamed milk, topped off with foamed milk.

Caffè Mocha: A squirt of chocolate syrup on the bottom of the cup, then espresso topped by steamed milk, a crown of whipped cream and a sprinkle of cocoa powder.

Cappuccino: Espresso topped with steamed milk and a generous cap of foamed milk.

Frappuccino: A cold and creamy low-fat blend of fresh-brewed Starbucks Italian roast coffee, milk and ice. Variations: with a shot of espresso (**Espresso Frappuccino**), with dark chocolate syrup (**Mocha Frappuccino**), or with a protein and vitamin supplement (**Power Frappuccino**).

The Glossary of Coffee Tasting Terms and Specialty Coffee Drinks was provided courtesy of **Starbucks Coffee Company**.

WINE SAVVY

THE EMERGENCE OF CALIFORNIA WINES

Though immigrant families started it in the late nineteenth century, California's wine industry did not flourish until the 1970s, when it fostered a new American interest in wine and a healthy increase in per capita consumption. California wine was thought to come of age at a blind tasting in Paris, where eminent French judges chose several California wines over those produced in France. The American media seized on this with a vengeance, much to the delight of the California wine industry. .

Meanwhile, others trends took hold in the popular segment of the wine market, including the seemingly unquenchable thirst for "a glass of **Chardonnay**, please." By the early 1980s, there was an influx of new talent into the California winemaking industry. Many of these new winemakers had been educated in viticulture and enology at UC-Davis, while others were cellar rats who learned through on-the-job training. These young winemakers were committed to producing quality wine through better viticulture practices, proper utilization of soil and climate and better winemaking techniques.

A number of these winemakers struck out on their own, experimenting with different types of grapes while challenging the "varietal imperialism" of **Cabernet** and **Chardonnay**. Wines made from **Rhone Valley varietals**, like **Syrah, Grenache** and **Mourvedre**, became increasingly popular and offered different flavors than the previous spectrum of California red wines. Plantings of **Italian varietals**, such as **Nebbiolo**, **Sangiovese** and **Malvasia** sprang up in order to take advantage of the Mediterranean-like growing climate of California.

The winemaking business fractured into many segments. While giant corporate wineries gained their market share, smaller artisan wineries also found their niche. Given the time and money, dreamers could build winery empires based on individual winemaking philosophies, whereas thirty years before, the rules of the game had seemed far more proscribed.

Today, California winemakers now understand that certain climates and soils that are good for, say, Cabernet, are not good for Pinot Noir. As more acreage is planted or grafted over, the most appropriate varietals are planted in the most appropriate environment. This not only increases the quality of the wines, but also furthers the movement of specialty wineries to the forefront. In essence, wineries no longer sell half a dozen different wines, but concentrate on only two or three—the best grapes from the best varieties that the region has to offer.

TODAY: MORE WINE, BETTER VINTAGES, AND LOWER PRICES

In the late '90s, we are quite possibly entering the "Golden Age" of California winemaking. A new generation of vintners is fashioning wines with an intensity of flavor that is California's birthright, owing to its sunny climate and rich soils. They are refining their techniques to preserve the innate characteristics of the fruit, while at the same time building in more structure and complexity to enhance drinkability and longevity. Through their meticulous attention to detail, they are eliminating distracting elements from the wine in favor of creating a harmonious variety of complex aromas and flavors.

Today, in the best vintages, the wines are still powerful but now tempered with suppleness, finesse and depth. The most recent California grape harvest was a windfall for California winemakers. The 1997 crush was 2.87 millions tons, far outstripping the previous record set in 1993. For consumers, this translates as not only more wine but better wine (weather and growing conditions were near ideal) at lower prices, particularly for premium wines in the $10-$20 range. True, there will always be high-ticket "trophy" wines, like **Opus One**, **Dominus** and **Cardinale**. Good, solid, lower-priced wines that meet the needs of the everyday dining table, however, are also plentiful, due to both the bounty of the harvest and the recent influx of inexpensive imports.

In red wines, **Cabernet Sauvignon** is still king, though vintners are trying to catch up to the demand for **Merlot** by feverishly planting hundreds of new acres yearly. More interestingly, **Pinot Noir**—made in a smooth and silky style—has come of age, with excellent examples produced now in Santa Barbara, Carneros and the Russian River Valley (and Oregon's Willamette Valley). After a string of great vintages, **Zinfandel** is on the comeback trail, and is now being made in a more food-friendly style. Upstart red varietals, which have a long heritage in France and Italy, have taken their rightful place beside old standbys on wine lists: look to **Sangiovese, Nebbiolo, Syrah, Mourvedre** and **Cabernet Franc** for intriguing flavors.

In white wines, the thirst for **Chardonnay** is seemingly unquenchable; it's far and away the white wine of choice. However, **Sauvignon Blanc**, at half the price, partners better with a wide variety of dishes, including many featuring seafood and chicken. A host of **Rhone**-style varietals, such as **Viognier, Marsanne** and **Roussanne,** are beginning to penetrate the marketplace, as consumers discover there is life beyond Chardonnay. The floral aromas of these wines are beguiling, and their flavors follow through with bright, refreshing fruitiness. Likewise, Italian varietals in California—like **Pinot Grigio** and **Tocai Friulano**, also offer unique flavor profiles, with a crispness and high acidity that cleanses the palate.

GUIDE TO CALIFORNIA REGIONS

It's been said that there are no climatic differences in California wine growing regions, as there are in Europe, and thus "every year is a vintage year" in California. Nothing could be further from the truth. For proof, merely contrast a 1989 Napa Valley Chardonnay (where it rained at harvest) and a 1989 Central Coast Chardonnay (where it didn't). The myth of statewide sunny weather also needs dispelling. There are certain pockets of land in California (usually associated with mountain ranges) that have vastly different weather and climatic conditions than the rest of the state. And from a viticultural standpoint, certain grape varieties that do well in one environment do not perform well in another. Check out a Pinot Noir from the Sanford and Benedict Vineyards in the (very cool) Santa Ynez Valley versus one from the (hot) Calistoga area of Napa Valley. Where the wine comes from *does* make a difference—the difference between a balanced, complex wine and a harsh, unpleasant one.

ALEXANDER VALLEY

A largely unpopulated area of northern Sonoma County, the Alexander Valley is warmer than the rest of the county. There has been success here with Cabernets as well as Bordeaux style blends (white and red). The Chardonnays can be interesting.

AMADOR/SIERRA FOOTHILLS

Just east of Sacramento, Amador County is home to some of the oldest continuously producing vineyards in the state. The principal wine is Zinfandel and its ubiquitous offspring, White Zinfandel. There is also Cabernet and Barbera, along with experimental acreage planted for Rhône varietals like Syrah, Mourvedre and Grenache.

CALIFORNIA

The use of this geographical term indicates only that all the grapes came from within the confines of the state.

CARNEROS

At the southernmost end of Napa and Sonoma Counties, this recently developed area borders on the cool San Pablo Bay. Perhaps the coolest area in either county, the climate is perfect for Pinot Noir and Chardonnay.

CENTRAL COAST

This is a very broadly defined area that covers coastal wine-growing regions from Santa Cruz on the north to Santa Barbara on the south. An entire spectrum of grape varieties is grown here, depending on which particular varietal is suitable for the individual microclimate.

CENTRAL VALLEY

Another broad area that covers the inland wine growing area from Sacramento to Bakersfield. This is the hottest, driest grape-growing region in the state. A wide variety of wines are made, most of them passable but few of them distinctive.

DRY CREEK VALLEY

Parallel to and west of the Alexander Valley in Sonoma County, its relatively warm climate has produced good red wines, particularly Zinfandel and Cabernet. Chardonnay is a drawing card, too.

MENDOCINO/LAKE COUNTIES

The northernmost grape growing counties share a fairly cool growing season. Chardonnay, Pinot Noir, Gewürztraminer and Riesling can be particularly impressive.

MONTEREY

The cooling influence of the Monterey Bay has created a great environment for Chardonnay, while Pinot Noir has been less successful. Further inland, individual pockets of land have produced good Cabernets.

NAPA VALLEY

The most famous wine-growing region in California and a top tourist attraction. The name "Napa" is synonymous with quality. Its long-lived Cabernets have achieved worldwide notoriety. Chardonnay, Pinot Noir, Sauvignon Blanc and sparkling wines have also proven themselves here.

RUSSIAN RIVER VALLEY

A district of widely varying soils and climate in western Sonoma County; the cooler regions enjoy a reputation for Chardonnay, Pinot Noir and sparkling wine.

SANTA BARBARA COUNTY

Home to the Santa Ynez and the Santa Maria Valleys, it is the only region in California that has an east-west mountain range funneling cool ocean fog and breezes to the vineyards. That fact belies its southern California heritage that says it's too warm for grape growing. Pinot Noir, Chardonnay, Riesling and Syrah are prominent.

SONOMA COUNTY

Encompassing several different valleys with varying microclimates, it is probably the most versatile grape-growing region in California. Cabernet, Merlot, Pinot Noir, Chardonnay, Sauvignon Blanc and sparkling wine do well here.

TEMECULA

This southernmost grape-growing region, halfway between L.A. and San Diego, is also the most recently planted. Thus far its best efforts have been with Chardonnay and sparkling wine, while the red wines are on the rustic side.

WINE TOURING

Visiting the wineries of Northern California can provide a pleasant day or two's break from the excitement of the city. The selected wineries below have tasting rooms and are open to the public on a regular basis. Nevertheless, you'll do well to phone ahead before setting out on your wine touring adventure. For comprehensive information on the wineries of California and Mexico, see Gayot/Gault Millau/AAA's **The Best Wineries of North America**. (Order form in the back of this book). See Wine Touring in the Wine Country, Peninsula, San Jose and Monterey/Carmel Chapters.

GLOSSARY OF TASTING TERMS

Acidity: a principal component of wine that shows up as a sharpness or tartness, giving it snap.

Aroma: the smell the wine acquires from the grapes themselves and fermentation process.

Astringency: the mouth-puckering quality found in many young red wines.

Austere: a wine unusually high in acidity; lacking roundness or wholeness.

Balanced: no individual component of the wine stands out; all the elements contribute to a harmonious whole.

Berry: taste characteristic found in many red wines, it resembles the taste of fruit like blackberry, blueberry and cherry.

Body: the weight of the wine in the mouth; usually manifested by a richness, fullness or viscosity.

Bouquet: the smell that develops from the process of aging wine in the bottle.

Buttery: a component that gives white wines a rich, roundness that resembles the taste of butter.

Chewy: a rich red wine with big body and dense flavor.

Clarity: the appearance of a young wine should be clear, not cloudy.

Complex: a wine that displays many levels of flavor.

Dry: a wine with no apparent residual sugar. Novice wine drinkers may describe this as "sour."

Earthy: positive characteristics of loamy topsoil, mushrooms or truffles sometimes found in red wines. In French, "goût de terroir."

Fat: a wine with good fullness and length, although it may lack finesse.

Floral: flowery aromas and tastes, usually associated with white wines.

Fruity: the taste of the fruit of the grapes themselves; it often manifests itself as other fruit flavors, such as apples, strawberries or black currants.

Grassy: an herbaceous flavor, like new-mown grass, common to Sauvignon Blanc; negative if extreme.

Hard: a wine that does not have generous flavors; applied to red wines that have excessive tannins.

Herbaceous: a general term descriptive of various herbal flavors in wine, recognized by aroma and taste.

Hot: a wine in which the high level of alcohol is out of balance with the other elements.

Intense: powerful, dense, and rich in flavor

Jammy: in red wines, intense fruitiness combined with berry-like flavors.

Nose: all the elements detected by the sense of smell, including both the aroma and bouquet.

Oaky: flavors of the oak in which the wine is fermented and/or aged.

Smoky: a roasted aroma or taste characteristic attributable to aging in oak barrels.

Spicy: descriptive of the spice-like flavor elements found in wine such as pepper, cardamon, clove and cinnamon.

Supple: a wine that tastes soft and smooth; easy to drink.

Tannic: a mouth puckering astringency found in young red wines.

GLOSSARY OF GRAPES

Red Wine Varietals

CABERNET SAUVIGNON

The king of red wines in California, Cabernet's reputation was established by wineries in the Napa Valley, although it has proved distinctive in other regions as well. While sometimes a bit harsh in its youth, it has the ability to mature into a most complex and full-bodied wine, much like the great wines of Bordeaux. Its flavors are comfortable with simple grilled meats as well as more complex dishes like venison in mushroom sauce. Great and consistent producers of Cabernet can be found in the Napa and Sonoma Valley, as well as Australia, Chile, Argentina and, of course, the châteaux of Bordeaux which produce the true benchmark of this varietal.

MERLOT

This variety was once relegated to blending into other lots of red wine. But in the last twenty years it has taken on an identity of its own. Merlot has herbal and fruity flavors similar to Cabernet, but it has a smooth and supple character in the mouth without the bite of tannins. It complements the same type of foods that Cabernet does, albeit less distinctively. Top producers hail from Bordeaux (where the wine is mostly blended, but sometimes bottled separately, depending on the region) Chile, Argentina, Napa, Sonoma and Washington State.

PINOT NOIR

Pinot Noir has the potential to be the most seductive, beguiling red wine in existence. Unfortunately past examples from California left a lot to be desired. In the past decade or so, however, Pinot Noir has shown the greatest increase in quality of any varietal. The perseverance of younger winemakers and traditional winemaking methodology is resulting in Pinots that can stand side by side with the wines of Burgundy. Lighter than Cabernet, Pinots have a richness and intensity of fruit that is unparalleled. The best of them drink like velvet and accompany a wide variety of foods. Top French Burgundies are bottled under a variety of different names and labels, depending on region, vineyard and producer. In America, considerable success with this Burgundian varietal has been from Napa, Sonoma (Carneros), Santa Barbara and Oregon.

SYRAH

The great grape of the Rhône Valley has become more widely planted in California in the last ten years. Highly aromatic wines with meaty, smoky, spicy flavors are the trademark of the Syrah grape. When made in a lighter style, it's a good quaffing wine to pair with simple bistro type food. When made in a richer style, it's a good accompaniment to lamb and all manner of wild game. Syrah is the grape found in French Côte Rotie, St. Joseph and Cornas, and plays a major role in the spicy Châteauneuf-du-Papes of the southern Rhône too. In California, the Syrah grape is being cultivated in such diverse regions as Santa Barbara, Sonoma, Monterey, the Amador Foothills and Yolo County.

ZINFANDEL

Real Zinfandel is red, a fact many wine drinkers are redis-covering now that the trend for "white" zinfandel has stabi-lized. "Peppery," "briary," "brawny" and "chewy" are only a few of the adjectives used to describe this mouth-filling wine. It has a real zest for matching up with tomato-based pasta dishes and other highly herbalized preparations. There is no European counterpart for this variety; it is one that the first Italian wine-makers propagated and cultivated when they came to California. Its origins are obviously European, but today it's a grape variety that is unique to California. Vintners in Napa, Sonoma and Amador seem to do the best job with it.

White Wine Varietals
CHARDONNAY

In the '80s it became de rigeur to ask for "a glass of Chardonnay" in a restaurant and passé to simply request "a glass of white wine." Chardonnay is the most popular wine in California for a reason: it's cold, fruity and easy to drink. It's pleasant with just about any dish involving cheese, eggs, fish or fowl. Winemakers have divided into two camps over the style of Chardonnay; one school of thought emphasizes the high-toned, steely, fruit-like qualities of the wine through little or no use of oak, while the other school emphasizes barrel and malo-lactic fermentation in addition to the fruit characteristic, which lends the wine a rounder, buttery taste. Benchmarks for Chardonnay are (rich and extracted) white Burgundies and (steely and crisp) Chablis. In California, there are fine Chardonnays from just about every region, including Napa, Sonoma, Mendocino, Monterey and Santa Barbara.

GEWÜRZTRAMINER

This so-called "aromatic" varietal is making a minor comeback in California. "Gewürz" translates as "spice" and it's immediately detectable when poured into a glass. The flavors echo the fragrant and flowery nose echoes, while providing an additional punch from a piquant, spicy component. Made with some residual sweet-ness, the wine seems to be a good counterpoint for spicy Chinese and Thai dishes. The Alsatian region of France has about four centuries of experience in producing these wines in the tradition-al style. In California, the cooler growing regions, like Sonoma, Mendocino and Santa Barbara, do well with this grape.

RIESLING

Another "aromatic" that is finding a home in California again, Riesling can be a particularly refreshing alternative to the Chardonnay/Sauvignon Blanc white wine tandem. Unlike its cousin, Gewürztraminer, this varietal has little spice and instead relies on its delicate aromas and subtle flavors for its special niche. Usually lighter in style and sometimes with resid-ual sweetness, it's better paired with lighter fare. The Riesling is a mainstay of German winemaking and also ripens to full maturity in Alsace. The top California producers have generally been those who have also had success with Gewürztraminer.

SAUVIGNON BLANC

This variety is often considered the poor man's Chardonnay; it can be vinified similarly but costs only half as much. But Sauvignon Blanc has a number of identities ranging from a clean, slight grassy white wine to a herbaceous, full-bodied wine backed up with oak aging. It does its best service at the table when paired with strong, forceful, herbal flavors like goat cheese and raddichio salad. Unheralded but excellent examples come from Sancerre and Pouilly-Fumé in the Loire Valley. In California, just about every region produces a Sauvignon Blanc, although the North Coast counties seem to have a real knack for it.

SPARKLING WINES

Domaine Chandon (owned by Moet & Chandon) set up shop in Napa Valley around twenty years ago, and after its initial success, almost every French Champagne house has come to California to establish its foothold. The main reason for their interest in the New World is that Champagne is a geographically limited area which is almost fully planted, and California was almost virgin territory for sparkling wine. While the legacy of Champagne seems to be tiny pinpoint bubbles that reveal delicate and subtle flavors, their California counterparts are more often bold, upfront and fruity with their flavors. The prevailing wisdom is that the delicate nuances of the wine (in particular, Champagne) get lost when paired up with hearty, complex or highly seasoned dishes. It's certainly the perfect aperitif wine. All the California sparklers are of high quality so it seems to be a matter of house style as to what is preferred. Names to remember are Domaine Carneros, Domaine Chandon, Gloria Ferrer, Mumm-Napa, Piper-Sonoma, Mirassou, Roederer Estates, Scharffenberger, Schramsberg, Iron Horse, Handley, Cordonui, J, and Maison Deutz.

VINTAGE WINE CHART

VINTAGE CHART: The World's Wines																		
FRANCE												GER.	ITALY		CALIFORNIA			
Red Bordeaux	White Bordeaux	Sauterne	Red Burgundy	White Burgundy	Beaujolais	Côtes du Rhône	Provence	Alsace	Loire: Anjou, Muscadet	Pouilly, Sancere	Champagne	Rhine, Moselle, Nahe	Piedmonte	Chianti	Cabernet Sauvignon	Chardonnay	Pinot Noir	Zinfandel
1995 5	4	3	3	4	4	5	4	5	4	4	—	4	4	3	5	5	4	Ex
1994 4	3	2	2	4	3	3	4	5	3	3	—	4	2	3	Ex	5	5	Ex
1993 4	3	3	3	3	4	3	4	4	4	4	—	5	4	2	5	5	4	5
1992 3	3	3	3	5	2	3	3	3	3	3	—	5	3	2	5	5	4	5
1991 3	3	2	4	4	Ex	4	3	3	1	3	1	4	2	2	4	5	4	5
1990 5	4	5	Ex	4	4	5	5	5	5	5	Ex	5	5	5	5	5	4	5
1989 5	4	Ex	5	5	Ex	5	5	Ex	5	5	5	5	5	2	4	3	4	4
1988 4	4	Ex	5	5	4	4	5	4	4	5	5	5	5	3	5	4	4	4
1987 3	4	1	4	3	2	1	2	3	3	2	3	4	4	2	4	3	4	5
1986 5	5	5	3	3	3	3	3	4	4	4	3	4	3	4	5	5	4	4
1985 5	5	2	Ex	5	5	5	3	5	5	5	5	4	5	Ex	4	4	4	5
1983 5	5	Ex	3	5	—	5	4	Ex	4	4	5	5	2	3	3	4	4	3
1982 Ex	4	3	2	4	—	4	—	2	5	5	5	3	5	4	4	4	4	3
1981 4	5	4	—	—	—	3	—	3	5	5	5	4	3	3	4	4	4	4
1979 4	4	3	3	5	—	4	—	—	—	—	5	4	4	2	4	4	3	4
1978 4	5	—	Ex	5	—	Ex	—	—	—	—	4	2	5	4	5	4	4	4

EX: EXCEPTIONAL
5: VERY GREAT
4: GREAT
3: GOOD

2: MEDIUM
1: PASSABLE
—: SMALL YEAR

* This is only meant to be a general guide. Start by learning which regions and years are better than others; once you develop a good knowledge, buy according to your preferences.

The European wines are categorized by the region in which the grapes were grown. This is their "appellation," displayed on the label along with the phrase *Appéllation controlée or Denominazione di origine contrallata* to guarantee the wine's authenticity. The California wines are categorized by grape name, as they are throughout the United States.

CALIFORNIA
FOOD & WINE EVENTS
& SEASONAL FOOD TIPS
(Dates vary with the year)

We've put together a calendar of the more prominent and/or interesting Northern California food and wine events (dates are provided when possible and should be confirmed).

JANUARY

New Year's Resolutions
- Volunteer with Food Runners, a community organization that picks up excess food and delivers it to more than 100 food programs in San Francisco for the needy. To get involved, call 415-929-1866.
- Countymeals-on-Wheels, in Alameda County, delivers hot food and visits the elderly. A donation provides meals for the needy. Write to
- Countymeals-on-Wheels, 8000 Edgewater Dr., Oakland CA 94621, or call 510-567-8056.

FEBRUARY

- Masters of Food and Wine, Carmel (last week in February) Convene with great chefs and winemakers at this annual food and wine extravaganza at Highlands Inn in Carmel 831-624-3801. Tickets are from $60-$175 depending on how many events one attends.
- Chinese New Year Festival & Parade (mid to late February) Besides the spectacular parade, traditional foods like sweet bean buns and dumplings are sold at this festive time.

MARCH

- Shuck and Swallow Oyster Challenge (end of March) A fun event held at McCormick & Kuleto's restaurant in San Francisco's Ghirardelli Square. Chefs compete to see who can shuck and consume the most oysters in ten minutes. Following the free contest there is an oyster and wine pairing. Tickets are $20 and proceeds benefit a charity. Information:

  415-929-1730.
- Celebrate with Heart in San Francisco (end of March, beginning April) This annual black-tie-optional benefit gala at the Westin St. Francis Hotel is hosted by the American Heart Association. Festivities include live entertainment, delicious cuisine and auctions with getaway packages and fine wines. The price per person begins at $95. Information: 415-433-2273.

- Farm Day, Marin County (third week in March) In celebration of National Agriculture Week, Farm Day allows children under 12 to tour an open-air farmers' market and meet over 70 regional food growers, ranchers and food purveyors at the Marin Civic Center Exhibit Hall and Fairgrounds, San Rafael. There are dozens of hand-on agricultural displays, farm animals and participatory presentations. Information: 415-456-3276 or 800-897-FARM.
- Napa Valley Mustard Festival (starts late January through March)
- Every year this Wine Country festival has grown. It encompasses towns from Napa to Calistoga. Enjoy free cooking demonstrations, mustard and wine tastings, art and photo exhibits. Information: 707-259-9020.

APRIL

- Monterey Wine Festival (late March, early April) The country's oldest and most lavish wine event, this four-day weekend in Monterey includes a wine and golf tournament, new release and barrel sample tastings, a benefit dinner and more. Information: 800-656-4282.
- Easter Basket Sale for AIDS (before Easter) In the Marina District, San Francisco, restaurants and food producers donate baskets for sale to benefit smaller AIDS organizations. Baskets are priced from $20 to $500. The event is held in the Fort Mason Center. Information: 415-441-1282.
- Macy's San Francisco Annual Flower Show (beginning of April) Wander into Macy's on Union Square to take in the spectacular colors and breathtaking fragrances of the flowers starring in this free event. The flowers are on display until they begin to droop —usually for two weeks—and during this time, there are urban gardening seminars, flower arranging classes, talks on entertaining and chef demonstrations. Information: 415-393-3724.
- Meals on Wheels Gala & Auction, San Francisco (usually the end of April or early May.
- This premier food and wine benefit in San Francisco is the largest fundraiser for Meals on Wheels, which raises money to feed homebound seniors. The Bay Area's finest chefs participate along with top California wineries. Cocktails, dinner and silent and live auctions. Black tie optional. Tickets are $175. Information: 415-920-1111.

MAY

- Cinco de Mayo, (first weekend in May)Festivals abound in Northern California. There are usually colorful parades in the Mission District of San Francisco and San Jose. You can expect arts, crafts, food and music. Information: 415-826-1401.
- Olive Oil Festival, Sonoma (end of April or early May) With more and more olive oil now being pressed in California, this is a fun, low-key festival where you can sample various olive oils, talk to the growers and have a nice day in the country. The event costs $12 and is held at B.R. Cohn Winery, which also produces olive oil. Information: 707-938-4064.

- Discover Alexander Valley (first Sat. in May) The eight wineries in the Alexander Valley host an afternoon-evening food-and-wine pairing to lure visitors to the beautiful area. The wineries are spread out over seven miles along Highway 128. Tickets, priced at $25, are limited. Information: 707-433-2319.
- Paso Robles Wine Festival (mid-May) This annual festival includes tastings from over 30 wineries, food, jazz and even a golf tournament. The tasting is held in downtown Paso Robles between Spring and 12th Streets. Information: 800-549-WINE.
- Festival of Greece, Oakland (mid-May on Friday, Saturday & Sunday) The annual Greek festival features food, live music, tours, exhibits and dancing—it's one of the livliest food & wine events in the Bay Area. There's usually a cooking demonstration by a celebrity chef. Greek Orthodox Cathedral of the Ascension, 4700 Lincoln Ave., Oakland. Tickets: $5-$10. Information: 510-531-3710.
- Taste of the Nation, San Francisco This prestigious food event is the annual benefit for SOS, Share Our Strength, a non-profit, hunger-fighting organization which includes many food professionals. Many top restaurants and wineries participate. Tickets are usually $75 to $85. Information: 415-495-2331.
- Carnival San Francisco This spectacular multi-cultural celebration features a parade, music, dancing in the streets and food in San Francisco's Mission District. Information: 415-824-8999.

JUNE

- Union Street Spring Festival, San Francisco (early June) San Francisco City arts and crafts fair between Gough and Steiner. Californian and European wines, music, food and live entertainment. Free; from 10 a.m.-6 p.m.
- Napa Valley Wine Auction (first Thursday through Sun in June) Serious wine connoisseurs flock to St. Helena annually to visit the Meadowood Inn & Resort and participate in a series of prestigious dinners, tastings, auctions and more that raises a million dollars for Napa Valley charities. The cost of the entire four day event is $1,800 per couple. Tickets to individual events, like the Vintners Ball or the Barrel Tasting and Auction, can be purchased individually. Information: 707-942-9783 ext. 901. North Beach Street Fair (mid-June)

- The oldest and probably biggest street festival in San Francisco salutes the Italian and artistic heritage of this traditional neighborhood. Lots of good food, music and crafts. Information: 415-403-0666

JULY

- Jazz & Art on Fillmore Street (July 4th weekend) This annual San Francisco street fair has arts and crafts, food, wine and live entertainment. Free.

- Connoisseur's Marketplace, Menlo Park (late July) This annual festival features gourmet food, California wines, chef demonstrations from top Peninsula restaurants, over 200 arts and crafts booths, live entertainment and children's activities. On Santa Cruz Ave. Admission and parking are free; tastings from $1 to $6. Information: 650-325-2818.

- Gilroy Garlic Festival (last weekend in July) You won't believe the endless uses of the stinking rose until you've been to this festival in the world capital of garlic growers. There's garlic ice cream, garlic pizza, even garlic drinks. Dance to live music, and attend cooking and craft demonstrations. General admission is $10, $5 for children ages 6-12 and seniors. Information: 408- 842-1625.

AUGUST

- California State Fair, (CalExpo) Sacramento (mid-August-early September) Food competitions, wine tastings, county exhibits, nature demonstrations, displays, live entertainment plus Hispanic Cultural Day and Asian-Pacific Cultural Day. And horse racing. Adults $7; children ages 5-12 $4. Information: 916-263-3247.

- Mendocino Bounty (mid to late August) Over 60 brewpubs, farm-fresh produce growers, restaurateurs, fish and livestock producers, wineries and specialty food producers come to Hopland to showcase the food and drink of Mendocino County. The event is held at the Fetzer's Tasting Room at Valley Oaks in Hopland. Tickets are $25 in advance, $30 at the door. Information: 707-468-9886.

- Day In the Park, Lafayette (late August) This fund-raiser/tasting event helps children in risk of or with life-threatening illnesses. Over 30 wineries, 6 microbreweries and 30 restaurants participate. At the Taylor Estate (old Kaiser Estate), 940 Reliez Station Lane, Lafayette. The cost is $145 per person. Information: 925-937-7947.

SEPTEMBER

- A La Carte A La Park (Labor Day weekend) San Francisco's premier outdoor festival of food and music raises money for Shakespeare in the Park. Microbrew and wine tastings, food, chef demonstrations and live music all for $8 adults, $6 for seniors; children under 12 are free. The event is held at the Sharon Meadow Golden Gate Park. Information: 415-383-9378.

- Sonoma Valley Wine Auction (Labor Day weekend) Celebrity chef dinners, entertainment, gourmet lunches, barbecue, wine tastings, plus silent and live auctions. Prices vary depending on how many events one attends: the main auction costs $135; the vintners' dinner is priced at $110 per person. Information: 707-935-0803.

- Millbrae Art & Wine Festival (Labor Day weekend) Artists and craftspeople, international foods, beer and wine gardens, live music, farmers' market and street performers gather in Millbrae to have fun. Tastes are priced from $1-$6. Information: 650-697-7324.

OCTOBER

- MacArthur Park Wine Festival (first or second weekend in October)This outdoor festival, brings 90 vintners' wines along with oakwood-smoked barbecued baby back ribs, mesquite-grilled chicken and house-made sausages to downtown Palo Alto. Silent auction and live music. Proceeds benefit American Red Cross. Cost is $45 for the food, tastings and music. Hosted by MacArthur Park Restaurant, 27 University Ave. in Palo Alto. Information: 650-321-9990.

- Sonoma County Harvest Fair (first weekend In October)There's food, award-winning wines, cooking demonstrations by the county's top chefs, agricultural and animal exhibits, a grape-stomping contest, arts and crafts shows and free activities for the children. Adults are $5. Information: 707-545-4203.

- Great Chefs of Marin Black Tie Dinner (end of September, beginning of October)This annual event supports the Marin Assn. for Retarded Citizens. Tickets are priced at $125 and up per person. Information: 415-472-2373.

- Half Moon Bay Art & Pumpkin Festival (mid-October)Over 250 artisan vendors set up shop on Main Street in Half Moon Bay, selling fine art, unique crafts, photography and jewelry. Scores of food booths featuring every pumpkin goodie imaginable plus snacks feed the thousands that attend. There's entertainment, a costume contest, a pumpkin-pie-eating contest and the great pumpkin weigh-in. Free admission. Information: 650-726-9652.

NOVEMBER

- March of Dimes Gourmet Gala, San Francisco (end of October beginning of November)World-renowned chefs are linked with leading interior designers or top food writers from across the country to create special designer settings with matching food. The sets and food are judged and all the proceeds go to charity. Tickets are $150-$200. The event, which includes dinner, dancing and first release wines, is usually at the Fairmont Hotel. Information: 415-788-2202.

FOOD & WINE PAIRINGS

Consider the myriad foods available at our grocers and food preparations that can be enjoyed in our restaurants. Then consider the number of varietal wines available and all their styles. It quickly becomes clear that the enterprise of pairing food and wine can be as complicated as you wish to make it. If you'd like some rules of thumb to help you sort out the possibilities, here are two that have stood the test of time. Rule One: Drink red wine with meat, and white wine with fish and poultry. Rule Two: Forget about Rule One and marry any food with any wine you wish; when it comes to personal preferences, there are no rights and wrongs.

There are, of course, some classic food and wine matches that satisfy again and again. And there are exciting new standards being discovered daily as the range of foods and wines available continues to expand. Based on our experience, the following matches of widely available dishes and cuisines with the wines of North America are worthy of special consideration. One caveat: Sauces can change everything, so ask the cook or a waiter for a flavor forecast.

APPETIZERS & FIRST COURSES

ANTIPASTO
Pinot Gris, (Dry) Chenin Blanc, Sauvignon Blanc, Pinot Blanc, Gamay Beaujolais, Barbera

ASPARAGUS
Sauvignon (Fumé) Blanc, (Dry) Riesling, Vidal Blanc

CARPACCIO (BEEF)
Barbera, Cabernet Rosé, Rhône Blends

CARPACCIO (TUNA)
Sauvignon (Fumé) Blanc, Vin Gris

CAVIAR
Brut Sparkling Wine

CLAMS (RAW OR CASINO)
Sauvignon (Fumé) Blanc, Brut Sparkling Wine, (Dry) Chenin Blanc, Pinot Blanc, Seyval Blanc

COLD MEATS
Vin Gris, Riesling, Gamay Beaujolais, Barbera, Seyval Blanc, (Dry) Vignoles, Chambourcin Rosé

CRUDITÉS
Pinot Blanc, Chenin Blanc, Chardonnay, Gamay Beaujolais

FOIE GRAS
Brut Sparkling Wine; Late-Harvest Riesling, Sauvignon Blanc, or Gewürztraminer, Muscat, Pinot Noir

NIÇOISE SALAD
Sauvignon (Fumé) Blanc

NUTS AND/OR OLIVES
Brut Sparkling Wine

OYSTERS (RAW)
Sauvignon (Fumé) Blanc, Brut Sparkling Wine, Pinot Gris, Chardonnay, (Dry) Riesling, Pinot Blanc, Chenin Blanc

PASTA SALAD
Sémillon, Sauvignon (Fumé) Blanc, (Dry) Chenin Blanc, (Dry) Riesling

PASTA WITH CREAM SAUCE
Chardonnay, Pinot Blanc

PASTA WITH SHELLFISH
Sauvignon (Fumé) Blanc, Chardonnay

PASTA WITH TOMATO SAUCE
Barbera, Sangiovese, Zinfandel, Rhône Blends

PASTA WITH VEGETABLES
Pinot Blanc, Dry Riesling, Sauvignon Blanc, Viognier, Gamay Beaujolais, Barbera

PATÉS
Gewürztraminer, Seyval Blanc, Gamay Beaujolais, Riesling, Brut Sparkling Wine, Cabernet Franc, Vin Gris

PROSCIUTTO AND MELON
Pinot Blanc, Riesling, Late Harvest Riesling or Gewürztraminer, Muscat

QUICHE
Riesling, Chenin Blanc, Chardonnay, Viognier, Gamay Beaujolais

SCALLOPS
Sauvignon (Fumé) Blanc, Chardonnay, Brut Sparkling Wine, Pinot Noir, Sémillon

SMOKED FISH (TROUT, HERRING)
Riesling, Gewürztraminer, Pinot Blanc, Brut Sparkling Wine

SOUPS
Usually none, or (Solera) Sherry

FISH & SHELLFISH

CRAB
Sauvignon (Fumé) Blanc, Brut Sparkling Wine, Chardonnay

LOBSTER
Brut Sparkling Wine, Chardonnay

MUSSELS
Chenin Blanc, Pinot Blanc, Pinot Gris, Sauvignon (Fumé) Blanc

RED SNAPPER
Chardonnay, Sauvignon (Fumé) Blanc

SALMON
Pinot Noir, Sauvignon Blanc, Pinot Gris, Sémillon, Vin Gris

SALMON TARTARE
Brut Sparkling Wine, Pinot Gris

SASHIMI, SUSHI
Brut Sparkling Wine, Semi-Dry Riesling

SCALLOPS, OYSTERS, CLAMS
See appetizers

SHRIMP

Pinot Blanc, Chenin Blanc, Sauvignon (Fumé) Blanc, Chardonnay, Colombard, Vidal Blanc

STRIPED BASS

Chardonnay, Pinot Blanc, Viognier, (Dry) Vignoles

SWORDFISH

Sauvignon (Fumé) Blanc, Brut Sparkling Wine, Vin Gris, Pinot Noir

TUNA

Sauvignon (Fumé) Blanc, Pinor Noir, Merlot, Vin Gris, Chardonnay

OTHER WHITE FISH

Chardonnay, Viognier, Dry Riesling, Semillon

MEAT & POULTRY

CHICKEN

Chardonnay, Vin Gris, Riesling, Merlot, Gamay Beaujolais, Chenin Blanc, Pinot Noir, (Lighter) Cabernet Sauvignon

CHICKEN SALAD

Riesling, Chenin Blanc, Gewürztraminer, Pinot Blanc

CHICKEN (SMOKED)

Vin Gris, Pinot Noir, Zinfandel

DUCK

Pinot Noir, Merlot, Rosé Sparkling Wine, Cabernet Sauvignon, Zinfandel

FRANKFURTER

Riesling, (Chilled) Gamay Beaujolais

HAM

Vin Gris, Gamay Beaujolais, Merlot

HAMBURGER

Cabernet Sauvignon, Gamay, Syrah, Chancellor, Barbera, Zinfandel, Rhône Blends

LAMB (GRILLED, BROILED)

Meritage, Cabernet Sauvignon, Merlot, Pinot Noir, Marechal Foch, Chancellor, Zinfandel

PHEASANT

Pinot Noir, Syrah

QUAIL

Pinot Noir

RABBIT

Riesling, Pinot Noir, Barbera, Merlot, Zinfandel

SAUSAGE

Riesling, Brut or Rosé Sparkling Wine, Barbera, Gamay Beaujolais, Norton or Cynthiana, Syrah, Zinfandel

STEAK (GRILLED, BROILED)

Cabernet Sauvignon, Merlot, Rhône Blends, Zinfandel, Meritage, Norton or Cynthiana, Brut Sparkling Wine

TURKEY

Zinfandel, Merlot, Chardonnay, Gamay Beaujolais

VEAL

Chardonnay, Barbera, Merlot, Cynthiana

VENISON

Syrah, Rhône Blends, Petite Sirah, Zinfandel, Pinot Noir, Norton, Chancellor, Cabernet Sauvignon

OTHER MAIN COURSES

COUSCOUS
Cabernet Franc, Merlot, Petite Sirah, Rosé Sparkling Wine, Syrah, Vin Gris

CURRY, FISH OR CHICKEN
Riesling, (Chilled) Gamay Beaujolais, Sauvignon (Fumé) Blanc, Zinfandel

MOUSSAKA
Merlot, Sangiovese, Barbera, Zinfandel

PIZZA
Barbera, Zinfandel, Sangiovese, Brut or Rosé Sparkling Wine, Cabernet Rosé

SPICY CHINESE
Dry (and off-dry) Riesling, Pinot Gris, Pinot Blanc, Brut or Rosé Sparkling Wine, Merlot

SPICY MEXICAN
Dry (and off-dry) Riesling, Vin Gris, Chenin Blanc, (Chilled) Gamay Beaujolais

THAI
Chenin Blanc, Pinot Blanc, Riesling, Gewürtraminer, Brut or Rosé Sparkling Wine

CHEESES

GOAT
soft: Brut or Rosé Sparkling Wine, Sauvignon (Fumé) Blanc, Cabernet Sauvignon, Merlot, Pinot Noir

hard: Pinot Noir, Merlot, Syrah, Cabernet Sauvignon

COW & SHEEP
medium: Pinot Noir, Petite Sirah

hard: Cabernet Sauvignon, Petite Sirah, Zinfandel, Port Blue, Late-Harvest Riesling, Chenin Blanc, Gewürtraminer, Muscat, Zinfandel

DESSERTS

APPLE PIE, TART & BAKED
Late-Harvest Riesling, Various Ice Wines, Muscat, Demi-sec Sparkling Wines, Blueberry Wine

BERRIES
Brut Sparkling Wines, Demi-sec Sparkling Wines, Late-Harvest Riesling, Muscat, Zinfandel

CHOCOLATE
Late-Harvest Riesling, Raspberry Wine, Black Muscat, Cabernet Sauvignon

CAKES
Demi-sec Sparkling Wines, Late-Harvest Riesling, Muscat, Various Ice Wines

CREAMS, CUSTARDS, PUDDINGS
Demi-sec Sparkling Wines, Late-Harvest Riesling, Muscat, Various Ice Wines

FRESH FRUIT
Late-Harvest Chenin Blanc, Riesling, Gewürtraminer, Muscat

ICE CREAMS, SORBETS
Usually none, perhaps fruit wine or fruit liqueurs

NUTS
Port, Brut Sparkling Wine, Angelica

TIRAMISU
Angelica

WATER SAVVY

Knowing Your Bottled Water

The bottled-water boom over the past decade and a half has transcended the elements of fashion, and has made bottled water a staple in American homes and restaurants. In 1995, according to Beverage Marketing Corp., bottled-water sales increased 8 percent, making it the fastest-growing segment of the beverage industry. Today, yearly sales of bottled water total about $3.4 billion. What spurred this need among consumers to buy what you can get out of the tap for free?

Baby boomers are maturing, and their tastes, as well as concerns over their waistlines, are guiding them toward more natural, less caloric beverages than the Cokes, Buds and margaritas they enthusiastically consumed in their younger party days. America's passion for fitness, combined with, in some cases, a near-prohibitionist attitude toward alcohol, has also driven consumers to seek PC beverage alternatives. Furthermore, the deteriorating taste and quality of tap water—and the fear of the contaminants it may contain—have made bottled water not just a choice for some people, but a necessity.

Trouble at the Tap

The basic belief that American tap water is safe to drink may no longer hold water. Virtually every day, the media reports incidents of contamination and pollution of our municipal water sources. Water quality varies from city to city, street to street and tap to tap. New York City is said to have better-tasting tap water than Los Angeles. Yet both are subject to such chemical treatments as chlorination, which kills bacteria but can produce trihalomethanes (THMs) when it interacts with organic matter in water. THMs have been found to be carcinogenic. From toxic dumps leaking into the aquifers to agricultural pesticides seeping into our reservoirs, our taps are under constant threat. Even the very delivery system that brings tap water from the reservoir to the glass has been found to contain contaminants: lead, copper, radon and a potpourri of other elements that can cause everything from severe headaches to cancer.

When we turn our taste buds to bottled water, we have a long list of "don't wants," but only a hazy idea of what things we do want in our water. Understanding all the bottled water options is the first step.

Not All Water is Created Equal

Within the bottled-water business there are two distinct divisions. The biggest, by volume, is the 5-gallon or jug-water business. Deer Park and Great Bear are among the leaders in this field. Bottlers also are capitalizing on consumers' fondness for their office water coolers, selling two-and-a-half as well as one-gallon containers in supermarkets. This type of bottled water is sold as an alternative to tap water. Premium—or "gourmet"—bottled waters, such as San Pellegrino, Poland Spring and Perrier, are sold as alternatives to soft drinks and alcohol. Packaging ranges from six-ounce to two-liter bottles, from custom glass and PET plastic to aluminum cans. These waters are sometimes carbonated and may have added essences, juices or flavorings.

To make an informed choice about which of the various types of bottled waters is for you, scrutinize the labels. European bottled mineral waters come from springs, which are simply underground water sources that flow naturally to the surface. Waters labeled "spring water" must come from a spring source. Federal labeling standards in the United States, which came into force in May, 1996, now require that bottlers disclose on the label where the water originated.

Purified water is a different story—it's usually produced by distillation, de-ionization or reverse osmosis. This water can originate from either the tap or from ground water. Often labeled "purified" or "drinking water," this processed water often has minerals added to it to give it taste. If the water is produced by vaporization and condensation, it may be labeled "distilled water".

Eight Glasses a Day Keeps the Doctor Away

In Europe, bottlers tout the reputed healthful properties of good water. Almost every European bottled water is "bottled at the source," which means that it comes from a spring where people have gone for hundreds of years to "take the waters" in curative spa treatments. Spas like Vittel and Contrexeville have medical programs designed to address specific ailments. Most spa treatments involve consuming more than eighty ounces of water a day, which is said to remove toxins from the body and to be effective in the treatment of obesity. In Europe, these bottled waters—with their mineral contents listed on the label—are sold not only in supermarkets but also in pharmacies. Doctors even prescribe certain mineral waters for specific ailments.

In the U.S., however, bottled water is marketed with an emphasis on taste, its contribution to fitness regimens, and in some cases, its trendiness. The U.S. Food and Drug Administration does not recognize any therapeutic values of bottled water because the existing medical research does not conform to FDA guidelines. However, the therapeutic value of certain bottled waters is becoming a subject of discussion in American scientific and medical circles.

The Taste of H20

We have approximately 100,000 taste buds, each one connected to our brain by a nerve. Each taste bud senses four basic stimulations from various parts of the tongue; saltiness and sweetness are experienced from taste buds on the tip of the tongue; sourness is perceived on the outer edge of the tongue, and bitterness is perceived on the rear surface of the tongue. Aiding the total tasting experience are two nerves in the upper passage of the nose. The aromatics of a substance pass through the nose when we exhale. Experiment: pinch your nostrils closed and notice how much less vivid your sense of taste is. When evaluating water, it is important to draw the water into the mouth and cover all your taste-sensitive areas with it.

Tap-water taste varies depending on where you live and how your municipal water supply treats or processes the water. The slightly acidic taste of chlorine is one of the most commonly perceived tastes in municipal tap water. Chlorine and other chemicals can affect the taste of beverages, ice cubes, soups and even vegetables. Water impurities can also affect the taste of foods and beverages. Certainly, tea and coffee's natural aromatic constituents will diminish when made with poor-tasting tap water. In fact, Julia Child once said that her Santa Barbara tap water turns her "Chinese tea into mud."

When Carl Rosenberg became the chief baker at the Century Plaza Hotel in Los Angeles, he was asked to duplicate the famous dinner rolls baked at the Olympic Hotel in Seattle. Rosenberg tried out the recipe in Los Angeles, but the rolls' distinctive flavor and texture were both missing. He rechecked the ingredients, and all were correct and of the highest quality. "Could it be the water?" he wondered. After ordering several gallons of Seattle tap water, Rosenberg tried the recipe again. This time the rolls were perfect. Since it was not practical to ship Seattle water each time he baked the rolls, Rosenberg used distilled water, which produced better dough fermentation than L.A. tap water.

But though distilled water may be better to cook with than tap water, it does not score well in water tastings. At a recent "Homage to H20" held by The American Institute of Food and Wine, ten non-carbonated bottled waters were judged in a blind tasting. The distilled bottled water scored the lowest number of points, and judges used words like "dull" and "flat" to describe its taste. People tend to prefer drinking spring water because it tastes better than distilled water. Use distilled water to fill your car battery and steam-iron.

The taste of spring water reflects the different geologic strata underground, where the water absorbs minerals and trace elements—some over a year or two, and others over centuries. These minerals are described in the water's mineral analysis (printed on the label) and are perceived in its taste. Highly mineralized water can sometimes taste metallic; highly bicarbonated water can taste salty. Water with a high content of hydrogen sulfide tastes like rotten eggs, and water with a high concentration of iron can taste like a rusty nail. People tend to prefer their non-carbonated water with a range of 30 to 100 parts-per-million of total dissolved solids—that being the measure of these minerals and trace elements. For carbonated waters, higher levels of minerals are acceptable.

The taste of water can be affected not only by what's in the water, but what the water is in: Lower-grade plastic bottles can impart a plastic taste to the water. If the bottles are stored in the sunlight, the plastic taste can become even stronger.

Bubbly Water

The taste of carbonated water is effected by its level of carbonation—the more carbon-dioxide gas present, the more acidic the water's taste. This sensation, sometimes described by tasters as "bracing," "sharp" and "spritzy," can be positive or negative, depending upon which minerals are in the water. Certain minerals bind the carbonation into the water. Seltzers tend to lose their carbonation quickly because of the lack of minerals. In bottled-water tastings, the more highly mineralized carbonated waters have scored best.

Become bottled-water savvy with this brief primer about popular brands available in New York restaurants.

The Major Brands

Calistoga

Nestled at the north end of Napa Valley, Calistoga is a spa-resort town where a geyser second in size only to Yellowstone's Old Faithful shoots up from the ground, and people have been coming to "take the waters"—in pools and in mud-baths—since before the turn of the century. Of the town's three commercially bottled waters, Calistoga comes from water which emerges from the ground at 212 degrees Fahrenheit and is then cooled to 39 degrees F for bottling. The hydrogen-sulfide aroma is removed from the water at the bottling plant by filtering it through sand. The finished water is then ozonated and carbonated. Calistoga also bottles a non-carbonated water sourced from a Napa County spring.

Crystal Geyser

Also bottled in the town of Calistoga, Crystal Geyser water comes from an aquifer 240 feet below the bottling plant. The water surfaces at a temperature of 140 degrees F, and through a method of heat exchanges, is cooled, filtered to remove sediment, ozonated, carbonated and bottled. The company also produces the non-carbonated Natural Alpine Spring water near the town of Olancha, California. Its source is high in the Sierra Mountains, where glacial waters have seeped over eons through cracks in the granite rocks. Crystal Geyser also produces Natural Alpine spring water, which comes from a source near the base of Mt. Whitney.

Dannon Natural Spring Water

You know the name "Dannon" from the company's line of milk products. Now you'll find it on bottles of non-carbonated water. The source this newcomer to the bottled-water biz is a spring in the Laurentian region of Quebec, Canada. Test-marketed in Florida and Colorado, initial results showed that Dannon's brand name and moderate pricing produced positive sales, as consumers associate the name with taste, trust and natural products.

Deer Park

Deer Park's source is a spring 3,000 feet above sea level surrounded by hundreds of acres of woodlands in the Allegheny Mountains, near Deer Park, Maryland. When it was first bottled in 1880, the non-sparkling water was called Boiling Spring because of the action of the water as it bubbled through white sand. The Deer Park Hotel and Spa, which opened in 1873, became a watering ground for distinguished guests, including U.S. Presidents Garfield, Cleveland, Harrison and Taft.

Evian

This famous non-sparkling European water comes from Source Cachat in France, where the water emerges from a tunnel in the mountain at 52.88 degrees F. The source is fed from the melted snow and rain that filters through glacial sand from the Vinzier Plateau over a period of 15 years. The glacial sand is surrounded by clay which protects the water from pollution. The water is bottled at a nearby bottling plant, which is highly automated and exceptionally hygienic.

Ice Mountain

Early Indians were the first to discover Ice Mountain Spring, located in the remote woodlands of Mt. Zircon, near Rumford, in central Maine. They noticed it seemed to rise and fall with the cycles of the moon and called it Moon Tide Spring. The water was first bottled by the Abbott family In 1859, and is now bottled as both still and sparkling.

Mountain Valley

This water springs from a source in a 500-acre forest in the hills between Glazypeau and Cedar Mountains, in Arkansas.

Adjacent is a timberland preserve, all of which protects the Mountain Valley aquifer. It was first bottled in 1871 and has been continuously bottled since then, both as carbonated and non-carbonated water. Mountain Valley's source emerges at 65 degrees F; the bottling plant draws approximately 50 gallons per minute from the spring. The source's aquifer is estimated to be at 1,600 feet below earth's surface, where the water filters through levels of shale, Blakely sandstone and limestone.

Perrier

Dating back more than 100 million years to the Cretaceous Period, when limestone deposits began to form faults and fissures that captured water deep within the earth below what is now Vergèze, France. Hannibal's Carthaginian army is said to have paused by the spring, Les Bouillens, in 218 B.C. Remains in the area suggest that the Romans also refreshed themselves in the waters of Perrier, which have a bit of natural carbonation. When it is bottled, extra fizz is created by adding filtered CO_2 gas captured at a nearby natural source.

Poland Spring

The history of Poland Spring, Maine, dates back to 1793, when the area around the spring was first settled and the Ricker family opened a small inn. Soon afterward Joseph Ricker lay dying, and to ease his fever someone fetched water from the spring. The story is that Ricker drank it and lived another fifty-two years to tell the tale! Iin 1845, Hiram Ricker began to bottle the water and, in 1893, Poland Spring was awarded the Medal of Excellence at the World's Columbian Exposition in Chicago. Today, Poland Spring comes both still and sparkling.

San Pellegrino

The spring of San Pellegrino is sequestered in the mountains north of Milan, Italy, and was first made famous by quenching the thirst of Leonardo da Vinci. Today the Fonte Termale, an opulent marbled drinking hall is a monument to the glamour of "taking the waters." San Pellegrino's sources are three deep springs which emerge from the ground at 69.8 degrees F. The waters come from an aquifer 1,300 feet below the surface, where limestone and volcanic rocks impart unique minerals and trace elements. Among its several bottled waters, San Pellegrino also bottles and imports to the U.S. Acqua Minerale Naturale Panna, a still water that comes from a spring in the hills of Tuscany near Florence.

Saratoga

In the southern foothills of New York's Adirondack Mountains is the famous town of Saratoga Springs, where, in the Gay '90s, celebrities like Lillian Russell and Diamond Jim Brady drank Saratoga's carbonated water from monogrammed cups. Saratoga's original source was a hand-drilled well that went through 30 feet of sand and 150 feet of rock. Natural carbonation occurs in the water, although the water is re-injected with additional carbonation during the bottling process.

Solé

The Fonte Solé Spring is located in the foothills of the Lombardy region of the Italian Alps, and has been revered for its health-giving waters since Roman times. In the Middle Ages, the source was controlled by a monastery when both plague and pestilence threatened the population. A belief grew up that those who drank from the spring would be . Today, the water is recognized as being low in sodium. The University of Pavia has declared it as being microbiologically pure. Solé is packaged in green glass bottles, both non-carbonated and lightly carbonated. The latter, be warned, is not the best mixer to use for spritzers because of the fragility of its bubbles.

Spa

First discovered by the ancient Romans, the source for Spa's non-sparkling mineral water is located in Belgium's Ardennes Valley. Spa was the first town to develop an international bottled water industry (in 1583, the water was exported to none less than King Henri II of France). In the process, the town inadvertently exported its name; since then, "spa" has been synonymous with most natural springs and health resorts. On the edge of the High Venn near Spa is the spring called Reine (the Queen's Spring). Rain and melted snow falls on a moss area of La Fagne, a plateau 575 meters above sea level. It percolates down through layers of clay, slate, flint, sand and quartz where it finally surfaces at 440 meters above sea level.

Tynant

Springing from a source in Wales' Cambrian Mountains, this carbon-filtered sparkling water first made a name for itself in London's high-end hotels in 1989. Today, the lightly carbonated beverage is more widely distributed, and imported to the United States as well. Tynant is recognizable by its striking blue glass bottles, the hue that apothecary bottles were colored during the Victorian era.

Vittel

This still mineral water comes from three springs in the small town of Vittel, protected within a 5,000 hectare forest in the Vosges Mountains in Northeastern France. Vittel Grande Source comes from an immense underground aquifer where rock strata and sandstone charge the water with calcium, magnesium and sulphates. The spring surfaces at 11.1 degrees C. and its waters are renowned for its stimulating effects on the kidneys, gall bladder and liver.

By Arthur von Wiesenberger, the author of a number of books about water, the most recent, The Taste of Water (Best Cellar Books). He is also a consultant to the bottled-water industry.

RESTAURANT INDEXES

RESTAURANTS BY CUISINE

AMERICAN

Kate Mantilini
Lawry's The Prime Rib
McCormick & Schmick's
Mr. Chow
Nic's Martini Lounge & Restaurant

AFGHAN

The Helmand
Kabul (P)

AMERICAN

Atlas Café
The Avenue Grill (M)
Balboa Café
Bayview Restaurant (WC)
Bergman's (WC)
Bette's Oceanview Diner
Big Three Fountain (WC)
Bighorn Grill (EB)
Bill's Place
Birk's (P)
Bitterroot
Bix
Brannan's Grill (WC)
Bubba Gump (MC)
Bubba's Diner (M)
Buckey Roadhouse (M)
Buck's Restaurant (P)
Buffalo Grill (P)
Café Flore
Café for All Seasons
Camera Café (SJ)
Casa Orinda (EB)
Cityscape
Chow
Christophe
Delancey Street Restaurant
Dottie's True Blue Café

Eddie Rickenbacker's
Ella's
Empire Grill & Tap Room (P)
The Flatiron (M)
The Fly Trap
Fog City Diner
The Fountain at the Fairmont (SJ)
The Grill at Meadowood (WC)
The Grill on the Alley (SJ)
Hard Rock Café
Harry Denton's
Hayes Street Grill
Hobee's (SJ)
Horn of Zeese (WC)
Jack's
Johnny Rockets
John's Grill
Just For You Café
Kate's Kitchen
Liberty Café & Bakery
Livefire Grill & Smokehouse (WC)
MacArthur Park (P)
Max's Diner
McCormick & Kuleto's
The Meetinghouse
Mel's Drive-In
Mendocino Showplace Restaurant
Miss Millie's
Momo's
Mo's Gourmet Burgers
Moss Beach Distillery (P)
Napa Valley Wine Train (WC)
Nepenthe
North Star Restaurant
The Oasis (P)

Pacific Blues Café

Park Chow

Parkside Grille (P)

Peninsula Fountain & Grill (P)

Perry's

Planet Hollywood

Red Devil Lounge

Rick & Ann's (EB)

The Roadhouse (WC)

Rob's Rib Shack (WC)

Rosine's (MC)

Rutherford Grill (WC)

Sears Fine Foods

Tarpy's Roadhouse (MC)

Tides Wharf Restaurant (WC)

Union Ale House

Vintners Court

Walker's Restaurant & Pie Shop (EB)

Washington Square Bar & Grill

Whole Foods (P)

Yes Burgers & Malts

AMERICAN/BREAKFAST

Café Fanny (EB)

The Diner (WC)

Doidge's

Joann's Café (P)

Mamma's on Washington Square

Millie's Kitchen (EB)

Village Corner (MC)

AMERICAN/BREWPUB

Beach Chalet

Buckhorn Saloon (WC)

Downtown Joe's (WC)

Gordon Biersch (P,SJ)

Gordon's (WC)

Magnolia Pub & Brewery

Pyramid Alehouse (EB)

AMERICAN/ECLECTIC

Bill's Café (SJ)

ARGENTINEAN

Evita Café

ASIAN NOODLES

Zao Noodle Bar (P)

BARBECUE

Big Nate's

Brother-in-Law's Bar-B-Que

Doug's (EB)

Henry's World Famous Hi-Life (SJ)

Moonshine

Rasta Dwight's Barbecue (WC)

The Roadhouse (WC)

San Francisco Bar-B-Q

BASQUE

Des Alpes Restaurant

BRAZILIAN

Bahia Cabana

Canto do Brasil

Terra Brazilias

Lasalette (WC)

BURMESE

Burma Super Star

Irrawaddy Burmese Cuisine

Mandalay

Nan Yang Rockridge (EB)

BURMESE/CHINESE

Rangoon

CAFÉ

Mendocino Bakery & Café (WC)

CAFÉ/DESSERTS

Caffè Trieste

CAFÉ/SNACKS

North End Caffè

CAFETERIA

Pluto's (SF, P)

CALIFORNIA

Agenda Restaurant (SJ)

All Seasons Café & Wine Shop (WC)

Alta Plaza

A.P. Stumps (SJ)

CALIFORNIA/ITALIAN

Aperto
Ca' Bianca Restaurant (WC)
Café Da Vero (WC)
Café Four-Eleven (EB)
Kuleto's Trattoria (P)
Lo Spuntino: An Italian Taste (WC)
Puccini & Pinetti

CALIFORNIA/ MEDITERRANEAN

Equus (WC)
Oberon
Taste Café & Bistro (MC)
Zigzag (MC)

CALIFORNIA/MEXICAN

Boonville Hotel (WC)

CALIFORNIA/SEAFOOD

Grasing's (MC)

CALIFORNIA/SOUTHERN

Catahoula (WC)

CALIFORNIA/SOUTHWESTERN

Rio Grill (MC)

CALIFORNIA/VEGETARIAN

Late for the Train (P)

CAMBODIAN

Angkor Borrei Restaurant
Battambang

CARIBBEAN

Chicken! Chicken! (P)
Mango Café (P)

CHINESE

Atrium (M)
Chef Jia's
Dragon Well
Eliza's
Empress of China
Ever Rain (M)
Firecracker
Fook Yuen (P)
Gary Chu's (WC)
Great Eastern
Harbor Village Restuarant
Hong Kong Flower Lounge (P)
House of Lee (M)
House of Nanking
Hunan Restaurant
The Mandarin
North Sea Village (M)
Ping's (M)
R&G Lounge
Shanghai 1930
Shen Hua (EB)
Taiwan (SF, SJ)
Uncle Yu's (EB)
Yet Wah (M)
Yuet Lee

CHINESE/DIM SUM

Chef Chu's (P)
Green Garden (EB)
Ming's (P)
Restaurant Peony (EB)
Yank Sing

CHINESE/BARBECUE

Kam Po Hong Kong Kitchen

CHINESE/FRENCH

Tommy Toy's Cuisine Chinois

CHINESE/HAKKA

Ton Kiang

CHINESE/SEAFOOD

Mayflower

CHINESE/SHANGHAI

Fountain Court

CHINESE/VEGETARIAN

Kowloon Vegetarian Restaurant
Lotus Garden
Lucky Creation

CONTEMPORARY

Black Cat
Boulevard

Café de Paris L'Entrecôte
Café Florio
Café Jacqueline
Campton Place
Cassis Bistro
Chapeau!
Christophe (M)
City of Paris
Clementine
Filou (M)
Fleur de Lys
Fresh Cream (MC)
Fringale
Hyde St. Bistro
Jeanne d'Arc
Kincaid's Bistro (MC)
La Boucane (WC)
La Folie
La Maison (EB)
La Note (EB)
La Toque (WC)
L'Amie Donia (P)
Le Central
Le Charm
Le Marquis (EB)
Le Mouton Noir (P)
Le Papillon (SJ)
Left Bank (M, P)
L'Olivier
Masa's
Ovation at the Opera
Piaf's
Restaurant Sent Sovi
The Ritz-Carlton Dining Room
South Park Café
Voulez-Vous (EB)

FRENCH/CALIFORNIA
Charles Nob Hill
The French Laundry (WC)
Grand Café
Jardinière
Pastis
Pinot Blanc (WC)
Rubicon

FRENCH/CONTEMPORARY
Club XIX—Inspired by

Hubert Keller (MC)
Obelisque

FRENCH/CRÊPES
Ti Couz

FUSION
Arco-Iris
AsiaSF
Bridges Restaurant & Bar (EB)
Café Akimbo
Citrus Club
Entros
Eos Restaurant & Wine Bar House
Mes Trois Filles (WC)
Ooodles
Oratalia
Roy's at Pebble Beach (MC)
Silks
Soizic (EB)
The Waterfront Restaurant
Yo Yo Tsumami Bistro

FUSION/SEAFOOD
Brix (WC)

FUSION/SUSHI
Higashi West (P)

GERMAN
Elbe (P)
Germania Restaurant at the Hochburg (SJ)
Speckmann's
Suppenküche

GOURMET BAR FOOD
Bubble Lounge
Harry Denton's Starlight Room

GREEK
Evvia Estiatorio (P)
Kokkari

HOFBRAU
Pluto's

HUNGARIAN
Hungarian Sausage Factory

ICE CREAM PARLOR
The Big Dipper (WC)
Bombay Ice Cream & Chaat

INDIAN
Ajanta (EB)
Amber Indian
Restaurant (P)
Bombay Ice Cream & Chaat
Gaylord India Restaurant
Madras (EB)
North India
Sue's Indian Cuisine (P)

INDIAN/CALIFORNIA
Indian Oven

INDONESIAN
Jakarta
The Rice Table (M)

INTERNATIONAL
Pomelo

IRISH/SEAFOOD
Moby's Fish & Chips

ITALIAN
Acquerello
Alioto's #8
Antica Trattoria
Baraonda
Basta Pasta
Brazio (EB)
Buca di Beppo (P)
Bucci's (EB)
Ca' Bianca (WC)
Café Citti (WC)
Café Fina (MC)
Café La Scala (P)
Café Niebaum-Coppola
Café Pecatore
Café Prima Vera
Café Tiramisu
Caffè Delle Stelle (EB)
Caffè 817 (EB)

Caffè Macaroni
Caffè Sport
Cantinetta at Tra Vigne (WC)
Capp's Corner
Carpaccio (P)
Cento Stelle (M)
Columbus Ristorante
Cucina Jackson Fillmore (M)
Dalla Torre
Fior d'Italia
Firewood Café
Frantoio (M)
Gambardella's (P)
Giglio (EB)
Gira Polli (M)
Il Davide (M)
Il Fornaio (SF, M,P, SJ, MC)
Il Porcellino (EB)
Jackson Fillmore Trattoria
Kuleto's
La Gondola (MC)
La Felce
La Traviata
Little City Antipasti Bar
L'Osteria del Forno
Mangiafuoco
Marin Joe's (M)
Mario's Bohemian Cigar Store
Mazzini Trattoria (EB)
Maye's Original Oyster House
Mescolanza
Mio Vincino (SJ)
Montecatini (EB)
North Beach Restaurant
Original Joe's (SF, SJ)
Palio D'Asti
Pane e Vino
Paolo's (SJ)
Parma Ristorante
Pasta? (P)
Pasta Pomodoro (SF, EB)
Pasta Prego Trattoria (WC)
Pazzia
Piatti Ristorante (WC, P, MC)
Postino (EB)

PAN-ASIAN/SEAFOOD
Stillwater Bar & Grill

PERUVIAN
Fina Estampa
Rincon Peruono

PIZZA
Arinell Pizza
Amici's East Coast Pizzeria (M)
Cheese Board (EB)
Mary's Pizza Shack (WC)
Mulberry Street Pizzeria (M)
Pauline's Pizza
Tomatina (WC)
Vicolo Pizzeria
Willow Street Wood-Fired Pizza (SJ)
Zachary's Chicago Pizza (EB)

POLISH
Old Krakow

PORTUGUESE
Lasalette (WC)

RUSSIAN
Katia's, A Russian Tea Room

SALVADORAN
Amelia's (P)
El Zocalo

SEAFOOD
A.Sabella's Restaurant
Alamo Square Seafood Grill
Alioto's #8
Barbara's Fish Trap (P)
Blue Point Restaurant
Butterfield's
Crustacean
The Fish Market (P)
Franciscan
Hayes Street Grill
Maye's Original Oyster House
McCormick & Kuleto's
Miramar Beach Restaurant (P)
Pacific Café (M)

Plouf
Scoma's
Scott's Seafood (SJ)
Swan Oyster Depot
Yabbie's

SEAFOOD/GRILL
Sam's Grill
Sardine Factory (MC)
Scott's Seafood Grill & Bar
Tadich Grill

SINGAPOREAN
Strait's Café (P)

SOUTHERN/SOUL
Powell's Place
Roscoe's Chicken & Waffles (EB)

SOUTHWESTERN
Left at Albuquerque (P)

SPANISH
Alegerías
Barcelona
Bolero (M)
Cesar (EB)
Esperpento
Patio Español
Tapas Sevilla (EB)
Thirsty Bear
Timo's
Zarzuela

SPANISH/CATALAN
Vinga

STEAKHOUSE
Alfred's Steakhouse
Blake's Steakhouse & Bar
Harris'
House of Prime Rib
Izzy's Steak & Chop House
Marin Joe's (M)
Morton's of Chicago

STEAK/SUSHI
Anzu Nikko

SWISS
Matterhorn Swiss Restaurant

THAI
Bangkok 16
Basil
Jhan Thong (M)
Khan Toke Thai House
Lalita
Manora's Thai Cuisine
Marnee Thai
The Royal Thai
Thai Basil #2
Thep Lela (M)
Thep Phanom
Vulcan Café (EB)

TIBETAN
Lhasa Moon

VEGAN
Herbivore
Organica

VEGAN/CALIFORNIA
Millenium

VEGETARIAN
Greens
Valentine's Café
White Lotus Restaurant (SJ)

VIETNAMESE
Crustacean
Elephant Bleu
Golden Turtle
Jasmine House
Khanh's GardenRestaurant
Le Cheval (EB)
Le Colonial
The Slanted Door
Thanh Long

VIETNAMESE/FRENCH
New Aux Delices

WINE BAR
Hayes & Vine

RESTAURANTS
BY NOTABLE FEATURES

WE'VE INCLUDED ONLY THE BEST IN EACH CATEGORY

BREAKFAST
BRUNCH
BUSINESS DINING
KID FRIENDLY
HOTEL DINING ROOMS
LATE-NIGHT DINING
LIGHT & HEALTHY DINING
LIVE MUSIC/ENTERTAINMENT
OUTDOOR DINING
PLACES TO MEET FOR A DRINK
ROMANTIC
VIEW
WINE LIST

BREAKFAST
Auberge Du Soleil (WC)
Bette's Oceanview Diner (EB)
Bill's Café (SJ)
Bubba's Diner (M)
Buck's Restaurant (P)
Café Fanny (EB)
The Diner (WC)
Doidge's
Dottie's True Blue Café
Gordon's (WC)

Joann's Café (P)

Late for the Train (P)

Mendocino Showplace Restaurant (WC)

Millie's Kitchen (EB)

Oakville Grocery Café (WC)

Original Joe's (SJ)

Paolo's (SJ)

Park Grill

Postrio

Rick & Ann's (EB)

The Ritz-Carlton Terrace

Roscoe's Chicken & Waffles (EB)

Sears Fine Food

Village Corner (MC)

BRUNCH

Absinthe

Beach Chalet

Blackhawk Grill (EB)

Café Cuvée

Campton Place

Carnelian Room

Cityscape

Empire Grill & Tap Room (P)

Fandango (MC)

Garden Court

Greens

Lark Creek Inn (M)

Nepenthe (MC)

Pacific

Pacific's Edge (MC)

Park Grill

The Restaurant at Meadowood (WC)

Restaurant Zibibbo (P)

The Ritz-Carlton Terrace

BEST BUSINESS DINING

Agenda Restaurant (SJ)

A.P. Stumps (SJ)

Aqua

Bay Wolf (EB)

Blake's Steakhouse & Bar (SJ)

Boulevard

Campton Place

Carnelian Room

Charles Nob Hill

Farallon

Fleur de Lys

Fresh Cream (MC)

Garden Court

Globe

The Grill on the Alley (SJ)

Hawthorne Lane

Jack's

Jardinière

John's Grill

Kokkari

Kyo-Ya

La Folie

L'Olivier

Mama's on Washington Square

Masa's

Montrio (MC)

Morton's of Chicago

One Market

Pacific

Palio D'Asti

Paolo's (SJ)

Park Grill

Postrio

Restaurant Zibibbo (P)

The Ritz-Carlton Dining Room

Rubicon

Sam's Grill

Scala's Bistro

Silk's

Spago Palo Alto (P)

Splendido

Stars

Stokes Adobe (MC)

Tadich Grill

Zaré

Zigzag (MC)

KID FRIENDLY

Bill's Café (SJ)

Bubba Gump (MC)

Bubba's Diner (M)

Buca Di Beppo (P)

Buckeye Roadhouse (M)

Byblos Restaurant

Menara Moroccan Restaurant (SJ)

Moonshine

Pacific Blues Café (WC)

Pacific's Edge (MC)

The Palace (P)

Piaf's

Red Devil Lounge

Rob's Rib Shack (WC)

Rose Pistola

BEST OUTDOOR DINING

Applewood Inn & Restaurant (WC)

Aram's

Auberge Du Soleil (WC)

Bouchon (WC)

Brava Terrace (WC)

Ca' Bianca Restaurant (WC)

The Café at Château Souverain (WC)

Café Niebaum-Coppola

Cantineta at Tra Vigne (WC)

Domaine Chandon (WC)

Elroys

Empire Grill & Tap Room (P)

The French Laundry (WC)

Gordon Biersch

Kelly's Mission Rock

Lark Creek Café (EB, P)

Lark Creek Inn (M)

Le Charm

Madrona Manor (WC)

Nepenthe (MC)

Park Grill

Piatti Ristorante (WC)

Pinot Blanc (WC)

Postino (EB)

The Restaurant at Meadowood (WC)

Restaurant Zibibbo (P)

The Ritz-Carlton Terrace

Santa Fe Bar & Grill (EB)

Showley's (WC)

Spago Palo Alto (P)

Tra Vigne (WC)

Ventana (MC)

BEST PLACES TO MEET FOR A DRINK

Absinthe

Agenda Restaurant (SJ)

Alta Plaza

A.P. Stumps (SJ)

AsiaSF

Backflip

Balboa Café

Betelnut Pejiu Wu

Bighorn Grill (EB)

Bix

Black Cat

Blake's Steakhouse & Bar (SJ)

Boulevard

Bubble Lounge

Carnelian Room

Carpaccio (P)

Cesar (EB)

Cypress Club

E&O Trading Company

Eastside West

Eddie Rickenbacker's

Elroys

Entros

Farallon

Fog City Diner

Goeffrey's Inner Circle (EB)

Gordon Biersch (SF, P, SJ)

Harry Denton's

Harry Denton's Starlight Room

Hayes & Vine

Jardinière

Kenwood Restaurant & Bar (WC)

Le Colonial

MacArthur Park

Maye's Original Oyster House

Mecca

Momo's

One Market

The Palace (P)

Paolo's (SJ)

Palomino Euro Bistro

Postrio

BEST WINE LIST

Acquerello
Alioto's No. 8
All Seasons Café & Wine Shop (WC)
A.P. Stumps (SJ)
Applewood Inn & Restaurant (WC)
Aqua
Auberge Du Soleil (WC)
Basta Pasta
Black Cat
Boulevard
Café Niebaum-Coppola
Chapeau!
Chez Panisse (EB)
The Covey at Quail Lodge (MC)
Fandango (MC)
Fleur de Lys
The French Laundry (WC)
Girl & The Fig (WC)
Grasing's (MC)
The Grille at Sonoma Mission Inn (WC)
Hawthorne Lane
Hayes & Vine

Hayes Street Grill
Insalata's (M)
La Folie
La Toque (WC)
Lark Creek Inn (M)
Masa's
Napa Valley Grille (WC)
One Market
101 Main Bistro & Wine Bar (WC)
Park Grill
Plumpjack Café
Postrio
The Restaurant at Meadowood (WC)
Restaurant Lulu
The Ritz-Carlton Dining Room
Rose Pistola
Rubicon
Rue de Paris (SJ)
Sardine Factory (MC)
Sierra Mar (MC)
Silk's
Spago Palo Alto (P)
Stillwater Bar & Grill (MC)
Terra (WC)

RESTAURANTS BY AREA

SAN FRANCISCO

BERNAL HEIGHTS
Hungarian Sausage Factory
Liberty Café & Bakery

CASTRO
Café Cuvée
Café Flore
Chow
Dame, A Restaurant
Firewood Café
Fuzio Universal
Mecca
2223 Restaurant

The Zodiac Club

CHINA BASIN
Kelly's Mission Rock
Momo's

CHINATOWN
Alfred's Steak House
Chef Jia's
Des Alpes Restaurant
Empress of China
Great Eastern
House of Nanking
Kam Po Hong Kitchen
Kowloon Vegetarian

Chinoise
Zaré

FISHERMAN'S WHARF
A.Sabella's Restaurant
Alioto's No. 8
Café Pescatore
Franciscan
Scoma's

GHIRADELLI SQUARE
Gaylord India Restaurant
The Mandarin
McCormick & Kuleto's

HAIGHT-ASHBURY
Cha Cha Cha
Citrus Club
El Balazo
Eos Restaurant & Wine Bar
Grandeho Kamekyo
Hama-Ko
Indian Oven
Kate's Kitchen
Magnolia Pub & Brewery
Moby's Fish & Chips

HAYES VALLEY
Alamo Square Seafood Grill
Caffè Delle Stelle
Evita Café
Hayes & Vine
Hayes Street Grill
Powell's Place
Suppenküche
Terra Brazilis

INNER SUNSET
Ebisu
House
Organica
Park Chow
PJ's Oyster Bed
Pluto's

JAPANTOWN
Isobune
Juban
Korea House

Mifune
Yo Yo Tsumami Bistro

LOWER HAIGHT
Botana
Thep Phanom

MARINA
Alegrías
Aya Sushi
Baker Street Bistro
Bistro Aix
The Brazen Restaurant
Byblos Restaurant
Café de Paris L'Entrecôte
Café Marimba
Columbus Ristorante
Curbside Too
Dragon Well
Greens
Irrawaddy Burmese Cuisine
Izzy's Steak & Chophouse
Lhasa Moon
Mel's Drive-In
North India
Parma Ristorante
Sweet Heat
Trap Door
World Wrapps
Zeil Noodle Club
Zinzino

MISSION
Alejandro's La Polleria
Arinell Pizza
Atlas Café
Bangkok 16
Bitterroot
Bombay Ice Cream & Chaat
Brisas de Acapulco
Bruno's
Café Ethiopia
Charanga
Delfina
El Farolito
El Nuevo Fruitlandia
El Zocalo
Elephant Bleu

Esperpento
Fina Estampa
Firecracker
Flying Saucer
Herbivore
La Cumbre
La Rondalla
La Taqueria
La Traviata
Mangiafuoco
Pancho Villa Taqueria
Pauline's Pizza
Rincon Peruono
Roosevelt Tamale Parlor
Sacrifice
The Slanted Door
Taqueria San Jose
Ti Couz
Timo's
Tokyo Go Go
Trattoria Contadina
Truly Mediterranean
Universal Café
Vineria
Woodward's Garden

NOB HILL
Acquerello
Charles Nob Hill
Fournou's Ovens
Nob Hill Terrace
The Ritz-Carlton Dining Room
The Ritz-Carlton Terrace

NOE VALLEY
Fattoush
Firefly
Miss Millie's
Speckmann's
Valentine's Café

NORTH BEACH
Albona Ristorante
Basta Pasta
Black Cat
Café Jacqueline
Café Niebaum-Coppola

Caffè Macaroni
Caffè Sport
Caffè Trieste
Campo Santo
Capp's Corner
Cypress Club
Enrico's Sidewalk Café
Fior d'Italia
Gira Polli
The Helmand
Hunan Restaurant
La Felce
Little City Antipasti Bar
L'Osteria del Forno
Mama's on Washington Square
Mario's Bohemian Cigar Store
MC2
Moonshine
Mo's Gourmet Burgers
North Beach Restaurant
North End Caffè
Pasta Pomodoro
Ristorante Ideale
Rose Pistola
Sushi on North Beach
Tavolino
Tommaso's
Washington Square Bar & Grill
Zax

OUTER MISSION
Angkor Borei Restaurant
Patio Español

OUTER SUNSET
Thanh Long

PACIFIC HEIGHTS
Alta Plaza
Elite Café
Jackson Fillmore Trattoria
Osome

POLK GULCH
Bistro Zare
Crustacean

California Culinary
Academy

Original Joe's

UNION SQUARE

Anjou

Anzu Nikko

Brasserie Savoy

Café Akimbo

Campo Santo

Campton Place

Christophe

City of Paris

E&O Trading Company

Farallon

Fleur de Lys

Grand Café

Harry Denton's Starlight
Room

Jeanne D'Arc

Kuleto's

Masa's

Morton's of Chicago

Oodles

Oritalia

Pacific

Plouf

Postrio

Rubicon

Scala's Bistro

Sears Fine Food

UPPER HAIGHT

Pomelo

VAN NESS

Golden Turtle

Hard Rock Café

Harris'

House of Prime Rib

Matterhorn Swiss Restaurant

Osaka Grill

WEST PORTAL

Bocca Rotis

Café for All Seasons

Cityscape

Old Krakow

WESTERN ADDITION

Brother-inLaw's Bar-B-Que

Café Kati

The Meetinghouse

MARIN COUNTY

CORTE MADERA

Atrium

David's Finest Taquería

Il Fornaio

Marin Joe's

Ultra Lucca

INVERNESS

Manka's Inverness Lodge

KENTWOOD

Half Day Café

Pacific Café

LARKSPUR

Bolero

Lark Creek Inn

Left Bank

Yet Wah

MILL VALLEY

The Avenue Grill

Bistro Alsacienne

Buckeye Roadhouse

El Paseo

Frantoio

Gira Polli

Joe's Taco Lounge & Salseria

Robata Grill & Sushi

Thep Lela

NOVATO

Ever Rain

SAN ANSELMO

Bubba's Diner

Cucina Jackson Fillmore

Filou

Insalata's

Rossetti Osteria Romana

Yahiro Sushi Bar &
Restaurant

Restaurant Indexes - Restaurants by Area

SAN RAFAEL
Amici's East Coast Pizzeria
Casa Mañana
Cento Stelle
The Club at McGinnis
The Flatiron
House of Lee
Il Davide
India Village
Jhan Thong
Kasbah Moroccan Restaurant
Mulberry Street Pizzeria
Ping's
The Rice Table
Sushi to Dai For
Yes Burgers & Malts

SAUSALITO
Christophe
Mikayla
North Sea Village

TIBURON
The Caprice
Guaymas

EAST BAY

ALAMEDA
Arco-Iris
Commodore's Waterfront Café
ALBANY
Kathmandu
Walker's Restaurant & Pie Shop

BERKELEY
Ajanta
Bette's Oceanview Diner
Café at Chez Panisse
Café Fanny
Café Rouge
Cesar
Cheese Board
Chez Panisse
Ginger Island
Le Bayou Cajun & Creole Café

Lalime's
La Note
Mazzini Trattoria
O Chame
Picante Cocina Mexicana
Pyramid Alehouse
Rick & Ann's
Rivioli Restaurant
Santa Fe Bar & Grill
Santa Fe Bistro
Shen Hua
Zachary's Chicago Pizza

CASTRO VALLEY
La Maison

CONCORD
Korea Palace

DANVILLE
Blackhawk Grill
Brazio
Bridges Restaurant & Bar
Café Four-Eleven
Tapas Sevilla

EMERYVILLE
Bucci's
Doug's Barbecue
Townhouse Bar & Grill
LAFAYETTE
Le Marquis
Millie's Kitchen
Postino
Uncle Yu's

LIVERMORE
Wente Vineyards Restaurant

OAKLAND
Autumn Moon Café
Battambang
Bay Wolf
Cactus Taqueria
Café Rustica
Caffè 817
Garibaldi's On College
Geoffrey's Inner Circle
Giglio

363

Downtown Joe's Restaurant & Microbrewery

Foothill Café

La Boucane

Mustards Grill

Napa Valley Wine Train

Pasta Prego Trattoria

Pearl

Uva Trattoria Italiana

Vintners Court

OAKVILLE

Oakville Grocery Café

PETALUMA

Twisted Vines

RUTHERFOD

Auberge Du Soleil

La Toque

Rutherford Grill

SANTA ROSA

Ca' Bianca Restaurant

Café Lolo

Equus

Gary Chu's

John Ash & Co.

Lisa Hemenway Bistro

Mistral

Mixx

Mixx Pastry & Accessories

Willowside Café

SEBASTOPOL

Café da Vero

101 Main Bistro & Wine Bar

SONOMA

Babette's

Café La Haye

Deuce

The General's Daughter

Heirloom

Lasalette

Lo Spuntino: An Italian Taste

Mary's Pizza Shack

Piatti Ristorante

Rob's Rib Shack

ST. HELENA

Ana's Cantina

Bergman's

The Big Dipper

Brava Terrace

Cantineta at Tra Vigne

The Grill at Meadowood

Pairs Parkside

Pinot Blanc

The Restaurant at Meadowood

Roadhouse 29

Showley's

Terra

Tomatina

Tra Vigne

The Wine Spectator Restaurant

YOUNTVILLE

Bistro Jeanty

Bouchon

Compadres Mexican Bar & Grill

The Diner

Domaine Chandon

The French Laundry

Gordon's

Livefire Grill & Smokehouse

Napa Valley Grille

Pacific Blues Café

Piatti Ristorante

PENINSULA

BURLINGAME

Café La Scala

Chicken! Chicken!

Kuleto's Trattoria

CUPERTINO

Kathmandu West

HALF MOON BAY

Miramar Beach Restaurant

LOS ALTOS

Chef Chu's

MENLO PARK
Carpaccio
Flea St. Café
Gambardella's
Late for the Train
Left Bank
Max's Bakery & Kitchen
The Oasis
Scala Mia House of Garlic

MILLBREA
Fook Yuen
Hong Kong Flower Lounge
Osho

MOSS BEACH
Moss Beach Distillery

MOUNTAIN VIEW
Amber Indian Restaurant
Sue's Indian Cuisine
PALO ALTO
Bravo Fono
Buca Di Beppo
Elbe
Empire Grill & Tap Room
Evvia Estiatorio
The Fish Market
Gordon Biersch
Higashi West
Il Fornaio
L'Amie Donia
Left at Albuquerque
MacArthur Park
Mango Café
Max's Opera Café
Ming's
Miyake
Pasta?
Peninsula Fountain & Grill
Piatti Ristorante
Pluto's Hofbrau
Rangoon
Restaurant Zibibbo
Spago Palo Alto
Straits Café
Whole Foods
Zao Noodle Bar

PESCADERO
Duarte's Tavern

PORTOLO VALLEY
Parkside Grille

PRINCETON BY THE SEA
Barbara's Fish Trap

REDWOOD CITY
Amelia's

SAN CARLOS
Creola—A New Orleans
Bistro
Kabul

SAN MATEO
Buffalo Grill
231 Ellsworth
Viognier

SANTA CLARA
Birk's
Taqueria La cumbre

SARATOGA
Le Mouton Noir
Restaurant Sent Sovi

SOUTH SAN FRANCISCO
Joann's Café

SUNNYVALE
Faz Restaurant & Catering
The Palace
Thai Basil #2

WOODSIDE
Bella Vista Restaurant
Buck's Restaurant
The Village Pub

SAN JOSE

Agenda Restaurant
A.P. Stumps
Bella Mia
Bill's Café
Blake's Steakhouse & Bar
Café Prima Vera

Camera Café
Emile's
Eulapia Restaurant & Bar
The Fountain at the Fairmont
Germania Restaurant at the Hochburg
Gordon Biersch
The Grill on the Alley
Henry's World Famous Hi-Life
Hobee's
Il Fornaio
Johnny Rockets
Khanh's Garden Retaurant
Le Papillon
Mio Vincino
Menara Moroccan Restaurant
Original Joe's
Paolo's
Red Sea Restaurant
Rue de Paris
Scott's Seafood
71 Saint Peter
Spiedo Ristorante
Stratta Grill & Café
Taiwan
White Lotus Restaurant
Willow Street Wood-Fired Pizza

MONTEREY/ CARMEL

BIG SUR
Nepenthe
Sierra Mar
Ventana

CARMEL
Anton & Michel

Casanova
The Covey at Quail Lodge
Il Fornaio
Grasing's
Kincaid's Bistro
La Bohème
La Gondola
Mondo's Trattoria
Piatti
Rio Grill
Village Corner
Zigzag

CARMEL HIGHLANDS
Pacific's Edge

MONTEREY
Bubba Gump Shrimp Co.
Café Fina
Cibo Ristorante Italiano
Fresh Cream
Montrio
Rosine's
Sardine Factory
Stokes Adobe
Tarpy's Roadhouse

PACIFIC GROVE
Cypress Grove
Fandango
Pablo's Mexican Restaurant
Petra Restaurant
Taste Café & Bistro
Vito's

PEBBLE BEACH
Club XIX—Inspired by Hubert Keller
Roy's at Pebble Beach
Stillwater Bar & Grill

INDEX

Index

Index

THE WORLD DINING & TRAVEL CONNECTION

Want to keep current on the best bistros in Paris? Discover that little hideaway in Singapore? Or stay away from that dreadful and dreadfully expensive restaurant in New York? André Gayot's *Tastes* newsletter gives you bi-monthly news on the best restaurants, hotels, nightlife, shopping, airline and cruise-line information around the world.

PLEASE ENTER/RENEW MY SUBSCRIPTION TO TASTES NEWSLETTER FOR:

☐ Six bi-monthly issues at the rate of $30 per year & $35 outside U.S./Canada.

☐ 12 bi-monthly issues at the rate of $55 for two years US & $60 outside US/Canada.

☐ Enclosed is my check or money order made out to GaultMillau, Inc. for $ _____.

☐ Please charge my credit card: ☐ VISA* ☐ MasterCard ☐ AMERICAN EXPRESS*

Card # _____

Exp. ___/___ Signature _____

Telephone _____

Name_____

Address _____

City _____ State____ ZIP _____

Country_____

321/99

FOR FASTER SERVICE CALL I (800) LE BEST I

GAYOT | PUBLICATIONS

GAYOT PUBLICATIONS GUIDES ARE AVAILABLE AT ALL FINE BOOKSTORES WORLDWIDE.

INTERNATIONAL DISTRIBUTION IS COORDINATED BY THE FOLLOWING OFFICES:

MAINLAND U.S.
Publishers Group West
1700 Fourth St.
Berkeley, CA 94710
(800) 788-3123
Fax (510) 528-3444

CANADA
Publishers Group West
543 Richmond St. West
Suite 223, Box 106
Toronto, Ontario
M5V 146 CANADA
(416) 504-3900
Fax (416) 504-3902

HAWAII
Island Heritage
99-880 Iwaena
Aiea, HI 96701
(800) 468-2800
Fax (808) 488-2279

AUSTRALIA
Little Hills Press Pty. Ltd.
Regent House,
37-43 Alexander St.
Crows Nest (Sydney)
NSW 2065 Australia
(02) 437-6995
Fax (02) 438-5762

TAIWAN
Central Book Publishing
2nd Floor, 141, Section 1
Chungking South Rd.
Taipei, Taiwan R.O.C.
(02) 331-5726
Fax (02) 331-1316

HONG KONG & CHINA
Pacific Century
Distribution Ltd.
G/F No. 2-4
Lower Kai Yuen Ln.
North Point, Hong Kong
(852) 2811-5505
Fax (852) 2565-8624

UK & EUROPE
World Leisure Marketing
Unit 11, Newmarket Court
Newmarket Drive
Derby DE24 8NW
(01332) 573737
Fax (01332) 573399

FRANCE
GaultMillau, Inc.
01.48.08.00.38
Fax 01.43.65.46.62

SOUTH AFRICA
Faradawn C.C.
P.O. Box 1903
Saxonwold 2132
Republic of South Africa
(11) 885-1787
Fax (11) 885-1829

TO ORDER THE GUIDES FOR GIFTS, CUSTOM EDITIONS OR CORPORATE SALES IN THE U.S., CALL OUR TOLL-FREE LINE.

ORDER TOLL-FREE
1 (800) LE BEST 1

GAYOT PUBLICATIONS

on the Internet

GAYOT PUBLICATIONS / GAULTMILLAU IS PROUD
TO FEATURE RESTAURANT, HOTEL AND
TRAVEL INFORMATION FROM OUR BOOKS AND
UPDATES ON MANY INTERNET WEB SITES.

We suggest you start surfing at:

www.gayot.com
www.digitalcity.com
www.perrier.com

We welcome your questions and comments
at our e-mail address:

gayots@aol.com